# MUSIC AND THE BRAIN

The Composer as Artist   W. H. Crotch

Julius Caesar's Tower at Windsor Castle

The Bridge at Datchet (Reproduced by kind permission of Dr. and
Mrs. Simon Holland)

*(Both drawings in black chalk and watercolour)*

# MUSIC AND THE BRAIN

*Studies in the Neurology of Music*

Edited by

## MACDONALD CRITCHLEY

*Honorary Consulting Physician, the National Hospital for Nervous Diseases,*
*Queen Square, and King's College Hospital, London.*
*Emeritus President, World Federation of Neurology.*

and

## R. A. HENSON

*Physician in Charge, Neurological Department and Chairman, Section of*
*Neurological Sciences, The London Hospital.*
*Physician, The National Hospitals for Nervous Diseases, Maida Vale, London.*
*Honorary Consultant Neurologist to the Royal Society of Musicians of Great*
*Britain.*

*With a Foreword by Sir Michael Tippett*

Charles C Thomas · Publisher
*Springfield · Illinois*

First published 1977
© Macdonald Critchley & R. A. Henson 1977
ISBN 0-398-03653-5

Printed in Great Britain

# Contents

# Contributors

BENTON, A. L.
> Professor of Neurology and Psychology, University of Iowa.

BLAU, J. N.
> Physician, The National Hospitals for Nervous Diseases, Queen Square and Maida Vale, London.

CRITCHLEY, MACDONALD
> Honorary Consulting Physician, The National Hospital for Nervous Diseases, Queen Square, and King's College Hospital, London.
> Emeritus President, World Federation of Neurology.

DAMÁSIO, A. R.
> Associate Professor of Neurology, University of Iowa.
> Formerly Professor of Neurology, University of Lisbon, and Chief, Language Research Laboratory, Centro de Estudos Egas Moniz, Portugal.

DAMÁSIO, HANNA
> Instructor in Neurology, University of Iowa.
> Formerly Research Fellow, Centro de Estudos Egas Moniz, Portugal.

DEUTSCH, DIANA
> Associate Professor, Department of Psychology, University of California, San Diego.

GOODDY, W.
> Physician, The National Hospital for Nervous Diseases, Queen Square, and University College Hospital, London.

HARRER, G.
> Professor, Department of Psychology, University of Salzburg.

HARRER, H.
> Research Fellow, Department of Psychology, University of Salzburg.

HENSON, R. A.
> Physician in Charge, Neurological Department and Chairman, Section of Neurological Sciences, The London Hospital.
> Physician, The National Hospitals for Nervous Diseases, Maida Vale, London.
> Honorary Consultant Neurologist to the Royal Society of Musicians of Great Britain.

HOOD, J. D.
> Director, Medical Research Council Hearing and Balance Unit, The National Hospital for Nervous Diseases, Queen Square, London.

KHAMBATA, A. S.

Consultant Surgeon in Diseases of the Ear, Nose and Throat, Dartford Group of Hospitals, Kent.

MEYER, A.

Emeritus Professor of Neuropathology, Institute of Psychiatry, University of London.

MOFFETT, ADRIENNE

Research Fellow, Section of Neurological Sciences, The London Hospital.

PHILLIPS, C. G.

Professor of Anatomy, University of Oxford.

PRATT, R. T. C.

Consultant Psychiatrist, The National Hospitals for Nervous Diseases, Queen Square and Maida Vale, London.

SCHIPKOWENSKY, N.*

Professor, Department of Neurology and Psychiatry, University of Sofia.

SCOTT, D. F.

Physician in Charge, Department of Electroencephalography, The London Hospital.

SEARS, T. A.

Professor of Neurophysiology, Institute of Neurology, The National Hospital for Nervous Diseases, Queen Square, London.

TRETHOWAN, W. H.

Professor of Psychiatry, University of Birmingham.

WERTHEIM, N.

Professor of Neurology, University of Tel Aviv.

WYKE, MARIA

Principal Psychologist, The National Hospital for Nervous Diseases, Maida Vale, London.

* Professor Schipkowensky died before publication.

# Acknowledgments

The authors listed below wish to acknowledge the help afforded them.

J. N. BLAU and R. A. HENSON are grateful to the patients who have permitted them to quote their case histories and to colleagues for access to their case notes.

DIANA DEUTSCH'S work was supported by United States Public Health Service grant MH-21001-04.

R. A. HENSON. Christopher Brown, Professor Norman Geschwind, Iris Hawes, Frances Henson, Dr. Robert Sherlaw Johnson, Dr. Anthony Milner, John Moutrie, Dr. Pamela Prior, Dr. Robert Simpson, Dr. Helmut Walcha. The Librarians of The London Hospital Medical College (J. P. Entract) and the Royal College of Physicians (L. M. Payne); the Staff of the Music Library, University of London; B.B.C. Audience Research Unit.

A. MEYER. Dr. Eliot Slater, Mrs. Ursula Baker, Dr. Raymond Hierons, Dr. Samuel Last, Dr. W. Pallie, Dr. S. F. Witelson. S. Karger, Publishers, for permission to reproduce figures.

W. H. TRETHOWAN. Professor E. W. Anderson, Dr. Howard Ferguson, Mrs. Joyce Finzi, Dr. Nigel Fortune, Mr. Michael Hurd, Mr. Robert Layton, Dr. Eric Sams, Mrs. Sue Savage, Dr. Eliot Slater.

MARIA WYKE. Mr. C. Gabriel, Miss A. Greenwood, Miss Eileen Ralph.

# Preface

MACDONALD CRITCHLEY and R. A. HENSON

When the Danube Symposium on Neurology met in Vienna in 1972 the topic "neurology of music" was regarded as particularly apt. This was the first occasion when the subject had been submitted to serious discussion, although the sedative and even therapeutic effects of music had been referred to on and off since the pre-homeric myth of Orpheus and Eurydice. There had, of course, been a few highly technical studies dealing with certain psychological aspects. The success of the Vienna meeting was so obvious to both of us, who were present as participants, that we realised there was a place for a more exhaustive neurological study dealing with musical perception and execution as pertaining to the medical sciences. Prompted by our colleagues, we decided to co-operate in editing a volume with chapters written by several authors.

Originally we had hoped to cover the whole field, but this has not proved practicable. No consideration has been given to the problem of absolute pitch, nor to the neurology of musical notation, but with these exceptions we submit that the ground has been covered in the present state of our knowledge.

Our collaborators are drawn from the ranks of neurological exponents, and include workers in the clinical fields as well as in the basic sciences — anatomy, physiology, pathology, psychology and otology — as far as they pertain to the nervous system. It so happens that one contributor has had a professional musical training, the others being amateurs of varying degrees of knowledge and competence. Our co-authors were requested to write for musical readers as well as neurologists. This task proved more difficult in the case of some chapters than others, but we hope that on the whole an adequate compromise has been effected so that the reading matter will interest teachers and students of music, as well as medical men. Our musical friends besought us not to "write down" to them, and we have tried to act upon this advice. In a compendium such as this some overlap was inevitable, and we have allowed it to persist where editorial expurgation would have interfered with the writer's argument.

The scheme of the book is straightforward. The first chapter is intended to be a general introduction, while the remainder of Part I deals with various aspects of nervous function involved in musical activity. Part II concerns the effects of nervous disease on musical functions, and also the converse state of affairs, namely, certain disorders which are provoked by music. The age-old topic of musical therapy is also critically discussed.

We are extremely grateful to Sir Michael Tippett for his kindness in sparing time to read the manuscripts and to write a preface. Dr. Geoffrey Bush, too, was good enough to peruse each chapter, thus saving us from a number of musical errors, but he must not be held responsible for any blemishes or *bêtises* which remain, or for the musical opinions expressed by the authors. Lastly, we thank our colleagues for their co-operation in this enterprise.

# Foreword

## SIR MICHAEL TIPPETT

The human practice of music is so ancient an art that the semantics are inevitably bedevilled by history. Thus 5th-century Augustine's *De Musica* is chiefly about what we would *now* call poetry. The 16th-century Agrippa who tried to relate 4-part vocal harmony to other quaternities such as that age-old earth-water-air-fire, belonged to the late Renaissance group of men, Bruno, Kepler, Fluid et al. who thought in a complex. A complex, some of whose elements even then could have been distinguished as religious reformation; post-Galen medicine; alchemy-music. In the historical manner the complex has since divided out we can feel that the semantics of medicine and science have become increasingly precise, while those of religion and aesthetics are still perhaps inevitably ambiguous. For example, when R. A. Henson writes "The use of microtones in contemporary music makes greater demands on the hearing powers of an audience than more traditional works," we must assume that the sounding of the microtones could be verified acoustically as factually accomplished, yet once we permit ourselves to listen musically (the crucially difficult word) then, in my opinion, we shall experience the microtones as no more than expressive divergences from an unconscious, or innate or whatever, notion of (tempered) whole tones and semi-tones. But this is not to suggest that medicine does not have, even now, somewhat similar difficulties. I can imagine that the answer to: what is memory?, just as to: what is music? though immediate to subjective experience is locked in a vicious circle to discursive description.

Attempting to make some general observation from my un-medicated subjective obsessional experience of composition, I think the composer has, as it were, to exacerbate both sides of the psychosomatic equation. He must activate the nervous system in order to produce the effect (to be transmitted through performance independent to himself) so continuously as to engineer periodic nervous collapse. (I guess what he is activating is the neurological "clock" described by W. Gooddy.) At the same time in order to imagine, he must activate the psyche towards the more dream-like state, where "regression" to thinking in a complex is possible. It is a curious irony that all the enrichment of knowledge I have received from this book can only enter my music by an alchemy which transmutes the experience of reading into metaphor; submitting once more to that "divine madness", to use Plato's jargon.

The book of course is the product of research. But medicine is chiefly a daily practice of therapy. Music too can be directly therapeutic; whether on the body or the emotions (or the reverse, as reported by Macdonald Critchley and D. Scott). But music is only tangentially a therapy. So there are two directions in the book – towards music, towards medicine. Yet so much overlaps, join, divides. Like the image of Yeats' gyres I often had a vision while reading of a tidal pulse – inwards from music into the body; outwards from the body into music. Or to quote a more passionate metaphor:

> *Marbles of the dancing floor*
> *Break bitter furies of complexity*

of body, of mind. Music to calm, perhaps,

> *That dolphin-torn, that gong-tormented sea.*

# PART I

# 1

R. A. HENSON

# Neurological Aspects of Musical Experience

The neurological literature on music is commonly dull and lacking in interest to the general reader. There is a wealth of distinguished writing by neurologists on philosophical and literary matters, and music has fared ill by comparison. The reasons are not too far to seek, they include inadequate musical knowledge and a proper apprehension of venturing into difficult fields where traditional scientific guidelines are often unavailable. Even Henry Head limited his work on music to observations on the effects of brain damage on musical functions, although he had a good knowledge of music and the intellect and imagination to make a major contribution. Brain (1959) made some brief, perceptive comments, but his main interests lay elsewhere and he never pursued the subject of music in any depth.

On the other hand, the literature of music is rich. From the great days of Greece up to the present time philosophers, theologians and musicians have provided a stream of theory and criticism. After the commentaries of Plato, Aristotle and other Greeks, the early Christian fathers recorded their views on music and its relationship to life and worship; St. Augustine (A.D. 354–430) provided a remarkable analysis of musical experience in the sixth volume of his *De Musica*. Inevitably the Christian Church remained dominant in writings on music until the Renaissance, but from this time onwards the literature enlarged widely. Interested persons have a notable collection of antique and contemporary literature of high quality at their disposal. Furthermore, musicians have rightly made their own studies in practical or applied neurology. Teachers have expounded their ideas on motor activity and voice production as they relate to performance, hitherto with little assistance from neurophysiologists. Others have recorded their views on memory, an area where neurological knowledge is enlarging and increasingly capable of helping the musician.

Music as we know it today is some eight centuries old, although its origins lie deep in history. The polyphonic style reached its first known flowering in the thirteenth century with the composition of the canon *Summer is i-cumen in*; the earliest extant complete setting of the Ordinary of the Mass by one composer is Machaut's (*c.* 1300–*c.* 1372) *Messe de Nostre Dame* (Hughes, 1953). Development has proceeded at differing rates since this time and modern composers continue the exploratory process with new ideas on style and performance. In confining this study to serious Western music only a segment of musical history is covered, but the neurological substrate of musical experience does not change, and it is hoped that the ideas and conclusions contained will prove capable of wider interpretation.

## The Nature, Development and Prevalence of Musical Ability

Billroth, the Viennese surgeon, was one of the first to attempt definition of the substrate of musical ability or talent. His *Wer ist musikalisch?* was published in 1894. Later, many psychologists have explored the subject in depth, devising tests of musical aptitude and studying the development of talent. Notable among early workers was Seashore, the fruit of whose long experience is contained in his *The Psychology of Musical Talent* (1919) and *Psychology of Music* (1938). Many other important contributions have been made in more recent years and Shuter (1968) has provided a valuable review of these.

The essential auditory requirements for rewarding expressive or receptive musical activity include the capacity to perceive tones and tonal relationships, not simply the specific acoustic properties of a note, such as pitch, duration, timbre and intensity, but the sounding of notes consecutively, melody, tones sounded simultaneously, harmony, and tones sounded in terms of time, rhythm (Hanson, 1942). The musician must also be able to recognise the horizontal relationship of tones or counterpoint. Memory is essential for musical appreciation and performance, and an emotional response is necessary for full experience. While generalisations of this sort can be validly made, it is a truism to recall that the requirements differ according to the individual and that there are wide variations in any unselected group of persons. The majority are able to enjoy music in one form or another and are sufficiently equipped to sing a tune. For the composer, professional performer, amateur executant and serious listener other attributes are needed. The professional performer must possess exceptional motor skills and motivation and persistence in practice, while the composer must have a deep understanding of musical form and structure and the imagination or inspiration to energise his professional expertise.

Musical aptitude and talent declare their presence early in life (Chapter 11), and professional executive potential is usually evident in the first decade. According to Révész (1953) almost one half of the children he tested showed musical aptitude by the age of five. Shuter (1968) traced the development of musical ability from infancy to maturity. A favourable home or educational environment naturally encourages the process, while absence of such stimulus can delay the appearance and recognition of unusual talent. Musical capacity continues to enlarge during the third decade. Middle and old age form no barrier to new experience or creative ability if the mental faculties are preserved.

The prevalence of musical talent and interest is a matter of social and neurological concern. Serious musical enjoyment was the prerogative of the few until comparatively recent times. Though the common people of the Middle Ages had their folk music and dance, with entertainment from wandering minstrels of different types, and material deriving from these sources played an important part in musical development, it was the Church, royal courts and establishments of other rich and powerful people which were the main repositors of good music. Later the area of performance widened with the emergence of a wealthy merchant class ready to dispense patronage and the spread of private music-making. The first public concerts, in the modern sense of the term, were arranged by the violinist John Banister in London in 1672. When this series ceased in 1678 Thomas Britton, a Clerkenwell charcoal hawker, inaugurated his concerts which continued for thirty-six years. For the first time performances of serious music by outstanding musicians, such as Purcell and Handel, were open to the public. However, Purcell was probably best known by the public from his theatre music and Handel from his oratorios and music performed in the Pleasure Gardens. Music by leading composers was played to large audiences at Gardens like Vauxhall, particularly in the eighteenth century when Glee clubs and other private music groups flourished.

There was a rapid expansion of musical societies and educational facilities in the Victorian Age, but the advent of gramophone and radio in particular has awakened latent interest and increased knowledge and enjoyment among the population at large. On the educational side improved facilities for instrumental training and enthusiastic teachers in schools have shown that there is a large reservoir of musical skills among the young. The proliferation and enlargement of school choirs and orchestras has been a remarkable phenomenon over the past twenty-five years, and standards of performance are often high.

A B.B.C. Audience Research Report (1964) investigated the public for serious music. The final sample of 1250 persons over fifteen was explored by lengthy interview and questionnaire. It was concluded that the serious music public had been successfully sampled, but the remainder of the population may have been less accurately represented. Forty per cent. claimed to have been taught to play an instrument in childhood, but only four per cent. still did so in adult life. Musical knowledge was scanty in the majority; fifty-four per cent. had little or no contact with music in childhood and denied knowing anything about it as adults, while a further twenty-one per cent. were ill-informed. A small best-informed group of 7·5 per cent. was largely drawn from the middle class, but the ill-informed or ignorant constituted a proportionate cross section of the population. Persons professing little interest were shown to make up about a quarter of concert audiences, and there were few in the sample who did not state a liking for music in general. Sadly, serious contemporary music ranked lowest in terms of music liked in all groups of the sample.

## The Early Medical Literature

References to music and medicine are common in the Greek and Latin literature, but as one would expect their interest is largely historical or literary. Early writers were concerned with the therapeutic effects of music; for example, Pliny (1513) reported that Cato had preserved an incantation for the cure of sprains and Varro another for gout. Caelius Aurelianus (1529) mentioned the use of music in the general treatment of insanity and locally in the management of sciatica; "A certain piper would play his instrument over the affected parts and these would begin to throb and palpitate, banishing the pain and bringing relief." Caelius was sceptical and quoted an alternative view, "anyone who believes a severe disease can be banished by music and song is the victim of a silly delusion".

Henricus Cornelius Agrippa (1533) attempted to relate the four voice parts to cosmic elements, bass with the earth, tenor with water, alto with air and soprano with fire. He proceeded to compare the Dorian mode with water and phlegm, the Phrygian with fire and yellow bile, the Lydian with air and blood, and the Myxolydian with earth and bile.

Music played a part in the so-called dance manias which began in the Middle Ages and continued until the eighteenth century. Schedel (1497) described the chorisants who would dance for half a day, believing they would cure themselves of illness. Kircher (1654) and others made detailed case histories of patients with tarantism and of the use of the tarantella in treatment of tarantula bites.

Robert Burton (1632) covered the usual ground of ancient accounts of the effects of music in his Anatomy of Melancholy. His reference to music presents the art as a remedy for morbid states of mind. "Many men are melancholy by hearing music, but it is a pleasing melancholy that it causeth, and therefore to such as are discontent, in woe, feare, sorrow or dejected, it is a most pleasant remedy. It expels cares, alters their grieved minds, and easeth in an instant."

## The Neurological Literature

The latter half of the nineteenth century saw the beginning of modern neurology and the development of concepts of localisation of function within the brain. Several important German neurologists analysed disturbances of musical function in patients with brain disease and attempted to site the responsible lesions. Knoblauch (1888) introduced the term "amusia" to mean impaired capacity for musical activity and the word is acceptable in this sense. Sensory amusia comprises inability to hear, read or understand music, while motor amusia predicates difficulty in singing or writing music or in instrumental performance (Chapter 22). Knoblauch (1888), Wallaschek (1893) and Edgren (1895) classified the amusias, while Probst (1899, 1901) published clinico-pathological studies on amusic persons. Many later authors have trodden similar paths, pursuing the goal of localisation of musical functions or studying the relationship between aphasia and amusia (Auerbach, 1906; Henschen, 1920, 1926; Kleist, 1928, 1962; Head, 1926). Kleist (1962) went to extremes in his attempts to localise; for example, he linked comprehension and execution of melody in singing and playing and textual comprehension and appreciation of melody with adjoining but architectonically different cortical areas on the basis of lesions there. Feuchtwanger (1930) made a notable contribution in a treatise which deals with the whole subject of amusia.

This early concentration of neurologists on the effects of focal brain lesions has yielded a mass of interesting material, the German literature being especially fruitful in this respect. Among reports in English Head's (1926) series is notable, while Souques and Baruk (1926, 1930) provided a thorough account of an amusic French piano teacher. Important studies on brain damaged composers have come from Alajouanine (1948), who reported his findings on Ravel, and Luria et al. (1965), who recorded the effects of a stroke on Shebalin.

The peculiar effects of a thalamic lesion on musical experience were mentioned by Head (1920): "Music is peculiarly liable to evoke a different reaction on the two halves of the body. One of our patients was unable to go to a place of worship because 'he could not stand the hymns on his affected side', and his son noticed that during the singing his father constantly rubbed the affected hand." Other examples of this strange phenomenon are recorded in the same book. Roeser and Daly (1974) described an unusual example of altered musical perception in a patient with a left-sided thalamic syndrome and hemiparesis due to a presumed right thalamic tumour; she thought her hi-fi apparatus was defective, for music sounded "fuzzy and blurred".

Apart from excessive concentration on problems of cerebral localisation, much of the early published work can be faulted for failure to take account of premorbid musicality or to test patients adequately. Imperfect musical knowledge on the part of the neurologist has compounded the situation. Ustvedt (1937) and Wertheim (1963) have made these points and devised detailed methods of testing their amusic patients.

Advances in clinical neurology and modern techniques have made more dynamic investigations possible in recent years. Clinical and electroencephalographic studies on epileptic patients have provided useful information. Auditory hallucinations are heard as part or whole of an epileptic event by some 16 per cent. of sufferers from temporal lobe seizures (Currie et al., 1971) and the experience is musical in a proportion of these. Reviewing his experience of electrical stimulation of the cerebral cortex in patients undergoing resections for epilepsy Penfield (Penfield and Perot, 1963) found that musical hallucinations were evoked in seventeen out of forty "experiential responses" among a total series of 1132. This response was only encountered with stimulation of the superior or lateral surface of the first temporal convolution on either side, but more right than left. Stimulation of the primary auditory area produced buzzing or whistling. Evidently the superior temporal gyrus has direct or indirect associations with the storage of musical experience.

Although the amusias were commonly ascribed to lesions of the left or dominant cerebral hemisphere by early writers, several recognised that the right hemisphere plays a part in musical activity. Milner (1962) provided a sound basis for this belief. Using the Seashore tests she showed that right temporal lobectomy, performed for epilepsy, made certain kinds of auditory discrimination difficult, comparison of tonal patterns and judgments of tone quality being most conspicuously impaired. No such loss was found after left temporal lobectomy. The problem of laterality was taken further forward by Gordon and Bogen (1974), who demonstrated that right intracarotid injections with amylobarbitone caused defects in singing, whereas speech remained relatively intact. With left-sided injections speech was more affected than singing. Both Smith (1966) and Gott (1973) observed that patients who had undergone dominant hemispherectomy for tumour were able to sing much more effectively than they could speak. Dichotic listening techniques were employed by Kimura

(1964) to study melody identification. In general when dichotic tests with words or digits were used subjects showed an ability to identify these with the right ear, while melodies tended to be discerned with the left ear. These results were supported by Shankweiler's (1966) observation that patients who had undergone right temporal lobectomy showed selectively impaired perception of dichotically presented melodies. However, Gordon (1970) found that the left ear was superior for dichotically presented chords, but not for melody. The discrepancies in the results between these and other workers may be explained by the complex nature of music. Recognition of music depends on several factors, for example, melody, metre, rhythm, harmony, dynamics and sometimes words, as in opera or song. There may be shifts of superiority from one ear to the other, but both combine for full experience in the normal individual. Here the value of investigation of normal persons rather than mere examination of brain damaged patients is clearly shown.

## The Perceptual Situation

In the remainder of this chapter a number of neurological processes important in musical experience will be considered. Some of these are accessible to neurological study, others barely so or not at all.

Most musicians would surely agree that music has a meaning beyond perception of the structure and content of a composition. Musicality is a complex function involving the special senses and intellectual and emotional functions. The emotional response can be depressed or disordered in brain disease, a phenomenon mentioned earlier in relation to thalamic lesions but also evident in persons with diffuse cortical damage or affective disorder. Important observations on autonomic functions during musical activities have been made by the Harrers (Chapter 12). The problem of the language of music is pursued in Chapter 14.

There are three persons, or groups of persons, concerned with any musical event, the composer, the performer or performers, and the audience, which may consist of one or many individuals. When the composer plays his own music to himself he only is involved in the perceptual situation. More often two people participate, the performer and the composer, though the latter may be dead, for example, when a pianist plays a Beethoven sonata for his own enjoyment. Three groups are involved in many circumstances, as when an orchestra presents a symphony concert containing works by more than one composer to an audience in a hall or over the radio. Thus, composer, performer and listener must be considered in further neurological analysis, remembering that the same individual may be placed in each category at different points in time.


## The Role of the Special Senses

### *The Auditory System*

There are certain basic auditory requirements for the pursuit of music, and the physiology of hearing is discussed in Chapter 3. In the present context it is worth recalling that while tonotopic organisation is evident in the cochlea of the inner ear and inferior colliculi of the brainstem there is reduced relationship between the frequency of neural activity and stimulus intensity in the auditory cortex, although some such organisation persists at this level. Important discriminations made by auditory mechanisms depend on cortical function. The expectation that the patterns underlying auditory experience exist entirely within the input signals is misplaced (Creel et al., 1970).

Absolute or perfect pitch is the ability to identify a musical sound without the help of a reference sound. Music teachers commonly differentiate between active and passive absolute pitch; the former is the ability to produce a pitch at will, while the latter is the capacity to identify a sounded pitch or key. Active pitch is much rarer than the passive form; however, relative sense of pitch is quite adequate for most musical activities. Most people can perceive an interval of a semitone, with training or a better ear quarter tones may be heard. The use of microtones in contemporary music makes greater demands on the hearing powers of an audience than more traditional works. Too fine a sense of pitch can mar the hearer's appreciation of musical performances save the best; for example, the delicate ear suffers agony when hearing a group of amateur string performers playing out of tune. It is now generally believed, however, that listeners recognise slight differences of unison tuning as characteristic of massed effects in music, for example, orchestral strings or ranks of organ pipes coupled together. Makers of electronic organs actually incorporate a device, a frequency-separator, to bring about minute differences in the tuning of unisons.

Full analytical musical enjoyment requires the ability to hear the individual parts of a choral or orchestral piece. It is comparatively simple to listen to the sections of an orchestra playing baroque and classical compositions; progressively greater auditory development is required to hear the different parts of a romantic or modern work. An example of exceptional auditory development is afforded by those conductors who are celebrated for their skill in detecting players' errors in complex, dissonant pieces involving unlikely instrumental combinations.

Although deafness comes as a terrible blow to any musician, the composer may still be productive after hearing has been lost. The prodigious output of Beethoven during the years of complete deafness is the most remarkable example (Cooper, 1970). Smetana went on composing and conducting after his deafness became severe, though he gave up conducting in 1881, three years before his death. He was also afflicted by persistent tinnitus which added to his difficulties. Fauré was entirely deaf for the last six years of his life. During this time he composed several important chamber works, three song cycles, and pieces for piano. His style became more introspective as he explored different ways of expression, phenomena comparable to those manifest in Beethoven's late string quartets, but it would be over-simplification to ascribe the change to the effects of deafness alone. Tinnitus, that is noise in the ears, may seriously interfere with musical activity of itself, though there is usually accompanying deafness. In one personally known case the almost intolerable tinnitus linked with deafness due to bilateral Ménière's disease inhibited both auditory imagery and the enjoyment which might otherwise have derived from playing keyboard instruments.

Auditory imagery constitutes an important item in the musician's mental equipment. Some persons are quite unable to imagine any tune, but all musicians possess the capacity, though in varying degrees (Seashore, 1938). It is possible to hear with the "inward ear" without external stimulus; the music appears in as many different readings or performances as one has experienced and memorised.

Auditory imagery naturally plays an important part in composition. William Byrd described the part played by a text in provoking auditory images. In the preface to the first volume of his *Gradualia* (1605) he wrote of his feelings for sacred texts; "there is in those very sentiments, as I have learned by experience, a mysterious hidden power so that to anyone who considers divine things . . . the fittest possible measures occur of their own accord in some strange way and offer themselves copiously even when one's mind is sluggish and inactive." Mendelssohn conceived the idea of "writing an overture in the form of two separate tableaux" on reading Goethe's *Meerstille* and *Glückliche Fahrt*. He did not commit a note to paper but wrote, "I have the whole thing already in my head, and the great waves will be represented by double bassoons." However, the overture *Calm Sea and Prosperous Voyage* was not performed until four years later and was presumably worked on during the intervening years (Blunt, 1974a). Schubert responded with remarkable facility to a text; in setting one song

he "took the verses to the window . . . read the poem through twice with
deep attention . . . and turning with a smile said, 'I have it, it's done
already, and it will do very well'" (Hellborn, 1869). Of course, Schubert
was a remarkably rapid composer of songs; longer and more complex
works are surely only sketched in this fashion (Chapter 14). Auditory
imagery can be stimulated in many other ways, including sight of a score,
by visual images, emotional experiences or by voluntary effort.

Auditory imagery is part of the stock in trade of performers and
particularly conductors or directors of performances. Reid (1961) told how
Beecham realised throughout his first public orchestral concert in London
that he was failing to obtain the tone, style and general effect he wanted,
"Somehow or other the sound of the music was strangely different from
the concept of it in my brain . . ."; the failure may have stemmed from
faulty expectation on the part of a young conductor or from the inability of
the players to produce the sounds he wanted.

## The Visual System

Vision obviously plays an important part in some musical activities. Opera
can only be fully enjoyed if the performance is seen. The sight of an
orchestra or solo performer enhances auditory experience. A beautiful
woman brings an extra dimension to a lieder recital; conversely, a singer
with an ugly style can impair enjoyment. Vision of the movements and
gestures of conductors and performers can heighten appreciation of time
and rhythm, reinforcing auditory perception. A more complex role was
played by the eyes in the case of the deaf Beethoven directing a
performance of his *A minor quartet* (Op. 132); an English observer wrote,
"He took off his coat, the room being warm and crowded. A staccato
passage not being expressed to the satisfaction of his eye (for alas he could
not hear) he seized Holz's violin and played the passage a quarter of a tone
flat" (Cooper, 1970).

Another aspect of seeing and hearing is found in score reading. Score
reading is influenced by the type and style of the publication. The sight of
an artistically written autograph, say one of Bach's, or a clearly printed and
attractively presented work brings visual pleasure to enhance or enlarge
the strictly musical experience. Notation brings its own influence to bear
on the reader, for example, most people will react in contrasting ways to a
page of plainsong and a Bach fugue or Beethoven sonata. The inhibiting
effect of complex patterns of notes of different values on the tyro pianist is a
well known phenomenon; conversely, a passage in uniform notation may
well engender misplaced confidence. On a larger scale, there is visual
grandeur in the full score of a major orchestral or choral work. The faculty

of score reading is variably developed and while there are many musical persons who can read and hear a known work, or one which is unknown but not too complex, there will be comparatively few who can successfully read an unknown composition by, say, Stravinsky (see Chapter 14). Even fewer persons would read and hear a new piece by a member of the avant-garde employing newer or idiosyncratic notational forms. On the other hand, there are competent professionals engaged in popular music who cannot read musical notation. In one personal case a child's incapacity to read music was not discovered until the age of ten, by which time he was playing the piano exceptionally well; the boy had been learning his pieces "by ear". Many years later he finds it easier to learn a work by listening rather than reading, which he still finds difficult.

Score reading reinforces auditory impact and this heightens experience, particularly when the reading listener is hearing masses of sound, as in Bach's *B minor Mass* or Bruckner's symphonies. Thus both eye and ear combine in musical experience. Schumann put the point rather differently; "He is a good musician who understands the music without the score, and the score without the music. The ear should not need the eye, the eye should not need the outward ear."

Blindness does not necessarily form a barrier to musical performance or composition. Several sightless musicians have been keyboard virtuosi, from the German Conrad Paumann (*c.* 1410–1473) and the Spaniard Antonio de Cabezón (1510–1566), who were both organists and composers, to Helmut Walcha, the contemporary German organist, who has made authoritative recordings of the organ and keyboard works of J. S. Bach and is also a composer. Blindness makes exceptional demands on the individual's capacity to learn and retain. Before the introduction of Braille, and perhaps the special notation devised by Rousseau, the problems of the blind player were even greater than they are now. Celebrated blind musicians have commonly lost sight early in life. John Stanley, the British eighteenth century organist, was blinded in an accident at the age of two. It is recorded that his aural memory was sharpened, ". . . he could perform a composition from memory after a couple of hearings . . . he frequently directed an oratorio evening without sight of the score" (Boyd, 1974). Stanley's virtuosity was such that people would walk from one church to another to hear him play. He was a competent composer of modest dimensions.

## Somatic Motor and Sensory Systems

Somatic motor and sensory activities naturally play a decisive part in any musical performance, but they have a wider importance than this. Musical experience is certainly incomplete without the sensorimotor skills and training needed for at least modest performance, and one reason for teaching children to play instruments is that this discipline will help them to listen to music. The individual who has never played or sung in an instrumental consort or a choir is at a distinct disadvantage in the perceptual situation compared with a practising musician. Any member of an amateur string quartet stands in a different category from the informed non-string player where works for this combination are concerned, and it is likely that the gulf cannot be bridged. In other words, performing skills yield rewards beyond performance.

Although performers in an audience will more deeply share the motor activities of singers and players, the whole listening group responds by motor responses. The sight of gestures and other movements can reinforce auditory perception; additionally, the dynamics of a performance, not to speak of the effects of orchestral size and composition and of individual instruments, bring about changes in the percipient's motor state. In public there is rarely overt motor activity, good concert manners preclude this, but rather sensations of movement, a succession of postural adjustments or even offensive foot tapping; in private the listener can allow himself more freedom, responding with spontaneous movements or mining the attitudes and techniques of conductor or instrumentalist.

It seems generally agreed that rhythm depends on subcortical activity, and full appreciation demands an intact motor system at least on one side of the body. A hemiplegic musician may be able to conduct or play the piano with one hand to concert performance level, but the minor hemisphere is usually affected in such cases. Cerebellar or basal gangliar dysfunction might be expected to interfere with rhythmic sense, but there does not appear to be any published work on this point. Gordon and Bogen (1974) found little or no impairment of rhythmic sense in patients subjected to unilateral, intracarotid amylobarbitone injections. The basis of rhythm learning is not fully understood; Ustvedt (1937) and Ettlinger and Moffett (1970) were unable to demonstrate defects in dysphasic patients. In contrast to rhythm and tempo the sense of metre or measure was impaired in Ustvedt's (1937) patients, who mostly suffered from left-sided vascular hemispheric lesions with aphasia.

## Synaesthesiae

Synaesthesiae, which may be regarded as a sort of sensory overflow, play an important part in musical experience for some persons (Chapter 13).

Both musical and literary men have described the ways in which they related colours to different keys or notes. Rimsky-Korsakow and Scriabin left records of the colours they associated with different keys, and these coincided in about a third. Attempts have been made to combine music and colour by using specially devised or adapted instruments. Scriabin composed his *Promethée, Poème de Feu*, with an accompaniment of coloured lights projected on a screen according to directions contained in a line of the score. This work is rarely played with its visual components but there was only a small attendance at a recent London performance at the Royal Albert Hall, which suggests a sparse public response. There is also a notated part for colour in Schoenberg's *Die glückliche Hand*. Synaesthesiae are often cutaneous, various paraesthesiae are felt at the back of the neck, down the spine and sometimes throughout the trunk and limbs. The stimulus is generally a musical piece heavily loaded with affect, either of itself or because of its associations.

## Memory

Memory is most important in all aspects of music (Chapter 7). Indeed, it is not possible to undertake a simple musical task such as singing a tune without employing memory. The enjoyment of the listener in hearing any piece of music is conditioned by his remembrance of similiar melodic and harmonic passages based on the same tonal relationship (Scholes, 1955). Remote memory must be intact so that the store of past auditory and emotional experience can be drawn upon, while recent memory is needed to identify references to previous material within a movement or whole work. For all musicians the store of auditory imagery required for creative work and informed listening depends on intact, efficient memory processes. Sensorimotor and visual memories are particularly necessary for performance, but these are reinforced by theoretical skill in formal and harmonic analysis and by knowledge of composer style.

There are many records of remarkable feats of musical memory, and those two geniuses, Mozart and Mendelssohn, figure frequently in popular examples. Both composers wrote down Allegri's *Miserere* after hearing it in the Sistine Chapel. This work was sung in Holy Week and few copies existed outside the Vatican. Composed in nine parts for two choirs it was elaborately ornamented. There are differing accounts of Mozart's achievement in 1770 when aged fourteen; he is variably reported as having heard the *Miserere* twice or six times, and the number of mistakes he made is also uncertain. However, it was a display of the boy's virtuosity. Mendelssohn rehearsed the first performance of the *St. Matthew Passion* after Bach's death without a score and rewrote his *A Midsummer Night's Dream Overture* when the score was left in a London cab. Even more notably, at a musical evening in his home, he reproduced directly a Hungarian folksong and three or four complex variations after the initial performance by Liszt (Blunt, 1974b). The capacity for rapid learning and memorising possessed by some performers is quite remarkable. Menuhin (1972) witnessed Enesco's skill in this direction when rehearsing a new sonata for violin and piano by Ravel. After playing the work once Enesco asked that they might run through it once more to be on the safe side, "Ravel agreed and to our amazement Enesco put the score down and . . . played every note from memory." Von Bülow memorised a Stanford symphony on a train journey so that on arrival he was able to conduct the work without the score; he also played all Beethoven's piano works from memory (Scholes, 1955). Scholes (1955) cited the achievement of Sir Frederick Gore Ouseley, the Victorian musician and cleric, who "once played Beethoven's Septet on the piano, stating the instruments to which each passage was assigned, and this after only two hearings of it, one of them ten years before (and never having seen the score )".

Contemporary soloists often play without the book and members of string quartets sometimes do so; this places early accounts of similar achievements by nineteenth century performers in perspective. Although many executive musicians have this ability, some prefer not to exercise it in order to escape an avoidable source of anxiety in performance.

The ability to learn a work "by heart" is not possessed by all persons with good or exceptional memories for figures, words or musical performance. Such individuals, although good readers, have great difficulty in learning and retaining simple works for, say, piano. The possession of an elaborate number form has not proved helpful in a personal case with this problem.

## Discussion

There are obvious limits to what the neurological sciences can achieve in understanding or explaining musical experience. This is also unfortunately true of the neurological study of any art form, auditory, visual or literary. As Gilford has remarked, the great difficulty in the scientific study of the arts is that human perception of qualities and patterns is far ahead of anything which science can apprehend at the present time; and with perception comes the emotional response which is quite undefinable in neurological terms. Early neurologists studied music and the brain by observing the effects of focal lesions on musical activities. Their observations have provided useful information on parts of the brain particularly concerned with the components of musical life, the capacities to read, comprehend, compose or perform; they are also helpful to the physician who cares for musicians suffering from the effects of strokes and other forms of brain disease. However, this classical method has proved of limited value in the long term, not least because investigation is restricted to the sick. Much has been made of the way in which some patients bereft of speech are able to sing, and it is certainly a bizarre experience to hear a dysphasic person sing. It is common knowledge that a completely dysphasic individual may be capable of ejaculatory speech in response to emotional stimuli, such as anger, fear or pain; similarly, the capacity to sing may represent better preservation of emotional language. The dysphasic singer, however, is grossly handicapped in musical terms. There is no apparent record of any professional vocalist who was able to perform acceptably with permanent dysphasia, though there are examples of careers terminated by this disability (e.g. Head, 1926). According to Luria et al. (1965), Shebalin composed to his previous standard in spite of dysphasia following a stroke, but surely there must have been problems over word-setting. On the receptive side the musician with speech disturbance must be handicapped when listening to opera or song.

The dispute between those workers who regarded speech as localisable within the brain and those who took a holist view has not been reflected in the literature on music, save by a few writers (e.g. Feuchtwanger, 1930). Contemporary neurologists generally take a viewpoint intermediate between the extremes. It is almost a hundred years since Jackson (1879) pointed out the error of trying to localise a cerebral function; he believed that focal brain damage led to general dedifferentiation of function. Lesions of different parts of the brain result in a variety of dysphasic syndromes, but Jackson could not accept that abruptly demarcated areas of cortex stand for any kind of representation or that faculties reside in such places, "since speech and words enter into thought it is incredible that speech could reside in a limited spot". Head extended this view by his contention that brain disease "however localised can never affect speech and speech only". Certainly, the musical defects which occur in persons with brain damage from injury or disease are commonly, and one suspects invariably, associated with other manifestations of disturbed cerebral function. For example, an attempt to find an acceptable reported case of loss of ability to read musical notation without dyslexia or other evidence of disordered higher brain function has proved unsuccessful.

It is not possible to localise creative activities such as composition or performance within the brain. Only elementary psychological functions can be assigned to different areas of cortex; more complex activities depend on the several, appropriate parts of the brain, and these are linked by subcortical and interhemispheric pathways. Composition, performance and listening demand the sense of sight and hearing, intellectual and emotional functions and sensorimotor activity. This implies wide involvement of the cerebral cortex, subcortical motor and sensory nuclei and the limbic system in the intact musician.

Head's conception of speech as a process of symbolic formulation and expression is no longer acceptable to many neurologists, but the notion can be usefully applied to music, though some assert that only notation is truly symbolic. With music, as with speech, appropriately sited lesions may interfere with the basic individual psychological, sensory and motor events which combine in musical experience. Diffuse brain disease impairs musicality through intellectual deterioration and altered emotional response, apart from any derangement stemming from lesions affecting specific areas.

## Conclusion

In recent years neurologists have shown a new and welcome interest in the study of musical functions in normal people. Further investigations on such topics as the mechanisms of musical memory and of reading and learning music should yield information valuable in musical education. Neurophysiologists can assist teachers and performers as they explore the mechanisms of breathing, voice production and movement. Examination of the skills of composers and performers by neurophysiological and neuropsychological methods would be rewarding although a difficult exercise to mount. However, there is an ultimate mystery of musical experience which is not susceptible to neurological study, and the last word can be left to Richard Hooker (1597) who wrote that music is "a thing which delighteth all ages, and beseemeth all states; a thing as seasonable in grief as in joy . . ."

## REFERENCES

AGRIPPA, H. C. (1533) De occulta philosophia, sive de magia libri tres. Cologne.

ALAJOUANINE, T. (1948) Aphasia and artistic realisation. *Brain*, **71**, 229–241.

AUERBACH, S. (1906) Beitrag zur Lokalisation des musikalischen Talentes im Gehirn und am Schädel. *Arch. Anat. Physiol. (Anat. Abt.)*, 197–230.

AURELIANUS. (1529) Tardarum passionum Libri V. Basle.

B.B.C. (1964) *The Public for Serious Music.* An Audience Research Report.

BILLROTH, T. (1894) *Wer ist musikalisch?* Deutsche Rundschau.

BLUNT, W. (1974a) *On Wings of Song. A Biography of Felix Mendelssohn.* London, Hamish Hamilton, 88.

— (1974b) Ibid., 210–211.

BOYD, M. (1974) John Stanley's Voluntaries. *The Musical Times,* **115,** 588–599.

BRAIN, LORD (1959) *The Nature of Experience.* London, Oxford University Press, 55–57.

BURTON, R. (1632) *The Anatomy of Melancholy.* Oxford.

COOPER, M. (1970) In: *Beethoven, the Last Decade 1817–1827.* London, Oxford University Press, 71.

CREEL, W., BOOMSLITER, P. C. and POWERS, S. R. (1970) Sensations of tone as perceptual forms. *Psychol. Rev.,* **77,** 534–545.

CURRIE, S., HEATHFIELD, K. W. G., HENSON, R. A. and SCOTT, D. F. (1971) Clinical course and prognosis of temporal lobe epilepsy. A survey of 666 patients. *Brain,* **94,** 173–190.

EDGREN, I. G. (1895) Amusie (musikalische Aphasie). *Dtsche. Z. Nervheilkh.,* **6,** 1–64.

ETTLINGER, G. and MOFFETT, A. M. (1970) Learning in dysphasia. *Neuropsychol.,* **8,** 465–474.

FEUCHTWANGER, E. (1930) *Amusie. Studien zur pathologischen Psychologie der akustichen Wahrnehmung und Vorstellung und ihrer Struckturgebiete besonders in Musik und Sprach.* Berlin, Springer-Verlag.

GORDON, H. W. (1970) Hemispheric asymmetries in the perception of musical chords. *Cortex,* **6,** 387–398.

GORDON, H. W. and BOGEN, J. E. (1974) Hemispheric lateralisation of singing after intracarotid amylobarbitone. *J. Neurol. Neurosurg. Psychiat.,* **37,** 727–738.

GOTT, P. S. (1973) Language after dominant hemispherectomy. *J. Neurol. Neurosurg. Psychiat.,* **36,** 1082–1088.

HANSON, H. (1942) Musician's point of view towards emotional expression. *Am. J. Psychiat.,* **99,** 317–325.

HARDING, R. (1942) *An Anatomy of Inspiration,* 2nd edit. reprinted with minor corrections, 1967, London, Frank Cass and Co., p. 73.

HEAD, H. (1920) *Studies in Neurology.* Vol. 2, 560, Oxford Med. Publn.

— (1926) *Aphasia and Kindred Disorders of Speech.* Vol. 1, 379–380, 409; vol. 2, 248–258, Cambridge University Press.

HELLBORN, K. von (1869) *Life of Franz Schubert,* 2 vols. Trans. A. D. Coleridge, London, Longmans Green & Co., vol. 2, 160–161, quoted by Harding, R. (loc. cit.)

HENSCHEN, S. E. (1920) Aphasie, Amusie und Akalkulie. In: *Klinische und anatomische Beiträge zur Pathologie des Gehirns.* Vol. 5, Stockholm, Nordiska Bokhandeln.

— (1926) On the function of the right hemisphere of the brain in relation to the left in speech, music and calculation. *Brain,* **49,** 110–123.

HOOKER, R. (1597) *Fifth Book of Laws of Ecclesiastical Polity.* See Harrison, F. L.

(1968), *The New Oxford History of Music*. Vol. IV, 468, London, Oxford University Press.

HUGHES, A. (1953) *History of Music in Sound*. Vol. III Ars Nova and the Renaissance, p. 18, London, Oxford University Press.

JACKSON, H. (1879) On affections of speech from disease of the brain. *Brain*, 1, 304–330.

KIMURA, D. (1964) Left-right differences in the perception of melodies. *Quart. J. exper. Psychol.*, 16, 355–358.

KIRCHER, A. (1654) Magnes sive de arte magnetica opus tripartitum. Ed. 3, Rome.

KLEIST, K. (1928) Gehirnpathologische und lokalisatorische Ergebnisse über Hörstörungen, Geräuschtaubheiten und Amusien. *Mschr. Psychiat. Neurol.*, 68, 853–871.

— (1962) *Sensory Aphasia and Amusia. The myeloarchitectonic basis*. Trans. F. J. Fish and J. B. Stanton, Oxford, Pergamon Press.

KNOBLAUCH, A. (1888) Über Störungen der musikalischen Leistungsfähigkeit infolge von Gehirnläsionen. *Dt. Arch. klin. Med.*, 43, 331–352.

LURIA, A. R., TSVETKOVA, L. S. and FUTER, D. S. (1965) Aphasia in a composer. *J. Neurol. Sci.*, 2, 288–292.

MENUHIN, Y. (1972) In: *Theme and Variations*, pp. 61–62. London, Heinemann.

MILNER, B. (1962) *Laterality Effects in Audition in Hemispheric Relations and Cerebral Dominance*. Ed. V. B. Mountcastle, pp. 177–195, Baltimore, Johns Hopkins Press.

PENFIELD, W. and PEROT, P. (1963) The brain's record of auditory and visual experience. *Brain*, 86, 595–696.

PLINY, the Elder (1513) *Historiae naturalis, Libri xxxvii*. Venice.

PROBST, M. (1899) Über Lokalisation des Tonvermögens. *Arch. Psychiat. Nervkrankh.*, 32, 387–446.

— (1901) Über einen Fall von vollständiger Rindenblindheit und vollständiger Amusie. *Mschr. Psychiat. Neurol.*, 9, 5–21.

REID, C. (1961) *Thomas Beecham: an independent biography*, p. 45. London, Gollancz.

RÉVÉSZ, G. (1953) *An Introduction to the Psychology of Music*. London, Longmans Green and Co.

ROESER, R. J. and DALY, D. D. (1974) Auditory cortex disconnection associated with thalamic tumour. A case report. *Neurology*, 24, 555–559.

SCHEDEL, H. (1497) Liber Chronicorum (Nuremberg Chronicle). Augsburg.

SCHOLES, P. (1955) *Oxford Musical Companion*. Oxford University Press, 630, 631, 632.

SEASHORE, C. E. (1919) *The Psychology of Musical Talent*. New York, Silver Burdett.

— (1938) *Psychology of Music*. New York, McGraw-Hill.

SHANKWEILER D. (1966) Effects of temporal lobe damage on perception of dichotically presented melodies. *J. Comp. Physiol. Psychol.*, 62, 115–119.

SHUTER, R. (1968) *The Psychology of Musical Ability*. London, Methuen.

SMITH, A. (1966) Speech and other functions after left (dominant) hemispherectomy. *J. Neurol. Neurosurg. Psychiat.*, 29, 467–472.

SOUQUES, A. and BARUK, H. (1926) Un cas d'amusie chez un professeur de piano. *Rev. neurol.*, **33**, 1, 179–184.

— (1930) Autopsie d'un cas d'amusie (avec aphasie) chez un professeur de piano. *Rev. neurol.*, **37**, 1, 545–556.

USTVEDT, H. J. (1937) Über die Untersuchung der musikalischen Funktionen bei Patienten mit Gehirnleiden, besonders bei Patienten mit Aphasie. *Acta med. Scand. Suppl.*, **86**, 7–737.

WALLASCHEK, R. (1893) Die Bedeutung der Aphasie für die Musikvorstellung. *Z. Psychol. Physiol, Sinnesorg.*, **6**, 8–32.

WERTHEIM, N. (1963) Disturbances of the Musical Functions. In: *Problems of Dynamic Neurology*, pp. 162–180. Ed. L. Halpern, Jerusalem, Rothschild Hadassah University Hospital.

# 2

R. T. C. PRATT

# The Inheritance of Musicality

The scientific study of the inheritance of musicality offers particular difficulties, and no firm conclusions can be reached at the present time.

## GENERAL AND METHODOLOGICAL PROBLEMS

### 1. Biochemical genetics

The striking advances this century in the study of genetics have established the biochemical basis of inherited characters. In 1902 Garrod, in a paper entitled "The incidence of alcaptonuria: a study of chemical individuality", assembled certain features of this disorder (its frequent occurrence in sibs, its all-or-none character, the raised frequency of parental consanguinity, and its persistence throughout life), and concluded that it was determined by a mendelian mode of inheritance and that genetically-determined biochemical abnormalities would prove to be common. Progress in biochemical genetics was initially slow with respect to human disorders, but the work of Onslow (1925), Scott-Moncrieff (1939) and Haldane (1939) on the biochemical basis of inherited flower pigmentation, and of Beadle and Tatum (1941) on *Neurospora*, demonstrated the generality of Garrod's conclusions and encouraged further work on man. By the use of improved methods of chemical analysis, in particular chromatographic techniques, very many inherited metabolic disorders have now been analysed in man. Of the various expositions on this theme, that of Harris (1975) on Human Biochemical Genetics merits particular commendation. Its special interest in the present context is that it is the fourth version of a book on the subject by the same author, the first appearing in 1953 as Number 37 of the Eugenics Laboratory Memoirs, on the back cover of which were listed the contents of earlier numbers of the same series, including some published before 1914. Number 6 (1909) dealt with "Diabetes insipidus, split-foot, polydactylism, brachydactylism, tuberculosis, deaf-mutism, and legal ability", Number 9 (1909) with "Angioneurotic oedema, hermaphroditism, deaf-mutism, insanity, commercial ability", and Number 12 (1911) with "Haemophilia". Galton (1869), a pioneer of such studies, had considered abilities as diverse as mathematics and rowing. This juxtaposition of a variety of disorders and talents reads strangely nowadays with the benefit of hindsight. The concern in this country of the pioneers of the study of inheritance was variously distributed amongst a continuum of characters, some of which (e.g. alcaptonuria) are now regarded as due to a specific biochemical abnormality (a changed base in a DNA molecule causing an incorrect amino-acid to be inserted into the corresponding polypeptide chain), and others which appear to defy interpretation in biochemical terms. It naturally proved disappointing that a group of disorders of considerable social importance, such as alcoholism, or of great academic interest, such as legal ability, fall into the latter category; they seem most unlikely to have a simple biochemical basis or to yield to the approach that currently attracts the greatest scientific attention. Unfortunately for our present subject musicality falls into this category.

Yet there are indications that some higher cerebral functions may be dominantly inherited in an all-or-none fashion. The possession of a number-form, the faculty of visualising numbers as each occupying a particular and idiosyncratic position in space (Galton, 1883), may well fall into this category, although it is difficult to imagine the intermediate steps between a base substitution in a stretch of DNA and a complicated form of visual imagery. Galton also explored the normal range of visual imagery, extending from a vividness equalling reality to its complete absence (except in dreams). Casual enquiry reveals there is a similar range with auditory imagery, some gifted people being able to "hear" a symphony in their imagination as clearly as at an actual performance, whereas others can hear nothing. The way this faculty runs in families would repay study.

## 2. Heterogeneity of diseases and qualities

Early studies attempting to interpret the familial concentration of mental deficiency encountered many difficulties that were overcome only when it was fully recognised that many separate causes might lead to mental deficiency, and that no single mechanism could explain its occurrence in every case. For example birth injury leading to brain damage could cause mental defect in the absence of any predisposing genetical factor whatsoever. In those instances where genetical factors were the main cause the large number of individual metabolic errors responsible was not recognised for some time. It is probable that in a similar fashion positive attainments may be reached by a variety of routes.

## 3. Monogenic and polygenic inheritance

In the simplest examples of disorders that are entirely genetically determined a single pair of genes is involved. In dominant inheritance only one of the pair involved is abnormal, and the disorder tends to appear in successive generations, being inherited from one or other parent. In recessive inheritance both genes of the pair are similarly abnormal and the disorder appears on an average in 25 per cent. of brothers and sisters, the parents (and children) being normal, though all of them are carriers of one abnormal gene.

Other disorders and qualities depend not on a single pair of genes but on many pairs; this mechanism (polygenic inheritance) is likely to be the genetical basis of qualities that are continuously distributed in the population (for instance height, weight, intelligence), rather than being present or absent in a straightforward all-or-none fashion. It is plausible that musicality falls within this category. The likelihood of polygenic inheritance being responsible for the familial concentration of certain continuously-distributed qualities can be tested by the resemblance between parent–child pairs, sib pairs and husband and wife. The correlation between husband and wife would be zero with random mating, but in practice assortative mating disturbs the zero correlation, and musical talent might be expected to play no small part in influencing the choice of a marriage partner.

A further complication with polygenic inheritance is the threshold effect, best evaluated in infantile pyloric stenosis by Carter (1961). This disorder is more common in males, and females require a stronger genetical predisposition to develop it, as reflected in the raised frequency of the disorder in relatives of females, the less commonly affected sex, as compared with the relatives of males. In either sex once the threshold is crossed the disorder appears; in this way a polygenically-determined disorder will manifest in an all-or-none fashion.

### 4. The influence of environment

There is a complex interplay between heredity and environment in almost every situation. A person genetically unable to metabolise the muscle relaxant succinyl-choline will be free from disability unless exposed to the drug. Some cultural environments may be entirely lacking in the stimuli necessary for the development of an inborn talent, whether it be for physics or music. Furthermore, it is plausible that practice and application may enable a person of low intellectual calibre to reach a modest level of achievement in, for example, arithmetic, but no amount of practice would allow him to gain mastery in calculus. Conversely, intense practice and application may enable a person to achieve his full potential, but the limit will have been fixed by his genetical endowment.

## 5. *The accuracy of recorded pedigrees*

There is a tendency in recording pedigrees for unaffected (or undistinguished) persons to be omitted; even those investigations concerned primarily with the mode of inheritance have not escaped errors. An abnormal gene carried on the Y chromosome would be inherited in an unusual way, namely, only males would be affected, and they would pass it on to all their sons and none of their daughters. The classic (and probably unique) instance of this mode of inheritance, quoted in many text-books, was reinvestigated by Penrose and Stern (1958), who showed that the pedigree when corrected after consulting parish registers and other sources was incompatible with the long-accepted Y-linked inheritance. The tendency for pedigrees, in particular those from earlier centuries, to be unreliable, and especially for unaffected members to be omitted, thus weakening evidence for segregation, makes it unwise to draw firm conclusions from such evidence, and regretfully it has been largely disregarded here.

## 6. *Twin studies*

Monozygotic (identical) twins are born with identical genetical endowment, whereas dizygotic (non-identical) twins resemble each other genetically no more than they do a sib who is not a twin. Twins are therefore a most important group for the study of the relative importance of heredity and environment, since dizygotic twins are exposed to very similar environments although differing genetically, whilst in the rare instances of monozygotic twins brought up apart their environments differ although their genetical endowment is the same. This field is one that has received only limited attention with respect to the inheritance of musicality but promises much. There are, however, two particular disadvantages. Twins are slightly more subject to minor brain injury at birth and, if present, such injury might well accentuate or diminish intrapair differences. Secondly, twins are as a group of only average musical ability, and the practical difficulties of this kind of study are increased by the rarity of twins in the extreme ranges of ability, who are more likely to illuminate the problems of heredity than those of average ability.

## 7. *What is inherited?*

In the case of intelligence, factor analysis of test results has led to the belief that they can be accounted for on the basis of a general factor (g) and a number of specific factors (for example spatial ability). It is likely that this is also the case with musicality, but not enough work has been done on this aspect (Shuter, 1968), and the validity of factor analysis in other fields has been criticised. There is no reason to believe that if an aspect of music were unitary from a musical point of view (a possible example is genuine absolute pitch), its inheritance would be genetically unitary. The various tests of musicality have been fully reviewed by Shuter (1968). There is no evidence that tests of basic specific sensory qualities (as in the Seashore battery) have simpler or stronger genetical basis than higher and more direct tests of musicality (e.g. musical memory in the Wing battery); in fact the Wing tests appear to be both more reliable and to be more valid in the sense of corresponding with independent teachers' ratings, and of forecasting success with an instrument. The Wing tests are also relatively uninfluenced by previous training and are therefore more likely to reflect innate capacities more directly.

## EVIDENCE AND OPINIONS

### 1. Anatomical and neurophysiological considerations

Post-mortem studies of the brains of distinguished men have hitherto been valueless. Language is represented in the left cerebral hemisphere in 99 per cent. of right-handers, but it is only recently that claims have been made that structural differences between the two sides may underlie language laterality, and even the lateralisation of musical ability. Scheid and Eccles (1975) report that the planum temporale is larger on the left side in 65 per cent. of brains, on the right side in 11 per cent. of brains, and equal in 24 per cent. They say, "We would therefore suggest that the enlargement of the right planum temporale is a measure of the musical ability built into the brain by genetic coding, just as we would assume that the left planum temporale is a measure of the linguistic abilities similarly built prenatally ready for linguistic use. Since the asymmetries can be observed so easily macroscopically, it should be a simple matter to test this hypothesis out by post-mortem examination of brains both from subjects who were distinguished by musical abilities and from those who were not. It is important to realise that these special developments of the temporal lobe have already occurred by the time of birth. No amount of training could make a subject with a poorly developed musical area a competent performer in any musical field! It is of course general knowledge that people vary widely in their musical sensitivity and ability. It is not just a matter of experience and practice. These 'gifts' are generally regarded as inborn, and of course we can now postulate it has a structural counterpart in the enlargement of the appropriate area of the temporal lobe."

Such investigations have hitherto been performed on the brains of persons whose handedness was not recorded. Now that a reliable test of language laterality is available, using unilateral ECT (Pratt and Warrington, 1972), it is known that in left-handers there is no relationship between degree of left-handedness and language laterality (Warrington and Pratt, 1973). The hypothesis of Scheid and Eccles is, as they say, simple to test, but in the present climate of knowledge is likely to be refuted. There is nevertheless strong evidence of an innate capacity to respond to specific auditory stimuli; in a study of cerebral evoked responses Winter (1972) found that certain cortical cells in the squirrel monkey respond less to simple stimuli than they do to monkey calls.

## 2. Pedigree studies

Galton (1869) in his book *Hereditary Genius* included musicians amongst his men of eminence. The Bach family naturally features prominently in any survey of this sort, but the pedigrees as published (e.g. Révész, 1953, p. 193) give rise to suspicion on several counts: they contained few females (talented or not), they recorded a suspiciously high proportion of talented persons, and they were totally unrepresentative of the generality of musicians. More random samples of families were recorded by Davenport (1911), who found that with both parents of superior musical ability the children were superior to medium, and none was poor; with both parents poor all children were poor. When parents were dissimilar in ability the children varied between the two extremes. Révész (1953) summarised the findings of two large surveys by questionnaire made by Heymans and Wiersma (Table 1, Column 1), and by Haecker and Ziehen (Table 1, Column 2).

In view of the fact that the graded abilities were classified into three arbitrary groups, agreement is surprisingly close (although differing from the findings of Davenport). Disregarding for the moment the influence of environment, these findings support a polygenic mode of inheritance, as

*Table 1* Musical ability of parents and children

| Parents | Children Musical | | Intermediate | | Unmusical | |
|---|---|---|---|---|---|---|
| | 1 | 2 | 1 | 2 | 1 | 2 |
| Musical × Musical | 84 | 86 | 6 | 6 | 10 | 8 |
| Musical × Unmusical | 59 | 59 | 5 | 15 | 36 | 26 |
| Unmusical × Unmusical | 30 | 25 | 8 | 16 | 62 | 59 |

does Révész's observation that the offspring of two gifted parents are rarely as gifted, showing the expected regression towards the mean. Polygenic inheritance is also supported by the observation that in a musical family the gifts are often distributed in various directions, for example, composer, performer, conductor, or maker of instruments, rather than being confined to one limited aspect of music. In summary, although the evidence from pedigree studies for a familial concentration of musical ability is strong, it is not possible to assess how great a part musical environment rather than genetical endowment may have played.

### 3. Test results within families

With the development of a variety of musical tests it is possible to study the level reached by a single person on a number of tests, to begin to assess whether one or many factors contribute to musicality, and to measure the correlation between the results of various degrees of relative within a family. Earlier studies were reviewed and admirably extended by Shuter (1968), who used the reliable Wing tests. The musical quotients (MQ's) of both parents when averaged gave a correlation approaching 0·5 with the child, as did the sib–sib correlation. The correlations were, however, considerably lower when individuals, and the individual tests, were considered. Procedures of this kind do not allow the effects of heredity and environment to be separated, even when, as in Shuter's investigation, an independent assessment of the musicality of the home environment was made.

### 4. Twin studies

Twin studies again have been reviewed by Shuter (1968), who found in comparing MQ's that the correlation was 0·84 for monozygotic and 0·72 for dizygotic, same-sexed child pairs, lower figures than are found for intelligence tests. Shuter was also able to test five identical pairs brought up apart and found considerable similarities, but again not as great as are found with intelligence tests. Further studies on twins and their sibs are greatly needed and are likely to throw more light on the interplay between inheritance and environment.

### 5. Absolute pitch

The possession of absolute pitch would seem to be a profitable subdivision of musicality to study genetically, but the name itself is misleading, as Révész (1953, pp. 95–111) pointed out in distinguishing "genuine absolute pitch" from approximations to it, where, for example, the ability may be restricted to a limited range of notes or to a particular musical instrument (see also Wynn, 1973). Its accuracy also varies according to the menstrual cycle (Wynn, 1971) and it is possible for it to be learned by an ungifted subject "in 365 hard lessons" (Brady, 1970). Baggaley (1974) stressed the importance of measuring the speed of performance as well as accuracy in the assessment of absolute pitch. The early development of absolute pitch (in some instances by three years of age) again suggests an inborn gift, but the evidence collected by questionnaire by Sergeant and Roche (1973) argued conclusively in the opposite direction. In over a thousand professional musicians the possession of absolute pitch was related to the age at which training on a musical instrument began. Of those who began training before the age of four years 95 per cent. possessed absolute pitch, whereas of those who started training between 12 and 14 years only 5 per cent. possessed it (correlation coefficient 0·98). This finding is reminiscent of the critical period for imprinting in animals and man (Ackroyd, et al., 1974).

## 6. *Tune deafness*

An ingenious approach to the inheritance of musicality was made by Penrose, Fry (1948) and Kalmus (1968), who investigated the tune-deaf (tone-deaf). Twenty-five popular tunes were each presented with its pair, either the same or differing by one or two wrong notes so that the incorrect version is readily selected by 95 per cent. of people, with a clear segregation of scores from the 5 per cent. tune-deaf. Segregation was also found within families, but no clear-cut mode of inheritance could be discerned.

## 7. *Sex-ratio*

There is a pronounced variation in the sex-ratio in various branches of music, vocal soloists for example reaching an equality of acclaim that has not been achieved by composers. There is no obvious genetical interpretation of this. An environmental explanation is suggested by the recent emergence in Great Britain of women composers of high repute contemporaneous with the growing equality of opportunity in musical education.

## 8. *Environmental effects*

In situations where an environmental factor can be shown to be highly important, the genetical contribution is thereby diminished, but, as was emphasised earlier, the relative importance of genetical and environmental factors may well be different when various levels of achievement are selected. The clearest demonstration of environmental influence is in Sergeant's work on absolute pitch quoted above, but it is important to remember that his information was obtained from professional musicians. The influence of training on a random cross-section of the population (cf. Brady, 1970) might well emphasise a greater importance of genetical factors.

Contrary to a strongly held belief, the Welsh do not appear to be innately gifted by their very race, according to studies by McLeish and Thomas (1971) on three groups matched for intelligence and consisting of Welsh speakers living in Wales, bilingual Border residents and an English group from Cambridge.

## CONCLUSION

Numerous studies have clearly emphasised the importance of home environment and parental attitudes on the development of musical and artistic talent in children (Freeman, 1974). Shuter (1968) reviewed the scientific evidence on this subject and concluded, "A musically stimulating home is certainly likely to help children to make the best use of whatever potential talent they may happen to possess. It would be over-optimistic, however, to hope that parents could substantially improve the ability, as opposed to the taste, with which their children have been endowed."

## REFERENCES

ACKROYD, C., HUMPHREY, N. K., and WARRINGTON, E. K. (1974) Lasting effects of early blindness: a case study. *Q. Jl. exp. Psychol.*, **26**, 114.

BAGGALEY, J. (1974) Measurement of absolute pitch: a confused field. *Psychology of Music*, **2–2**, 11.

BEADLE, G. W. and TATUM, E. L. (1941) Genetical control of biochemical reactions in *Neurospora. Proc. natn. Acad. Sci. USA*, **27**, 499.

BRADY, P. T. (1970) Teach yourself absolute pitch in 365 hard lessons. *J. acoust. Soc. Am.*, **48**, 88 (8).

CARTER, C. O. (1961) The inheritance of congenital pyloric stenosis. *Br. med. Bull.*, **17**, 251.

DAVENPORT, C. B. (1911) *Heredity in Relation to Eugenics*. New York, Dover Reprint, 1972.

FREEMAN, J. (1974). Musical and artistic talent in children. *Psychology of Music*, **2–1**, 1.

FRY, D. (1948) An experimental study of tone deafness. *Speech*, **12**, 4.

GALTON, F. (1869) *Hereditary Genius*. London, Murray.

— (1883) *Inquiries into Human Faculty and its Development*. London, Macmillan, Everyman Edition, 1951.

GARROD, A. E. (1902) The incidence of alcaptonuria. *Lancet*, **2**, 1616.

HALDANE, J. B. S. (1939) The biochemistry of the individual. In: *Perspectives in Biochemistry*, p. 1. Ed. J. Needham and D. E. Green, Cambridge University Press.

HARRIS, H. (1953) *An Introduction to Human Biochemical Genetics*. London, Cambridge University Press.

— (1975) *Principles of Human Biochemical Genetics* (2nd ed.). Amsterdam, North Holland.

KALMUS, H. (1968) The world of the colour blind and the tune deaf. In: J. M. Thoday and A. S. Parkes, *Genetic and Environmental Influences on Behaviour*, p. 206. Edinburgh, Oliver & Boyd.

McLEISH, J. and THOMAS, C. (1971). Nationality and musicality used to test the Lamarckian hypothesis. *Nature, Lond.*, **230**, 337.

ONSLOW, M. W. (1925) *The Anthocyanin Pigments of Plants*. 2nd ed., Cambridge University Press.

PENROSE, L. S. and STERN, C. (1958). Reconsideration of the Lambert pedigree. *Ann. hum. Genet.*, **22**, 258.

PRATT, R. T. C. and WARRINGTON, E. K. (1972) The assessment of cerebral dominance with unilateral ECT. *Br. J. Psychiat.*, **121**, 327.

RÉVÉSZ, G. (1953) *Introduction to the Psychology of Music*. London, Longmans Green.

SCHEID, P. and ECCLES, J. C. (1975) Music and speech: artistic functions of the human brain. *Psychology of Music*, **3–1**, 21.

SCOTT-MONCRIEFF, R. (1939) The biochemistry of flower colour variation. In: *Perspectives in Biochemistry*, p. 230. Ed. J. Needham and D. E. Green, Cambridge University Press.

SERGEANT, D. and ROCHE, S. (1973) Perceptual shifts in the auditory information processing of young children. *Psychology of Music*, **1–2**, 39.

SHUTER, R. (1968) *The Psychology of Musical Ability*. London, Methuen.

WINTER, P. (1972) *Neurosci. Res. Prog. Bull.*, **10**, 1, 72.

WYNN, V. T. (1971) "Absolute" pitch – a bimensual rhythm. *Nature, Lond.*, **230**, 337.

— (1973) Absolute pitch in humans. *Prog. Neurobiol.*, **1**, 113.

WARRINGTON, E. K. and PRATT, R. T. C. (1973) Language laterality in left-handers assessed by unilateral ECT. *Neuropsychologia*, **11**, 423.

# 3

J. D. HOOD

# Psychological and Physiological Aspects of Hearing

While all the higher vertebrates and indeed many primitive animals possess a highly specialised organ, the ear, for the reception of sound, its functional utility in man has attained a pre-eminence which finds its highest expression in our ability to communicate by means of the spoken word and in our appreciation of music. It does not of course follow that hearing in man is in any way exceptional, in fact in terms of the range of frequencies which can be perceived, it seems likely that man has the most limited range of all mammals. Thus, whereas human hearing extends from some 16 Hz, approximating to the lowest register of an organ pipe, to at most 20 000 Hz, the sound of grasshoppers, certain rodents and bats have hearing ranges encompassing an additional two octaves to frequencies as high as 100 000 Hz. It is highly probable that the auditory characteristics of each species have evolved in ways most suited to the animals' requirements, which at times take on a remarkable specificity. Rats for example have been shown to possess particularly acute hearing in a very narrow ultrasonic band of frequencies which corresponds precisely to the frequency spectrum of sounds emitted by the young, and the inference is that it is by this means that the mother and offspring are able to locate each other in the dark. The characteristics of human hearing on the other hand are uniquely suited to the reception of speech sounds, so much so that there can be little doubt that speech communication has been its prime evolutionary objective, while music in its turn has been a natural by-product of the development of speech and language. Despite marked functional differences, the hearing mechanism itself is strikingly similar in all higher mammals and consists essentially of an outer ear, a middle ear and an inner ear (Figure 1).

## THE OUTER EAR

The auricle or pinna is the visible portion of the ear. In order that it can collect and deflect sound into the ear it is a matter of physical acoustics that its dimensions be at least comparable to or larger than the wave length of the sound reaching it. Wave length varies inversely with frequency, and in man this condition prevails only at the highest audible frequencies. Bats and other animals, however, which are highly dependent upon hearing in the ultrasonic range of frequencies have funnel shaped pinnae, the musculature of which is highly organised for the directional receptivity of sounds of high frequency with consequently very short wave lengths. On

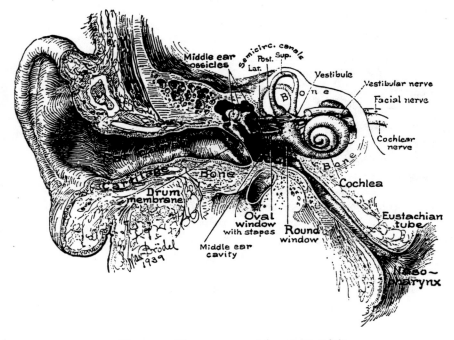

Figure 1    The anatomy of the ear (Brödel)

this account most textbooks maintain that in man the pinna is a useless appendage, and this is supported by the fact that those of us who have any ability at all to move our ears are the exception rather than the rule. However, the collection of sound may not be the only function of the pinna since there is now strong evidence that it may play an important role in sound localisation. Thus it has been shown that by progressively eliminating different ridges and valleys of the pinna, localisation ability can be appreciably reduced, and the evidence now is that its convolutions introduce time delays in arrival between direct sound and sound reflected from its folds which can be meaningfully interpreted by the brain in directional terms. This has obvious relevance to musical appreciation since, in view of the complexity of the wave form of music, it would be surprising if the pinna did not exert a modifying influence upon the quality of the music perceived particularly in respect of stereophonic listening.

Of particular interest in this respect are the results of some recent experiments carried out in Germany in which a dummy head was constructed equipped with artificial pinnae, each terminating in a separate microphone connected to a two-channel tape recorder. Recordings were then made of orchestral concerts performed in different auditoria and the output of each channel of the recorder ultimately delivered to headphones worn by a listener. Under these conditions it is claimed that not only are the acoustics of the different auditoria faithfully retained in the recording but, moreover, the stereophonic effect is so strikingly enhanced that the location in space of individual instruments of the orchestra can easily be identified.

Incoming sound reaches the middle ear by way of the ear canal or external auditory meatus, a slightly curved tube about one inch in length terminated by the ear drum, or tympanic membrane, which separates the outer from the middle ear. The ear drum has a conical appearance with the apex directed inwards. The meatus and pinna in combination have a slight resonating effect over a limited band of frequencies around 3500 Hz.

## THE MIDDLE EAR

The tympanic cavity, an air filled space in the temporal bone, lies beyond the ear drum. In it are housed three articulated bones, the malleus, the incus and the stapes, known collectively as the ossicular chain. The malleus is attached to the interior surface of the tympanic membrane and articulates in turn with the incus and the stapes, the footplate of which is attached to an opening in the bony labyrinth known as the oval window by means of a cartilaginous surround or annular ligament. The cavity and structures contained within it comprise the middle ear, the function of which is the efficient transmission of sound energy from the outer ear to the inner ear by way of its point of entry, the oval window. The oval window has a surface area about 1/20 that of the tympanic membrane and is faced on its innermost side by the fluid of the inner ear. In other words it presents what is commonly known as a high impedance to incoming sound and in isolation would reflect most of the sound energy reaching it. Indeed, in certain pathological conditions in which the ossicular chain is absent or impaired, appreciable deafness results so that only very loud conversation can be heard. In order, therefore, that the relatively large excursions of the tympanic membrane, a low impedance source, can be translated to the oval window, a so-called impedance matching device is called for, and this is provided by the lever action of the ossicular chain so that with relatively little loss in efficiency most of the energy reaches the inner ear.

The ossicular chain is maintained in a remarkable state of equilibrium by a number of ligaments, the two most important being the tensor tympani and the stapedius muscles which are applied to the malleus and stapes respectively. When the ear is stimulated with a loud sound there occurs a strong reflex contraction of the tympanic muscles which markedly reduces the efficiency of transmission. In consequence it has long been held that their function is to protect the delicate receptors of the inner ear against the assault of noise of traumatising intensity. This view, however, is not completely in accord with known facts.

In the first place, the time taken by the tympanic muscles to contract is too long to afford any protection against sounds of sudden onset and, furthermore, they fatigue fairly rapidly in the presence of loud noise sustained for any length of time. Finally, the deafness that is common in workers exposed to ·industrial noise is evidence that the ear has not really any adequate protective device. A much more likely explanation of the function of the tympanic muscles stems from recent studies which have shown that they are brought into activity not only during but prior to vocalisation. This means that the sensitivity of our hearing to the sound of our own voices is in a state of continuous reflex regulation. We have only to alter the transmission characteristics of our hearing by blocking our ears with our fingers and attempt to speak in such circumstances to realise how heavily dependent voice control is upon hearing. Actually, we hear the sound of our own voices by two routes, one the usual air conduction route and the other by so called bone conduction. In the latter, the skull itself is set into vibration and these vibrations are transmitted directly to the inner ear, by-passing the middle ear mechanism. Contraction of the middle ear muscles, while reducing the efficiency of transmission by the air conduction route, will tend to increase bone conduction thereby preferentially enhancing the hearing of our voices. Experiments have in fact shown that we do seem to hear our own voices at a higher level than would be perceived by a listener close by. This arrangement makes a good deal of sense. If two vocalists, for example, are singing in close harmony each can exert control over his own voice only if he can hear it above the level of his neighbour's. In the absence of a system which favours the hearing of one's own voice a bizarre situation would develop in which each singer would continually attempt to out-vocalise the other. When we consider both the exquisite voice control called for in singing and the very considerable volume of sound emitted by an opera singer some form of hearing sensitivity regulation might be considered not only desirable but essential.

The proper functioning of the tympanic membrane is dependent upon equality of air pressure being maintained at each of its surfaces. The tympanic cavity, however, is lined with pneumatised mastoid cells which absorb oxygen and in the absence of a pressure regulating device this would soon give rise to a negative pressure in the middle ear. This function is performed by the Eustachian tube, a slender canal which connects the lower portion of the tympanic cavity to the upper part of the throat. It opens during the act of swallowing allowing air to enter or leave the middle ear. Additionally it serves to equalise pressure variations which occur with change in altitude, as for example when we climb or descend a hill or fly in an aeroplane. This is why it is customary on certain air lines to hand out boiled sweets prior to take-off and landing, the aim being to stimulate frequent swallowing and thus alleviate the uncomfortable feeling of fullness in the ears and transitory deafness that occurs even nowadays despite cabin pressurisation.

## THE INNER EAR

The peripheral organ of hearing is housed within the bony labyrinth located in the temporal bone. The labyrinth is comprised of three parts, the vestibule, the semicircular canals and the cochlea. Of these, only the latter is concerned with hearing, the first two having to do with the sense of balance. All three communicate with each other and in consequence it is not unusual to find deafness accompanied by disorders of balance, the most classical example being Ménière's disease, in which fluctuating attacks of giddiness and deafness are the rule.

The cochlea is a spiral shaped tube of about $2\frac{1}{2}$ turns in man and $1\frac{1}{2}$ inches in length and bears a remarkable resemblance to a snail's shell; hence its name. In cross section Figure 2 it can be seen to be divided by a partition, the basilar membrane, into two parts the so-called scala vestibuli and scala tympani. These two canals are filled with fluid called perilymph and communicate with each other at the apex of the cochlea by way of an opening termed the helicotrema. At the basal end the scala vestibuli is terminated by an opening into the middle ear, the oval window in which is housed the footplate of the stapes. The scala tympani has a similar opening, the round window which is covered by a thin membrane.

When the stapes is set into motion by sound reaching the ear drum, inward movement gives rise to an increase in pressure of the fluid of the inner ear, and this is relieved by an outward bulging of the round window membrane. These movements are reversed with outward movements of the stapes. The resulting pressure variations in turn give rise to a travelling wave which passes along the length of the basilar membrane. Although the analogy is not a true one the form of vibration is similar to that of a length of rope held in the hand at one end and waved up and down. With low pitched sound the whole of the basilar membrane is set into vibration, whereas with very high pitched sound only a very small portion at the base near the oval window vibrates.

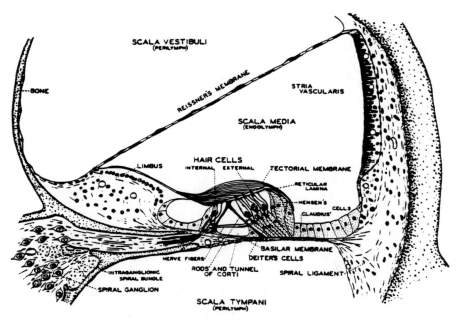

Figure 2    Cross section of the cochlea

The basilar membrane is comprised in part of a fibrous membrane, the fibres of which run transversely across the membrane. Their elasticity varies throughout the length from base to apex in a ratio of about 1 : 100. Its width varies similarly being five times greater at the apex than at the base. This arrangement of course is remarkably similar to the tuned strings of a piano, and it was considerations of this kind that led Helmholtz to propose his classic resonance theory of hearing in which it was supposed that each fibre was tuned to a particular frequency, the lower tones being subserved by the broad fibres at the apex, the high tones by the shorter fibres at the base. While, as will be seen later, this hypothesis is no longer tenable certain authorities still maintain that some form of resonance activity takes place in the cochlea. The vital structure responsible for the transduction of sound vibrations into nervous impulses is the Organ of Corti, which lies upon the basilar membrane. It is bathed in a fluid, endolymph, which is separated from the perilymph by a delicate membrane called Reissner's membrane to form the cochlear duct.

The Organ of Corti is shaped like a triangular tunnel composed of arches in which are embedded the auditory receptors or hair cells. There are three rows of outer hair cells and a single line of inner hair cells. These connect at their base with auditory nerve fibres which traverse the basilar membrane to reach the axis of the cochlear spiral where they collectively form the auditory nerve. At their upper ends the hair cells terminate in fine hairs called cilia which are embedded in a gelatinous like membrane termed the tectorial membrane. When the basilar membrane vibrates in response to incident sound the tectorial membrane moves transversely across the Organ of Corti causing the cilia to bend, and it is this bending action which is thought to be the triggering action which initiates the nervous response of the hair cells.

The external hair cells and the internal hair cells have been shown by means of electron microscopy to be structurally quite different from each other. Since on purely physical grounds it can be argued that the external hair cells will be brought into activity in advance of the inner hair cells, and in addition have been shown in general to be more vulnerable to damage by loud noise, disease or toxic agency, it has always been believed that they subserve hearing for low intensity sounds, while the inner hair cells respond only at higher intensities. Recent studies have revealed, however, that 95 per cent. of all fibres innervating the cochlea reach the inner hair cells and these are largely afferent, that is to say they carry impulses from the periphery to the brain. Of the remainder reaching the external hair cells 90 per cent. are efferent, carrying nerve impulses in the opposite direction. This of course implies that the external hair cells are under some form of central influence, and although the functional significance of this remains speculative there are good reasons for supposing that the role of the external hair cells has largely to do with the extremely fine pitch discrimination of which the ear is known to be capable.

## CENTRAL AUDITORY PATHWAYS

Nervous impulses from the sensory receptors in the cochlea are relayed by way of junction points termed synapses along the VIIIth nerve to make connection with what are known as second order neurons. From these the auditory pathways proceed up the brainstem interrupted by further synaptic relays en route to the cerebral cortex. A simplified diagram of the auditory connections is shown in Figure 3. The fibres from the cochlea all terminate in the cochlear nucleus in the brain stem, where they form synaptic connections with second order neurons. A small number ascend to the higher centres on the same side, but the majority cross the mid line and proceed to the opposite side to make connection with the third order neurons converging in the medial geniculate body, and thence by way of the fourth order neurons through the auditory radiations to the auditory cortex. It will be observed, therefore, that both cochleae are bilaterally represented not only in the brain stem but also in the cortex. An important consequence of this is that a lesion in the brainstem above the level of the cochlear nucleus cannot give rise to deafness unless the tracts on both sides are involved. Furthermore, removal of one cerebral hemisphere produces no obvious auditory impairment at either ear since the remaining hemisphere continues to receive impulses from both ears. This indicates that both the crossed and uncrossed central connections are equivalent at least with respect to auditory acuity.

Within the brainstem itself, the fibre tracts of the auditory system are arranged tonotopically so that the frequency organisation of the cochlea is maintained at all levels from the auditory nerve to the cortex. In this way

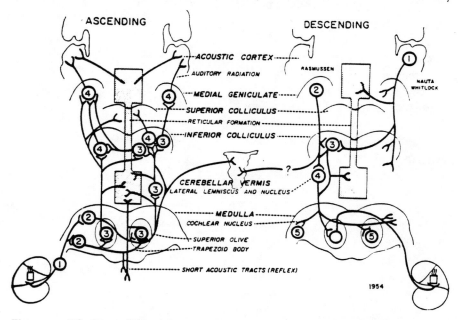

Figure 3   The ascending and descending connections of the auditory pathways (Galambos, R. (1957) *Laryngoscope,* **68,** 338)

tones of different frequency produce maximum excitation at different places though such places may be multiple in any one nuclear area, and indeed this multiplicity seems to increase at higher levels so that in the cortex at least four separate areas offer representations of the cochlea.

How auditory information is processed centrally is far from clear. Most auditory neurons are spontaneously active and in response to cochlear stimulation this activity may be either excited, suppressed or even unchanged. All three modes of activity have to be considered within the context of the extraordinarily complex auditory information which constantly assails the ear. In this respect what we have to deal with is not the response of a single neuron to a single pure tone but rather with the manner in which it may interact with tones of neighbouring frequency and differing phase relationships. Thus, for example, two or more frequencies can often produce exquisite resolution by a neuron that would otherwise be only indifferently responsive to a single tone. Interactions of this kind are commonplace in the auditory system but our knowledge of their functional significance is, at the present time, rudimentary.

## THEORY OF HEARING

Theories of hearing that have been put forward in the past, beginning with Helmholtz resonance theory, are too numerous to detail here and in any event the majority are now of little more than historical interest. Instead, attention will be given to certain well established facts and the inferences that may be derived from them. In the analysis of sound performed by the ear two aspects have to be considered: first, pitch with its physical attribute frequency; and second, loudness with its physical attribute intensity.

All sounds in air consist of rapid vibrations of the air particles which move backwards and forwards, imparting this movement to their neighbours so that waves of sound energy are propagated which on reaching the tympanic membrane set it into sympathetic vibration. The number of complete vibrations per second is said to be the frequency in cycles per second now, by international agreement, commonly designated in Hertz (Hz). Low pitched tones have a low frequency, high pitched tones a high frequency. Tones of only a single frequency are called pure tones, the simplest example being the sound of a tuning fork when struck very gently, and are rarely encountered in everyday life. Instead all sounds consist of complex combinations of a multitude of different vibrations. Some of these are periodic in nature, others aperiodic. The latter are perceived as noise, the former have a wave-form with a repetitive character and are perceived as tones. A feature of any periodic wave, however complex it may be, is that it can be analysed according to what is known as Fourier's Law into its component pure tones the frequencies of which bear to one another the ratios 1 2 3 4 5 and so on. The first of these is known as the fundamental and in general imparts the particular aspect of pitch which the sound may possess, the remainder are known as overtones and give to the sound by virtue of their relative magnitudes its particular quality or timbre. In this way we are able to distinguish the tone of a violin from a piano and so forth. These components can readily be identified and measured by physical means, and it is a remarkable feature of the ear that it carries out just such an analysis according to what is known as Ohm's Law of hearing. The precise manner in which this analysis is accomplished remains a matter of speculation, but we can be reasonably certain that the first stage of the process is a place analysis. Thus it will be recalled that the travelling wave set up on the basilar membrane is dependent upon the frequency of the incident sound wave, low frequencies setting the whole of the membrane into vibrations and high frequencies only a restricted portion at the base. In other words, the basilar membrane itself appears to be performing a mechanical form of frequency analysis, and if this is so one would expect the high frequency receptors to be located at its base with the low frequency receptors extending progressively throughout its length. Electrophysiological and histological studies on both animals and humans have confirmed precisely this kind of arrangement. In particular, hair cell damage restricted to the basal end of the cochlea consistently gives rise to deafness confined to the high frequencies.

Nevertheless, the observed forms of vibration of the basilar membrane, although showing a surprising degree of selectivity, cannot in themselves account for the superlative pitch discrimination possessed by the ear, and on this account it has been found necessary to postulate a second and more refined stage of tuning, the most likely site being the external hair cells. For low frequencies, however, a purely mechanical form of frequency analysis appears to be less obvious since the whole of the basilar membrane is set into vibration, and in consequence most of the receptors throughout its length will be brought into activity. An additional form of frequency analysis has therefore been suggested for which there is in fact substantial experimental evidence. This has come to be known as the Volley Hypothesis.

If recordings are made from the auditory nerves of animals exposed to pure tones of varying frequency, then the impulses generated in the nerve are found to be synchronous in frequency with that of the pure tone up to a frequency of about 4000 to 5000 Hz. Now as it happens the maximum rate at which any one fibre can respond does not much exceed 300 impulses per second. The auditory nerve of course is made up of thousands of nerve fibres and what appears to be happening is that as the frequency is raised from say 300 to 600 Hz the individual fibres respond in alternation, half at one cycle of the stimulus frequency and the other half at each succeeding cycle, so that although their individual maximal rate of response never exceeds 300 the net result at the level of the auditory nerve will be a response synchronous with the tonal frequency.

With further increase in frequency, groups of fibres will respond in rotation to every 3rd, 4th or 5th cycle of the stimulating tone and so on so that synchrony of the total nerve discharge is maintained. This means in effect that the frequency of the nervous response reaching the cortex could carry information concerning the pitch of a sound. How the brain interprets this information is not clear, but it is perhaps worth noting that recordings of nerve impulses in the higher centres of the auditory system indicate that synchrony is progressively lost the higher one ascends. It is possible that place and frequency both play a part in pitch perception, the latter being of greater importance for low frequency sounds.

The sensation of loudness is related to the total sound energy reaching the ear and, although the subjective aspects will be dealt with in greater detail later in this chapter, it is worth noting here that increasing the intensity of a tone results not only in an increase in the rate of response of individual fibres but also in a spread of activity along the basilar membrane with a recruitment of additional receptors. In consequence there occurs a progressive increase in the total flow of nervous impulses per unit time which is apparent not only at the periphery but also in the higher centres. While this clearly provides the basis for loudness perception it is pertinent to recall that high frequencies stimulate only a very restricted portion of the basilar membrane at its base, so that the availability of additional receptor numbers must be more severely restricted than in the case of low frequency sounds which involve the whole length of the basilar membrane.

## DIRECTIONAL HEARING

Reference has earlier been made to the role of the pinna in sound localisation, and its importance is evidenced by the fact that persons with hearing in only one ear are nevertheless able to localise sounds, although their ability to do so is usually reported to be much impaired. Other contributory factors therefore need to be considered in terms of binaural cues to account for the enhanced localising ability possessed by those of us with normal hearing in both ears. In this context it is important to note that sound waves are not restricted, as are light waves, to linear propagation.

Instead they are able to bend round obstacles and undergo multiple reflections from the surroundings. It is for this reason that a unilaterally deaf person can still hear a sound even though his deaf ear may be turned to its source. In these circumstances, however, the sound will appear less loud both on account of the head shadow effect and the fact that the sound waves have a greater distance to travel.

To a binaurally hearing person, therefore, information on the direction of the source of sound can be obtained from the relative intensities at the two ears. Actually the head shadow effect is much less apparent at frequencies below 500 Hz which, because of their long wave length, can readily bend round the head. It so happens, however, that at these low frequencies phase differences assume importance. Thus at the onset, say, of a pure tone the sound will arrive in advance at the ear nearest the source. In other words it is said to be out of phase with the tone in the contralateral ear. For example a phase difference of half a cycle or 180° implies that at a particular point in time the stapes footplate will be moving inwards at one ear and outwards at the other. Nervous impulses are only initiated at a particular point in the cycle, namely the outward movement of the stapes, so that the time delay between the impulses at the two ears faithfully reflects the phase difference. In view of the fact that the time taken by these impulses to reach the cortex is of the order of 20 m sec it is remarkable that time differences of the order of 60 $\mu$ sec can be discriminated. It appears, however, that these time delays are of importance only at the onset of sounds and therefore localisation is possible only with sounds of short duration. However, the majority of sounds encountered in everyday life including music are constantly changing and of a transient nature and fall into this category.

The wave length of frequencies above about 1200 Hz becomes progressively less than the distance between the two ears so that phase differences for the higher frequencies assume a complete irrelevance, since once they exceed a complete cycle they can provide no meaningful directional clues. For these higher frequencies, therefore, localisation is heavily dependent upon intensity differences brought about by the diffraction of the head.

It will be clear from the foregoing that sounds located in the median plane, whether to the front, above or behind the head, cannot be localised on this basis and this in practice has been found to be the case. This, however, only applies if the head is maintained stationary. In fact the head is in a constant state of movement and there can be little doubt that this considerably enhances our localisation ability. One final word of caution, however, is called for. The above conclusions have been derived for the most part on the basis of laboratory experiments carried out with headphones to which sound stimuli applied to each ear separately have been artificially delayed in time or varied in intensity. In these circumstances quite striking directional effects may be demonstrated, but the localisation appears to be curiously confined within the head itself and unrelated to the common experience of spatial localisation. It may well be that there are other factors concerned with sound localisation which have not yet come to light. More information is certainly needed on the way in which the higher centres collate and process directional cues, particularly in respect of the complex and competing information which reaches the cortex. How, for example, we are able to direct our attention to one single voice submerged in the babble of a cocktail party has yet to receive a satisfactory explanation.

## SUBJECTIVE ASPECTS OF LOUDNESS PERCEPTION

Although loudness is the subjective attribute of intensity the two terms are by no means synonymous, since one refers to a particular aspect of sensation as determined by the discriminatory responses of a normal human observer while the other is a physical quantity which can be measured with the aid of instruments and expressed in terms of energy and pressure. The relationship between the two has been studied at some length and shown to be extraordinarily complex. Thus two tones of different frequencies but identical sound energies may impart entirely different loudness sensations. This is because first the ear is most sensitive to those frequencies which are of importance for the understanding of speech in the middle part of its range and considerably less sensitive at the higher and lower frequencies, and second the rate of change of loudness with intensity varies over the whole of the spectrum. In its most sensitive region the amount of energy required to elicit the faintest sensation of sound is incredibly small, indeed it has been calculated that at these levels the amplitude of movement of the basilar membrane is only of the order of magnitude of the diameter of the hydrogen atom. The sensitivity is such that it is highly likely that any further enhancement would serve no useful purpose, since the ear would then become receptive to the random molecular movement of the air particles themselves. At the upper end of the scale loudness perception is limited first by feelings of discomfort and finally by the intrusion of actual pain in the ears. The intensity range over which the ear operates from the faintest to the loudest sounds encompasses a billionfold change in energy. This vast energy range is not of course matched by a comparable range of loudness perception, instead the ear conforms in general terms to a rule applicable to all sensation known as Weber's Law, which states that the energy change required to produce a detectable change in sensation is a constant fraction of the original energy. In other words a faint sound can be made just perceptibly louder by a much smaller energy increase than would be required for a loud sound or, put more generally, loudness varies as the logarithm of the sound energy. Because of the great range of intensities involved it has now become conventional to express sound energies in logarithmic units termed decibels. The decibel scale was derived originally from the bel scale, named after Alexander Graham Bell the inventor of the telephone.

1 bel represents a tenfold change in sound energy,

2 bels one hundredfold,

3 bels one thousandfold, and so on.

In practice the bel was found to be too large a unit so that each bel was divided into ten decibels.

If, therefore, a sound of energy $E_1$ is increased to one of energy $E_2$ the increase in decibels $= 10 \log E_1/E_2$.

It is of particular importance to note that sound energy expressed in decibels represents a *ratio* of two energies, that is to say one energy level is said to be so many decibels above or below a particular reference level. The reference level in question is arbitrary and must always be specified or implied. A convenient reference level frequently used in this context in physiological acoustics is $10^{-12}$ Watt/m$^2$, which approximates to the energy required to elicit the very faintest sensation of sound, the so-called threshold of hearing at 1000 Hz.

The lowest curve shown in Figure 4 is the sound energy curve in decibels referred to this level for the threshold of hearing at all frequencies within the audible range. It will be seen that the sound energy required to elicit a sensation of hearing at 100 Hz is almost 40 db or 1000 times greater than at 1000 Hz. The remaining curves are equal loudness contours. These curves were determined by establishing the energy of tones at all frequencies which equate in loudness to that of a reference 1000 Hz tone, first at 10 db then at 20 db and so on. These are purely subjective scales of loudness and the levels are referred to as phons. Because 1000 Hz is taken as the reference tone the decibel and the phon level are by definition identical at this frequency.

Consideration of these contours leads to conclusions of some importance to musical appreciation. It will be seen, for example, that with higher phon levels the curves tend to flatten out so that at levels of about 110 phons equal sound energies at all frequencies evoke approximately equal sensations of loudness. By contrast, as has been mentioned earlier, the sound energy required to elicit the faintest sensation at 100 Hz is some 40 db greater than at 1000 Hz. This means that once the sound has become audible the energy has to be increased only some 70 db to attain a loudness of 110 phons. In other words an energy range of 70 db at 100 Hz encompasses the same loudness change as an energy range of 110 db at 1000 Hz. This has important consequences in musical reproduction. If a studio recording or a radio sound transmission is played at the receiving end at a lower sound

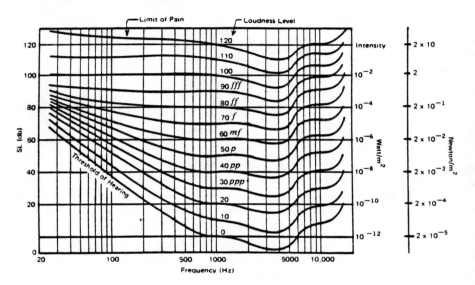

Figure 4 Curves of Equal Loudness (After Fletcher and Munson (1933) *J. acoust. Soc. Amer.*, **5**, 82. In: *Introduction to the Physics and Psychophysics of Music* by J. G. Roederer)

level than that which prevails in the studio, then all other things being equal the low tones will be differentially attenuated and suffer accordingly. If on the other hand the received loudness level is greater than that in the studio the reverse will be the case, and the bass frequencies because of their more rapid loudness growth will become accentuated.

In fact, given an ideal system which reproduces all frequencies equally effectively, the original quality can only be maintained if the intensity level of the reproduction is identical to the intensity level of the original. Since one has no knowledge of the studio acoustics or particular recording techniques this can never be achieved in practice. It is, therefore, worth remembering that when the Hi-Fi enthusiast, striving for perfection with his sophisticated equipment, twiddles his knobs and dials, all he is doing is to impose upon what he hears a quality which he finds aesthetically pleasing to himself. In view of the very considerable number of variables involved it is highly unlikely that he will arrive either by design or by chance at just that correct combination which faithfully matches the original.

## Acknowledgments

Grateful acknowledgment is made to the authors and publishers for permission to reproduce the figures 1–4.

# 4

# Brains and Hands

A brain scientist who cannot himself compose or perform music may well despair of his ability to "enter the mind of", that is to say define the specific cerebral aptitudes of even the humblest musician, let alone those immortals whose achievements mark some of the summits so far scaled by living brains. He can take comfort, however, in the certainty that a musician-neurologist who himself had cultivated these highest aptitudes would be no nearer to an understanding of the brain structures and brain processes on which these aptitudes depend.

What can we know of the brain of a Mozart, whose childhood genius flowered into a maturity in which he could declare that a whole new composition would be *simultaneously* present in his mind, so that he could survey it, like a fine picture or a beautiful statue, at a glance? He could then, at convenient moments, translate the whole imagined fabric of rhythm, melody, harmony, counterpoint and tone colour into visual symbols on paper by a *succession* of movements of his hand. He could also have sung any of the parts separately, or, by a different succession of movements of his hands, could have reproduced the whole sense of the work, if not all of its notes, at the keyboard. One can assume that he would have been unconscious of all these movements but that he could have attended to them if he had wished to do so, though at the risk of distraction from the overriding musical goals. Consciousness would normally have been filled by the auditory imagery of the work as a whole, of the threads running through it, the coming climaxes, the final close.

On reading the symbols he wrote on the paper, highly trained musicians can hear the whole work in their heads, sometimes claiming that the experience has the advantage of freedom from the blemishes of an actual performance. Of their ability to reproduce an orchestral score at the keyboard, they may say that they hear all the sounds in their heads and reproduce as many as they can in the time available. Conscious attention may be momentarily focused on part or whole of what is in progress, but must usually be running ahead. What is not attended to will be performed apparently automatically. It is unlikely that any attention will be spared for the positions and movements of the hands. Some considerable attention, however, was necessary at the earlier stages of the long training which makes it possible for those with the essential natural aptitudes to carry out such skilled performances.

Those less gifted, or perhaps one should say differently endowed, can achieve fragments only of the total skill. Thus, some find it possible to read and to memorise a single part without being able to perceive, in detail and at all times, the composition as a whole. Possibly they could never train themselves to manage counterpoint at the keyboard. They may cultivate tone-production by voice, stringed or wind instrument, achieving beautiful sounds involving high degrees of muscular skill. Beauty of tone and expression are their overriding objectives: it seems generally agreed that the muscular skills are always "instrumental" and subsidiary. Yet pupils and teachers may have to preoccupy themselves with their cultivation, at least in the early years of study.

We have little idea of the nature of the long-term brain-storage of a complex piece of music, whether composed and memorised before it is ever exteriorised; whether memorised from reading the score (as when v. Bülow conducted Stanford's *Irish Symphony* in Berlin without a score, having memorised it in the train from Hamburg); or whether memorised from hearing a single performance (as by Mozart when he wrote out Allegri's *Miserere* and by the blind eighteenth-century organist John Stanley who could accompany any new oratorio after hearing it only once). Nor have we much idea how a "*static*" store could release the appropriate *dynamic sequences* of movement, whether of writing or performing. Nor do we know how the successive reading of visual symbols can trigger the appropriate movements of the hands of a performer who is playing at sight. Our knowledge of the fine structure and of the chemical and electrical properties of brain cells is advancing steadily; we are building up detailed maps of the major nerve-paths which transmit excitation and inhibition from one brain region to another; we are beginning to discover how the new interconnections may be formed that could be the basis of learning and memory; but it is a very far cry from a partial understanding of some of these elemental structures and processes to a complete understanding of the modes of interaction of the $10^{10}$ nerve cells of the human cerebral cortex with their unimaginable wealth of possible interconnections. Such understanding is a goal that is endlessly worth pursuing, however much we may suspect that it will prove to be unattainable. Even if only few and simple answers are forthcoming, a brief, general and very incomplete survey of two parts of the problem-area may have some interest. These are concerned with the nervous organisation of our postures and movements and of our perception of them.

*     *     *     *     *

The evolution of the human forelimb can be traced back across some sixty million years, to the adoption of an arboreal mode of life by ancestral insectivorous mammals in Eurasian and North American forests. The selection-pressures would have included safety from ground predators, the presence of clouds of insects and an abundance of fruit. Survival, in arboreal locomotion, would have been favoured by improved vision, especially by stereoscopic vision, and by improved prehension. In arboreal leaping, adults, guided by vision, must grab branches with hands and feet, and infants too large to be held in the jaws must cling to their parents' fur. Food beyond the reach of the mouth must be grasped and pulled in. Unfamiliar objects would need to be explored by finger-touch instead of with the muzzle.

Except in size, there has been relatively little change in the structure of the forelimbs as between these tiny ancestors and ourselves, This, at first sight, may seem surprising. The primitive five-fingered limbs have retained what Le Gros Clark called their ancient simplicity of structure and function. (Compare the forelimbs of the horse, with their specialisation for rapid terrestrial locomotion.) Indeed, Le Gros Clark drew attention to an actual (but advantageous) *retrogression*: the sharp, hollow claws degenerated into flattened nails, which provide support for the padded, sensitive finger-tips and allow the prehensile hands to mould themselves more accurately to surfaces of varying size, shape and texture, in arboreal acrobatics.

The fact is that the evolution of Primates, which we consider to culminate in Man, has been pre-eminently cerebral and behavioural. Enlarging brains have commanded increasingly refined and versatile performances from bones, joints and muscles that have remained morphologically primitive. The sense-organs in the skin, joints, muscles and tendons have gained access to greatly enlarged areas of the brain and cerebellum. The "receiving areas" allocated to hand, face and foot, and especially to hand, have enlarged disproportionately to those for trunk, shoulder and thigh. The areas of cortex which discharge motor commands to these parts have enlarged correspondingly. Elliot Smith believed that the acquisition of skilled movements, and the correlation of these with vision, were the leading factors in primate evolution, and that arboreal life had tended to develop the tactile, kinaesthetic and visual senses and to link their cortical receiving areas in more intimate associations with one another and with the motor areas of the cortex. None of these neural changes, of course, can be traced in the fossil record, but the general enlargement of forebrain and cerebellum is abundantly documented by the size of the fossil skulls. Man's brain has increased in size by 50 per cent. in the space of 0·5 million years – or, as Darlington has put it, in 20 000 generations: a brief moment indeed on the time-scale of Evolution. Fire, tools, speech, agriculture, the rest – all products of increasing size and *organisation* of the brain; conferring evolutionary advantages on their possessors; creating unremitting selection-pressures for yet further increases in cerebral organisation. Further increase in size is constrained already, by the width of the canal through which the baby's head must be born into the world.

We may be sure that the same principle is true of hearing. Our ears are marvellous instruments but they are equalled and in some respects excelled by those of some lower mammals. It is the related brain developments that are responsible for the musician's ability to train his powers of auditory discrimination, analysis and imagery. Where a musician speaks of someone having "a good ear", a neurologist might speak of his having good auditory "receiving" and "association" areas of cortex.

No longer an arboreal primate, man stands and walks on his legs, leaving his arms and hands free for exploration, prehension, manipulation and construction in the service of his brain. In the series of living primates, which have their counterparts in fossil series and may be regarded in some ways as having become arrested at particular stages of evolution, the most primitive (Prosimians) show only the simplest prehensive pattern: divergence and straightening of all the fingers as the hand approaches an object, flexion and convergence as they close together upon it. In *Monkeys, Apes and Man*, Napier has drawn attention to the differentiation of *power* and *precision* grips: *power*, for supporting weight or wielding heavy objects; *precision*, for picking-up food and manipulating small objects with the thumb and index finger, whose tips can be brought accurately into contact with one another ("opposition").

Primitive primates do not appear to make much use of their hands for exploring the shapes and textures of objects, but this active exploration is prominent in the life of the higher forms.

Use of the hands in man has progressed to include music-making which goes far beyond the functions of prehension, tactile exploration and simple manipulation and construction. In the actions of everyday life, the modern musician shapes his hands into prehensive patterns and grips, like those of other people; at the keyboard he shapes them into chords, that is into patterns representing complex sounds, before they touch the keys.

$$*\qquad*\qquad*\qquad*\qquad*$$

Computer engineers now speak of overriding "programmes" and subordinate "subroutines". An equivalent hierarchy of organisation is implicit in the conception of overriding and subsidiary goals, which we have already introduced. The principle of hierarchical organisation has been familiar to neurologists for about a century, since Hughlings Jackson first graded performances along a scale ranging from "least automatic" to "most automatic", and divided the central nervous system into three main functional levels, of which the "highest" was responsible for "least automatic" performances and the "lowest" for "most automatic" performances. "Least automatic" would include the overriding organisation of skilled performances (their "programmes"): "most automatic" would include those stereotyped patterns of movement that are determined by genetically-endowed neural structure — rhythmic respiration, postural and protective reflexes, the elemental components of locomotion, and so forth. These postures and movements are complex combinations and recombinations of the simplest fixations and movements of individual joints brought about by the few muscles acting at each joint. The "lowest level" is also a functional concept; structurally, it corresponds to the brainstem and spinal cord.

The elemental fixations and movements are also available to the higher functional levels of the brain and cerebellum, for varying combination and recombination in the service of "higher level" performances. Sherrington's studies of the brains of apes pointed to the importance of the so-called motor area of the cerebral cortex in the synthesis of new patterns of movement. Hughlings Jackson had designated this area as the "middle level". It is generally supposed that in the learning of new performances, extending over many years, and best begun when the brain is young, the "highest" and "middle" levels can build up new combinations and sequences of postures and movements in the service of new "goals". These "less automatic" performances become eventually "more automatic" in the sense that they can be carried out without conscious attention. New combinations are built up successively and the "units" of performance become larger and more complex. Thus the skilled executant operates with scales, chords, arpeggios and harmonic progressions and not with the movements of individual fingers. In the slang of the modern psychological laboratory, he operates with larger and larger "chunks" as his skill increases. The individually acquired postures and movements are integrated with the inherited ones. Head and body are "more automatically" supported and the centre of gravity is shifted appropriately to maintain balance as the arms and hands are moved "less automatically" from one position to another and the fingers play their notes.

The location of the "highest level" is probably not confined to any single brain structure. Contemporary brain research finds that all areas of the cerebral cortex are connected to the basal ganglia of the forebrain and to the cerebellum. Most of the output of basal ganglia and cerebellum is funnelled back to the motor area of the cortex through the thalamus. In monkeys carrying out simple movements to earn a reward, nerve cells in cerebellum, basal ganglia, thalamus and motor cortex have been found to become active in advance of the movements. We do not know if it is sensible to speak of movements being "initiated" in any one of these structures rather than in any other. We know that injury to the cerebellum delays the onset of movements, weakens their power, makes them erratic in force and speed, and makes them overshoot or undershoot their targets. Injury to part of the basal ganglia may abolish all voluntary movement. Injury to the motor area of the cortex ("middle level") and its nerve-paths to brainstem and spinal cord ("lowest level") does not abolish all voluntary movement, but one of its effects is to make it difficult or impossible to move the fingers separately or to straighten them voluntarily, or to relax their grasp.

The major nerve path from the "motor cortex" to the spinal cord, the cortico-spinal tract, is relatively insignificant in most mammals, which use their muzzles for exploration and prehension, but is massive in man. It includes a special component which brings cortical nerve cells into direct synaptic contact with the motor nerve cells which work the muscles. In the evolution of primates this cortico-motoneuronal component has enlarged in relation to the increasing wealth of precision patterns of the hands: in monkeys its contacts with the nerve cells which operate the muscles which are responsible for the precision grip of thumb and index finger are especially dense. The synaptic endings in the spinal segments which control the hands are densest in man. By this direct connection with the "middle level", these motor nerve cells of the "lowest level" are made preferentially accessible to what Hughlings Jackson called "processes representing movements" – whether these originate in the "association areas" of the cerebral cortex or in the related neural networks of the basal ganglia, cerebellum or thalamus.

This direct mode of addressing these particular motor cells by-passes the complex neural apparatus of the "lowest level", but the cortico-spinal system also addresses brain-signals to all other parts of this apparatus. Thus, it can adjust the sensitivity and discrimination of the sensory signals which travel from skin, muscles and joints to the cerebral cortex and cerebellum. It can also enhance or suppress the activity of the local reflex networks. The motor cells form a common output pathway which is shared by local reflex commands from the outside world and by brain-commands from the "middle level".

The simplest movements are those that are brought about by the two or more muscles which act at a single joint. The arrangement of the neural networks which interconnect the clusters of motor cells which drive these muscles is therefore interesting and important. So is the distribution to these cells and networks of the signals which enter the central nervous system from the moving muscles. These networks and feedback circuits form the common basis of our "least automatic" as well as of our "most automatic" movements.

The muscles act by bending, straightening or fixing joints, and are associated in patterns whose complexity increases in proportion to the number of degrees of freedom of movement at the joints and the number of joints across which the particular muscles can act. These complexities are greatest where mobility is greatest – in the shoulder, forearm and hand. Let us, however, simplify matters by considering a hypothetical pair of antagonistic muscles. Muscle A bends, and muscle B straightens, a single hinge-like joint. Each muscle is driven by its cluster of nerve cells, A or B, in the spinal cord. These clusters are interconnected by clusters of inhibitory cells, in such a way that when the brain drives cluster A to make muscle A bend the joint, cluster B is automatically inhibited; so that muscle B (which is passively lengthened when the joint is being bent) remains relaxed. For fixation of the joint, the inhibitory cells can themselves be switched off by the brain, so that muscles A and B can be switched on together.

Attached to the sides of some of the muscle fibres are small receptor organs, the muscle spindles. Their nerves transmit signals of the length and rate-of-change of length (= velocity) of the muscle. The importance of this information for our awareness of the positions and movements of our limbs will be considered later: our concern at this point is with the automatic governing of movements by feedback from the moving muscles.

When muscle A bends its joint, its spindles are shortened, and this depresses their signalling. Such depression, however, can be offset by another set of spinal nerve cells, the fusimotor cells. If cluster A and its associated fusimotor cells are switched on together by the brain, the signalling from the spindles of muscle A can be sustained throughout the bending of the joint. The effect of the spindles' signals is to add to the excitation of cluster A, and to excite the cells which inhibit the antagonistic cluster B.

This arrangement provides for the possibility of what P. B. C. Matthews has called the "servo-assistance" of movement. Suppose that the bending of the joint encounters resistance during its course. The active shortening of muscle A will be checked. Since the depressing effect of the shortening on the spindles' signalling will be thereby removed, that signalling will suddenly increase. This feedback will add to the excitation of cluster A and the inhibition of cluster B, and the extra output of power will tend to overcome the resistance.

When muscle A bends the joint, the passive lengthening of muscle B increases the signalling from B's spindles. This would tend to excite cluster B and inhibit cluster A, and thus to oppose the bending of the joint. The brain, however, can inhibit fusimotor cells, and can thereby reduce the sensitivity of muscle B's spindles to passive stretch; it can also selectively inhibit cluster B. All this can be improved by learning. The tendency to stiffening of "unwanted" muscles in the early stages of learning a skill, and their relative relaxation in the later stages, is well known to every music teacher.

There is evidence that the output of the "middle level", as well as that of the "lowest level", is subject to automatic governing by feedback from the active muscles of the arm and hand, in monkeys and in man. When a movement is resisted during its progress, the muscles increase their output in two surges. In man, the first of these begins about 25 milliseconds after the start of the resistance. This corresponds with the time of transmission of the signal in the circuit from spindles to motor cells and back to the muscles ("lowest level" loop). The second begins about 50 milliseconds from the start of the resistance: this time allows for transmission in the circuit from spindles to cortex, thence to motor cells and back to muscles ("middle level" loop). It is interesting that transmission through both loops, but especially the "middle level" loop, can be enhanced or depressed by a prior instruction to "resist" or "let go" when the movement is opposed by the experimenter. This means that the "transmissibility" of the circuits can be pre-set by the subject: he cannot react quickly enough to adjust them during the actual disturbance.

The fingers of the player of a well-made keyboard instrument ought not to encounter sudden resistances or inequalities of touch, but one can imagine that the tracker action of some ancient organ – for whose testing, toccatas might have been composed – could confront the player with unexpected loads which would give ample scope to his servo-assistance mechanisms. Mechanical coupling of manuals could well add to the challenge.

Contemporary psychological research on human performance is trying to establish which movements, and carried out under what conditions, are dependent throughout their course on feedback from the moving parts (closed-loop operation); which are wholly ballistic, that is to say, launched from an internal programme and not subject to external modification during their course (open-loop operation); or partly ballistic, and subject only to intermittent correction during their course, or (in the case of repeated movements) subject to correction during some repetitions only. Contemporary neurophysiology cannot investigate such complex performances, but knowledge of brain structure, derived from electro-physiological as well as from microscopical studies, can offer some suggestions about their possible neural basis.

We know that loss of input from the limbs makes "least automatic" movements impossible in the absence of vision, and grossly defective when vision is allowed. This implies that feedback, as well as internal programmes, is normally involved. There are many areas of interconnection, and therefore of possible interaction, between descending nerve paths to the spinal cord, including the corticospinal pathway, and ascending pathways carrying information of limb positions and movements to the cerebellum and cerebral cortex. At every site of interaction, any mismatch between the motor "command" and the "expected" movement could, in principle, be detected and fed back to the appropriate "sub-routine", to lead to some corrective modification of subsequent "commands". In musical performance, an overriding correction should be derived from the perception of incorrect sounds – for example, of faulty intonation by a string player. Thus, we might distinguish corrections derived from errors in the overall performance referred, as it were, to the "programme", and those derived from errors in the actual movements, referred to the "sub-routines".

The faster the movements, the less time will be available for correction. The minimum reaction time to a sound – the interval between hearing the sound and pressing a telegraph key – is about 150 milliseconds. The "lowest level" and "middle level" loop times are about 25 to 50 milli-seconds. In collaboration with a physiologist, the late James Ching found that his most rapid rate of repetition of a single note on the piano with a single finger was ten times per second. This means that each downward stroke takes about 50 milliseconds.

*          *          *          *          *

Our perception of the positions of parts of our bodies in relation to one another and to external objects within our reach, and our perception of their movements, depend on signals coming in from the muscles, tendons and joints, and rather less from signals coming in from the skin. The perceptions remain accurate when the skin sensations are disordered, but are disordered by selective injuries of the brain and spinal cord which leave the skin sensations unimpaired. Psychological experiment finds that our blindfold perception of the positions of our hands and arms is more accurate when these have been reached by our own active movements, than when they have been imposed passively upon us by the movements of the experimenter. Thus, our own effort contributes some part of the information on which our perception depends.

Throughout our long infancy our brains are building up internal models or schemas of our bodies and of the external world, and integrating the separate schemas, built up in relation to the different senses, into overall models of our bodies and of the world. To these models, and to expectations derived from them, the brain refers the impressions streaming in from our senses in the act of perception. As William James said, what we perceive comes as much from inside our heads as from the world outside. We can readily imagine that a musician's brain, in the course of his long learning, builds up internal schemas of the shape of his instrument, and of the sounds it produces, which become intimately related to the schema of his body that was built up during infancy and childhood. In his attack, the skilled string player can assume a posture, and execute movements, that will sound the required note with little or no error; correcting his intonation, if necessary, by hearing. The advantages of beginning this learning process at the earliest possible' age are admitted by everyone. Neural plasticity diminishes with increasing age.

What are the immediate sources of information of position and movement, when vision is excluded by blindfolding? The joints seem obvious candidates. Their capsules are well supplied with receptor nerve-endings, and from these signals travel to receiving areas of the cerebral cortex, adjacent to the "motor" area, conveying information of the angle through which the joint has been moved; but without these signals, on which normal perception no doubt partly depends, a person can still perceive his positions and movements. Surgeons can now replace diseased joints by artificial ones, without depriving the patient of his perceptions. This surprising fact turns our attention to the muscles and tendons. It is interesting that patients with artificial finger joints experience normal awareness of movement when their fingers are passively wiggled up and down, which stretches muscles, but not when they are wiggled from side to side, which does not.

We have seen that the muscle spindles supply information of muscle length ("static") and of change of length and velocity ("dynamic"). For many years it was believed that these signals do not arouse perceptions. Part of the basis for this opinion was that no signals from muscles could be shown to reach the cerebral cortex. Modern work has discovered the cortical area which receives these signals. It lies immediately adjacent to the "motor" area, and partly overlaps the adjacent receiving areas for skin and joints. All these areas are mutually interconnected by short neural linkages.

The muscle spindles contain receptors of two types: the primaries, which give a mixed signal of length and velocity, and the secondaries, which signal only length-at-any-instant. The primaries are so exquisitely sensitive to movement that they can be selectively stimulated by vibrating the tendon of a muscle. This creates a vivid illusion of movement, even if no movement has taken place. Our natural movements do not give rise to illusions, and additional sources of information are available. Correct perception of passive movements could depend on additional information from the joints and from the length-measuring secondary receptors of the spindles. For the correct perception of active movements, still further information would be available. The sensitivity of the spindle receptors can be increased by fusimotor activity. The tendons contain nerve-endings which are extremely sensitive to the active pull of the muscle fibres. As we have seen, "copies" of the motor "commands" are anatomically available for comparison with incoming messages on their way up to the brain. The actual messages could be "interpreted" in the light of the messages that would have been "expected" to result from the correct execution of the "commands".

Thus, there is a wealth of information on which the learning of positions and movements could be based, and for which vision is unnecessary. It might be advantageous if every educational piano were provided with a screen which would prevent the pupil from seeing his arms. It might help him to learn his positions and movements more quickly, and relegate them as soon as possible to a "more automatic" level of performance so that his attention could be concentrated on the overriding auditory objectives.

# 5

A. S. KHAMBATA

# Anatomy and Physiology of Voice Production: The Phenomenal Voice

## INTRODUCTION

The original nature of the larynx is entirely at variance with the faculty of speech. The primary function of the larynx is that of a valve of the pulmonary air tract by virtue of the sphincteric action of its muscular folds. It has, however, come to occupy a unique position of importance in Man as the organ of communication through speech. The larynx is composed of a number of cartilages, connected by ligaments and moved by muscles. The muscles can move the larynx as a whole in relation to its adjacent structures, extrinsic muscles, and the cartilages themselves in relation to each other, intrinsic muscles.

## THE LARYNGEAL CARTILAGES

The largest of the cartilages is the thyroid which consists of two quadrilateral alae fused anteriorly in the midline along their whole length except at the top where a notch, the thyroid, is left. The upper and lower angles of the free posterior borders continue upwards and downwards respectively as the superior and inferior cornua or horns. The angle at which the alae meet is very wide in children, less so in the adult female, and much smaller in the adult male. In the male the fused anterior borders form the projection known as "Adam's apple". The outer lateral surface of the thyroid ala or lamina is marked by an oblique line along which there are attached the thyrohyoid, sternothyroid and inferior constrictor muscles. The inner surfaces of the alae are covered by mucous membrane. At the angle formed at the junction of the laminae anteriorly are attached the thyro-epiglottic ligaments, the vestibular and vocal ligaments, the thyro-arytenoid, thyro-epiglottic and vocalis muscles. As age advances the thyroid cartilage ossifies, sometimes to an almost complete degree. The cricoid cartilage, which lies immediately below the thyroid cartilage and articulates with it, forms the lower part of the larynx. It is shaped like a signet ring having a narrow anterior arch and a broad quadrilateral posterior arch. It is of great importance in maintaining the patency of the trachea. The paired arytenoid cartilages are pyramidal in shape, their bases articulating with the cricoid cartilage. Each has an anteriorly placed vocal process to which the vocal ligament is attached, and a laterally placed muscular process to which are attached the lateral crico-arytenoid muscle anteriorly and the posterior crico-arytenoid posteriorly. The small corniculate cartilage, or cartilage of Santorini, articulates with the flattened medially directed apex of the arytenoid cartilage on each side. In front of this is placed the small cuneiform cartilage, or cartilage of Wrisberg. These two cartilages are enclosed within the mucous membrane of the ary-epiglottic fold on each side. These small cartilages are involved in supporting the ary-epiglottic folds and assist the oesophagus in opening during sphincteric closure of the larynx. The flattened leaf-like epiglottis is attached at its narrow lower end by the thyro-epiglottic ligament to the inner surface of the angle of the fused thyroid laminae below the thyroid notch. The superior margin is free. The mucous membrane of the tongue passes in continuity on to the anterior surface of the epiglottis. The glosso-epiglottic fold in the midline further attaches it to the tongue, and the lateral glosso-epiglottic folds on either side attach it to the pharyngeal wall. The hyo-epiglottic ligament in the midline attaches it to the hyoid bone in front. The ary-epiglottic folds pass down on either side to the arytenoid cartilages. The thyro-hyoid membrane and thyro-hyoid ligament connect the upper border of the thyroid laminae to the hyoid bone above. The crico-thyroid ligament and conus elasticus connect the lower margin of the thyroid laminae to the cricoid cartilage. The superior edge of the lateral part of the crico-thyroid ligament is free and is thickened to form the vocal ligament. The quadrangular membrane extends between the epiglottis and the arytenoid cartilage. It is poorly developed, and its free lower edge extends downwards to the vestibular fold, in which a thickening of fibrous tissue forms the vestibular ligament. The laryngeal ventricle separates the upper quadrangular membrane and the crico-thyroid ligament, the free superior edge of which forms the vocal ligament. The cricoid cartilage is connected to the first tracheal ring by the crico-tracheal ligament. The larynx is thus connected to the hyoid bone and the tongue above, and is continuous with the trachea below.

## LARYNGEAL MUSCLES

The muscles of the larynx are divided into intrinsic and extrinsic groups.

*Extrinsic muscles*

These are the sterno-thyroid, thyro-hyoid, stylo-pharyngeus, palato-pharyngeus and the inferior constrictor. The sterno-thyroid is the principal depressor of the larynx, and the thyro-hyoid the principal elevator of the larynx. The stylo-pharyngeus, though its main action is to raise the lateral wall of the pharynx, also raises the larynx. The palato-pharyngeus raises and shortens the wall of the pharynx, and also helps in tilting the larynx forward during deglutition. The muscles which raise the hyoid bone will also raise the larynx, mylo-hyoid, stylo-hyoid and genio-hyoid, while the sterno-hyoid and omo-hyoid will depress it.

*Intrinsic muscles*

These are the paired crico-thyroid, posterior and lateral crico-arytenoids, thyro-arytenoid, and vocalis, ary-epiglottic muscles, the oblique inter-arytenoids and the unpaired transverse interarytenoid muscle. The thyro-arytenoid muscle on each side is in the form of a sheet. The lower part of the muscle is thicker, and this forms a distinct bundle, the vocalis muscle; many of whose fibres arise from the vocal ligament. The parts of the vocalis muscle that directly adjoin the vocal cord have a better capillary circulation and may have a special function. By virtue of its attachment to the vocal ligament the vocalis can tighten the anterior part of the vocal ligament. The thyro-arytenoid and vocalis muscles adduct the vocal cords. The lateral and posterior crico-arytenoids act in opposition to each other. The posterior crico-arytenoids are abductors of the vocal cords, while the lateral crico-arytenoids are adductors of the vocal cords. The aryepiglottic and inter-arytenoid muscles approximate the arytenoid cartilages and thus close the inter-cartilaginous part of the rima glottidis. The crico-thyroid muscles act in opposition to the thyro-arytenoid and vocalis muscles, tightening the vocal ligaments while they are elongated at the same time. All the intrinsic muscles of the larynx are supplied by the recurrent laryngeal nerves except the crico-thyroid which is supplied by the external branch of the superior laryngeal nerve. The rima glottidis is the elongated fissure between the vocal cords anteriorly and the vocal processes and bases of the arytenoid cartilages posteriorly. The average length of the rima glottidis varies from 16 mm in the female to 25 mm in the adult male. The anterior three-fifths of the rima is called the intermembranous part and the posterior two-fifths the intercartilaginous part. In adduction the intermembranous part is reduced to a narrow slit, while the intercartilaginous part is triangular in shape. In abduction the intermembranous part is triangular while the intercartilaginous part is triangular with the apex posteriorly. The outline of the rima glottidis thus becomes lozenge shaped. During phonation the membranous part of the vocal cord vibrates, whereas the arytenoids' intercartilaginous part remains in apposition.

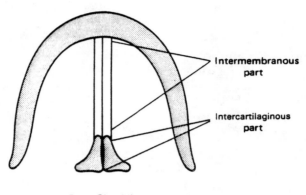

**Rima Glottidis**

## THE VOCAL CORDS

The vocal cord is a flat band, pearly white in colour but whiter in the female than in the male. It extends from the internal surface of the thyroid cartilage near the midline to the vocal process and part of the body of the arytenoid, being continuous below with the conus elasticus. It consists of a mesh of yellow elastic tissue, in which many fat cells are embedded. The free medial border is covered by squamous epithelium, while it is bound laterally by the thyro-arytenoid muscle. A few of the muscle fibres of the thyro-arytenoid arising from the arytenoid cartilage are inserted into the vocal cord and constitute the ary-vocalis or vocalis muscle. It is triangular in cross section. The average length of the vocal cords is 17–25 mm in the male and 12·5 to 17 mm in the female. The ratio of the length of the vocal cord to the antero-posterior diameter of the larynx is 1 : 2·3 at birth. This decreases rapidly to 1 : 1·5 at 9 months. The ratio of 1 : 1·5 is maintained in the female and until puberty in the male. At puberty in the male the ratio is altered to 1 : 1·3 over a short period of time due to the increase in length of the vocal cords. Because of the sudden transition, control of the voice is temporarily lost, and the voice tends to crack until such time as it has completely broken and settled. After this change vocal control is regained in a lower key than before, by as much as an octave at its lowest limit.

*Castrati* do not show similar changes and consequently retain a boyish voice in the original higher key. In the female not only are the cords shorter than in the male, but the free medial edge is sharper whereas in the male this is more rounded, and a greater area comes into apposition with the other cord. The anatomical differences are responsible for the characteristic quality of the voice in the male and the female. It is not only the length of the cord which determines the pitch of the voice but also the total mass of vibrating cord.

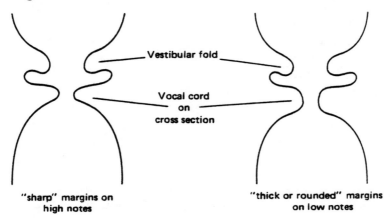

Vestibular fold

Vocal cord
on
cross section

"sharp" margins on
high notes

"thick or rounded" margins
on low notes

## VOICE PRODUCTION

The production of the voice by the larynx involves two essential mechanisms:

### 1. *The respiratory bellows*

This is provided by the lungs and the muscles of expiration in the thorax and abdominal wall. When the intrathoracic and infraglottic pressures reach an adequate level the vocal cords are set in vibration with the production of a laryngeal tone. The controlled act of respiration is of prime importance in singing. The lungs must be capable of filling rapidly and emptying at a steady controlled rate, correct breathing being the basis of all good singing. The intratracheal pressure during normal conversation is 15–25 mm of $H_2O$ and may rise up to 95 cms of $H_2O$ during loud shouting.

### 2. *The reeds or vibrating mechanisms*

The human voice is a wind instrument, the reeds being the vocal cords; but, unlike those in other instruments, these reeds are mobile, alterable in shape and dimension. A wide range of notes of varying pitch, quality and intensity can be produced. As the column of air is forced through the narrow aperture of the glottis the vocal cords, and particularly their edges, are set in vibration. Segmental vibration of the cords adds harmonics to the basic tone produced.

The mechanism of the larynx has been studied by the use of laryngoscopy, stroboscopy, cineradiography, tomography, cinematography and oscillography. The adducted vocal cords are set in vibration during phonation. When studied in slow motion, the vocal cords are seen to execute a movement in which the free margins are rolled upwards and outwards, the surfaces in contact being forced apart from below upwards. This is particularly well seen during the production of low tones. The cord movements have a vertical as well as a horizontal component. The vibrations may involve the entire length of the vocal cords or only segments of the same. The duration of the closed contact of the cord varies with the pitch of the note produced, the lower the note, the longer the period of closure. The airstream is thus cut up into a series of very rapid puffs, hence producing a tone (Punt, 1967). The frequency of these phases governs the pitch, whereas the force or power of the airstream determines the volume or loudness of the tone, according to the aerodynamic or tonic theory of tone production. The other theory postulated is that the movements are due to the rhythmic contraction and relaxation of the thyro-arytenoid muscles and are independent of the airstream. The return of the cords that have been forced apart by the airstream has been attributed to passive elastic force within the cords, suction created by the passage of air under pressure through the glottic chink, or rhythmical active muscle contraction.

## PITCH

The pitch of the tone is determined by the length and tension of the vibrating segments of the cords, the configuration of the contact areas of the cord edges and the air pressure. The length and tension of the cords are controlled by the thyro-arytenoid muscles and indirectly by the crico-thyroid muscles. The latter are involved in production of high pitched tones, above 650 Hz. In the production of the lowest tones, the so-called *chest register*, the cords are broad, their tension is relatively low and the whole length vibrates. Progressing up the scale, a rise in pitch is achieved by bringing into play an increasing number of motor units of the thyro-arytenoid muscle, but contraction of the thyro-arytenoids alone raises the pitch to a lesser degree than does the contraction of the crico-arytenoids (Rubin, 1963). The subglottic air pressure which governs the intensity and loudness of the tone has a very slight effect on the pitch, there being a tendency for the note to "sharpen". This is particularly noticeable in the production of the *messa di voce* and the gradual *crescendo* and *decrescendo* on a held note; the tendency to "sharpness" is corrected by a corresponding reduction in the tension of the cords in the well-trained singer. As the tones produced rise in pitch a gradual lengthening of the vocal cord is observed, this being achieved by the crico-thyroid muscle. As the pitch of the tones produced rises, there is a tendency, which is generally held to be undesirable in singing, for the larynx as a whole to rise. This leads to a reduction of the size of the supraglottic resonating cavities with deterioration of the tonal quality. Most well trained singers will have corrected this tendency during their period of training.

## VOLUME

The loudness of a note is governed largely by the subglottic air pressure. However, a well-trained singer can sustain a note sung *forte* for as long as one sung *piano*. Hence the volume is not determined by air pressure alone but possibly by other factors as well. It is believed that the intensity of contraction of the tensor muscles, thyro-arytenoid and crico-thyroid, plays a contributory part in governing the volume (Rubin, 1963).

### The resonators

The pure laryngeal sound in itself is thin and weak. Several anatomical factors influence the quality or timbre of the voice. The most important of these are the thoracic cavity and tracheo-bronchial tree, larynx, pharynx, soft palate, oral cavity, nose and nasopharynx, paranasal sinuses, and lips and tongue.

### The thoracic cavity

Perhaps all parts of the thoracic wall and particularly the sternum act as sounding boards. Slow, controlled escape of air from the lungs causes the least degree of alteration in size of these lower resonators. Hence sufficient air capacity and the efficient control of breathing give the best results in singing, the latter being acquired through training.

### The pharynx

During phonation the pharynx is open in varying degrees. The capacity and shape can be varied by movements of the tongue and action of the constrictor muscles. Elevation of the larynx when singing up a scale greatly reduces the size and dimensions of the pharynx. Contraction of the muscular walls of the pharynx can greatly influence the quality of the voice. When the larynx is elevated there is usually an attendant contraction of the palato-pharyngeus muscles, drawing the posterior pillars of the fauces together, and the soft palate tends to contract at the same time resulting in a *closed throat*. The presence of enlarged adenoids and diseased tonsils tends to alter the quality of voice further. The latter can impede the movements of the muscles and soft palate, thus affecting quality. Tonsillectomy in trained singers may need to be followed by renewed study and practice.

## The soft palate

The soft palate can shut off the nasal and nasopharyngeal resonators from the larynx and is hence of considerable importance. It is raised in all pure vowel sounds. Many famous teachers and singers lay particular emphasis on correct positioning of the soft palate, particularly Mathilde Marchesi and Jean de Reszke.

## The oral cavity

The oral cavity has a semi-rigid roof, the hard and soft palate, and its outer walls and floors are composed of soft tissue. The dimensions of the hard palate, particularly the length and degree of doming, affect the quality of the voice. Racial characteristics may play a part in this feature of the supraglottic resonators. Negro singers by virtue of the dimensions of these resonators often have a characteristic quality of voice. The position of the tongue can appreciably alter the capacity of the oral cavity. It is often stated by singers that if the tongue is kept flat, with the tip in contact with the posterior aspect of the lower incisor teeth, it ensures that the capacity of the oral cavity is kept at a maximum and maintains an *open throat*. Elevation of the tongue is a frequently encountered fault in untrained singers. The lips, teeth, and tongue are of particular importance in articulation of consonants. The trilled "r", as in Italian, is produced by the tongue tip tapping rapidly against the teeth. The uvula trilled "r", as in French, consists of a rapid succession of contacts and releases between the uvula and the back of the tongue (Negus, 1929).

## Nose and nasopharynx

These two resonators are inseparable. The effect of the nose as a resonator is great, and this can be exercised even when the nasopharynx is shut off or partially obliterated, for the rigid hard palate which forms the floor of the nose has considerable influence in allowing sympathetic vibration. The nasal cavities act as resonators because the contained air is thrown into forced vibrations. Hence, anatomical defects such as a deviated nasal septum or inflammatory processes can affect the timbre of the voice. In spite of the frequently mentioned term *sinus tone* amongst singers and vocal teachers, the paranasal sinuses themselves do not appreciably alter the resonance of the voice (Negus, 1929; Punt, 1967).

## THE REGISTERS

As variations in pitch occur during singing, certain changes are observed in the vocal cords themselves. In the very lowest notes, the whole length of the vocal cords vibrate and the free edges are thickened and rounded. With a rise in the pitch there is progressive thinning or sharpening of the opposing vibrating edges, and in the highest notes, the so called *head register*, only the membranous parts of the cords vibrate, the arytenoids being held firmly together, and the amplitude of the vibrations diminishes as the pitch rises. It must be remembered that the characteristic sound of a note in a particular register depends not only on the changes in the vocal cords but on the resonators called into play. Hence in the *chest register* the singer experiences a maximum sense of vibration in the thoracic cavity, while in the uppermost notes in the *head register* this appears to be experienced mainly in the head. Some singers refer to a *middle register* (in addition to these two main registers). In the inadequately trained singer the listener can often hear a distinct "break" as the voice passes from one register to another. In addition, most of the great singers of the "golden age" of *bel canto* had a highly developed and cultured *falsetto* function. This use of the *falsetto* persisted well into the 19th Century. Correct training and the intelligent use of the voice enable the artist to pass from one register to another with no audible break and a resultant *seamless scale*, the voice having the same quality throughout its range. This is perhaps most enjoyably demonstrated in the recordings by the soprano Rosa Ponselle from Spontini's opera *La Vestale*. Register breaks occur when the singer has difficulty in making the alterations in bulk and tension within the larynx, necessary at the limits of the registers.

Mention must be made of the *falsetto* voice. This is particularly a feature of the male voice. What is usually meant by *falsetto* is a slender sound of little volume, but characterised by a core to the tone. The singer often describes the sound as being placed forwards on the incisor teeth of the upper jaw, whereas the typical head note appears to be placed high up in the head. During production of the *falsetto* voice, the arytenoids are held together and there is minimal contact of the sharpened edges of the vocal cords; only the anterior segments of the cords appear to move. Unless the *falsetto* is carefully and skilfully blended into the basic or full voice, a tonal break occurs; but with proper schooling, the *falsetto* can be employed to advantage in the production of a well gradated *messa di voce*. Most female voices can produce *falsetto* tones, particularly on the high pitches. This mechanism can prove very useful in the production of *pianissimo* effects on the highest notes of the soprano voice, and for placing a note prior to employing the full voice.

The *falsetto* voice has in the past been used extensively in the performance of Church music and it is the basis of the modern counter-tenor voice. A whole breed of church singers evolved at the end of the 15th Century specialising in the use of the *falsetto*. Spanish falsettists were much in demand and were widely heard in cathedrals and chapels all over Europe for over a century, until they were eclipsed by the advent of the *castrati* in the seventeenth century. Contralto voices in the Church were, however, still provided by falsettists until the end of the last century. Giovan Riccardo Daviesi (1839–1921) the distinguished 'contralto' singer of the Sistine Chapel in the 19th century was perhaps the last of the great falsettists. He was a close friend of Liszt and Rossini and studied laryngology with Sir Morell Mackenzie in London in the 1870s. This type of voice must not be confused with the *castrati* contralto, as it is not the product of eviration.

The *haute-contre* voice, to which leading male roles in French opera from Lully to Rameau were assigned, is now generally agreed to have been an exceptionally high tenor who normally sang in a natural voice but had a *falsetto* extension at the top of the range. The modern counter-tenor voice

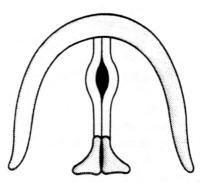

**The "Falsetto" Voice**

on the other hand is produced throughout its range by the *falsetto* mechanism, the normal voice of the performer being a baritone or bass. It is perhaps the nearest approximation to the falsettist contralto voice of the past that we still hear today.

## The coup de glotte

Good singing requires that the tone should start rapidly and smoothly and be accomplished in such a manner that the throat offers no resistance to the outflowing breath. Many celebrated singers and singing teachers have taught the *coup de glotte* as the best starting point in the training of the voice. Amongst them were Garcia, Duprez, Viardot-Garcia, Fauré, and Lablache. In this, "before the onset of tone, the air accumulates under the tightly closed vocal cords being released by a sharp opening and closing of the glottis" (Husler and Rodd Marling, 1965). If the mechanism of the larynx is not clearly understood by the singer, this method can cause damage. When, however, the mechanism is fully understood, as it was by these great singers, the onset of voice will be instantaneous and smooth. It must not be practised without expert knowledge and guidance. When correctly performed "the glottis is opened and closed without movement of the arytenoid" (Goesttler, 1950). It is taught as a necessity for the acquisition of the *staccato* in singing technique.

## The trill

When properly produced the trill has been called the crowning glory of *bel canto*. It consists of the even sounding of two notes a semitone apart in pitch, though the baroque trill involves an interval of a tone. When required, the singer should be able to produce a well gradated *messa di voce* while vocalising the trill, or hold it for several measures without losing pitch or evenness in production. The ability to trill naturally is, alas, infrequently encountered and many eminent singers have only been able to essay an approximation of it. The production of the trill requires that the larynx be kept free of all forms of obstructive stiffness; it is said to consist of a "shaking movement" of the larynx. The reader is referred to the recordings of Adelina Patti (particularly Lotti's *Pur Dicesti*), Sigrid Onegin and Selma Kurz, for demonstration of the flawless trill. Modern male singers appear to find it particularly difficult to trill, though it was a prerequisite in the 18th and early 19th centuries. This could be attributed to the general change in taste in music and the decline of extensive vocal training with the arrival of the *Romantic* and *Verisimo* schools of music drama. It is however heard to advantage in certain recordings of the tenors Herman Jadlowker, Fernando de Lucia and the great bass Pol Plançon.

## Whispering

In whispering the pitch is high and above that of normal speech. The sound though gentle is capable of considerable amplification. In whispering the inter-arytenoid muscles do not contract, and the arytenoid cartilages remain separated. The glottis is partly open and the vocal processes of the arytenoids are rotated medially.

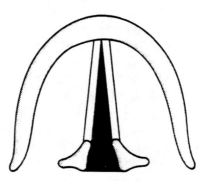

The glottis during whispering

## Ventricular band voice or "double voice"

In this mechanism not only do the vocal cords come into apposition but the ventricular bands come together, both sets being set in vibration.

Good singing depends on the co-ordinated action of a great many muscles, some of which are under the conscious control of the singer, while others respond passively to the control of the mind. Vocal training is essentially an unlocking process. The good singer is one who has obtained the key that gives him free access to his vocal organ which he then uses with intelligence and musicality.

## Muscles concerned in singing (adapted from Negus, 1929)

Muscles of the nose, muscles of the mouth, muscles of the lower jaw, muscles of the tongue, muscles of the soft palate, muscles of the pharynx, supra-hyoid and infra-hyoid muscles, intrinsic muscles of the larynx, anterior and lateral muscles of the neck, muscles of the back, muscles of respiration including the diaphragm and muscles of the abdominal wall.

In conclusion let us not forget that there is little difference between the larynx of a great singer and that of a "voiceless" person. The commission which performed the autopsy on the great tenor Francesco Tamagno, Verdi's original Otello, reported as follows on the larynx: "The organ differs from that of a normal person only in that it exhibits an unusually large number of scars on the wall of the pharynx caused by catarrh" (Hagen, 1917).

## THE PHENOMENAL VOICE

In normal speech the range of the adult voice may extend from frequencies of 80 Hz in men to as high as 400 Hz in women. During normal conversation the overall range of the voice is barely an octave. These ranges are, however, extended considerably in the trained singing voice. Lucrezia Agujari, called *La Bastardina*, was celebrated for her *acuti* and is reported to have sung C''''. Michael Kelly, Mozart's first Don Basilio, states that Mozart's sister-in-law Aloysia Lange had an even wider range. The American soprano Ellen Beach Yaw, who was active in the early years

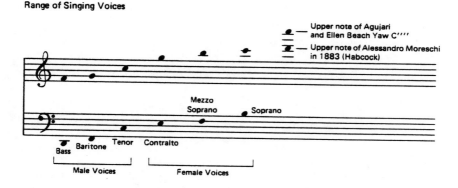

Range of Singing Voices

of this century, and more recently Erna Sack and Yma Sumac have laid claim to the same territory. The gramophone recordings of Ellen Beach Yaw further demonstrate an amazing ability to produce a trill, if that is the correct term, between notes a third and a fifth apart. The ability to produce tones in the "stratosphere" of singing has been the chief claim to fame of a number of singers, to the exclusion of beauty of tone, ease of production, musicianship and interpretive powers. It is a *rara avis* indeed who combines all these attributes.

It was, however, that unique breed of singers, the *Castrati* or *Evirati*, who flourished in the 17th and 18th centuries, who attained the greatest fame in the art of *bel canto*. Originally employed as singers in churches, as women were believed to have been expressly forbidden to sing in churches by St. Paul in the words "*mulier taceat in ecclesia*", the castrati rose to pre-eminence with the advent of opera as an art form. The use of the male soprano and contralto voices in opera generally fell out of favour in the early 19th century. Giovanni Battista Velluti was the last of the great *castrati*; following his debut in 1800 he went from success to success. In 1814 he appeared in Rossini's *Aureliano in Palmira* and in 1825 sang in London in Meyerbeer's *Il Crociato in Egitto*. He sang in public concerts until the 1830's, eventually dying in 1861 at eighty years of age. His last years were employed as a gentleman farmer, but he retained his interest in music and is believed to have helped the younger Garcia in writing his manual of singing.

Velluti never attained the prodigious fame of Carlo Broschi known as Farinelli (1705–1782); on hearing him sing a lady uttered the memorable phrase "One God, one Farinelli!" and this at a time which saw and heard Senesino, Carestini, Guadagni, for whom Gluck wrote the part of Orpheus, Cafferelli, Manzuoli and others. Burney describes a famous occasion when Farinelli was involved in a contest with a trumpet player; "He was seventeen when he left Naples to go to Rome, where during the run of an opera, there was a struggle every night between him and a famous player on the trumpet in a song accompanied by that instrument; this, at first, seemed amicable and merely sportive, till the audience began to interest themselves in the contest, and to take different sides; after severally swelling a note, in which each manifested the power of his lungs, and tried to rival the other in brilliancy and force, they had both a swell and a shake together, by thirds, which was continued so long, that both seemed to be exhausted; and in fact, the trumpeter, wholly spent, gave up, thinking however, his antagonist as much tired as himself, and that it would be a drawn battle; when Farinelli, with a smile on his countenance, showing he had only been sporting with him all that time, broke out all at once in the same breath, with fresh vigour, and not only swelled and shook the note, but ran the most rapid and difficult divisions, and was at last silenced by the acclamations of the audience. From this period may be dated that superiority which he ever maintained over all his contemporaries". He was invited to Madrid to soothe the melancholic Philip V of Spain with his singing. In Spain his power at court was considerable, and he became virtual prime minister of the country in that reign and the succeeding one of Ferdinand VI.

Castration was performed in young boys with promising or beautiful voices in an attempt to retain these qualities at a number of centres in Italy, particularly in Apulia, Norcia, Naples and Bologna. These aspiring singers then generally spent a period of six to nine years in one or other of the famous conservatoires being trained in the arts of the musician and singer. Castration was usually done just before the onset of puberty. It is said of the *castrati* that their bodies were usually well developed, though with a tendency to corpulence, Rossini referring to Velluti as the "*canoro elefante*" (harmonious elephant). The capacity of the lungs and the force of expiration of the *castrato* were equal to, if not greater than, those of a mature man, while the high-pitched boyish voice had the range of a soprano and often exceeded it. The voice changes are dependent on anatomical peculiarities deriving from arrested laryngeal development and not on physiological factors. The larynx in *castrati* develops more slowly and to a lesser degree than in the normal male, so that there is no sudden break; consequently continuous training can be undertaken. Habcock (1923) states that the mouth and nasal cavities of the *castrati* were of abnormal size. However, the angle of the thyroid cartilage is less prominent than in normal men, and the edges of the vocal cords are sharper and not so thick and rounded. Further, the changes which occur in the larynx of a normal man at 50 to 60 years of age, ossification of the cartilages, loss of elasticity, and some wasting of the muscles, do not take place in the *castrati*. The voice does, however, change in compass and timbre. Carestini initially had a soprano range up to C''' but this later deepened to an exceptionally low and rich contralto; he was famous for his singing of *Verdi Prati*, in Handel's *Alcina*, which ranges from D to G''.

It is not generally remembered that the *castrati* extended this vocal range by means of the *falsetto*, as do intact male singers. Tosi (1742) in his *Observations on the Florid Song* writes "A diligent master, knowing that a male soprano, without the *falsetto*, is constrained to sing within the narrow compass of a few notes, ought not only to endeavour to help him to it, but also to leave no means untried, so as to unite the feigned and the natural voice. . . . Many masters put their scholars to sing the contralto not knowing how to help them to the *Falsetto*, or to avoid the trouble of finding it." It is this extended *falsetto* which is probably described by Emma Calvé writing about Domenico Mustafa (1829–1912) who was director of the Papal music until 1895; "certain curious notes he called his fourth voice – strange, sexless, superhuman, uncanny". Calvé studied with him (Mustafa taught that these notes had to be practised with the mouth closed, and that it would take about four years truly to master them) and the sudden high, sustained, floating notes that she produces in her recordings of *Magali* and *Charmant Oiseau* (from David's *Perle du Brésil*) may well stem from Mustafa's teaching.

The last of the soloist *castrati* was Alessandro Moreschi (1858–1922), who performed at the funerals of Victor Emmanuel II and Umberto I of Italy. He has left a legacy of nine recordings made for the Gramophone and Typewriter Co. in Rome in 1902–3. To quote Desmond Shawe-Taylor "He was particularly famous in the part of the Seraph in Beethoven's *Christus am Olberge* . . . which would take him up to the C above the stave, with an alternative E two notes higher still." The voice is quite unlike that of a falsettist or counter-tenor. The discs are a fascinating legacy of a type of voice that once raised the cry of "Evviva il Coltello" in opera houses.

With the passing of the vogue for the *castrati* and the advent of Rossini, Bellini and Donizetti in the early 19th century a new type of tenor voice came into prominence. In the previous generations only the tenors Anton Raaff, Mozart's *Idomeneo*, and Annibale Pio Fabri attained anything like the fame of the *castrati*. The unique voice of the tenor Rubini exemplified the type of voice which now came into favour; the music which Bellini wrote for him in *I Puritani* calls for a voice capable of sustaining a high *tessitura*, with frequent excursions to the high C and D, and includes an F above the high C. This type of voice called into play a finely worked and developed *falsetto* mechanism of great sweetness of quality. Domenico Donzelli, the first Pollione in *Norma*, wrote to Bellini in 1831, ". . . My compass is almost two octaves: from D to high C, I employ chest voice to G only, but up to this pitch I can sustain a vigorous declamation. From this G to high C I employ a *falsetto* which, when used with art and strength, is extremely ornamental. I have adequate agility." It is evident that by "*falsetto*", Donzelli meant what we now term "*head voice*", whereas the extension up to high F used by Rubini was nearer to what we now term *falsetto*. Adolph Nourrit who dominated the French operatic scene until the advent of Duprez could perhaps be termed the last of the true *bel canto* tenors. He was much admired by Rossini. Nourrit, it is reported, always employed the *head voice* admixtured with *falsetto*, the resultant voice being of a sufficient strength and brilliancy to serve the music of Rossini, Meyerbeer and Halévy. Gilbert Duprez' famous *Do di petto* or *Ut de poitrine* in the passage *Corriam, Corriam* in Rossini's *William Tell* was the first time "chest supported" voice was used to produce the high C, an incident which produced a *furore* and started a new style in vocal technique which we have with us to this day.

It was not until the early 19th century that the operatic baritone voice as we know it today came into vogue, the lower male voice being generally sung by basses. Before Rossini's time it was called *tenore forte*, and his Figaro was designed for such a voice. It was Ronconi around 1830 who developed the possibilities of the baritone voice and named it. The word baritone derived from the Greek *barutonos* (heavy tone). The particular characteristics and vocal range of the baritones Felice Varesi (1813–1889) and Giorgio Ronconi (1810–1890), who were associated with the earlier operas of Verdi, influenced that composer's writing for this type of voice and led to the emergence of the so-called Verdi baritone, who is capable of prolonged vocal sojourn in the upper third of his range, with occasional excursions into tenor territory.

The increasing popularity of the Romantic school of music inevitably influenced vocal style as demands of a different type were made on singers. The latter in their turn obviously influenced the composers who wrote for them, no one more so than the mezzo-soprano Pauline Viardot-Garcia (1821–1910). The friend of Berlioz, Gounod, Liszt, Saint-Saëns, Meyerbeer and the Russian writer Turgenev she, more than any other singer, established the mezzo-soprano voice and lifted it in opera from hand-maiden to *prima donna*. She had a relatively short career and in her last years admitted that she had artificially enlarged the compass of her voice, bringing on its premature ruin, because "I wanted to sing everything".

The increasing popularity of Wagner's music has been said to have ruined the art of singing, but Verdi was similarly accused in his early days. It is true that on occasions he makes great demands on his singers' vocal and physical stamina, but a singer who can perform Mozart's *Donna Anna* or Bellini's *Norma* should have no technical problems with Wagnerian roles. Lilli Lehman often said that she would rather sing six performances as *Brunhilde* than one of *Norma*. Bernard Shaw, writing about Adelina Patti singing the music of *Elizabeth* in *Tannhauser*, said that she found her way instinctively to the correct interpretation of the music precisely because of her *bel canto* training, high praise indeed for her vocal method, for Shaw was no "canary-fancier". Patti's gramophone recordings, made after her retirement, afford but a glimpse of the voice that held undisputed sway from the 1860s to 1890 as "Queen of Song".

The clarion voiced Tamagno and Jean de Reszke held undisputed sway amongst male singers until the arrival of Caruso, perhaps the most famous tenor of all time. His unmistakable voice, fortunately well preserved for posterity by his gramophone records, was the product of intensive schooling. It was said of him, that a man who could build a "top" to his voice by sheer willpower could sing anything. His was a phenomenal voice indeed, but one made so by training, for in his own words great singing is "Ten per cent. natural voice, and ninety per cent. hard work."

Over the past three decades the revival of interest in music of the Baroque and earlier periods has led to the re-emergence of that peculiarly British institution the counter-tenor voice. This rather specialised category of male voice is perhaps a by-blow of the original *castrati soprani* and *contralti*, but it has lingered on through the tradition of Cathedral singing in this country in particular. This revival owes more to the counter-tenor Alfred Deller than to any other singer. The speaking and so-called normal singing voice of this breed of singer is generally of a baritonal colour, the particular characteristic of the counter-tenor voice being a well developed *falsetto* which is extended downwards into the *chest register*. As a general rule this category of voice is best heard when used in a concert hall of fairly modest size, for it tends to get lost in the larger spaces of a conventional opera house. The use of the *falsetto* in such a manner tends to produce a characteristic hooting quality in the voice, but there are notable exceptions, particularly that admirable singer James Bowman.

As we have seen, Wagner's vocal writing was often criticised as being the ruination of fine singers but his many champions, particularly Shaw, thought otherwise. Shaw's views on Wagner's music, though valid, are certainly of a partisan nature. What appeared to be almost unsingable is now accepted as a perfectly normal part of singers' training and repertoire. That most wonderful of instruments, the human voice, has risen to meet the demands made of it.

The development of serial and amelodic music has brought forward singers capable of dealing with the problems posed. The voice itself is often used as another instrument rather than as a conventional soloist. Perfect intonation and facility over a very large range is a pre-requisite. The demands made on the voice are considerable, but the instrument does meet these. Luciano Berio's music as sung by Cathy Berberian is a particular case in point.

Is there then any real limit to that phenomenal instrument, the human voice? Probably not.

## REFERENCES

BURNET, CHARLES (1776) *General History of Music*. London.

GARCIA, M. (1847) *Traité Complet de l'Art du Chant*. Paris.

— (1855) Observations on the human voice. *Proc. Roy. Soc.*

GOESTTLER, K. (1950) *Die Anordung, Histologie und Histogenese der quergestreiften Muskulatur im menschlichen Stimmband*. Leipzig.

HABCOCK, F. (1923) *Die Gesangskunst der Kastraten*. Vienna.

HAGEN, GOTTFR. (1917) *Musik u. Theater Archiv*. Munich.

HERIOT, A. (1956) *The Castrati in Opera*. London, Martin Secker and Warburg.

HUSLER and RODD MARLING (1965) *Singing. The Physical Nature of the Vocal Organ*. London, Faber and Faber.

KELLY, MICHAEL (1826) *Reminiscences of the King's Theatre*. London.

NEGUS, V. (1929) *The Mechanism of the Larynx*. London, Heinemann.

PUNT, N. (1967) *The Singer's and Actor's Throat*. London, Heinemann.

RUBIN, H. (1963) Experimental studies on vocal pitch and intensity in phonation. *Laryngoscope*, **73**, 973.

RUBIN, H. (1967) Vocal intensity, subglottic pressure and airflow in relationship to singers. *Folia Phoniat.* **19**, 393.

TOSI, PIETRO FRANCESCO (1742) *Observations on the Florid Song*. London.

# Some Neural and Mechanical
# Aspects of Singing

> Singinge he was or floytynge al the day
> He was as fresh as the month of May.
> Short was his gowne, with sleves longe and wyde.
> Wel coude he sitte on hors and faire ryde;
> He coude songes make and wel endite,
> Juste and eek daunce, and wel purtreye and write
> So hote he lovede that by nightertale
> He sleep no more than doth a nightingale
> Curteys he was, lowly and servisable
> And carf biforn his fader at the table.
>
> From the Prologue to the
> *Canterbury Tales*

In these few lines Chaucer expressively captured the need for man to move in order to satisfy his bodily needs, and to give outward expression to his mental state by action, word or song. Man's singing voice is his oldest musical instrument, rich in harmonic content, of wide tonal compass, eminently portable and completely idiosyncratic in performance being played by its owner alone. But whether man's state of mind is expressed in song, as with Chaucer's lusty Squire, or in propositional speech developing his point of view, the common factor in these different vocal activities is the controlled exhalation of air from the lungs.

Of course, every time we intend to speak or sing we do not have to say to ourselves "exhale". As with other complex motor skills, acquired during infancy and practised throughout life, the exhalation of speech and song is simply one component of a complete motor synergy under voluntary control. Only by a conscious act does one direct one's attention to an individual element of a motor synergy in order to improve its performance such as when learning a better "follow through" in tennis or a better "hand" for playing the piano. Breath control during singing is no exception. When cultivated to perfection it provides the cornerstone of supreme vocal achievement, but ideally remaining an unconscious part of it, so freeing the mind to dwell solely on artistic matters of interpretation.

Much has been written about the "correct" breathing for singing but all too often in such prosaic terms as to offer little direct help to the aspiring singer although possibly appropriate to the artistic goals conceived and set by the teacher. In this account, which could be accused of being "amusical", it is my purpose to describe mainly those aspects of our understanding of the nervous control of voluntary respiratory movements which should be of relevance to the kind of breath control required in singing. However, it would be pointless to attempt such a description without a corresponding account of the general mechanical properties of the system that is under nervous control, including those of the sound generator itself.

## Laryngeal sound source

The beautiful sounds created during singing depend mainly on voicing, the throwing into vibration of the vocal folds of the larynx. The source of sound is not the actual vibration of the vocal folds themselves, as implied in the description vocal cords, which suggests a function like that of a stringed instrument. Rather, as Helmholtz deduced, it derives from the regularly repeated interruption of air flow through the glottis, caused by the valving action of the vibrating vocal folds. Vocalisation is initiated voluntarily, following an inspiration, when the vocal folds are brought together (adducted) by the movement of the arytenoid cartilages and exhalation commenced. Providing there is an adequate sub-glottal (tracheal or alveolar) pressure, usually in excess of 2 cm $H_2O$, the adducted vocal folds are forced apart until the opening force is overcome by the combined effects of the tension in the vocal folds and the suction (Bernouille force) which occurs at the upper (pharyngeal) end of the glottis, thus bringing the vocal folds together once more. This cycle repeats itself all the while the sub-glottal pressure persists and the vocal folds are held in the adducted position. The frequency of vibration, which is perceived as the pitch of the voice, is determined principally by the length, mass and tension of the vocal folds. The Bernouille force mainly operates in the chest register when the vocal folds are relatively thick and present a longer restricted passage to the air flow.

In the absence of a driving sub-glottal pressure, the adducted vocal folds do not vibrate and no sound occurs. This dependence of phonation on sub-glottal pressure has been amply proved by experiments on excised, cadaveric human larynges. These produce rich full tones when actuated by a simulated sub-glottal pressure combined with a manually effected adduction of the vocal folds (Van den Berg, 1968).

Space does not allow a detailed description of the complex actions of the intrinsic and extrinsic (strap) muscles which cause the pitch and quality of the voice to be changed, nor for that matter of the articulatory jaw, tongue, palatal and mouth movements, which collectively are involved in singing (see Chapter 5). It is sufficient to say that the pitch of an individual voice is determined by the endowed natural length, mass and tension of the vocal folds and it is these properties which are in effect modified by direct and reflex control (Wyke, 1974). An increase in longitudinal tension in the vocal folds causes an increase in pitch, while for the low pitched voice typical of the chest register, the vocal folds and ligaments are relatively slack. The harmonic content of the voice derives from the particular shape changes undergone by the vocal folds during valving, but this is subject to further modification by the filtering and selective amplification in the resonators formed by the different parts of the pharyngeal and nasal cavities.

## Prosodic aspects of voicing

During voicing, the vocal folds and articulators are thrown into complex patterns of movement which change moment by moment to generate the continuous series of speech sounds (or segments) which are perceived as words, sentences or sung phrases. Little is known neurophysiologically about the specific mechanisms underlying the creation of a stream of speech sounds, this being an area of interest attracting mainly linguists and phoneticians. But there is one important aspect of voicing which needs to be emphasised and this is the way in which the sound produced by the larynx is continuously modified in intensity, fundamental frequency (pitch) and harmonic content (quality). These physical changes are responsible for the linguistically significant qualities of stress and intonation and together with tempo, rhythm and the duration of phonetic speech segments, comprise the *prosodic* qualities of speech (or singing). The prosodies link together the phonetically distinct but otherwise meaningless phonemes and thus give to the entire sequence of sounds (supra-segmental organisation) a complete structure which is (or should be) linguistically significant and semantically unambiguous. At the simplest level, prosodic features added to a single speech segment can completely modify meaning as in the three forms of "oh", "oh?" and "oh!". Similarly, the relative position or time sequence of prosodic features will transform nouns to verbs as in "insult" or "protest", or convert the declarative form to the interrogative. Intonation is recognised or perceived as a rise or fall in the fundamental frequency of the voice. It would appear from the work of Hirano et al. (1969) that three pairs of intrinsic laryngeal muscles were involved in the intonational change of the sentence "Bev bombed Bob" to "Bev bombed Bob?" as illustrated in Figure 1. It will be noted that the initial laryngeal adjustments occurred well before the onset of phonation, suggesting that, at least for the opening phase of the utterance, the mechanical properties of the sound generator were pre-set according to some preprogrammed pattern of command signals from the brain.

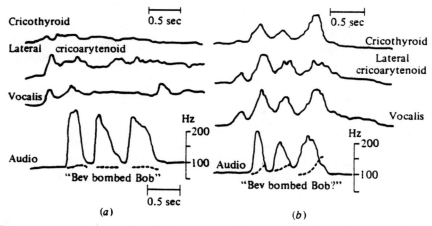

(a)  (b)

Figure 1    Integrated electromyographic signals (cricothyroid, lateral cricoarytenoid, and thyrovocalis muscles), fundamental frequency change (dashed lines) and associated microphone signals (audio) that were recorded as the speaker said the declarative and interrogative forms (parts a and b of the figure) of the sentence "Bev bombed Bob". (From M. Hirano, J. Ohala and W. Vennard, 1969. Journal of Speech and Hearing Research.)

Above all, in the present context, prosody is used to full effect in oratory and song, to convey with emotional impact the beliefs of the orator or the musical accomplishments of the singer. At this juncture it is convenient to emphasise an important difference between speech and song because of the implications it has for the variety of laryngeal and respiratory (sub-glottal pressure control) adjustments that need to be made for these two activities. For singing the word order is immutably fixed, tied as it is to the tempo and rhythm of the composed music (except of course for improvised song) so that creativity in singing can only really be expressed in the individuality of the performance in such matters as interpretation. In speech the word order, and with it the segmental and supra-segmental structure, is infinitely variable, constrained only by the grammatical rules of the language so that sentence after sentence is created as a novel event, calling forth remarkable adjustments of the speech apparatus through the most complex of organisations in the central nervous system.

Alajouanine (1948) described how Ravel, who suffered from Wernicke's aphasia, although having lost his ability to express himself musically, either by written composition or instrumentally, nevertheless retained his musical thinking. He could recognise errors of performance involving a detailed knowledge of the linking of bars. Given the first few notes of a composition of his own that he knew by heart, he could sing several of his own works or could play them well on the piano. However, Ravel's effective musical creativity was destroyed by his inability to order his musical thoughts according to the musical grammar necessary for expressing them in composition, while his aphasia impaired his analytical recognition of notes so that he could not name them.

Stress plays an important role in prosody and this is achieved mainly through direct control of the sub-glottal pressure; however, intonation and sound intensity are both used to highlight the perception of a speech segment. The acoustic intensity of voicing is proportional to the third or fourth power of the sub-glottal pressure, which means that doubling the pressure causes sound intensity to be increased eight or sixteen times (*vide* Cavanagh and Margaria, 1968). Some measure of control over sound intensity can be effected through intrinsic laryngeal mechanisms by regulating the duration and degree of glottal closure. This control, which is exercised through adjustment of the "opening quotient" (the time during which the glottis is open), is effective at low sub-glottal pressures.

As emphasised above, the principal determinant of sound intensity is the sub-glottal pressure. It is generally held that the speaker or singer determines the intensity of the sounds he wishes to produce by his sense of vocal effort in producing them, just as he probably does in his subjective assessment of other people's sounds. In fact, estimates of the subjective intensity of vocalised sound show this to be proportional to the sub-glottal pressure needed to produce it (Ladefoged and McKinney, 1963).

The "sense of effort" (muscular) is a subjective experience or sensory engram associated with voluntary movement. In effect the engram contains the complete history of the sensations associated with the previous attempt to achieve a particular motor goal, and this information is used to estimate the force required to achieve the present goal. As a sensory engram, the sense of effort is possibly generated by what is referred to as a "corollary discharge", conceived as a set of signals associated with the cerebral commands which convey the demand for movement to the motoneurons.

The sense of effort intermingles with the sensory information from the muscles and joints about the course of the movement. When through learning, habit and experience our movements become more and more automatic, then the total sensory experiences associated with them become one of "effortless" action and barely intrude into consciousness (Sears, 1974). But what has all this got to do with singing?

In recent years it has been established that the respiratory muscles, particularly those of the rib-cage, are subjected to a nervous control which is similar in both sensory and motor aspects to that of the limb muscles (for review see Sears, 1973), so one may now inquire "what is the role of 'sense of vocal effort' in singing?"

The sense of vocal effort in singing is expressed both in the prosody associated with the linguistic or emotional meaning of the words, especially in dramatic works, and also more generally in singing *piano* or *forte*, *crescendo* and *decrescendo*, *staccato* and *legato*, in *messa di voce*, indeed, whenever sound intensity is modified in a particular manner. The sense of vocal effort is also essential for a correct vocal attack, be this *coup de glotte*, the normal (clear) attack, or *mezza voce* (breath) attack. For the latter the tension in the vocal cords is slackened to allow the passage of a small amount of breath which does not contribute to the vibratory sound; the effect of this is to give light touch to the voice and hence to create, as a Lieder singer may wish to do, a dreamy or romantic mood. Overdone, this singing at reduced power will result in a breathy voice. With *coup de glotte* (closed glottis) the vocal folds are tightly approximated and as a consequence do not open — and then almost explosively — until the elevated vocal fold tissue tension is overcome by an adequately high sub-glottal pressure. This high pressure combined with the abrupt opening of the folds is responsible for the vital nature of this attack and the high sound intensity which can accompany it.

From the above account it will be recognised that the sounding of a note at a particular pitch and intensity, and with appropriate attack, depends upon a perfect sense of vocal effort. In turn this depends upon a quite remarkable coordination of sub-glottal (respiratory), laryngeal and supra-glottal (articulatory) movements, which occur in ever changing patterns as phoneme succeeds phoneme in the continuous streams of sounds comprising the sung phrase. This sense of vocal effort may be the only guide the individual singer has to judge his own sound intensity when singing in close proximity to other singers.

## The generation of sub-glottal pressure and its nervous control

As outlined above, the motive power for vocalisation derives from the sub-glottal pressure, which, since flow resistance in the normal airways is low, is the same as the alveolar pressure. When the glottis is open for voiceless sounds, the alveolar pressure also provides the source of power for the sounds created by articulatory movements. It is now appropriate to ask "how is the sub-glottal pressure generated and what are the principal features of its nervous control?"

Most descriptions of breath control during singing somehow manage to obscure the fact that it is the sub-glottal pressure which plays the vital role in regulating sound intensity. This is not surprising, of course, since it is only in the laboratory that we would actually dream of measuring pressure. Thus the voice teacher must inevitably resort to descriptions of the air flow and its control and attempt to relate these to where he expects the singer to perceive the location of his sense of vocal effort in order to achieve the desired vocal end result. There lies the possible source of much confusion. Without recourse to the measurement of pressures within the different compartments of the respiratory system, or the recording of the electrical activities of the muscles which form their boundaries (passive muscles are electrically silent), the perceived site of tension may falsely indicate which muscles are actively contracting.

### Mechanical aspects

During quiet breathing, when the glottis is open, the alveolar pressure fluctuates between zero and plus or minus about 2 cm $H_2O$. During conversational speech the sub-glottal pressure fluctuates between 2 and 12 cm $H_2O$, depending on the utterance. During singing the pressure can range between about 2·0 and 50 cm $H_2O$, the latter being reached in a maximally loud *crescendo*. The flow rates are commonly in the range 100–200 ml/second. This means that for a trained adult singer with a typical vital capacity (the maximal volume of air that can be expelled from the lungs following a maximal inspiration) of five litres, a steady tone could be sustained for about 40 seconds. Does this mean that the *castrati* who, it is claimed, could sustain a tone for one minute had large vital capacities, or were their vocal achievements a myth? We shall never know.

In order to understand how these pressures are produced it is simplest to refer to the "relaxation pressure curve" together with the aid of the diagrams in the excellent article by Proctor (1968) on voice training. The relaxation pressure curve describes the relationship between lung volume and the pressures which are developed in the airways against a closed glottis when the respiratory muscles are completely relaxed. As shown in the relaxation curve of Fig. 2a, at high lung volumes the combined elastic recoil of the lungs and chest wall produce a positive airway pressure amounting to 40 cm $H_2O$ at 100 per cent. vital capacity (VC) which potentially will promote expiratory air flow. At low lung volumes the

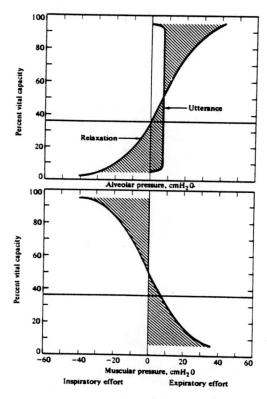

Figure 2 a. Lung volume – alveolar pressure relations during relaxation and during an isolated vowel utterance of normal loudness produced throughout most of the vital capacity. (Relaxation curve after E. Agostoni and J. Mead. "Statics of the respiratory system" in W. Fenn and H. Rahn (eds.) *Handbook of Physiology* (Washington D.C., Amer. Physiol. Soc., 1964).) Hatched area between the curves shows the muscular pressure required for the utterance.

b. Lung volume-muscle pressure relations replotted from data of the upper graph. Negative values represent net inspiratory forces and positive values represent net expiratory forces. (From T. J. Hixon (1973). In: *Normal Aspects of Speech Hearing and Language* (eds.) F. D. Minifie, T. J. Hixon and F. Williams. Prentice-Hall, New Jersey.)

weak tendency for the lungs to collapse (see Figure 3) is overcome by the strong tendency for the chest wall to expand with the net effect that a negative pressure is developed in the airways which potentially would promote inspiratory air flow. At about 40 per cent. VC, close to the normal end-expiratory volume, the opposing recoil forces of the lungs and chest wall are equal in magnitude and the total respiratory system is at its

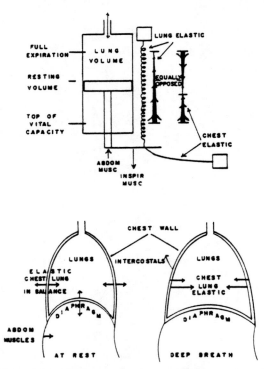

Figure 3   The diagram above shows the forces involved in breathing at indicated levels of the Vital Capacity. Below, a diagram of the muscular and elastic forces at resting volume (relaxation volume) and at the top of the vital capacity (100 per cent. VC). (From D. F. Proctor, 1968. Annals of the New York Academy of Sciences.)

mechanical mid-point, or relaxation volume, and the airway pressure is equal to atmospheric pressure (Figure 2a). Thus unless the recoil forces are opposed by an equivalent muscular pressure, net inspiratory above the relaxation volume and net expiratory below it (Figure 2b), the relaxation pressures will be released to generate sub-glottal pressures against the adducted vocal folds, or with glottis open, the supra-glottal articulators. For example, at full inspiration, as represented in Figure 3a by the piston at its lower limit, the positive relaxation pressure of 30–40 cm $H_2O$ would be more than sufficient for all but the loudest sounds. This position of the piston represents lung volume achieved by the maximum expansion of the rib-cage combined with the lowest descent of the diaphragm. However, if these muscles are completely relaxed to allow flow through the phonating glottis, lung volume steadily decreases, the relaxation pressure declines, and sound intensity rapidly falls until phonation ceases altogether when the sub-glottal pressure is insufficient to overcome the tissue forces in the adducted vocal folds – not exactly a sublime musical performance. Similarly, if the requirement is a long sustained note sung *piano* and needing a pressure, say, of 7·0 cm $H_2O$ (as in Figure 2a), then at high lung volumes the recoil pressure is greatly in excess of what is required, while at lung volumes below relaxation volume it would be acting in the direction of inspiratory flow, again, not exactly suitable for singing. Patients with high spinal lesions leaving them with only the innervation of the diaphragm intact, face difficulties exactly of this sort.

### Neural aspects

It should be evident from the foregoing that to generate a constant sub-glottal pressure for vocal requirements throughout the vital capacity requires an appropriately graded action of the inspiratory and expiratory muscles, as indicated by the changing hatched areas of the curve of Figure 2b. The basic principles of this control, which were outlined by Draper et al. (1960) and further developed from a mechanical point of view by Bouhuys et al. (1966), are illustrated from our own work in Figure 4. This shows, from above downwards, recordings of air flow, tidal volume and the electrical activity of sampled inspiratory and expiratory intercostal muscles, while the subject sang a note of attempted constant pitch and intensity. These records show two cycles of normal breathing prior to the intense activation of external (inspiratory) intercostal muscles as the thorax was expanded to 100 per cent. VC. At the onset of the note the inspiratory muscles of the rib cage remained in action, checking the release of the recoil pressure. In fact, immediately prior to the onset of the note there was a sudden reduction in electrical activity which represented the relatively abrupt release of the relaxation pressure required to produce the desired sound intensity. This, of course, is the moment of the "attack", judged subjectively by the singer through his acquired, and much practised, sense of vocal effort and accompanying which, according to the type of attack, would be the kind of anticipatory adjustments to the vocal folds illustrated in Figure 1. Thereafter, as the note continued, there was a progressive reduction in intercostal EMG activity, which through the graded release of relaxation pressure that it allowed, sustained a constant air flow (upper trace, Figure 4). Eventually, in the muscle sampled, the EMG activity ceased altogether at a lung volume of about 60 per cent. VC. From then on, the steady air flow depended on the progressively increasing activity of the expiratory intercostal muscles (supported by the abdominal muscles – not illustrated), these activities being needed to oppose the progressively

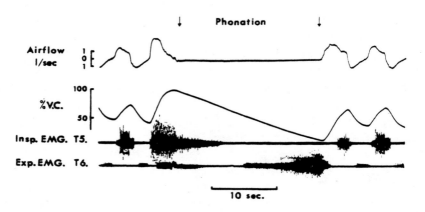

Figure 4  Electrical activity of the intercostal muscles during singing of a sustained tone FF. Inspiratory EMG recorded from external intercostal muscle in subscapular triangle (T. 5). Expiratory EMG from internal intercostal muscle in mid-axillary line (T.6). (From T. A. Sears and J. Newsom Davis, 1968. Annals of the New York Academy of Sciences.)

increasing recoil forces acting in the inspiratory direction (see Figure 2b). In such recordings we found that the higher the demanded sound intensity, the higher was the lung volume at which the inspiratory muscle became inactive and the expiratory muscle active. Furthermore, different regions of the rib-cage showed such patterns of activity at different lung volumes. Thus in Figure 4 the inspiratory EMG activity, which was contaminating the tracing from the 6th intercostal space, dropped out at a higher lung volume than the corresponding inspiratory EMG from the 5th intercostal space. This indicates that the sub-glottal pressure obtaining at a given instant depends on the integrated effect of many muscles acting in concert. From this it will be understood that the precise pattern of activity in the individual singer will be completely idiosyncratic, depending on many factors including the basic shape of his rib-cage and the manner in which he holds it when singing.

Perhaps the most important observation made by Draper et al., as it bears on the controversial question of the role of the diaphragm in singing, was that they found no evidence to support the view that the diaphragm contributes *actively* to breath control, except possibly at very high (?desirable) lung volumes. Bouhuys et al. (1966) have reached a similar conclusion based on a mechanical analysis of trans-diaphragmatic pressure. Thus the notion of diaphragm "support" for the breath would appear to be misleading from the viewpoint of mechanism, notwithstanding its probable value to voice teachers as a descriptive term. Is it possible to reconcile these apparent differences?

Elizabeth Schumann wrote of the expiratory breath as follows: "the feeling you have while expelling the breath or singing is of a steady push upwards of the diaphragm supported by the abdominal muscles, which must always be held in firmly" (cited from Auerswald, 1968). One cannot improve on this from the point of view of simplicity, nor deny the observation and experience of a great artist, but can one use her account to understand better the mechanism of perfect breath control in the light of the new facts?

If the abdominal muscles are not contracted as exhalation and phonation commence, then the weight of the abdominal viscera distends the abdominal wall outwards and through the slack diaphragm exerts an expiratory, collapsing force on the rib-cage. The importance of the abdominal muscle contraction, which can be initiated during the moment of suspension before the "attack", is that it supports the weight of the viscera and, by so doing, relieves the rib-cage (the chest in singing parlance) of an appreciable gravitational load. At the same time, by increasing the abdominal pressure the contracting abdominal wall *passively* tenses the diaphragm. In turn, this imposes a lifting force on the rib-cage, in effect allowing it to be held expanded by less inspiratory muscle force. This point will be returned to below. From this starting point of "tummy in, chest out", the singing expiratory breath can be accomplished in two ways. With rib-cage held high, a continuing thrust from the abdominal muscles will provide the basis of a steady tone, but only of relatively limited duration if the chest is not to move, as strongly advocated by Fuchs (1963). This is because a substantial fraction of the vital capacity depends on the rib-cage itself. In fact, the rib-cage almost invariably does move, but because of the large surface area which it exposes to the lungs its apparent motion may be small in relation to the volume of air exhaled. In practice, for long sustained notes, the abdominal compression is combined with compression of the rib-cage by intercostal muscle activity as illustrated in Figure 4.

Although the first method may be suitable for sustained notes of modest duration it is unsuitable for the more dynamic requirement of musical prosody where a little more action is required.

## Musical prosody

As already emphasised, stress plays an important role in prosody. This is achieved by a phasic increase in sub-glottal pressure superimposed on a baseline pressure relating to the linguistic surrounds of the speech segment that is being stressed. The dual aspect of this control is illustrated in Figure 5 which shows the EMGs recorded from an expiratory intercostal muscle

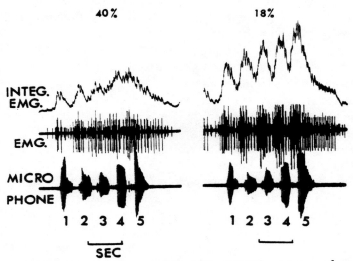

Figure 5    Recording of electromyographic (EMG) activity of expiratory intercostal (internal intercostal muscle) during counting from one to five, as indicated in the microphone trace, at the same attempted intensity. Counting initiated at 40 per cent. and 18 per cent. vital capacity. Upper trace, integrated EMG (rectified and smoothed).

when a subject counted "one, two, three, four, five" at two different lung volumes (40 per cent. and 18 per cent. vital capacity). At 40 per cent. VC each utterance, made at conversational loudness, was preceded by a burst of activity superimposed on background activity which itself steadily increased throughout the counting, as best seen in the integrated (rectified and smoothed) version of the original signal. Whereas the pulsed electrical activity reflects the utterance, the progressive increase in the baseline activity represents the need for more expiratory muscle pressure to overcome the increasing recoil pressure as lung volume diminishes (see Figure 2). When counting was initiated at 18 per cent. VC, each burst was of greater intensity and the baseline activity increased more steeply, reflecting the need for more muscular effort to oppose the steepening increase in recoil pressure. Thus the production of utterances involve the activation of the respiratory muscles in a specific pattern appropriate to the prosodic features of the utterance and the lung volume at which it is accomplished.

I have chosen to illustrate the counting of numbers rather than a singing staccato passage so that the reader (whether or not he is a singer) can more readily repeat the manoeuvre and with finger tips placed on the lower intercostal spaces feel the kind of pulsed action which occurs in the intercostal muscles associated with such EMG activity.

These recordings bring out two different aspects of the problem of creating similar speech sounds at different lung volumes, one being the need to overcome the volume-dependent elastic recoil forces; the other, to generate sub-glottal pressures appropriate to the intensity of the sustained tones or utterances. In their original description of the phasic activation of the chest wall in conversational speech, Ladefoged et al. (1958) found no such phasic activation of the abdominal muscles, except perhaps during very emphatic stressing, although the rectus abdominis muscle did show steadily increasing activity towards the end of a sustained utterance. To the best of my knowledge the EMG of these muscles has not been examined in trained singers, so that in view of what has been asserted above such studies should prove to be of great interest.

The importance of abdominal wall support to the chest can now be better understood. The abdominal wall/diaphragm compartment, under compression, forms a stable base or platform. Against this base below, and the resistance to airflow of the phonating vocal folds (up to 100 times greater than during quiet breathing from the figures of Klatt et al., 1968) above, the short, rapidly acting intercostal muscles can compress the rib-cage and lungs and thus increase sub-glottal pressure for the stressed segments of speech or song (Anderson and Sears, 1964). Without such a base, compression of the rib-cage by the intercostal muscles acting alone allows some volume displacement of the lungs into the abdominal compartment, mediated by displacement of the slack diaphragm, hence the change in alveolar pressure occurs more sluggishly. It should be understood that the kind of changes referred to above are in no sense essential to audible speech, or tolerable singing, but they would appear to be the probable physiological correlates contributing to the perfection in sound production which singers seek to achieve by practice but guided by their ears rather than the laboratory pressure gauge.

Draper et al. (1960) pointed out that the rapidity of fluctuations of EMG activity within a phrase indicates that the intercostal muscles must be comparable in their speed of action with the small muscles of the hand. These muscles have one thing in common, an abundance of muscle spindles, the receptors which signal information about muscle length to the central nervous system. Does this provide a clue to the special role played by the intercostal muscles in the prosody of speech and song?

The signals from muscle spindles and other receptors (Matthews, 1971, for a comprehensive review) are conceived as operating at two levels in the central nervous system, spinal and supraspinal. The former depends on the direct (monosynaptic) connections made on motoneurons by the afferent fibres from muscle spindle primary endings and the similar connections, newly discovered, made by the spindle secondary endings (Kirkwood and Sears, 1974). The latter level of operation involves the signalling to the brain (cerebral and cerebellar hemispheres) of information about the current state of affairs in individual muscles, which can be used by these higher centres to modify appropriately future muscular action. It is generally believed that through these two levels of operation the muscle spindles play an important role in the nervous regulation of movement and posture, particularly with regard to the learning of motor skills and their execution. Apart from these generalisations, it would not be appropriate here to go into more detail about the muscle spindle and its functions. It is sufficient to say that a considerable body of evidence has now accumulated from research on animals, and on man (Newsom Davis and Sears, 1970), to show that the nervous regulation of intercostal muscles is very like that of the limb muscles especially with regard to their load-compensating function (Sears, 1973, for review). This being so, we can see that by analogy with the small muscles of the hand, the muscle spindles of the rib-cage are admirably suited to the task of regulating sub-glottal pressure during speech and song.

Little is yet known about the way these control mechanisms are specifically disturbed by lesions of the central nervous system. It would, however, be most surprising if they were not found to contribute to the characteristic loss of prosodic features in the speech and song of patients with Parkinsonism, or the dysarthria of cerebellar disease. More subtle changes might also be expected to occur with cerebral lesions affecting the successive serial synthesis of percepts or movements which form what von Monakow called the "kinetic melody". Examples of this would be the perception of rhythmic or tonal melodies or their execution in song. The "kinetic melody" represents the way in which each individual element of a highly automated act becomes the stimulus for the next. Given the first few notes, Ravel would automatically complete the songs which he knew by heart, but he was unable to call on these words or notes to create new composition. The more automatic process of singing was preserved, while his speech function was not. We are not told, however, whether Ravel was able to add the prosodic features to his voice which could have given to each performance evidence of his emotional state of mind.

## Acknowledgments

The writer is grateful to authors and publishers for permission to reproduce figures.

## REFERENCES

ALAJOUANINE, TH. (1948) Aphasia and artistic realisation. *Brain*, **71**, 17–241.

ANDERSON, P. and SEARS, T. A. (1964) The mechanical properties and innervation of fast and slow motor units in the intercostal muscles of the cat. *J. Physiol.*, **173**, 114–129.

AUERSWALD, A. (1968) How singers think they sing. *Ann. N. York. Acad. Sci.*, **155**, Art. 1. 230–246.

BOUHUYS, A., PROCTOR, D., and MEAD, J. (1966) Kinetic aspects of singing. *J. Appl. Physiol.*, **21**, 483–496.

CAVAGNA, G. A. and MARGARIA, R. (1968) Airflow rates and efficiency changes during phonation. *Ann. N. York Acad. Sci.*, **155**, Art. 1. 152–164.

DRAPER, M. H., LADEFOGED, P. and WHITTERIDGE, D. (1960) Expiratory pressures and air flow during speech. *Brit. med. J.*, 1837–1843.

FUCHS, V. (1963) *The Art of Singing and Voice Technique*. London, Calder.

HIRANO, M., OHALA, J. and VENNARD, W. (1969) The function of the laryngeal muscles in the regulation of fundamental frequency and intensity of phonation. *J. Speech Hear. Research*, **12**, 616–628.

HIXON, T. J. (1973) *Respiratory function in speech*. In: *Normal Aspects of Speech, Hearing and Language*. Eds. F. D. Minifie, T. J. Hixon and F. Williams. Englewood Cliffs, New Jersey. Prentice-Hall, Inc.

KIRKWOOD, P. A. and SEARS, T. A. (1974) Monosynaptic excitation of motoneurones from secondary endings of muscle spindles. *Nature*, **252**, 243–244.

KLATT, D. H., STEVENS, K. N. and MEAD, J. (1968) Studies of articulatory activity and airflow during speech. *Ann. N. York Acad. Sci.*, **155**, 42–55.

LADEFOGED, P., DRAPER, M. H. and WHITTERIDGE, D. (1958) Syllables and stress. *Miscellanea Phonetica*, **III**, 1–14.

LADEFOGED, P. and McKINNEY, N. P. (1963) Loudness, sound pressure, and sub-glottal pressure in speech. *J. Acoust. Soc. Am.*, **35**, 454–460.

LURIA, A. R. (1966) *Human Brain and Psychological Processes.* New York, Harper & Row.

MATTHEWS, P. B. C. (1972) *Mammalian Muscle Receptors and their Central Actions.* London, Arnold.

NEWSOM DAVIS, J. and SEARS, T. A. (1970) The proprioceptive reflex control of the intercostal muscles during their voluntary activation. *J. Physiol.*, **209**, 711–738.

PROCTOR, D. F. (1968) The physiologic basis of voice training. *Ann. N. York. Acad. Sci.*, **155**, Art. 1, 208–228.

SEARS, T. A. and NEWSOM DAVIS, J. (1968) The control of respiratory muscles during voluntary breathing. *Ann. N. York. Sci.*, **155**, 183–190.

SEARS, T. A. (1973) Servo control of the intercostal muscles. In: *New Developments in EMG and Clinical Neurophysiology.* Ed. J. E. Desmedt. Basel, S. Karger.

— (1974) The afferent regulation of learned movements. *Brain Research*, **71**, 465–473.

VAN DEN BERG. JR. (1968) Sound production in isolated human larynges. *Ann. N. York. Acad. Sci.*, **155**, Art. 1, 18–27.

WYKE, B. D. (1974) Laryngeal neuromuscular control systems in singing. *Folia phoniat.*, **26**, 295–306.

# Memory and Attention in Music

## MEMORY IN MUSIC

It is clear from general considerations that musical memory must involve a highly complex and differentiated system, where information is retained simultaneously at many levels of abstraction. A detailed investigation of this system is only just beginning; and so far it has focussed almost exclusively on memory for pitch, or for abstractions based on pitch information. This chapter reviews the current state of knowledge in the field. The first part examines the organization of the pitch memory system: and the second part describes the various ways in which pitch information is recoded, and so retained in parallel.

### Organization of the Pitch Memory System

Various hypotheses may be advanced concerning the influences acting on pitch memory in storage. We may suppose, for instance, that such memory simply decays with time; or alternatively that pitch information is retained in a general system which is limited in terms of the number of items it can hold simultaneously. Another suggestion is that such information is retained in a specialized system, whose elements interact in specific fashion.

That time alone produces a decrement in memory for pitch has indeed been observed. When subjects are asked to make pitch comparison judgments between two temporally separated notes, such judgments become increasingly blurred as the time interval between the notes increases (Koester, 1945; Harris, 1952; Bachem, 1954, Wickelgren, 1969). However, memory decays only very gradually as a function of time alone. In the study by Harris (1952) subjects made pitch recognition judgments involving tonal stimuli of around 1000 Hz. After a retention interval of 15 seconds, the frequency discrimination threshold was still as good as 8 Hz. To place this in a musical context, a semitone in this frequency range is about 60 Hz; so the amount of memory blurring over this time period is small indeed.

On the other hand, a substantial decrement in pitch recognition occurs when other notes are interpolated during the retention interval. This impairment results even when instructions are given to the subjects to ignore the interpolated notes. An experiment which demonstrates this effect was performed by Deutsch (1970a). Subjects were selected for obtaining a score of 100 per cent. correct in comparing pairs of notes which were separated by a silent interval of six seconds, and which were either the same in pitch or which differed by a semitone. The same note pairs were then again presented; except that now eight notes were interpolated during the retention interval. The subjects were instructed to listen to the first test note, to ignore the eight interpolated notes, and then to judge whether the second test note was the same in pitch as the first or different. It was found that the interpolated notes produced a substantial decrement in recognition performance. The subjects, having achieved an errorless performance in the condition with no interpolated notes, now produced an error rate of over 40 per cent. Here a score of 50 per cent. correct represented chance performance; so the eight interpolated notes almost obliterated the subjects' ability to detect a pitch difference of a semitone.

We may now inquire why the interpolated notes produce a memory loss. One might hypothesize that these notes distract the listener, and so impair his ability to concentrate on the note he is trying to remember. If this interpretation were correct, then other interpolated materials which produced distraction of attention would have the same effect. Alternatively, we might suggest that there is a general memory store into which the pitch information is entered along with other information; and that this store is limited in terms of the amount of information it can accommodate. If this were so, then other interpolated materials which were also remembered should again impair pitch recognition. Yet another hypothesis is that information concerning pitch is retained in a specialized system. We might then expect that memory disruption would occur if other notes were interpolated, but not if different types of material were interpolated instead.

These various hypotheses were put to experimental test (Deutsch, 1970b). Subjects made pitch recognition judgments under three different conditions. In the first condition the subjects were asked to recognize a note following a retention interval of five seconds during which six notes were interpolated. In the second condition, instead of six notes, six spoken numbers intervened between the notes to be compared. These numbers were adjusted to appear equal in loudness to the notes, and they were spaced identically. In both these conditions, the subjects were asked to judge whether the test notes were the same or different in pitch, and to pay no attention to the intervening items. In the third condition, numbers again were interpolated, and the subjects were asked to recall them besides making the pitch recognition judgment. This ensured that the numbers had been attended to, and had entered memory.

The results of this experiment are shown on Table 1. It can be seen that the interpolation of notes caused a substantial decrement in pitch recognition; however, only a minimal decrement occurred when spoken numbers were interpolated, even when these numbers were also recalled. It will also be noted that number-recall when subjects were required to make pitch comparison judgments was as good as in a control condition where

Table 1

|  | Percentage errors | |
| --- | --- | --- |
| Condition | Pitch recognition | Number recall |
| 1. Pitch recognition with intervening notes ignored | 32·3 | |
| 2. Pitch recognition with intervening numbers ignored | 2·4 | |
| 3. Pitch recognition with intervening numbers recalled | 5·6 | 25·3 |
| 4. Number recall with no pitch recognition required | | 27·4 |

Percentage errors in pitch recognition as a function of type of material interpolated during the retention interval. Number recall was scored correct on any trial when all the numbers were recalled in the correct order. (From Deutsch, 1970b.)

this requirement was waived. It seems clear from this experiment that the memory decrement due to interpolated notes is not based on attention distraction, nor on displacement of material in some general memory store of limited capacity. We may therefore conclude that there exists a specialized system for the retention of pitch information.

Further experiments were addressed to uncovering the properties of the pitch memory system. One might still hypothesize that this system is one of limited storage capacity, except that it accepts only pitch information. On this theory, memory impairment would result from an overload produced by introducing too many notes. If this were correct, then the amount of memory impairment produced by an interpolated note would not vary as a function of its relationship to the note to be remembered. However, if one note can be shown to have a specific effect on memory for another depending on their pitch relationship, then this would suggest a system in which pitch memory elements interacted in a specific manner.

An experiment was therefore made to study the effect on pitch memory produced by a note which formed part of a sequence interpolated between two notes to be compared for pitch, when its relationship to the note to be remembered varied systematically along the pitch continuum (Deutsch, 1972a). Subjects compared for pitch two notes which were separated by a five second retention interval during which six other notes were played. Errors were plotted as a function of the pitch of a further note, which was placed in the second serial position of the intervening sequence, the relationship of which to the first test note varied from identity to a whole tone separation on the equal tempered scale. All other notes in the intervening sequence were at least $1\frac{1}{2}$ tones removed from the first test note. In a baseline condition no critical note was interpolated, and the note in the second serial position was chosen in the same way as the other notes in the intervening sequence.

Figure 1 plots error rates in pitch recognition judgment as a function of the pitch relationship between the first test note and the critical interpolated note. As can be seen, the disruptive effect of one note on memory for another does indeed vary as a function of their pitch relationship. This variation can be summarized in the following manner: memory is facilitated when the critical interpolated note is identical in pitch with the first test note. As the pitch difference between the first test note and the critical interpolated note increases, errors also increase. This increase peaks at $\frac{2}{3}$ tone separation, and then at distances greater than $\frac{2}{3}$ tone errors decrease again, reaching a baseline at around a whole tone separation. This experiment shows therefore that impairment in pitch memory occurs as a property of a processing mechanism which is organized in a precise and systematic manner. The functioning of such a system cannot be explained on the grounds of simple and undifferentiated storage capacity limitation.

A further experiment systematically explored the disruptive effect on pitch recognition which was produced by including within an interpolated sequence a note which was a semitone removed from the note to be remembered (Deutsch, 1973a). As shown in Table 2, when the test notes were identical in pitch, including a note which was either a semitone higher or a semitone lower produced roughly the same increment in errors. A substantially larger increment was produced when both these notes were included. When the test notes differed in pitch by a semitone, including a

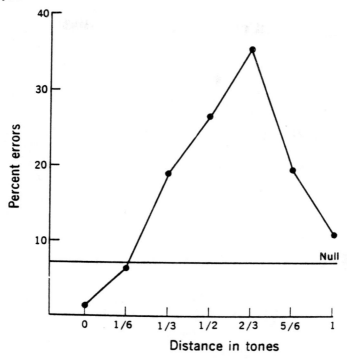

Figure 1   Per cent. errors in pitch recognition judgment as a function of the pitch relationship between the first test note and a critical interpolated note. The line labelled "Null" shows per cent. errors where no note in the critical range was included in the interpolated sequence. (From Deutsch, D., 1972, by permission of *Science,* **175,** 1020–1022. Copyright 1972 by the American Association for the Advancement of Science.)

note a semitone removed from the first test note also caused an increase in errors. However, a substantially greater increase occurred when the critical interpolated note happened to be identical in pitch to the second test note. (This effect appears to be due to deterioration of temporal or order information and this is discussed below.) And again, including both such notes produced a greater increase in errors than including either one alone. It was further found (Deutsch, 1975a) that when the test notes were identical in pitch, and a note that was a semitone higher or lower was included in a sequence of six interpolated notes, the disruptive effect was roughly constant whether the critical note was placed in the second or in the fifth serial position of the intervening sequence (Figure 2).

Such findings led to the construction of a theoretical model for the organization of pitch memory elements (Deutsch and Feroe, 1975). On this

*Table 2*

| Condition | Percentage errors |
|---|---|
| **TAPE I** | |
| **A. Test notes same** | |
| 1. Note a semitone higher included in intervening sequence. | 7·9 |
| 2. Note a semitone lower included in intervening sequence. | 6·9 |
| 3. Two notes, one a semitone higher and the other a semitone lower, included in intervening sequence. | 18·5 |
| 4. No note a semitone higher or lower included in intervening sequence. | 2·8 |
| **B. Test notes different** | 7·5 |
| | |
| **TAPE II** | |
| **A. Test notes different** | |
| 1. Note of the same pitch as the second test note included in intervening sequence. | 20·1 |
| 2. Note a semitone from the first test note, but on the opposite side of pitch continuum to the second test note, included in intervening sequence. | 7·4 |
| 3. Two notes, one as in Condition 1 and the other as in Condition 2, included in intervening sequence. | 25·2 |
| 4. No note a semitone removed from the first test note included in intervening sequence. | 3·2 |
| **B. Test notes same** | 6·6 |

Percentage errors in pitch recognition as a function of the presence in the intervening sequence of either one or two notes which were a semitone removed from the first test note. Tape I studied the effect in sequences where the test notes were identical in pitch, and Tape II where the first and second test notes differed by a semitone. (From Deutsch, 1973a.)

model, pitch memory is the function of an array the elements of which are activated by notes of particular pitch. These elements are placed along the array in such a way that elements which are activated by notes separated by the same distance in log frequency units are also separated by the same distance along the array. The hypothesis also proposes that these elements are linked as a recurrent lateral inhibitory network, analogous to those investigated by neurophysiologists in systems handling incoming sensory information (Ratliff, 1965).

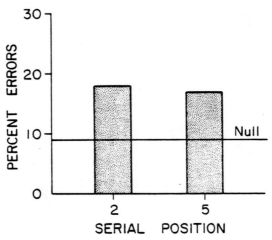

Figure 2   Per cent. errors in pitch recognition judgment where the first and second test notes were identical in pitch, and a note a semitone higher or lower than the test notes was included in the interpolated sequence. Errors are plotted separately for sequences where the critical interpolated note was placed in the second and the fifth serial position of a sequence of six interpolated notes. The line labelled "Null" shows per cent. errors in sequence where no such critical note was interpolated. (From Deutsch, 1975a.)

This hypothesis makes a specific prediction which would not be expected on other simple models. Thus, if a note which is inhibiting another note in memory were itself inhibited, this should release the originally inhibited note from inhibition. Such a phenomenon of disinhibition has been shown by neurophysiologists in sensory arrays. Applying such a model to the study of memory suggests that the inhibition of the inhibiting note would actually cause memory for the test note to return.

An experiment was carried out to test this prediction. Subjects compared for pitch two notes which were separated by a sequence of six interpolated notes. There was always placed in the second serial position of the intervening sequence a note which was $\frac{2}{3}$ tone removed from the first test note. Errors were then plotted as a function of a further note, placed in the fourth serial position, the relationship to the note in the second serial position varying systematically from identity to a whole tone separation. As shown in Figure 3, a systematic return of memory was indeed obtained. The error rate when the note in the fourth serial position was $\frac{2}{3}$ tone

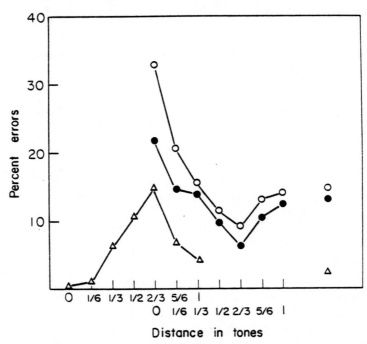

Figure 3  Per cent. errors in pitch recognition obtained experimentally and predicted theoretically. Open triangles display per cent. errors in the baseline experiment which varied the pitch relationship between a test note and a critical interpolated note. (Open triangle at right displays per cent. errors where no notes were interpolated in the critical range under study.) Filled circles display per cent. errors in the experiment where a note which was $\frac{2}{3}$ tone removed from the test note was always interpolated. Errors are plotted as a function of the pitch relationship between this note and a second critical interpolated note which was further removed along the pitch continuum. Open circles display per cent. errors for the same experimental conditions predicted theoretically from the lateral inhibition model. (Filled and open circles at right display per cent. errors obtained experimentally and assumed theoretically where no further critical note was interpolated.) (From Deutsch, D., and Feroe, J., 1975, by permission of *Perception and Psychophysics,* **17**, 320, 324. Copyright 1975 by the Psychonomic Society, Inc.)

removed from the note in the second serial position was significantly lower than in the baseline condition where the note in the fourth serial position was outside this range. A first-order inhibitory function was also obtained, using subjects selected by the same criterion as for the disinhibition experiment. This was used to calculate the theoretical disinhibition function, so that it could be compared with the function produced experimentally. These functions are also portrayed in Figure 3. It can be seen that there is a correspondence between the theoretically and empirically derived disinhibition functions. This is therefore strong evidence that the elements of the pitch memory system are arranged as a lateral inhibitory network, analogous to those handling sensory information at the incoming level.

*Octave generalization*

So far we have discussed interactive effects occurring in memory between notes which are separated by less than an octave. However, it becomes clear for many reasons that we code pitch not only along a monotonic dimension of "height" but also in terms of its position within the octave. We may therefore ask whether these interactive effects take place simply along a monotonic pitch continuum, or whether an abstracted octave array is also involved.

In one experiment (Deutsch, 1974a), subjects compared two notes for pitch when these were separated by a sequence of eight interpolated notes. The interpolated notes in any one sequence were either all in the same octave as the test notes; or they were all in the octave above; or in the octave below; or half were in the octave above and the other half in the octave below, the order of octave placement being random. Figure 4 shows how the rate of error varied for the different conditions. Interpolated notes in the lower octave produced fewest errors. Notes in the higher octave brought about an intermediate number of errors; whereas notes in the middle octave were responsible for an even greater number of errors. However, the mixed condition produced the most disruption. This study therefore demonstrates that accuracy in pitch recognition in a sequential setting depends upon the octave or octaves in which the other notes are placed.

We can also inquire what effect octave displacements have on specific disruptive effects in pitch memory. To this end, Deutsch (1973b) investigated two specific effects. The first occurs when the test notes are the same in pitch, and a note which is a semitone higher or lower is included in the interpolated sequence (Deutsch, 1973a). When both such notes are included this disruptive effect is substantially enhanced (Table 2); so this condition was studied here. A second disruptive effect occurs when the test notes differ in pitch, and a note which is identical with the second test note is included in the intervening sequence. Here the subject tends to mis-recognize the second test note as the same as the first (see below). The question investigated was whether such disruptive effects also occur when the critical interpolated note or notes are displaced by an octave.

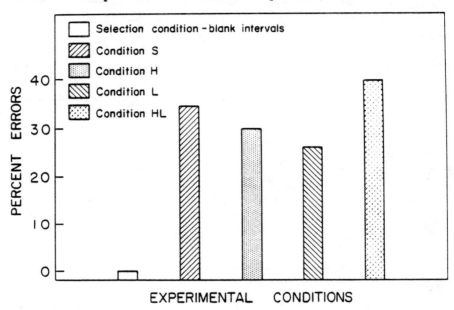

Figure 4    Per cent. errors in pitch recognition as a function of the octave in which the interpolated notes were placed. All sequences contained eight interpolated notes. Condition S: interpolated notes placed in the same octave as the test notes. Condition H: interpolated notes placed in the octave above. Condition L: interpolated notes placed in the octave below. Condition HL: half of the interpolated notes placed in the octave above and the other half in the octave below; the order of octave placement being random. (From Deutsch, 1974a.)

Table 3 illustrates the results of this experiment. It can be seen that both types of disruptive effect exhibit octave generalization. However, significant differences in the degree of these effects were found depending on the octave in which the critical interpolated notes were placed. When the critical interpolated notes were placed in the higher octave, then the disruptive effects were almost as great as when they were placed in the middle octave. However, when the critical interpolated notes were placed in the lower octave the disruptive effects were much weaker. From an analysis of the pattern of errors, it was concluded that these effects take place along both a monotonic pitch continuum, and also along an abstracted octave array.

## Repetition effects

Substantial effects on memory performance are produced by including in an interpolated sequence notes of the same pitch as one or other of the notes to be compared. Such effects may be either facilitary or disruptive.

*Table 3*

| Condition | Percentage errors |
|---|---|
| **Test notes different** | |
| 1. No note at pitch of the second test note, or displaced by an octave from this note, included in intervening sequence. | 4·6 |
| 2. Note at pitch of the second test note included in intervening sequence. | 26·7 |
| 3. Critical included note as in Condition 2, but displaced on an octave higher. | 20·2 |
| 4. Critical included note as in Condition 2, but displaced an octave lower. | 12·1 |
| **Test notes same** | |
| 5. No note a semitone removed from the test note, or displaced from such a note by an octave, included in intervening sequence. | 5·6 |
| 6. Two notes, one a semitone higher than the test note, and the other a semitone lower, included in intervening sequence. | 24·4 |
| 7. Critical included notes as in Condition 6, but displaced an octave higher. | 21·0 |
| 8. Critical included notes as in Condition 6, but displaced an octave lower. | 11·3 |

Percentage errors in pitch recognition as a function of the presence in the intervening sequence of notes displaced by an octave from those known to produce disruption. (From Deutsch, 1973b.)

If a note of the same pitch as the first test note is included among the interpolated notes, an improvement occurs in the recognition performance, which is highly sensitive to the serial position of the repeated note. In one experiment, subjects judged whether two test notes were the same or different in pitch when they were separated by a sequence of six interpolated notes (Deutsch, 1975b). It was found that when a note of the same pitch as the first test note was included in the second serial position of the intervening sequence, there resulted a substantial and highly significant improvement in performance. However, when the repeated note was placed in the fifth serial position, this improvement was insignificant. This was true both for sequences where the test notes were identical in pitch, and also where they differed (Figure 5).

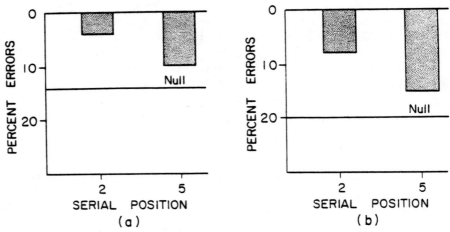

Figure 5   Per cent. errors in pitch recognition when a note of the same pitch as the first test note was included in the interpolated sequence. Errors are displayed separately for sequences where the repeated note was placed in the second and the fifth serial position of a sequence of six interpolated notes. The lines labelled "Null" display per cent. errors in sequences where the first note pitch was not repeated. (a) First and second test notes identical in pitch. (b) First and second test notes differed in pitch by a semitone. (From Deutsch, 1975b.)

A great increase in errors is produced in sequences when the test notes differ in pitch, and when a note that is identical in pitch to the second test note is included in the interpolated sequence. This effect depends largely upon the serial position of the repeated note: a far greater increase in errors occurs when this note is placed in the second serial position of a sequence of six interpolated notes than when it is placed in the fifth serial position

(Figure 6). However, no serial position effect is apparent in sequences where the test notes are identical in pitch, and where one of the interpolated notes is a semitone removed (Figure 2).

Such repetition effects are probably due to the deterioration of information along a time or order continuum. Deutsch (1972b) proposed an explanation for such effects and the way they vary with serial position.

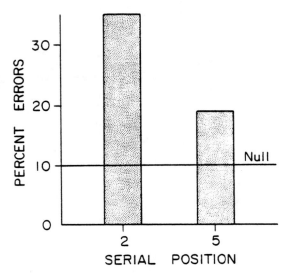

Figure 6  Per cent. errors in pitch recognition where the test notes differed in pitch by a semitone, and a note of the same pitch as the second test note was included in the interpolated sequence. Errors are displayed separately for sequences where the critical interpolated note was placed in the second and the fifth serial position of a sequence of six interpolated notes. The line labelled "Null" displays per cent. errors in sequences where no such critical note was included. (From Deutsch, 1975a.)

*Other systems*

Although little formal investigation has been made into the influences acting on other musical attributes in storage, it is tempting to speculate that the principles uncovered in the case of pitch also hold for other attributes. In the case of simultaneous and successive intervals, for instance, we may speculate that such memory is the function of a continuum the elements of which are activated by the simultaneous or successive presentation of tone pairs (Figure 7). We may further imagine that such elements are arranged according to the size of the ratio between the component frequences (i.e. in units of log $F_1$–log $F_2$), and that specific facilitative and disruptive effects take place between elements along this continuum, analogous to effects found in absolute pitch memory. Because of the perceptual similarity of simultaneous intervals which are inversions of each other (see below), we

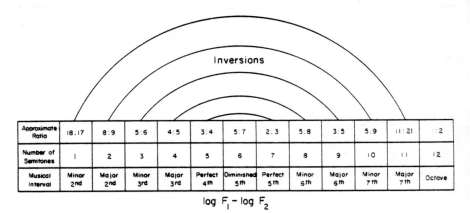

Figure 7   The interval size continuum. This is here divided into semitonal steps for purposes of clarity, but these steps simply represent arbitrary increments along the continuum.

would expect to find scallops in the curves plotting such interactive effects in the case of simultaneous note pairs. At present, however, this can only be proposed quite tentatively, and further work might yield interesting results.

## Higher-level encoding of pitch information

For most persons, absolute levels of performance in pitch recognition are remarkably poor (Pollack, 1952, 1964; Deutsch, 1970a, 1970b). Memory for pitch information must therefore depend largely upon abstraction of this information and its retention in recoded form. We shall therefore discuss the various ways in which such recoding is achieved.

At the first level of abstraction pitch information is coded as a set of features. Two types of encoding will be considered here in detail. The first designates the position of a note within the octave, and the second abstracts the relationships between units of a combination of pitches.

### Octave equivalence

Notes with waveform frequencies standing in the ratio of 2 : 1 are defined as an octave apart, and a perceptual similarity exists between notes which are separated by an octave or octaves. Generalization of response to notes separated by octaves has been demonstrated in conditioning situations, in both man and animals (Humphreys, 1939; Blackwell and Schlosberg, 1943). Moreover, those with absolute pitch may often relegate a note to the wrong octave, even though they name it correctly (Baird, 1917; Bachem, 1954).

The principle of octave equivalence forms an important basis for the traditional musical scale. This is composed of a set of notes within the octave, each of which is given a name (C, C#, D, etc.); and the entire scale consists of the repetitive presentation of these notes across successive octaves. Octave duplications in scales also occur cross-culturally, and the principle of octave equivalence may be regarded as a universal musical phenomenon (Nettl, 1956).

*Interval and chord equivalence*

When two notes are presented either simultaneously or in succession, a musical interval is perceived; and a perceptual similarity exists between intervals with component notes separated by the same frequency ratio. This principle forms part of the basis for the traditional musical scale, the smallest unit of which is the semitone, representing a frequency ratio of 18: 17. Note-pairs separated by the same number of semitones are considered as standing in the same relationship, and are given the same name in musical terminology. Figure 7 shows the set of intervals used in the traditional musical scale, together with their approximate frequency ratios. Attneave and Olson (1971) demonstrated under laboratory conditions that when subjects are asked to transpose a well-known melody, they do so by preserving the ratios between the successive notes. Further, examination of music in other cultures leads to the conclusion that such behaviour is not culture-dependent (Nettl, 1956).

The abstraction of relationships between simultaneously presented notes is not confined to note-pairs. We also classify together chords consisting of three or more notes; and chords with components standing in the same relationship are given the same name (major triad, minor triad, and so on). However, a chord cannot be defined simply in terms of the sum of its component intervals. For instance, a major triad and a minor triad sound quite different, yet in both cases their components stand in the relationships of a major third, a minor third, and a fifth (Figure 8). Thus the abstraction of chords consisting of three or more components involves more than the process of abstracting their component intervals.

In the case of simultaneous intervals and chords, a second shape recognition operation is also performed, known as inversion. Two chords are considered harmonically equivalent when their component notes are placed in different octaves. Thus, a simultaneous note-pair forming an interval of n semitones is perceptually similar to a pair forming an interval of 12-n semitones. The sets of note-pairs which are related by the operation of inversion are designated in Figure 7.

Experimental evidence for the perceptual similarity of inverted note-pairs was provided by Plomp et al. (1973). They required subjects to

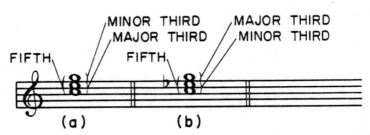

Figure 8   Root forms of the C major triad (a) and C minor triad (b); and their component intervals. In both cases, the components stand in a relationship of a major third, a minor third, and a fifth. However, in the major triad the major third lies below the minor third; and in the minor triad the minor third lies below the major third. (From Deutsch, 1969.)

identify the intervals formed by simultaneous pairs of notes, and found that confusions occurred between intervals which were musical inversions of each other. For instance, more confusions occurred between fifths and fourths than between either with diminished fifths. Confusions between seconds and sevenths were also common. Further evidence was provided by Deutsch and Roll (1974) who required subjects to make pitch comparison judgments when the notes to be compared were accompanied by other notes of lower pitch. When the test notes differed but formed the same interval, errors in recognition were quite pronounced. A significant increase in errors was also found when the relationship formed by the first test combination (a musical fifth) was an inversion of the relationship formed by the second test combination (a musical fourth). It was concluded that errors were due to the perceptual equivalence of the inverted interval.

The abstraction of specific features derived from pitch is analogous in many respects to the abstraction of spatial features in vision. There is good evidence that such abstractions in the visual system are achieved by a convergence of first-order units on to higher-order units, which in turn converge on to still higher-order units, and so on (Hubel and Wiesel, 1962). Deutsch (1969) proposed a mechanism for abstraction of features derived from pitch based on this principle of successive levels of convergence. Fundamentally, it assumes that pitch information is abstracted along two parallel channels, each of which consists of two levels of convergence. The first channel is concerned with abstraction of relational features. Here it is assumed that first-order units responding to notes of specific pitch are linked in groups of two and three to second-order units. These units therefore respond to specific intervals and chords. Three classes of such second-order units are defined: those responding to simultaneous stimulation only, those responding to ascending intervals, and those responding to descending intervals. These second-order units are then linked to third-order units in such a way that all units activated by notes standing in the same relationship are joined. Thus all units activated by thirds would feed on to one unit, all activated by fourths on to another, all activated by a major triad on to another, and so on. These third-order units therefore respond to abstracted intervals and chords (Figure 9).

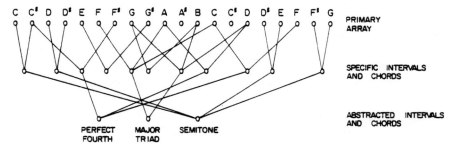

Figure 9   Two stages of abstraction along the transposition channel. Although units in the primary array are identified for purposes of clarity by musical notation, it is assumed that intervening units also exist, and that these are linked together in the same fashion. (From Deutsch, 1969.)

The second channel abstracts information concerning the position of a note within the octave, and also mediates inversion of chords. Here it is assumed that first-order units responding to notes of specific pitch are linked in such a way that there is convergence of notes separated by octaves on to the same second-order unit. In the second stage of transformation these units are linked to third-order units. It is assumed that these third-order units are activated by simultaneous rather than successive stimulus presentation. These units therefore underlie the perceptual equivalence of simultaneous intervals which are inversions of each other (Figure 10).

### Contour

There is good evidence that we recognize a melodic sequence, not only

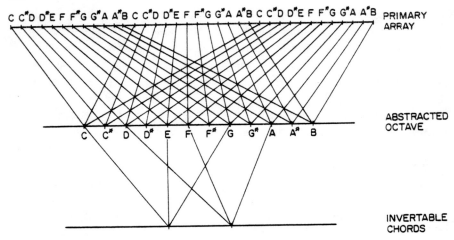

Figure 10   Two stages of abstraction along the octave channel. As in Figure 9, it is assumed that units intervening between those displayed here are also linked together in this fashion. (From Deutsch, 1969.)

because of its specific intervals, but also by global cues, such as its pitch range, and the sequence of directions of pitch change. Werner (1925) showed that people were able to recognize melodies when they were transformed on to extremely small scales, so that the interval sizes were grossly distorted. Furthermore, White (1960) found that melodies were recognized with fair accuracy when all the interval sizes were set to one semitone, leaving intact only the sequence of directions of pitch change. Indeed, in actual music a phrase is often transposed with distortion in the interval sizes, so as to conform to the elements of the scale; and such transposition is easily recognized (Figure 11).

*Scales and modes*

In the music of any given culture, melodic and harmonic sequences are composed out of small sets of pitch relationships, which are said to constitute their scale. The set of notes on the scale thus provides an alphabet in terms of which a melody or harmonic sequence may be defined. Thus transposition in a short-term situation often takes place along the scalar alphabet, so that the relative positions of the elements along the scale are preserved, but the intervals are therefore distorted (Figure 11).

For any given scale, one can determine a hierarchy of *a priori* probabilities of occurrence for notes standing in various positions along the scale. For instance, the note which occurs with greatest frequency is generally the tonic. In addition, one can determine a set of *transitional*

Figure 11    Transposition along the alphabet of the scale. A given melodic configuration is presented four times in succession, at different positions along the scale. Since the scale has unequal intervals, there results a variation in the set of intervals involved. (a) The sequence in musical notation. (b) The sequence plotted as log frequency versus time. The ladder at right displays the scale. (From Bach, J. S., *The Well-Tempered Clavier, Book I, Fugue V.*)

probabilities between the different elements of the scale. Thus in Western traditional music the leading tone is most often followed by the tonic, and so on. When the same set of pitch relationships is used as the basis for a different set of *a priori* and *transitional* probabilities, the scale is said to be in a different mode. Thus if we take the set of white notes on the piano and play them in ascending order, starting each time with a different note, the scales thus formed are in different modes (Scholes, 1950).

When we hear a piece of music, we quickly become sensitive not only to its scale, but also to the set of *a priori* and *transitional* probabilities for the elements of the scale. This is true both for linear successions of notes, and also for harmonic sequences. In traditional Western harmony there are strong *transitional* probabilities governing the root progressions of chords. For instance, the chord on the tonic (I) is most often followed by the chord on the subdominant (IV) or dominant (V); sometimes by the chord on the submediant (VI) and less often by the chord on the supertonic (II) or mediant (III) (Piston, 1948). At a higher organizational level, when modulating to a different key, the most probable modulations are to the dominant, subdominant, or relative major or minor.

The mapping of pitch information on to scales with strong *a priori* and *transitional* probabilities is of fundamental importance to musical memory, as it enables us to make use of a fund of highly learned information in recalling or recognizing a given sequence. The differences between attempting to recall a musical sequence in a familiar tonal system as compared with a set of notes chosen at random, is equivalent to the difference between trying to recall a sentence as compared with a set of nonsense syllables. Indeed, it has been demonstrated experimentally that short-term recognition of melodic patterns is greater when the melodies are in our tonal system than when they are not (Francés, 1972; Zenatti, 1969). Moreover, recognition of a melodic sequence which is preceded and followed by other notes is enhanced when the context notes establish a tonality (Miller and Cuddy, 1972). Recognition is greatest if the context notes are such that the entire sequence resolves to the tonic, which is the most probable resolution in our tonal system.

It is interesting to recall that modern serial music discards the traditional framework of probability relationships. Instead, every composition includes all twelve tones of the chromatic scale. For any given composition a particular ordering is adopted of these twelve semitones (known as the basic set, or row); and the entire harmonic and melodic material of the piece is drawn from this row, which may, however, be transposed, inverted or reversed according to the wishes of the composer. Thus each piece of music establishes its own set of *transitional* probabilities, and there is no set for this style of music in general. This necessarily imposes a much greater burden on memory than exists for tonal music (see also Meyer, 1967).

*Recognition of melodic sequences under various transformations*

A question of importance to musical memory concerns the extent to which a melodic sequence will be recognized when it has been subject to a given transformation. The case of transposition is clear. Here the entire sequence is presented in a different pitch range. Transposition takes place so readily that it is much easier to recognize a well-known tune than to determine in what key it is being played. Within a given piece of music transposition occurs in two different ways. First, the entire scale may be transposed, so that the set of intervals between successive tones is preserved. Or the sequence may be shifted along the scale so that the relative positions of the elements are preserved, but the pitch relationships are distorted. Figure 11 shows the same sequence repeated at four different pitch levels, involving three different set of intervals.

Other transformations used in music are known as inversion and retrogression. Inversion constitutes a systematic reversal of the directions of the successive intervals (this is different from the harmonic use of the term described above). In other words, all ascending intervals become descending intervals, and vice versa. Retrogression constitutes a reversal of the order in which the components of the sequence are presented. Musicians disagree widely on the question of perceptual equivalence of melodies transformed by these operations. This is particularly true of retrogression. Thus Piston (1949) wrote: "Retrograde forms are rarely employed since it is very difficult for the ear to recognize a motive played in this fashion" and described the canon in retrograde motion as "more an intellectual stunt than a purely musical effect." And Tovey (1957) wrote that retrogression "is of extreme rarity in serious music." However, Schoenberg (1951) took a different view. Drawing an analogy between inversion and retrogression in music, and inversion and mirror image reversal in visual shape perception, he said:

*The unity of musical space demands an absolute and unitary perception.* In this space . . . there is no absolute down, no right or left, forward or backward. . . . Just as our mind always recognizes, for instance, a knife, a bottle or a watch, regardless of its position, and can reproduce it in the imagination in every possible position, even so a musical creator's mind can operate subconsciously with a row of tones, regardless of their direction, regardless of the way in which a mirror might show the mutual relations, which remain a given quantity.

Given this disagreement, the question of perceptual equivalence of inverted or retrograde sequences is of considerable practical interest to musicians, as well as of theoretical interest to psychologists. In one experiment Dowling (1972) presented subjects with a standard five-note melody, and then with a comparison melody. In one set of conditions the comparison melody was either an exact transposition of the first or it was an inversion, retrograde, or retrograde-inversion of the first (in retrograde-inversion both the operations of inversion and retrogression were performed on the sequence); or it was unrelated. In another set of conditions the comparison melody was still more distorted so that the exact intervallic relationships were destroyed although the contour was preserved. It was found that although recognition performance for the transformed sequences was above chance, the subjects did not appear to distinguish between exact transformations and those that preserved contour alone.

Another experiment with bearing on this question involved long term recognition memory (White, 1960). Subjects were required to identify well-known tunes which were transformed in various ways. It was found that when the tunes were played backwards, recognition was again above chance; however, it was at about the same level as when the sequences were presented with all the pitch information removed so that the rhythm provided the only cue. Furthermore, the tunes were recognized better when the intervals were permuted randomly than when they were systematically reversed. This strongly suggests that the subjects were recognizing the retrograde sequences on the basis of their component intervals, rather than their orders.

A further question involves the principles of octave equivalence. One might suppose that since notes standing in an octave relationship are perceptually similar under various conditions, melodic sequences would also be perceptually similar when their components are placed within different octaves. To test this hypothesis Deutsch (1972c) played the first half of the tune "Yankee Doodle" to subjects under a number of conditions, with each hearing only one item. This tune was recognized by all subjects when it was played in any one of three octaves. However, when each note was chosen at random from these same three octaves (with the restriction that no two successive notes were taken from the same octave), recognition was actually slightly worse than when the tune was played as a series of clicks with the rhythm alone remaining. Similar findings have recently been reported by Dowling and Hollombe (1976) with the use of several tunes.

Deutsch (1972c) also found that when subjects were informed of the identity of the tune, they were able to follow the scrambled octaves sequence, and confirm that each note was indeed correctly placed within its octave. It was suggested that the subjects were able to imagine the tune simultaneously with hearing the distorted version, and so match each note with its octave equivalent. In this case, such an operation could be meaningfully performed in music if memory for the sequence were strong enough; or if the structure of the sequence were such that the displaced note was highly probable.

## Higher-level memory organization

The organization of music is essentially hierarchical. Notes combine to form phrases, which in turn form phrase-groups, which are in themselves successively combined until, at the highest level of the hierarchy, we obtain the composition's musical form (which often falls into one of those categories to which analysts give the name rondo, sonata, and so on).

Such hierarchical organization is important in retrieving musical information from memory. Experiments involving memory for many types of material, ranging from letters of the alphabet to patterns of lights, have demonstrated that retention is substantially improved if the material is hierarchically structured (Restle and Brown, 1970; Tulving and Donaldson, 1972).

Several theories of the organization of memory have assumed that information is retained along an internal hierarchy, and that it is retrieved by a systematic traversal of this hierarchy. This type of speculation can be usefully applied to music. However, it must be noted that cultivated music often involves the simultaneous presentation of several streams of notes. The information in each stream has its own structure, and the harmonic sequences produced by simultaneous notes are also systematically organized. An example of such multiple determinism is shown in Figure 12. In retrieving such information from memory several structures must be traversed in parallel; so it would be more useful to think of music in terms of multiple interacting hierarchies rather than a single hierarchy.

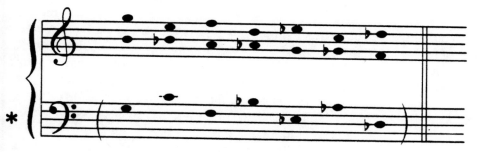

Figure 12   A complex musical sequence which is simultaneously determined by three types of progression. The top linear row may be described as a descending minor third repetitively transposed down a whole tone. The second linear row may be described as a descending run on the chromatic alphabet. And the harmonic sequence may be described as descending through the cycle of fifths. (From Fig. A1, Example 59, p. 168, of *Emotion and Meaning in Music* by L. B. Meyer. Copyright 1956 by the University of Chicago Press.) (* implied root progressions.)

## Attention in music

In listening to music, we do not as a rule attend with equal emphasis to all incoming stimuli, but rather, we focus our attention in various ways. Our attention strategies may change according to the type of music being played. For instance, when a solo instrument plays a simple melodic line there is no competition for attention. In contrapuntal music such as canons or fugues, we attempt as far as possible to attend to the various streams simultaneously. However, it is likely that we perceive such music instead in a fashion similar to Rubin figures in vision, where we fluctuate between alternative modes of figure-ground organization, rather than perceiving several figures and no ground. In other music, such as accompanied songs, one part serves generally as the figure and the other part as the ground. But even there ambiguities often emerge, and figure and ground may reverse their positions. Certain *avant-garde* music of today aims simply at creating textures – to produce a continuous stream of sound where no figure clearly emerges.

Much selective listening to music is voluntary; or at least it appears to be. We have the impression that we can chose at will which type of information to attend to. However, certain sounds capture the attention more than others. Loud notes will be noticed rather than soft; high notes rather than low. A contrasting sound which emerges from a homogeneous background will command attention. Notes with sharp attacks will be noticed in preference to notes with gradual onsets. A sound which is constantly modulating, for instance a note with *vibrato*, or a drum roll, will stand out from sounds which are smooth. Certain instruments are deliberately tuned so as to produce beats, whose constant waxing and waning serve to maintain the attention. For instance, most of the notes on the piano are produced by three strings which are struck by the same hammer; and these are tuned each to a slightly different pitch (Kirk, 1959). Another example is the Indonesian *gamelan* which is tuned in pairs, the pitch of each member of a pair being slightly different. Finally, certain specific sounds, such as the human voice, appear to be particularly attention-compelling.

One central factor in musical attention is the formation of sequential groupings. That is, in listening to music in which more than one note is presented at a time, the listener groups these notes into sequential configurations, which then form channels of attention. Listening to such music therefore involves a continuous process of decision as to which successive note to link with which. An important experimental question therefore concerns how such linkages are formed.

This type of question has been extensively investigated in the case of listening to simultaneously presented verbal material. Egan et al. (1954) required listeners to identify one of two simultaneous messages, and examined the conditions which reduced interference from the unwanted message. They found that high-pass filtering (i.e. omitting the high-frequency components) of either the accepted or the rejected message substantially improved intelligibility. Differences in loudness also helped, especially when the wanted message was the louder. Spatial separation led to markedly improved performance. Indeed, even a small amount of spatial separation has been found useful in focussing attention on one of two simultaneous verbal messages (Spieth et al., 1954; Triesman, 1964). Other studies have shown that the semantic content of the two messages may be important in determining selection (Gray and Wedderburn, 1960; Yntema and Trask, 1963; Deutsch and Deutsch, 1963). This would have its counterpart in music in the set of *a priori* and *transitional* probabilities between notes (see above).

The technique most commonly employed in investigating selective attention to verbal materials is known as dichotic listening. Here two simultaneous sequences are presented through earphones, with a different sequence to each ear. The subject is then instructed in various ways; for instance, to report what he heard, or to attend selectively to one message rather than the other. By examining the subject's performance, one can explore the principles underlying the formation of attention channels; examine what attributes are most attention-compelling; determine how much information can be attended to at any one time, and so on. Similarly, this technique can be applied to musical sequences. The subject can be presented with two simultaneous sequences of notes one to each ear, and the resultant percept examined in various ways.

The technique was used in a recent set of experiments, employing computer-controlled sine-wave tones of equal amplitude, and with simultaneous onsets and offsets. Subjects were presented with dichotic tonal sequences, and asked to report what they heard. The results were quite surprising, and demonstrate the operation of two different channelling principles for musical sequences.

### Spatial location

The tonal pattern first employed is shown in Figure 13(a) (Deutsch, 1974b, 1974c). It can be seen that this consisted of a sequence of notes which alternated in pitch from one octave to another. The same sequence was presented simultaneously to both ears; however, when one ear received the high note the other ear received the low note and vice versa. This pattern was continuously presented without pause for 20 seconds; and listeners heard the sequence with earphones placed first one way and then the other.

Surprisingly, none of the 86 subjects employed in this experiment was able to guess what this simple stimulus was. Further, people differed radically in the way the sequence was perceived. The majority of listeners

Figure 13   (a) Representation of the dichotic tonal sequence producing the octave illusion. (b) Representation of the illusory percept most commonly obtained. (From Deutsch, 1974c.)

obtained the illusory percept which is displayed in Figure 13 (b). It can be seen that this consisted of a single note the apparent location of which shifted back and forth from ear to ear; and the apparent pitch simultaneously shifted back and forth from one octave to the other. Again, for most of these subjects, when the earphones were placed in reverse position the apparent locations of the high and low notes remained fixed. This created the illusion that the earphone which had been emitting the high notes was now emitting the low notes, and vice versa.

On analysis, it was found that the handedness of the subjects differed statistically in terms of the localization patterns for the two notes at the two ears. Right-handers tended strongly to hear the high notes on the right and the low notes on the left, but left-handers showed no such tendency. This pattern of results indicates that listeners tend to localize the high notes to the dominant side and the low notes to the nondominant.

In considering the possible foundations for this illusion, it was hypothesized that it was based on the operation of two independent decision mechanisms: the first mechanism determines what pitch we hear, and the second determines where the note appears to be coming from. More specifically, it was assumed that when presented with this dichotic sequence the listener attends to the sequence of pitches arriving at one ear and suppresses the other – more often the sequence arriving at the dominant ear is attended to rather than the nondominant. It was further assumed that the listener localizes each note at the ear receiving the higher frequency, regardless of which frequency is in fact perceived. The combined operation of two such decision mechanisms would give rise to the percept of a single note which alternated simultaneously in both pitch and localization, this percept being independent of the position of the earphone.

In order to test this hypothesis, a new dichotic sequence was devised (Deutsch and Roll, 1976). This sequence consisted of three high notes followed by two low notes on one channel, and simultaneously three low notes followed by two high notes on the other. This pattern was repetitively presented ten times without pause, and listeners were asked to report what they had heard. The position of the earphones was then reversed and the procedure repeated.

Only right-handers were employed in this experiment. It was found that most of the subjects reported sequences consisting of one note at a time; and in confirmation of the hypothesis, each note appeared to be localized at the ear which received the higher frequency. Furthermore, on any given stimulus-presentation, most subjects reported three high notes followed by two low notes, or two high notes followed by three low notes. They thus reported the pitch information delivered to one ear and ignored the other. And, also in confirmation of the hypothesis, there was a significant tendency to follow the pattern of pitches delivered to the right ear rather than to the left, for both earphone positions.

In further experiments the stimuli were presented through loudspeakers rather than earphones. Analogous effects were obtained, which shows that in perceiving such sequences the listener attends to the pitch information which emanates from one location in auditory space and "suppresses" the other. Furthermore, there is a tendency in right-handers to attend to the pitch information emanating from the dominant, rather than the nondominant, side of auditory space (Deutsch, 1975d).

*Frequency range*

The experiments so far reported involved a sequence of two alternating pitches. In a further experiment, a major scale was used instead as the basic stimulus pattern (Deutsch, 1974d, 1975c). As shown in Figure 14, this scale was presented simultaneously in both ascending and descending form; and switching from ear to ear so that when a component of the ascending scale was in one ear a component of the descending scale was in the other, and vice versa. This pattern was repeated ten times without pause, and subjects listened to the sequence with earphones placed first one way and then the other.

This sequence also produced a variety of perceptual illusions. Most commonly, subjects reported hearing two melodic lines; a higher one and a lower one, that moved in contrary motion. Moreover, the higher tones all appeared to be emanating from one earphone and the lower tones from the other. Right-handers (but not left-handers) tended significantly to hear the higher notes on the right and the lower notes on the left. Indeed, about half of the right-handers tested reported this pattern of localization with the earphones positioned both ways. Thus when the earphone positions were switched around, it appeared to these subjects that the earphone that had been emitting the higher notes was now emitting the lower notes and vice versa. Figure 14(d) illustrates this phenomenon. This reproduces the written report of a subject with absolute pitch. His written statement "reverse headphones/same result (high in rt. ear)" shows that the higher notes were localized in the right ear and the lower notes in the left, regardless of the positioning of the earphones.

A different result was obtained by other subjects. These perceived only a single stream of four notes, which repetitively descended and then ascended. They perceived little or nothing of the other stream. All these subjects, when asked to shadow the sequence by singing, shadowed the upper stream and not the lower one.

This sequence therefore demonstrates a different channelling principle in music. Here all listeners formed perceptual channels based on frequency range. They either heard only the higher notes and ignored the lower, or they heard the higher and lower notes as two simultaneous but separate musical channels. There was in addition a significant tendency among right-handers to refer the higher stream to the dominant side of auditory space, and the lower stream to the nondominant.

This principle of channelling information by frequency range has also been investigated using rapid sequences of single notes. Miller and Heise (1950) presented listeners with a sequence of two notes alternating at a rate of 10 per second, and found that if the frequencies of these notes differed by less than 15 per cent. the sequence was heard as a trill (i.e. as a single string of related notes). However, as the disparity in frequency between the notes

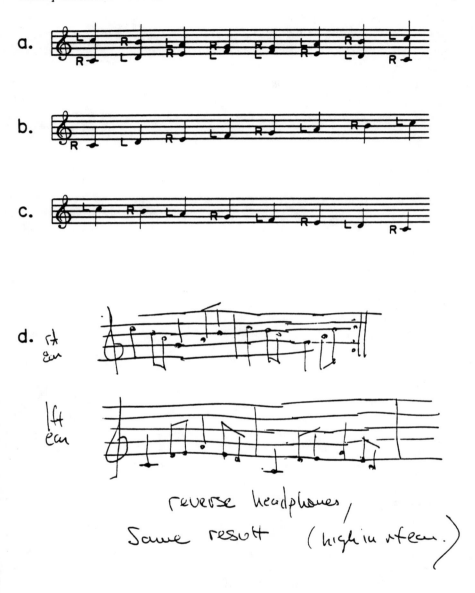

Figure 14 (a) Representation of the dichotic sequence producing the scales illusion. (b) The ascending component separately; (c) The descending component separately; (d) Illusory percept depicted by a subject with absolute pitch. This type of percept was most commonly obtained. (From Deutsch, D., 1975c, by permission of the *Journal of the Acoustical Society of America*, **59**, 1156–1160. Copyright 1975 by the Acoustical Society of America.)

increased, the sequence was heard instead as two interrupted and unrelated notes. This phenomenon has been termed "fission" by several investigators. Heise and Miller (1951) extended these findings to patterns of several notes, and found that if one of the notes in a rapid repetitive sequence differed sufficiently in frequency from the rest it was heard as isolated from the others — indeed, as appearing to emanate from a separate sound-source. Schouten (1962) also investigated this phenomenon, and found that as the separation between the frequency of successive notes is increased, a reduction in tempo is necessary in order to maintain temporal coherence between successive notes. Van Noorden (1975) made a systematic investigation into the relationship between frequency separation and tempo on the perception of temporal coherence. Subjects listened to melodic sequences and were required either to try to hear temporal coherence or to hear fission. It was found that when subjects were trying to hear coherence, decreasing the tempo from 50 to 150 m sec per note increased the frequency separation within which coherence can be heard from 4 to 13 semitones. However, when the subject was trying to hear fission, decreasing the tempo had little effect on performance. Between these two boundaries there existed a large region in which the listener could direct his attention at will, hearing either fission or temporal coherence.

The separation of tonal sequences by frequency range is extremely common in music. When a single instrument plays a melody and an accompaniment their pitch ranges are generally separate. Also, in contrapuntal music, each voice tends to be confined to a given pitch range. Composers of the early 18th century cleverly took advantage of this perceptual principle by their technique of pseudo-polyphony, or compound melodic line. Their compositions often included rapid sequences of single notes which were drawn from different pitch ranges, with the result that the listener hears two simultaneous melodies (Figure 15).

Dowling (1973) has demonstrated the importance of this principle of frequency separation by showing that when the notes of two well-known melodies are played alternately in rapid succession (at a rate of 8 per second) recognition of the individual melodies is very difficult if their pitch ranges overlap. As one of the melodies is gradually transposed, so that their pitch ranges diverge, recognition becomes increasingly easier. Correct identification is achieved at a frequency separation which leaves the range of the melodies not quite overlapping.

A further interesting property of rapid sequences of notes which are drawn from different frequency ranges was demonstrated by Bregman and

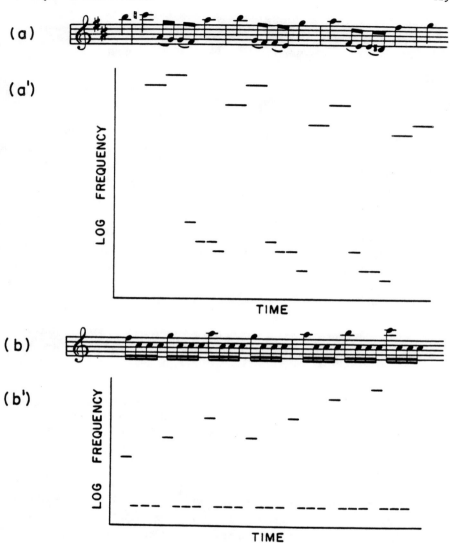

Figure 15 The grouping of melodic stimuli on the basis of frequency proximity. (a) and (b) display the sequences in musical notation; and (a') and (b') in plots of log frequency versus time. In sequence (a) we hear two parallel melodies, each in a different frequency range. In sequence (b) a single pitch is repeatedly presented in the lower range; and this provides a ground against which the figure in the upper range is heard. ((a) from Telemann, G. P., *Capriccio for Recorder and Basso Continuo*; (b) from Telemann, G. P., *Sonata in C Major for Recorder and Basso Continuo*.) (From Deutsch, 1975d, by permission of *Scientific American*, 1975, **233**(4), 92–104, Copyright 1975 by Scientific American, Inc.)

Campbell (1971). They found that it was easy to perceive the order of notes in a given frequency range; however, such perception was extremely difficult for notes drawn from different ranges.

*Timbre*

What happens when differences in timbre are introduced between successive notes? In much orchestral music, especially of the late eighteenth century, timbre is often used as a marker of sequential groupings; that is, adjacent phrases are played by different instruments. Further, in music for more than one instrument, such as duets, overlaps in pitch range commonly occur, and we have no difficulty in separating the different voices. This would imply that a sequence of notes of different timbres would not be heard as coherent, but one would hear fission instead. Indeed, Warren et al. (1969) and Warren and Obusek (1972) have shown that listeners find it very difficult to identify the order of elements in repetitive sequences of three or four unrelated sounds (hisses, buzzes and tones) played at a rate of five per second.

An experiment by Van Noorden (1975) shed interesting light on this question. It has long been known that a complex tone consisting of a number of harmonic components has a pitch which corresponds to the frequency of the fundamental, even when the fundamental is not present (Schouten, 1940). Van Noorden exploited this phenomenon to investigate whether temporal coherence between successive notes depends on their pitch similarity or on similarity between their frequency components. He found that, both when a pure tone alternated with a complex tone of the same pitch but which lacked the fundamental frequency, and also when two complex tones alternated which had the same pitch but whose frequencies lay in frequency ranges which did not overlap, fission was heard. However, if the two complex tones contained similar frequency components, temporal coherence was heard instead. Van Noorden therefore concluded that temporal coherence depended on contiguity between the underlying frequency components of the elements of the sequence, rather than on their perceived pitch.

*Other principles*

This review has focussed primarily on two channelling principles in music: chanelling based on spatial location and channelling based on frequency. There are without doubt many other principles. One that was mentioned briefly is loudness. Egan et al. (1954) have demonstrated that two simultaneous verbal messages interfere with each other less when these are presented at different loudness levels. Further, Dowling (1973) found that it was easier to separate interleaved melodies when these differed in loudness. We might also expect to find channelling based on other organizing principles of perception, for instance the Law of Good Continuation. Further, it is possible that familiar sequences, such as well-known melodies, might be treated as separate channels. However, these suggestions are at present no more than speculative.

## REFERENCES

ATTNEAVE, F., and OLSEN, R. K. (1971) Pitch as a medium: a new approach to psychophysical scaling. *American Journal of Psychology*, **84**, 147–165.

BACHEM, A. (1954) Time factors in relative and absolute pitch determination. *Journal of the Acoustical Society of America*, **26**, 751–753.

BAIRD, J. W. (1917) Memory for absolute pitch: Studies in psychology. In: *Titchener commemorative volume*. Worcester, p. 69.

BLACKWELL, H. R., and SCHLOSBERG, H. (1943) Octave generalization, pitch discrimination, and loudness thresholds in the white rat. *Journal of Experimental Psychology*, **33**, 407–419.

BREGMAN, A. A., and CAMPBELL, J. (1971) Primary auditory stream segregation and perception of order in rapid sequence of tones. *Journal of Experimental Psychology*, **89**, 244–249.

DEUTSCH, D. (1969) Music recognition. *Psychological Review*, **76**, 300–307.

— (1970a) The deterioration of pitch information in memory. Unpublished doctoral dissertation, University of California at San Diego.

— (1970b) Tones and numbers: Specificity of interference in short-term memory. *Science*, **168**, 1604–1605.

— (1972a) Mapping of interactions in the pitch memory store. *Science*, **175**, 1020–1022.

— (1972b) Effect of repetition of standard and comparison tones on recognition memory for pitch. *Journal of Experimental Psychology*, **93**, 156–162.

— (1972c) Octave generalization and tune recognition. *Perception and Psychophysics*, **11**, 411–412.

— (1973a) Interference in memory between tones adjacent in the musical scale. *Journal of Experimental Psychology*, **100**, 228–231.

— (1973b) Octave generalization of specific interference effects in memory for tonal pitch. *Perception and Psychophysics*, **13**, 271–275.

— (1974a) Generality of interference by tonal stimuli in recognition memory for pitch. *Quarterly Journal of Experimental Psychology*, **26**, 229–234.

— (1974b) An auditory illusion. *Journal of the Acoustical Society of America*, **55**, 518–19.

— (1974c) An auditory illusion. *Nature*, **251**, 307–309.

— (1974d) An illusion with musical scales. *Journal of the Acoustical Society of America*, **56**, 525.

DEUTSCH, D. (1975a) The organization of short term memory for a single acoustic attribute. In: D. Deutsch and J. A. Deutsch (eds.), *Short Term Memory*. New York: Academic Press.

— (1975b) Facilitation by repetition in recognition memory for tonal pitch. *Memory and Cognition*, **3**, 263–266.

— (1975c) Two-channel listening to musical scales. *Journal of the Acoustical Society of America*, **57**, 1156–1160.

— (1975a) Musical illusions. *Scientific American*, **233**(4), 92–104.

DEUTSCH, D. and FEROE, J. (1975) Disinhibition in pitch memory. *Perception and Psychophysics*, **17**, 320–324.

DEUTSCH, D. and ROLL, P. L. (1974) Error patterns in delayed pitch comparison as a function of relational context. *Journal of Experimental Psychology*, **103**, 1027–1034.

— — (1976) Separate "what" and "where" decision mechanisms in processing a dichotic tonal sequence. *Journal of Experimental Psychology: Human Perception and Performance*, **2**, 23–29.

DEUTSCH, J. A., and DEUTSCH, D. (1963) Attention: Some theoretical considerations. *Psychological Review*, **70**, 80–90.

DOWLING, W. J. (1972) Recognition of melodic transformations: Inversion, retrograde, and retrograde-inversion. *Perception and Psychophysics*, **12**, 417–421.

— (1973) The perception of interleaved melodies. *Cognitive Psychology*, **5**, 322–337.

— and HOLLOMBE, A. W. The perception of melodies distorted by splitting into several octaves: effects of increasing continuity and melodic contour. *Perception and Psychophysics*. (In press.)

EGAN, J., CARTERETTE, E., and THWING, E. (1954) Some factors affecting multi-channel listening. *Journal of the Acoustical Society of America*, **26**, 774–782.

FRANCÉS, R. (1972) *La perception de la musique*. Paris: Vrin.

GRAY, J., and WEDDERBURN, A. (1960) Grouping strategies with simultaneous stimuli. *Quarterly Journal of Experimental Psychology*, **12**, 180–185.

HARRIS, J. D. (1952) The decline of pitch discriminations with time. *Journal of Experimental Psychology*, **43**, 96–99.

HEISE, G. A., and MILLER, G. A. (1951) An experimental study of auditory patterns. *America Journal of Psychology*, **64**, 68–77.

HUBEL, D. H., and WIESEL, T. N. (1962) Receptive fields, binocular interaction and functional architecture in the cat's visual cortex. *Journal of Physiology*, **160**, 106–154.

HUMPHREYS, L. F. (1939) Generalization as a function of method of reinforcement. *Journal of Experimental Psychology*, **25**, 361–372.

KIRK, R. (1959) Tuning preferences for piano unison groups. *Journal of the Acoustical Society of America*, **31**, 1644–1690.

KOESTER, T. (1945) The time error in pitch and loudness discrimination as a function of time interval and stimulus level. *Archives of Psychology*, **297**.

MERRIAM, A. P. (1964) *The Anthropology of Music.* Evanston, Northwestern University Press.

MEYER, C. B. (1956) *Emotion and Meaning in Music.* Chicago, University of Chicago Press.

— (1967) *Music, the Arts, and Ideas.* Chicago, University of Chicago Press.

MILLER, G. A., and HEISE, G. A. (1950) The trill threshold. *Journal of the Acoustical Society of America,* **22**, 637–638.

MILLER, J., and CUDDY, L. L. (1972) Tonality as a cue for melody recognition. *Experimental Report 72–1,* Queen's University, Kingston, Ontario.

NETTL, B. (1956) *Music in Primitive Culture.* Cambridge, Harvard University Press.

PISTON, W. (1948) *Harmony.* London: Norton and Co., 2nd edition.

— (1949) *Counterpoint.* London: Gollancz.

PLOMP, R., WAGENAAR, W. A., and MIMPEN, A. M. (1973) Musical interval recognition with simultaneous tones. *Acustica,* **29**, 101–109.

POLLACK, I. (1952) The information of elementary auditory displays. *Journal of the Acoustical Society of America,* **24**, 745–749.

— (1964) Ohm's acoustical law and short term auditory memory. *Journal of the Acoustical Society of America,* **36**, 2340–2345.

RATLIFF, F. (1965) *Mach bands: Quantitative studies of neural networks in the retina.* San Francisco: Holden-Day.

RESTLE, F., and BROWN, E. (1970) Organization of serial pattern learning. In: G. H. Bower (ed.) *The Psychology of Learning and Motivation,* Vol. 4. New York, Academic Press, 249–331.

SCHOENBERG, A. (1951) *Style and Idea.* London, Williams and Norgate.

SCHOLES, P. A. (1950) *The Oxford Companion to Music.* London, Oxford University Press.

SCHOUTEN, J. F. (1940) The residue, a new component in subjective sound analysis. *Proc. Kon, Nederl. Akad. Wetensh,* **43**, 356–365.

— (1962) On the perception of sound and speech; subjective time analysis. *4th International Congress on Acoustics, Copenhagen Congress Report II,* 201–203.

SPIETH, W., CURTIS, J. F., and WEBSTER, J. C. (1954) Responding to one of two simultaneous messages. *Journal of the Acoustical Society of America,* **26**, 391–396.

TOVEY, D. F. (1957) *The Forms of Music.* London, Oxford University Press.

TRIESMAN, A. (1964) The effect of irrelevant material on the efficiency of selective listening. *American Journal of Psychology,* **77**, 533–546.

TULVING, E., and DONALDSON, W. (1972) *Organization of Memory.* New York, Academic Press.

VAN NOORDEN, L. P. A. S. (1975) Temporal coherence in the perception of tone sequences. Unpublished doctoral dissertation.

WARREN, R. M., OBUSEK, C. J., FARMER, R. M., and WARREN, R. P. (1969) Auditory sequence: Confusions of patterns other than speech or music. *Science,* **164**, 586–587.

WARREN, R. M. and OBUSEK, C. J. (1972) Identification of temporal order within auditory sequences. *Perception and Psychophysics,* **12**, 86–90.

WERNER, H. (1925) Uber Mikromelodik und Mikroharmonik. *Zeitschrift fur Psychologie*, **98**, 74–89.

WICKELGREN, W. A. (1969) Associative strength theory of recognition memory for pitch. *Journal of Mathematical Psychology*, **6**, 13–61.

WHITE, B. (1960) Recognition of distorted melodies. *American Journal of Psychology*, **73**, 100–107.

YNTEMA, D., and TRASK, F. (1963) Recall as a search process. *Journal on Verbal Learning and Verbal Behavior*, **2**, 65–76.

ZENATTI, A. (1969) Le developpement génétique de la perception musicale. *Monographies Françaises de Psychologie*, **17**, 1–110.

# 8

WILLIAM GOODDY

# The Timing and Time of Musicians

Time. See Tempo; Rhythm.
Tempo usually means "speed".
Rhythm. In its fullest sense it covers the ensemble of everything pertaining to what may be called the *time* side of music.

(*The Oxford Companion to Music*, 1970)

It usually proves to be a difficult task to get an accurate definition from musicians or from texts on music of what is meant by "time" in music. The quotations above indicate how often there is a circular approach to the subject; and the quest for definition often ends in feelings of exasperation on the parts both of the enquirer and the musician. Rather vague and subjective answers are often provided – "every musician knows what he means by 'time': a good sense of time is essential: either you've got it or you haven't: it's the beat, really, you must know where the beat is and then you can pull it about: many 'classical' players don't have as good a sense of time as the 'jazz' and 'pop' players: a scherzo is the same as a minuet except that it is much faster".

As the writer has pointed out in several publications, very many aspects of the word "time" lack accurate definitions and are taken for granted as innate awarenesses which are self-evident. Yet we are all aware that there is an important difference between our interior feelings of the passage of our life-time, our own personal time (PT) and our acceptance of public or government time (GT) by which we regulate those aspects of daily living in which we are obliged to associate with others. PT is always inner, personal, subjective and variable, dependent upon our mood, state of health, degree of fatigue, influence of alcohol or drugs or even the state of our bank balance. GT, by contrast, is impersonal, related to mechanical devices and unwavering.

The musician, on the least introspection or the completion of a printed page of music, must be especially aware of this double time situation. He recognises the value of verbal or metronome indications of time, while finding that he often may disregard a metronome marking (especially when practising); and he may be quite uncertain whether his notion of *poco allegro ma non troppo* is quite the same on Saturday evening as it was at noon on Wednesday.

It is easy to find examples of widely differing speeds of performances of works with metronome instructions by different soloists and orchestras; and we, as listeners, may have feelings that a work has felt much longer or shorter than it has been actually timed to be because of the style and impact of the performer upon our varying mood and alertness. Similarly musicians may admit that it is impossible to take exactly the same time for each performance of the same work; and indeed they hope never to do so because each performance is a re-creation and not a repetition (for which we need the disc, the tape or the piano-roll).

Perhaps the most surprising feature of any discussion about music is the finding that very often the musician has not realised (since such realisation at a conscious level is unnecessary for his performance – and anyway it formed no part of his formal instruction) that he always operates a marvellous system of creation and re-creation in four dimensions at once; and that he alone has perfected a scheme of notation for doing so. Similarly the neurologist and psychologist have not so far realised that music and musicians have for so long provided a great deal of clinical material relevant to the understanding of the space–time performances which the brain enables us to achieve.

In the visual sphere of activity the musician undertakes an extremely complicated mental transposition from planes of vision into space and time in the same act. On the page he sees notes arranged according to tradition or convention and in conformity with what the pen and the printing press and engraver can achieve. The vertical patterns signify the note or notes to be played at any one time by movements along a plane of his instrument. If we use the piano as an example, notes derived from a vertical position on the page have to be played all at the same moment on a horizontal keyboard, the top notes on the page corresponding with the keys on the right side of the keyboard. The rate of playing, the time of arrival of the next notes in time, depends upon that lateral horizontal relationship of the notes on the page. Subconsciously he suppresses the suggestion that adjoining keys horizontally are successive in time in the same way that adjoining notes on the page are. This point is merely one aspect of the complexity and dynamism which are implicit in the printed score. The page is an almost unique form of space-time, four-dimensional notation which the musician habitually takes for granted, scarcely ever being made explicit by the teachers or beginners or by great masters (either of whom may say, "I just know how to do it – and so must you – without all that introspection"). Yet it seems far more interesting and rewarding to be aware that in each musical act there is a splendid space—time achievement provided by an ultra-refined usage of the nervous system.

The composer has wanted to exteriorise for others the sounds his nervous system presents to his mind; and he has been dependent upon pen and paper. He has elaborated an intricate system of symbols denoting duration and emphasis of sounds over a wide range of frequencies related physically and mathematically to each other in a way that is acceptable to the senses of others. Discrete frequencies rather than continuous are almost invariably chosen, though the instrumental *glissando* and the vocal *portamento* (sometimes considered to be in dubious taste) may rarely be used for special effects. Presumably for the sake of reaching the awareness and performance of others the occurrences and durations of notes are grouped in patterns of bars, beats, phrases, keys and clefs so as to be compatible with the physical and emotional capabilities of the players and with the constructional form of the instruments to which the notes are referable.

We may now pass to an outline of an exposition of "timing" by the nervous system and its relevance to the "time" of musicians. We find that from the neurological point of view the musician trains himself to control vibrations so that they appear at so many beats each second. Whatever shape or size of instrument he decides to "play", by whatever form of muscular exertion, he aims to produce "notes" at a chosen frequency at the right moment in both public and his own internal time. The professional musician especially has to achieve such technical mastery that he is reliable enough to join other musicians in "concerted" output.

When experts play together in any numbers they agree to subject themselves to the discipline of a "conductor". The conductor, using hand or baton, makes motions of beating space (a form of vibration) though his activities are always described as "beating time". In this situation we see the proof of the space—time equivalence of movements, with the nervous system as the directing force. The conductor can beat space or time for a large number of players so that they produce their various vibrations by a diverse sequence of bodily movements, all of the utmost refinement, in relation to a system of notation. These physical activities are in conformity with the notions of the composer of the music who has so ordered, from a space—time notational system "in his head", the code system for the string, woodwind and brass, percussion and keyboard sections of an orchestra to make their fingers, arms, hands, lips, respiratory apparatus and perhaps feet act with almost unbelievable precision for half an hour or more. The whole orchestra, the singer, the instrumentalist, the chorus are driven to vibratory expression by the dots on the lines, the notes on the page, by means of co-ordinated actions mediated by the nervous system.

## The nervous control of vibrations

The musician may at first suppose that he relies almost entirely upon his ears for the control of vibrations. He certainly does detect a chosen pitch by ear and will aurally detect any falling away from such a standard; but the professional musician is wary of the player "by ear", relying himself on the stability and uniformity of the printed page. For the keyboard player (on a "tuned" instrument) there is mainly the matter of "right" or "wrong" notes, but for singers and players of stringed instruments there are the problems of intonation; but more important than audition alone are the mechanisms by which vibrations are set in accurate motion even before they reach the ears of the performer or listener. Whatever the form of instrument the sound produced depends upon the application of physical forces by the appropriate parts of the body. In singing there is the force of respiration acting upon the vocal cords to produce the correct volume and pitch of sound, which are then subjected to articulation and expression by the oral and facial muscles. Analogously the violin player depends mainly upon the forces of his upper limbs (though all musicians really use their whole bodies to play, with local emphasis according to the form of instrument which they are using). With the organ and some electronic instruments the power of the sound is controlled by levers, bellows, amplifiers and switches rather than purely bodily forces (though bodily motions originate the chosen sounds). There is also the visual means of getting correct notes, both in reading from a score for the desired notes and in checking visually that the note played is or is not the note written. Usually, however, after a piece has been "worked up", it is played from memory, with the player sometimes keeping his eyes shut. When he does this he is relying entirely on his muscular tension and space-awareness senses.

The nervous pathways which subserve sight, hearing, the senses of touch and vibration, and the awareness of muscle tensions and limb positions are well known. These pathways, nerves and nerve tracts ultimately reach the cognate parts of the brain via the spinal cord and brainstem, and provide the sensory information essential for initiation and control of movement. The subject of muscular control is treated in Chapter 4.

With this summary of the perceptual machinery for the control of the skilled movements which characterise the special talents of the musician we may pass to the consideration of the innate human mechanisms by which we are aware of the passage of time as we ourselves experience it, time which is personal to ourselves, varying with mood, age, health or illness. This form of time is entirely personal, and is accordingly abbreviated to

PT. It has to be completely differentiated and contrasted with public, non-personal forms of time devised for the convenience of society. This public form of time is provided from astronomical observations aided by a wide range of technological means (of which the metronome happens to be one) by national and international arrangements. This "government" time is abbreviated to GT. It is essential to have a clear awareness of the fundamental differences between these two forms of time. This subject has been set out by the author in detail in "Disorders of the Time Sense" in Volume 3 of the Handbook of Clinical Neurology (1969).

## Definition of a clock

For the understanding of any form of time we must first have a clear notion of what is a clock, for it is by various forms of clock that time is determined, measured and recorded. A definitional statement is provided by Einstein and Infeld (1947):

The primitive subjective feeling of time flow enables us to order our impressions, to judge that one event takes place earlier, another later. But to show that the time interval between two events is 10 seconds a clock is needed. By the use of a clock the time concept becomes objective. Any repeated physical phenomenon may be used as a clock provided it can be repeated as often as desired. Taking the interval between the beginning and end of such an event as one unit of time, arbitrary time intervals may be measured by repetition of this process. All clocks, from the simple hour-glass to the most refined instruments, are based on this idea.

It is exceptionally important to note that no clock mechanism fulfils its purpose as a clock unless its activity is perceived by an observer who understands the manner in which the clock possesses the attributes of a time-keeper, GT has to be provided as a public service since if everyone went by his own PT there would be an infinity of times, causing an irregular, unpunctual and indeed chaotic situation. We have only to imagine what would happen if each member of a large orchestra were to play a Beethoven symphony at his own speed without regard for the actions of his colleagues, or without any conformity with the conductor's indications.

GT is achieved by an engineering system in which observations of the regular actions of astronomic bodies (particularly non-human) are transformed into recording devices (clocks, watches) which specify how many fractions of the earth's rotation about its own axis in relation to the sun have passed since a selected point in the sky passed over a selected point on the earth (the meridian of Greenwich).

The clock of everyday use consists of a powered mechanism, driven by a coiled spring, or weight and pendulum, or by electricity. Two principles are used: (1) the continuous motion derived from the power source is broken up into intermittent motions of regular form, providing equal periods between each motion (equivalence of space with time), the moment of ending of one motion coinciding with the moment of beginning of the next; (2) the number of these periods or cycles is recorded.

A device known as the "escapement" permits the escape of movements of the clock-work, each of the same duration (being over the same spatial distance, in a manner similar to the movements of an orchestral conductor beating time). The movement takes place in a train of gear-wheels between the power source and the hands of the clock. In a domestic clock suitable gear ratios provide movements adjusted to fractions of movements of the earth about its axis (marked in hours, minutes and seconds). In an instrument such as a metronome the duration of the cycle is adjustable to a chosen interval by moving the weight on the arm up or down. The clock escapement also provides the energy which keeps its own mechanism in rhythmic action (in the balance-wheel and hair-spring). One of the latest forms of watch employs an electronically-activated tuning fork, thereby providing an analogy with the musical practice of a controlled vibratory system, as already outlined.

We find in the nervous system an exactly similar process, in which some *continuous* performance such as movement or sensation is transmitted by an *intermittent* process. It has long been recognised as a fundamental principle of nervous activity that all nerve units (neurons) transmit by impulse and not by any kind of continuous passage of any form of influence. Each neuron acts by an "all-or-none" response. A nerve impulse passes along a nerve fibre in an on-and-off manner, the rate of transmission being determined by a number of physiological factors which are specific for that nerve fibre, and which provide a specific rate of performance for each fibre. The whole subject is admirably set out in detail in *Nerve, Muscle and Synapse* by Katz (1966).

## Counting and recording the number of escaped cycles

The counting apparatus is provided by the passing of "hands" over the "face" of the clock which provides, in its marked subdivisions, intervals of space equivalent to intervals of time. The method is analogous to the division of a musical score into bars of equal duration, the duration being indicated at the start of the piece by means of a time signature.

In any clock we have the equation of space with time. From this fact we may deduce that (1) man, being equipped psychologically with senses of space and of time, must contain within himself internal chronometric mechanisms; (2) the brain may be seen as an organ for the equivalence of space and time; (3) the nervous system must be the principal mechanism for existence in space-time.

## Physiological clock mechanisms

There are two main groups of physiological clock mechanisms to be considered: (1) the non-nervous organs and systems which have rhythmic patterns of activity; (2) the nervous mechanisms which transmit the impulses from which the action of the non-nervous organs is detected. It is very important to note that all nervous mechanisms show intrinsic rhythmic activity, providing spatio-temporal patterns in the nervous system. The nature of this rhythmic activity has already been outlined, with special reference to the "all-or-none" signalling of the neuron.

(1) We need not examine in lengthy detail the large number of non-nervous organs and systems which contribute rhythmic and therefore time-provision information for the nervous system to integrate and report upon. The group includes the cardio-vascular system with the muscular activity of the heart and pulse transmission in the arteries. This system is minutely monitored by the nervous system with numerous mechanisms for adjusting activity to functional needs; for example, there is a cardiac and respiratory system for the regulation of heart output and breathing, partly controlling and partly controlled by biochemical adjustments in blood and tissue metabolism. The cardio-renal system regulates periodic output of soluble chemical substances in delicately adjusted volumes of fluid. The alimentary system has a rhythmic activity related to input of food, its transmission during digestion by rhythmic movements of the intestines and its periodic excretion. The glandular systems are well known for their cyclic endocrine activities in relation to hormone production, especially in relation to reproductive cycles, and in regulating bodily standards such as temperature, pulse and respiration (all with obvious rhythmic patterns). In one of these systems the production of cortisol is used experimentally to determine the peaks and troughs of bodily activity during the twenty-four hour cycle.

(2) In our present context it is the rhythmic activity in the elements of the nervous system, reporting on the activity of other systems and also reporting upon itself, which is the most important and interesting. Now we understand the system of rhythmic activity in the nervous system we may consider a new proposal about the function of the nervous system. The

proposal may be formulated thus: (i) because of the fundamentally rhythmic type of activity (associated with the "all-or-none" phenomenon of nervous transmission); (ii) because the nervous system mediates motor and sensory activity, and thus is completely integrated with the reception and creation of rhythmic phenomena (e.g. sound and light waves: habitual movements such as breathing, talking, walking, singing, playing musical instruments); (iii) because the nervous system is the final mediator of the individual's awareness of all the clock systems provided by rhythmic activity not primarily nervous; *therefore* the nervous system provides both the anatomical structure and physiological activity essential for satisfying the definition of a clock, and may be regarded as a clock; and the person with these mechanisms working normally and harmoniously has a reliable form of clock for the direction of all his activities. His final clock, by means of which he says he knows what time it is, how time is passing or how he uses a chosen time or timing in the execution of a piece of music, is, obviously, the abstraction, by mathematical summation, of all the subsidiary forms of time provided by the innumerable clock-forms which the body comprises.

If proof were needed in support of this contention of a high-level rhythmic abstracted clock-like indicator within the nervous system, it would be provided by the findings of the electroencephalogram (EEG). By this instrument (for amplifying the normal electrical activity of the brain) we find the brain in constant rhythmic activity. The EEG patterns alter with observable changes in the state of health and alertness of the subject under test. When "the clocks are stopped" or otherwise affected by, for example, injury, a fit, sleep, death, alcohol or other drugs or even by lack of sleep after long journeys, the brain rhythms will alter into patterns completely different from that subject's normal or habitual patterns.

We now see that personal time (PT) is a biological matter within each of us, dependent on all that we are, in ancestry and genetic make-up, in age and state of health, mood and present surroundings, alert or weary, satisfied with what we have been working on or worried by our apparent failure to achieve our aims in a professional or domestic career or in getting a few bars of music right as we practise them. In health PT is a self-adjusting, individual, vulnerable provision from the total of our living processes in each of us. It is in complete contrast with government time (GT) which is a standardised, specially non-human technological arrangement for the convenience of society in order to obviate the disorder which would result if public life were dependent upon the vagaries of innumerable personal times.

The changes or breakdown of PT in circumstances of emotional or physical disease have been set out by the writer (Gooddy, 1969, *loc. cit.*). Though it is here unnecessary to enumerate the wide range of disorders which may affect our senses of PT, it is perhaps worth pointing out that the musician is exceptionally vulnerable to any influences affecting his PT, for he is always attempting the difficult task of performing in his PT while his public background has to be of GT. At a certain age he has achieved such a standing that he has an engagement for a lesson, an audition, a concert. He will be expected to turn up "on time" (GT) and perform his music in relation to numerous standards of GT, such as length of programme or recording time, the metronome time, the teacher or pupil's time, the conductor's time, or tempo, for the work in question. Yet he will be playing the piece he has learned and adjusted to what he has felt best in his PT, so he has to make a careful and constant PT:GT adjustment throughout his playing. If he is giving a solo recital he may play mainly in terms of PT, but he has to pay some attention to "accepted" modes of performance, examples often being chosen from acceptable recordings of masters, sometimes even the composer's own recorded playing, and metronome markings or stop-watch timings for each piece. One of the most interesting points for the listener is to see what experts do with the printed notes of well known works. The wide range between performances of "the same work" by various players can be explained only by the differences in their individual PTs. In this connection the alteration of speed of playing with increase of age is often very striking; with an extreme example of Schweitzer's later playing of certain organ works of Bach compared with his version of the same works played twenty years earlier. On the other hand it is reported that Stravinsky's later recordings are often faster than his earlier ones. The listener to programmes comparing various versions of orchestral works performed under different conductors will be familiar with the astonishing variations in durations of movements and whole works for each conductor, even when specific time markings have been inserted in the score. In this connection it is interesting to observe how often Elgar the conductor, in his recordings, disagrees with Elgar the composer.

It is very much hoped that this sketch of nervous activity underlying the timing and time of the musician will be of interest and help to anyone facing, at any stage of his career, from beginner to *maestro*, the formidable problems of musical technique and interpretation. The greater the musician the more will he be permitted to play mainly in personal time instead of clock-on-the-wall time (GT). Perhaps his greatest skills and interpretative creativity may be seen in his interweavings of PT and GT in the most elegant and aesthetically satisfying manner; for, after all, he is representing for the listener the ideas originally mediated by the nervous system of the composer. The composer had his inspiration first in personal time; it was only later that he had to commit his ideas to paper for the publisher to print in government time.

# REFERENCES

EINSTEIN, A. and INFELD, L. (1947) *The Evolution of Physics*. London, Cambridge University Press.

GOODDY, W. (1969) *Handbook of Clinical Neurology*, ed. Vinken and Bruyn. Amsterdam, North-Holland Publishing Co., vol. 3, pp. 229–250.

KATZ, B. (1966) *Nerve, Muscle and Synapse*. New York, McGraw-Hill Inc.

9      ANTÓNIO R. DAMÁSIO and
HANNA DAMÁSIO

# Musical Faculty and
# Cerebral Dominance

## Introduction

The concept of cerebral dominance, long related to verbal language and regarded as a fixed state of neurophysiological arrangement, has undergone considerable changes in recent years. For one thing, dominance can no longer be defined for verbal language only and may correspond to languages other than verbal and to skills other than those of language reception and expression. Nor does dominance necessarily coincide with the function of the major (left) hemisphere alone. A dominance for visual and tactile processing or for aspects of emotion has been described, for instance, regarding the so-called minor (right) hemisphere (Kimura, 1963; Milner, 1965; Levy-Agresti and Sperry, 1968; Bogen, 1969a, 1969b; Benton, 1970; Fontenot and Benton, 1971).

The idea that dominance might be a fixed condition of the nervous system has also lost support. There is little doubt that abilities like processing verbal language probably relate to a prominent constitutional, morphophysiological gift (Kimura, 1967; Geschwind and Levitsky, 1968; Geffner and Hochberg, 1971; Geschwind, 1972; LeMay and Culebras, 1972; Tezner et al., 1972). However, this substrate is modified by training to such an extent that the fixed inheritance of an asymmetry becomes the mere base for a continued process of dominance acquisition (Knox and Kimura, 1970; Damásio, 1973; Damásio et al., 1975; Brown and Jaffe, 1975).

The relation of musical ability to cerebral dominance could thus be discussed as a reply to the questions: how do musical abilities relate to the classic concept of cerebral dominance for verbal language? And, is there a cerebral dominance for musical abilities? The answer to both questions requires a proper definition of musical ability in terms of human function, namely, its distinction from language ability. What, if any, is the core of essential characteristics of musical abilities that humans have in common and that may be relatable to a common human brain? Humming the national anthem is indeed an ability quite removed from professional singing on the operatic stage, and the correct playing of musical instruments, including very simple ones, always demands some sort of training. Moreover, the quality of professional performers varies widely according to their talents and training, and amateur performers may easily be distinguished as musical and non-musical, so disparate are their achievements. Conversely, no one will doubt that the same Mozart symphony is heard differently by the untrained listener, the Mozart lover or a celebrated Mozart conductor, like Beecham in his day. All this amounts to a denial of substantial similarity between verbal language and music in terms of a common denominator, performance capacity. However, it is possible to say that most normal human beings are able to enjoy music and to develop, by means of training, an ability to perform vocally or instrumentally.

On the other hand, the intimate characteristics of the musical code are quite different from the verbal language code. Unlike verbal language, musical "words" and "phrases" bear no immediate reference to environmental reality. In other words, and in the sense of Saussure (1906), music does not act as significant to any signified external object, nor, consequently, does it signal the internal nervous representation of any such object. The way musical words combine into phrases, and phrases are organised into larger structures, depends upon the rules of musical grammar current at the time of writing, and to which the composer normally feels obliged to conform. This syntax does not lend itself to translation in terms of the more frequent cognitive calculus operations. The symbolising power of music, by virtue of its lexical and syntactical nature, is thus restricted to the broad aspects of emotional states or general attitudes of problem-solving strategy. It does not translate things or relations between things in a transparent, linguistically effective manner. As a means of communication it does not serve the purpose of immediate conduction of behaviour, met by the languages of words and gestures: it is a language of emotion.

Regarding the possibility of a dominance for musical faculty, one may say that there are powerful arguments in favour of a relative lateralisation of nervous activity related to musical experience or execution. However, since this lateralisation has been ascribed to the hemisphere opposite the one related to language, several problems arise when one imagines the whole system performing as simple a musical act as singing a song with its lyric. Critchley (1972) has voiced reservations upon a duality of brain function concerned with music and language: "It is straining credibility to imagine that music, as comprising at one and the same time song and articulate language, should stem from the activities of opposite halves of the brain," and posed the pertinent question, ". . . if we talk with our major hemisphere and sing with our minor, by what cerebral legerdemain do we contrive to cope with those intermediate vocalisations, i.e. chanting and recitative?"

Summing up, one may say that music differs from verbal language both in its intimate structure as a code and in the way it may be used by humans in society. The fact that music is not a primary means of communication explains why people exhibit such differences in their ability to appreciate or perform music, and if verbal language itself should not be the object of crude localisational approaches musical faculty is an even worse target for piecemeal mechanicism. In short, we will assume that (a) there is no obvious reason why cerebral dominance for verbal language should involve cerebral dominance for the musical faculty; and (b) if there is a dominance for the musical faculty, this will be even less fixed than that of verbal language and, possibly, less consistent from person to person and closely related to the particular degree of musical ability exhibited by the subject.

## Behavioural studies

In contradiction to the assumptions stated above, however, music has been associated with language as a function of the left hemisphere and the amusias have been thought to result from almost the same lesions which produce aphasia. This has been the prevailing view in the literature in spite of reports – mainly anatomo-clinical studies – that were somewhat controversial and pointed to a functional divorce between music and language. A good example of the early literature on the subject is Edgren's study (1895) describing several possible combinations of aphasia and amusia. In his series of 50 patients aphasia plus amusia and aphasia without amusia were equally frequent, while amusia alone without aphasia seemed rare by comparison. Henschen, himself author of some of these early studies, was able to assert in 1926, "I have maintained, contrary to other authors, the opinion that most forms of amusia are localised in the left hemisphere only with the exception of some forms of instrumental music, which require the use of both hands (as the piano)." Henschen believed the musical faculty to be analogous to that of language and to have analogous pathological forms, "We have acoustic forms of amusia, that is inability to comprehend music as music, inability to sing, read and write music, and also to execute music, a form of musical apraxia . . . and each of these forms has its peculiar localisation in the cortex." He noted that the cases which seemed to point to a localisation of the faculty of singing in the right hemisphere were not conclusive evidence; but he conceded that in cases where the so-called left-sided centre for singing had been destroyed, the right hemisphere could apparently take over its functions. This is, indeed, how he interpreted the fact that in many cases of motor aphasia the ability to sing words was maintained in spite of complete failure to utter a single word in propositional speech. On the other hand, the comprehension of music was attributed to the left temporal pole, and it was assumed the right temporal pole could act as a substitute, at least in some cases, and compensate for the deficiency when the left side was damaged.

Similarly, and stressing the idea that dominance for music and language were one and the same thing, Feuchtwanger, in 1930, studied 34 patients with amusia, all of whom showed dysphasic disturbances. Ustvedt (1937), Wiesenburg and McBride (1935) and Nielsen (1946) have also held similar opinions, placing music and language together and naturally joining the amusias and the aphasias. Even more than Henschen, these authors admitted that there was a cerebral dominance for musical function and that this was as lateralised as, and coincident with, that of verbal language.

In more recent times some isolated case reports have contradicted these views. Thus Botez and Wertheim (1959) and Wertheim and Botez (1961) have presented cases of musicians who lost some aspects of their musical capacity in the face of relatively minor language impairment. It must be pointed out that the two cases were not entirely similar. The first one described musical disturbances in an "empirical" singer-accordionist who had sustained a lesion of the right frontal lobe and, although right-handed, certainly had a peculiar speech lateralisation. The second case was that of a professional violin player with a lesion in the left hemisphere; but both cases were extensively studied with the authors' own test battery for amusia (1959) and it is, therefore, possible to discuss differences and similarities of clinical features on a sound basis.

Although not dealing with music in particular, Spreen et al. (1965) have reported an unusual patient with an auditory deficit that precluded the recognition of any non-verbal sound but allowed for undisturbed perception of speech. Post-mortem examination of this case, which the authors described as "auditory agnosia without aphasia", showed a large lesion limited to the right hemisphere, predominantly involving the temporal lobe (mid portion and pole), the insula and restricted areas of the frontal and parietal lobes. Conversely, Luria et al. (1965), and quite recently Assal (1974), have presented cases of musicians who developed intense aphasic syndromes while remarkably preserving their capacities to conduct, compose, play the piano and generally recognise melodies. In both cases there was not even the question of a lower standard of performance, since several experts were willing to testify to the patients' unchanged powers of creation or executive ability. Yet Wertheim (1969), in virtually the latest paper on the subject, although he adopted a comprehensive view and reviewed the many controversial reports on anatomo-clinical correlation, thought it premature to comment in any conclusive manner on the functional localisation of musical faculty. He granted that the minor hemisphere may play a role in the expressive aspects of music – since, in some cases, lesions of F2 and of the pars triangularis of the right hemisphere were found to be associated with instrumental and vocal amusia – and he accepted the idea that cases of receptive amusia correspond with lesions of the dominant hemisphere, but the concept of a sort of cerebral dominance for musical abilities was not considered.

At the present time it seems possible to overcome some past limitations. Better tools for the study of higher nervous function, namely, the introduction of dichotic listening techniques in neurophysiological research, permit the investigation of dominance in the normal, in connection with several types of nervous processing. The considerable volume of experimental data gathered in the past decade makes it possible to formulate more cogent ideas.

## Studies of musical perception

Milner's suggestion (1962) that the right hemisphere is overwhelmingly concerned with musical ability was probably a turning point in the literature. Milner had studied patients after temporal lobectomies for epilepsy and realised, using the Seashore Measure of Musical Talents, that certain kinds of auditory discrimination became more difficult for patients who had had right-sided lobectomies. Subtests for timbre and tonal memory were remarkably impaired. Her original contribution was soon followed by a major study by Kimura (1964), who made use of the dichotic listening technique to investigate left-right differences in the perception of melodies. Small portions of solo instrument eighteenth century melodies (Mozart, Teleman, Vivaldi, Bach and Antonini) were played dichotically. All the subjects selected for the trials were normal volunteers (students and postgraduate nurses) with no particular musical aptitude. It was possible to demonstrate that the left ear was the preferred one for the optimal reception of melodies during two-channel simultaneous auditory stimulation. According to the explanatory theory of dichotic listening this meant that the right non-dominant hemisphere was processing melody perception in a more efficient way than the left. This too was a crucial paper for many a reason: it investigated normal subjects and not patients, it dealt with a series instead of a single instance, it made use of a well controlled experimental tool – dichotic listening – which in the years to come would prove to be a reliable method and contribute a considerable amount of new information. Last, but not least, by discovering a pattern which was the reverse of the one found for language, Kimura paved the way to provocative speculation and further research on the problem of interhemispheric sharing of nervous activity. Most of the ensuing work was reviewed in 1967 by Kimura herself in a comprehensive approach to the problem of functional asymmetry of brain activity.

Later, Shankweiler (1966) went back to a series of patients with temporal lobe damage and investigated the perception of dichotically presented melodies. This was a long study in which Kimura's tests were applied to 45 patients before and after temporal lobectomy. Twenty-one of the patients had left temporal lesions and 24 had right temporal lesions. Performance was severely disturbed after right temporal lobectomy. These data, combined with Milner's and Kimura's observations, made Shankweiler conclude that "together they provide substantial indications of the greater participation of the right temporal lobe in musical perception and further support for the hypothesis of a functional division of the two temporal lobes along the lines of the verbal non-verbal distinction." An interesting aspect of this study was the suggestion that the dominance effect for music was not strictly similar to the dominance effect for language. Indeed, when cases with similar temporal lesions in the right and left hemispheres were compared, it was noted that while right-sided lesions would always produce an extinction of the left channel in the test of melodies, left-sided lesions would not always determine a right channel extinction in the test of digits (the one used to evaluate verbal processing). It was concluded that dominance for language was of a higher level that could occasionally resist the impact of lesions, while dominance for musical ability, regardless of positive evidence, was of a weaker nature.

A relevant study concerning the factors capable of determining processing asymmetries was that of King and Kimura (1972). They worked with a population of students and evaluated the quality of perception of hummed melodies and human non-speech sounds. The melodies test reconfirmed the finding, by then well established, of left ear superiority/right hemisphere dominance, but the results with human non-speech sounds were of particular importance. Stimuli like laughing, crying, moaning and coughing were used. The result was similar to the test for melodies, showing the left ear superiority/right hemisphere dominance complex, significant at level $p < 0.05$. This was the first study to investigate the perception of vocally produced sounds other than speech sounds. It showed a marked lateralised processing for non-verbal vocal production, referred to the minor hemisphere, adding to the list of non-verbal auditory stimuli preferentially handled by the so-called minor hemisphere. Such data may be used to suggest that it is not the human voice *per se* that triggers the verbal language lateralisation in the left hemisphere – supporting the notion that the factor responsible for producing cerebral sharing of tasks is the verbal or non-verbal nature of the stimuli.

Working along the same lines, Spellacy (1970) sought to determine which musical characteristics brought about the right hemispheric dominance. Factors such as frequency, timbre and melody were evaluated. The paramount component was thought to be frequency, although evidence for this was not conclusive. In another study Spreen et al. (1970) investigated the same question for other factors like inter-stimulus intervals and intensity. Intensity level was found to be irrelevant, but, on the contrary, intervals were shown to be inversely correlated with dominance effect. In addition both studies confirmed the dominance effect in normals.

Within the context of these studies the contribution of Gordon (1970) produced some controversy. Gordon conducted a study on musical perception using dichotic listening tasks with digits, melodies and chords. The population selected for this study was made up of college musicians professionally engaged in musical performance. The results were as follows: in the test of chords there was a significant ($p < \cdot02$) superiority of the left ear over the right, but in the test of melodies, strangely enough, no such asymmetry was to be seen. Although both ears reached an above chance score ($p < \cdot01$), nevertheless the means did not differ significantly from each other ($p < \cdot1$). Such a finding was clearly discrepant from that which Kimura and Shankweiler had reported, with confirmation from other authors. Gordon's explanation for the divergent result obtained for chords and melodies invoked the existence of specific musical characteristics the processing of which might be differently lateralised by the brain; but no satisfactory explanation was offered for the fact that the test of melodies produced results which were so much in contrast with those of previous authors. Further on it will be argued that the main difference related to the type of subjects selected for the experiments and that their musical knowledge and training were the key factors in the phenomenon.

The concept that music may be processed differently by people with and without musical knowledge has been put forward by Bever and Chiarello (1974). They called attention to the possibility that, according to the subjects' contact with music, different nervous structures may be engaged in the processing of musical stimuli. The formulation behind their remarkable paper takes account of the fact that a melody, regardless of its being composed by a series of isolated notes, may be either perceived in terms of its overall melodic contour or as an organised arrangement of components. Bever and Chiarello cited several studies, both classic and modern, to the effect that naïve listeners do in fact perceive melodies in a *gestalt* fashion, while musically experienced listeners tend to approach sets of relation between musical elements (Werner, 1948; Meyer, 1956; Dowling, 1971; Deutsch, 1972). The authors then argued, in keeping with neo-Jacksonian views, that such a holistic apprehension is supposedly carried out by the right hemisphere, whereas the detailed, piecemeal analysis of the musical patchwork will be carried out by the left. They then proceeded to their hypothesis according to which "if a melody is normally treated as a *gestalt* by musically naïve listeners, then functional account of the difference between the two hemispheres predicts that melodies will be processed predominantly in the right hemisphere for such subjects". Understandably, the reverse is presumed to be true for musically sophisticated subjects.

The starting point for this hypothesis was apparently the finding, to which we have already called attention, that Gordon failed to report a left ear superiority for melody recognition when he used professional college musicians as subjects. Bever and Chiarello's results, even though they did not use dichotic listening and utilised instead a technique of monotic stimulation, fully support the assumption that the subjects' musical background was probably the relevant factor to explain Gordon's findings.

In short, the musically sophisticated listeners would achieve their best performance when using the right ear-channel, i.e. when they were predominantly conducting the perceptual process with their left hemispheres. On the other hand, the musically naïve persons performed better when the stimuli were coming via the left ear. Such findings, therefore, illuminate the results of Gordon and support those of Milner, Kimura and Shankweiler, while solving the apparent divergence.

One noteworthy aspect of Bever and Chiavello's paper is the notion that as capacity for musical analysis increases the left hemisphere dynamically "turns dominant" for musical processing. This is suggested by the observation that the relative superiority of the right ear for subjects (choirboys) of the same age, increases progressively and *pari passu* with experience in the choir. In the authors' own words there is a possibility that musical sophistication "has real neurological concomitants, permitting the utilisation of a different strategy of musical apprehension that calls on left hemisphere functions".

## Studies of musical execution

The neuropsychological studies reviewed so far have focussed on the evaluation of perceptive abilities. Understandably, objective evaluation of asymmetries related to expressive abilities has been rarely undertaken. Recent exceptions to this pattern include the papers by Smith and Burklund (1966) and Smith (1966), where musical performance following left hemispherectomy is reported. They showed how singing was maintained in the case of a 46 year old man whose dominant hemisphere had been excised for treatment of a glioma. The quality of melody reproduction and articulation was normal, contrasting with specific disturbances of speech. Similar findings were reported by Gott (1973), again in a case of left hemispherectomy in a young girl for recurrent tumour.

Recently we reported how singing of melodies was distorted and selectively impaired in a case of right hemispherectomy where most of the function of the ablated hemisphere had been effectively taken over by the remaining half of brain (Damásio et al., 1975).

In the face of these few references the papers of Bogen and Gordon (1971, 1974) assume a particular relevance because they represent the well planned study of singing ability in a series of six cases of "functional, pharmacological right or left hemispherectomy". By using the outline of the technique of Wada — unilateral injection of intracarotid amylobarbitone — they studied the singing performance of melodies, evaluating melodic quality, pitch variations and production of rhythmic patterns. When the injection was given in the right carotid, thus producing a depression of the right hemisphere, seven out of eight patients developed the equivalent of a transient expressive amusia which paralleled a transient hemiplegia. Speech defects were minor except in one of the patients who developed a transient speech-block. When the injection was given on the left the results were a transient right hemiplegia plus an aphasia, but the singing ability was unimpaired. It is important to note that the patients were required to sing familiar songs *without* words (hence no combination of lyric and melody was required which no doubt simplified the task). One patient who wanted to sing with the words did so, but with no recognisable melody. Verbal language ability was evaluated along with capacity to sing: they were required to execute simple verbal commands, repeat words, name objects or answer questions. The authors rightly concluded that singing either depends upon a lateralised process for which the right hemisphere is dominant, or else, more so than language, it depends upon a bilateral co-operation between the hemispheres, which is precluded by the right hemisphere amylobarbitone depression.

The importance of this investigation is obvious. The experimental situation, that of a "reversible hemispherectomy" as the authors call it, permits the immediate comparison between normal and pathological performances. Some details of the study also deserve further comment. Thus it was noted that the major defect leading to melodic distortion was disturbance in the production of correct pitch during right hemisphere depression. On the other hand, rhythm was not impaired, even when the patients were singing off-key. Oddly enough, rhythm was also normal during left hemisphere depression, which makes one speculate whether it results indifferently from right or left hemisphere function. One other major point was that pitch production for verbal non-singing utterances seemed to be unaffected by right hemisphere depression. In other words, when singing was distorted by right-sided injection verbal utterances were produced with normal tone and natural voice inflexions. The unavoidable conclusion is that, in contrast to the proposals of some authors, pitch control for music or verbal language is generated by different hemispheric structures. It seems probable, in view of the dysmelodic quality of language after left hemisphere depression, that pitch control for verbal language depends on the left hemisphere.

There is only one possible objection to the general validity of this study, stemming from the fact that the patients were epileptic, a condition which might have endowed them with a peculiar cerebral organisation. In the past this has been an argument against the value of some split-brain studies. However, by and large, the findings in severe epileptic patients prior to callosotomy or temporal ablation have been reproduced in non-epileptic subjects. The series in the Bogen and Gordon study, moreover, is quite homogeneous in terms of age and, presumably, pre-morbid musical ability.

If one takes a second look at the case reports of musicians with focal brain lesions, judging them in terms of the neuropsychological data above, the inconsistency of findings seems less extraordinary. Several factors explain and minimise the disparity, namely, the fact that procedures vary widely, that lack or presence of disturbances are differently ascribed to perceptive or motor aspects of musical performance, and that subjects were professionally quite dissimilar among themselves. Given the heterogeneity of the material we find the several reports much more consonant than they are generally believed to be. By and large, recent case studies have tended to separate aphasia and amusia, therefore denying the classical association of language/music disturbances while supporting modern neuro-psychological data. The well preserved ability to perform that some aphasic musicians manifest – Luria's composer-conductor (1965), Assal's light music pianist (1974) – also accords with the concept that the right hemisphere is paramount for qualified musical expression, rather more so than for musical reception. This dominance is only relative and in no way comparable in consistency or determination with the left hemisphere dominance for most aspects of language. On this point we still lack definitive experimental data concerning musicians and indeed the assumption rests on clinico-pathological evidence of musicians and non-musicians, and on the experimental study of Bogen and Gordon which was not conducted in a musical population. Bever and Chiarello's findings in no way run counter to the case studies since the Bever investigation concerned only the perceptual aspects of music. In point of fact, it would be interesting to know how some of the musician patients would fare in the Bever tasks. It is quite possible that they would give a comparatively poor performance but, again, if they proved normal it might be argued that, by means of overlearning, their professional training had "over-disseminated" the representation of some perceptual strategies.

## Conclusion

As one surveys the literature on the subject of musical ability and cerebral dominance, the difficulty in gathering precise data and formulating a coherent theory becomes evident. Since music is not really comparable with language it is only natural that old reports of amusiacs would pertain almost exclusively to patients who were musically gifted and in whom a deficit of musical listening or execution would be conspicuous, even if not deliberately sought by their physicians. Furthermore, we have seen to what extent the degree of musical sophistication may correspond with a different nervous organisation concerned with musical faculties. As a consequence it is understandable that more recent reports of cases of amusia do not coincide with some of the former observations. Another obvious source of divergence lies in the method of testing: with rare exceptions, whether clinical or experimental, few reports use standardised procedures capable of allowing further comparison. Nevertheless, in the light of new advances it is possible to explain some discrepancies and postulate that (1) musical faculty and cerebral dominance for verbal language are not intimately related; and (2) there is evidence for a sort of dynamic, developing cerebral dominance for certain features of musical faculty assuming the following aspects: (a) a right hemisphere dominance for musical execution, relatively independent of musical knowledge and training, and (b) a variable dominance for musical perception, to be ascribed to the right hemisphere in musically naïve subjects, and developing into a left hemisphere dominance in the case of musically sophisticated people.

Since high level training and knowledge of music in the population at large seem to be the exception rather than the rule, it is probably justifiable to assume that dominance for general musical faculty tends to develop in the right hemisphere first. A gradient theory would explain how, as training progresses, dominance would be gradually transferred to the opposite hemisphere for perceptual processing. Whether or not a similar shift might take place regarding the expressive aspects of music remains to be seen.

If cerebral dominance for music is of such a nature, how then are we able to sing a song with words? Is it believable that rival halves of brain combine in such a process? To answer the question one should realise that the sort of verbal language processing which enables the performer to sing the lyric is very different from the processing necessary for uttering the same words outside a musical or poetic context. The former process, concerned with words within the framework of a song or poem, operates out of an "appositional" store, and emerges in a global, *gestalt* way. The latter, which is concerned with most regular verbal utterances, stems from a "propositional" mechanism, resulting from a more analytical construction. The verbal language used in song is most probably generated by right hemisphere function and is therefore close to the origin of melody itself. There is no inter-hemispheric conflict: indeed, when one experimentally produces conflict, as in Bogen and Gordon's patient under the influence of amylobarbitone, the correct lyrics appear but inserted in an incorrect, distorted melody. In fact, one might propose that language and music do unite in the right hemisphere in order to escape inter-hemispheric rivalry. This could be why musical perception and expression commonly relate so closely to emotional experience and expression, hallmarks of right hemisphere function, remaining somewhat distant from the analytical processes that conduct reason from the left hemisphere.

## REFERENCES

ASSAL, G. (1974) Wernicke's aphasia without amusia in a pianist. *Rev. Neurol.*, **129**, 251.

BENTON, A. L. (1970) Hemispheric cerebral dominance. *Israel J. Med. Sci.*, **6**, 294.

BEVER, T. G. and CHIARELLO, R. J. (1974) Cerebral dominance in musicians and nonmusicians. *Science*, **185**, 537.

BOGEN, J. E. (1969a) The other side of the brain I: Dysgraphia and dyscopia following cerebral commissurotomy. *Bull. Los Angeles Neurol. Soc.*, **34**, 73.

BOGEN, J. E. (1969b) The other side of the brain II: an oppositional mind. *Bull. Los Angeles Neurol. Soc.*, **34**, 135.

BOGEN, J. E. and GORDON, H. W. (1971) Musical tests for functional lateralization with intracarotid amobarbital. *Nature*, **230**, 524.

BOTEZ, M. I. and WERTHEIM, N. (1959) Expressive aphasia and amusia following right frontal lesion in a right-handed man. *Brain*, **82**, 186.

BROWN, J. W. and JAFFE, J. (1975). Hypothesis of cerebral dominance. *Neuropsychologia*, **13**, 107.

CRITCHLEY, M. (1972), Inter-hemispheric partnership and inter-hemispheric rivalry. In: *Scientific Foundations of Neurology*, M. Critchley (ed.). London, William Heinemann Medical Books, p. 216.

DAMÁSIO, A. R. (1973) *Neurologia da Linguagem*. Lisboa, Livraria Buchholz.

DAMÁSIO, A. R., ALMEIDA LIMA, P. and DAMÁSIO, H. (1975) Nervous function after right hemispherectomy. *Neurology*, **25**, 89.

DAMÁSIO, H., DAMÁSIO, A. R., CASTRO-CALDAS, A., GROSSO, J. T., MARQUES, J. M. B. and FERRO, J. M. (1976) Age and culture as factors on dichotic listening performance. In preparation.

DEUTSCH, D. (1972) Octave generalization and tune recognition. *Percept. Psychophy.*, **11**, 411.

DOWLING, W. I. (1971) *Percept. Psychophy.*, **9**, 348.

EDGREN, J. G. (1895) Amusie (musikalische Aphasie). *Dtsch. Z. Nervenheilk.*, **6**, 1.

FONTENOT, D. J. and BENTON, A. L. (1971) Tactile perception of direction in relation to hemispheric locus of lesion. *Neuropsychologia*, **9**, 83.

GEFFNER, D. S. and HOCHBERG, I. (1971) Ear laterality performance of children from low and middle socio-economic levels on a verbal dichotic listening task. *Cortex*, **7**, 193.

GESCHWIND, N. (1972) Cerebral dominance and anatomic asymmetry. *New Engl. J. Med.*, **287**, 194.

GESCHWIND, N. and LEVITSKY, W. (1968) Human brain: left-right asymmetries in temporal speech region. *Science*, **161**, 186.

GORDON, H. W. (1970) Hemispheric asymmetries in the perception of musical chords. *Cortex*, **6**, 387.

GORDON, H. W. and BOGEN, J. E. (1974) Hemispheric lateralization of singing after intracarotid sodium amylobarbitone. *J. Neurol. Neurosurg. Psychiat.*, **37**, 727.

HENSCHEN, S. E. (1926) On the function of the right hemisphere of the brain in relation to the left in speech, music and calculation. *Brain*, **49**, 110.

KIMURA, D. (1963) Right temporal lobe damage: perception of unfamiliar stimuli after damage. *Arch. Neurol.*, **8**, 264.

— (1964) Left-right differences in the perception of melodies. *Quart. J. Exp. Psychol.*, **16**, 355.

— (1967) Functional asymmetry of the brain in dichotic listening. *Cortex*, **3**, 163.

KING, F. L. and KIMURA, D. (1972) Left-ear superiority in dichotic perception of vocal nonverbal sounds. *Com. J. Psychol.* **26**, 111.

KNOX, L. and KIMURA, D. (1970) Cerebral processing of nonverbal sounds in boys and girls. *Neuropsychologia*, **8**, 227.

LE MAY, M. and CULEBRAS, A. (1972) Human brain: morphologic differences in the hemispheres demonstrable by carotid arteriography. *New Engl. J. Med.*, **287**, 168.

LEVY-AGRESTI, J. and SPERRY, R. W. (1968) Differential perceptual capacities in major and minor hemispheres. *Proc. Nat. Acad. Sci.*, **61**, 1151.

LURIA, A. R., TSVETKOVA, L. S. and FUTER, D. A. (1965) Aphasia in a composer. *J. Neurol. Sci.*, **2**, 288.

MEYER, L. (1956) *Emotion and Meaning in Music.* Chicago, University of Chicago Press.

MILNER, B. (1962) Laterality Effects in Audition. In: *Interhemispheric Relations and Cerebral Dominance*, V. B. Mountcastle (ed.). Baltimore, Johns Hopkins Press, 177.

— (1965) Visually-guided maze learning in man: effects of bilateral, hippocampal, frontal, and unilateral cerebral lesions. *Neuropsychologia*, **3**, 317.

NIELSEN, J. M. (1946) *Agnosia, Apraxia, Aphasia: their Value in Cerebral Localization.* New York, Hoeber.

SAUSSURE, F. (1906) *Course in General Linguistics.* New York, Philosophical Library (1969).

SHANKWEILER, D. P. (1966) Effects of temporal lobe damage on the perception of dichotically presented melodies. *J. Comp. Physiol. Psychol.*, **62**, 115.

SMITH, A. (1966) Speech and other functions after left (dominant) hemispherectomy. *J. Neurol. Neurosurg. Psychiat.*, **29**, 467.

SMITH, A. and BURKLAND, C. W. B. (1966) Dominant hemispherectomy. *Science*, **153**, 1280.

SPELLACY, F. (1970) Lateral preferences in the identification of patterned stimuli. *J. Acoust. Soc. Amer.*, **47**, 574.

SPREEN, O., BENTON, A. and FINCHAM, R. (1965) Auditory agnosia without aphasia. *Arch. Neurol.*, **13**, 84.

SPREEN, O., SPELLACY, F. J. and REID, J. R. (1970) The effect of interstimulus interval and intensity on ear asymmetry for nonverbal stimuli in dichotic listening. *Neuropsychologia*, **8**, 245.

TESZNER, D., TZAVARAS, A., GRUNER, I. and HÉCAEN, H. (1972) L'asymétrie droite-gauche du planum temporale: á propos de l'étude anatomique de 100 cerveaux. *Rev. Neurol.*, **126**, 444.

USTVEDT, H. J. (1937) Uber die Untersuchung der Musikalischen Funktion bei Patienten mit Gehirnleiden besonders bei Patienten mit Aphasie. *Acta Med. Scand.*, Supp. 86.

WERNER, H. (1948) *Comparative Psychology of Mental Development.* New York, International Universities Press.

WERTHEIM, N. (1969). The Amusias. In: *Handbook of Clinical Neurology*, P. J. Vinken and G. W. Bruyn (eds.). Amsterdam, North-Holland Publishing Co., Vol. 4, 195.

WERTHEIM, N. and BOTEZ, M. I. (1959) Plan d'Investigation des Fonctions Musicales. *Encéphale*, **48**, 246.

—— (1961) Receptive amusia: a clinical analysis. *Brain*, **84**, 19.

WIESENBURG, T. H. and McBRIDE, K. (1935) *Aphasia, a Clinical and Psychological Study.* New York, The Commonwealth Fund.

# Musical Ability:
## a Neuropsychological Interpretation

I even think that *sentimentally* I am disposed to harmony. But *organically* I am incapable of a tune. I have been practising *"God Save the King"* all my life; whistling and humming of it over to myself in solitary corners; and am not yet arrived, they tell me, within many quavers of it.                 Charles Lamb

Those ideas that please me I retain in memory, and I am accustomed, as I have been told, to hum them to myself. If I continue in this way, it soon occurs to me how I may turn this or that morsel to account, so as to make a good dish of it. That is to say, agreeable to the rules of counterpoint, to the peculiarities of the various instruments, etc. . . . Nor do I hear in my imagination the parts successively, but I hear them as it were all at once (*gleich Alles zusammen*).
                          Passage from a letter attributed to Mozart*

This chapter attempts to review the contribution of psychologists to the field of music. However, it is centred entirely on the area of perceptual and cognitive functions. That is to say, other relevant factors such as the aesthetic, emotional and creative aspects of the musical experience have been omitted. The chapter is also selective in that it places emphasis on the analysis of those capacities which reflect functional asymmetries of the cerebral hemispheres in relation to musical ability.

The assessment of musical talent† has been one of the principal contributions of psychologists to the field of music. The approach has been twofold:

First, psychologists have been concerned with the measurement of the various elements that contribute to musical skill; secondly, they have attempted — using non-musical tests — to delineate the sensory, cognitive and performance capacities which are associated with musical talent.

## I. The assessment of musical ability

The measurement of musical ability (the field that has attracted most

---

\* From *Life of Mozart* by Edward Holmes: Everyman's Library.
† The terms "musical talent" and "musical ability" are here used interchangeably.

attention) has been hampered by the lack of agreement on the nature of musical skill (Lundin, 1953; Bentley, 1966; Lehman, 1968; Shuter, 1968). However, this problem has not deterred psychologists from devising tests for the quantification of musical ability. Lehman (1968) has pointed out that "intelligence could be measured before it could be defined and the same is true of musical aptitude". The result has been the construction of a variety of test batteries which include measurements of those elements that the respective authors consider as essential constituents of musical skill.

The different test batteries in current use can be divided into three main categories. Within the first are those tests which are based on classical psycho-physical measures of auditory perception with little recognisable musical content. Within the second are those which use musical material as a stimulus. On the whole these are similar to the "ear-tests" devised originally by musicians. Lastly comes the category of tests which evaluate complex aspects of music such as musical appreciation and recognition of musical passages.

An example of the first category is the Seashore Measure of Musical Talents published in 1919, the first music test battery to gain world-wide recognition (*see* Seashore, 1938).

The test in the 1940 revision (Saetveit et al., 1940) contains six measures[*] entitled:

*Sense of Pitch:* (Pairs of notes of different frequencies from 17 to 2 c.p.s: the subject is asked whether the second is higher or lower than the first.)

*Intensity Discrimination:* (Pairs of notes of different intensity from 4·0 to 0·5 decibels. The question asked: Is the second stronger or weaker than the first?)

*Sense of Time:* (Pairs of notes of different durations from 0·30 to 0·5 seconds: Is the second longer or shorter than the first?)

*Timbre:* (Pairs of notes, each of which is made up of fundamental and first five harmonics, the intensities of the third and fourth being varied: Are the two notes the same or different?)

*Tonal Memory:* (Pairs of note sequences, ten items each of three, four and five notes: Which note is different?)

*Sense of Rhythm:* (Pairs of rhythmic patterns: Are they the same or different?)

An example of the second category (based on musical material) is the Wing test of musical intelligence developed in 1933 (Wing, 1948). Wing's aim was to assemble a comprehensive series of tests, to assess their relative merits and to select those tests which were of a good diagnostic

---

[*] Sounds used in these tests were electronically produced.

value. The battery, in its present form, contains seven standardised tests:

*Chord Analysis:* (How many notes in a chord?)
*Pitch Change:* (Have the two chords been repeated exactly, or has a note moved up, or down?)
*Memory:* (Subject is presented with pairs of tunes and asked which note has been changed on the second playing.)
*Rhythm:* (Subject is presented with pairs of tunes and asked if the second is the same as the first, or, if it is different, which is the better version.)
*Harmony, Intensity and Phrasing:* (Tested in a similar way to rhythm, except that harmonisation, intensity or phrasing may have been altered.)

In the third category are the Oregon musical discrimination tests, which evaluate musical appreciation, and ability to recognise changes in musical passages. The subjects are presented with piano versions of classical pieces which have been altered in one way or another, and are presented along with the originals. The subject then has to say which one is the original piece, and the ways in which the other versions have been altered.

At present there are many standardised tests of musical ability (i.e. acquired skill), of musical capacity (i.e. inborn or native power) and of musical attainment.

*The nature of musical talent — factorial studies*
The historical development of the tests discussed above, and the critical evaluation of their validity and reliability, have been reviewed in great detail in various publications (for example, Bentley, 1966; Lehman, 1968; and Shuter, 1968) and will not be reiterated here. However, it is important, in so far as it is relevant to the understanding of the brain mechanism subserving musical ability, to comment on the work of McLeish (1950, 1968) who carried out a factorial analysis of musical cognition in the three basic types of test. McLeish tested 100 subjects with the Seashore test, the Wing test and the Oregon test of musical discrimination, together with a number of non-musical tests making a total of 22 variables. All these tests were given to the same group of subjects. Each battery was systematically analysed and compared with the others, using a summation factor analysis. Wing's battery and Seashore's battery were analysed separately, then in combination, then with all the other musical and non-musical tests.

Seashore had previously proposed that his test could not be regarded as a single unit but rather that it measured six different and independent abilities. Seashore's view was that a musical talent could manifest itself in a variety of patterns, depending on all possible combinations of high and low abilities in the six dimensions of musical skill. For the highest of musical talent, exceptional development was necessary in all six areas.

On the other hand Wing (1941), using a factorial analysis, demonstrated that there were marked intercorrelations in his seven measurements, thus suggesting the existence of a unitary mechanism of musical cognition.

McLeish's findings showed that, contrary to Seashore's view, his tests were not independent, but that there was a general factor running through all six measurements. He also confirmed the claim of Wing, namely that his tests proved the existence of a general factor of musical ability. Furthermore, McLeish's studies showed a most unexpected and surprising finding: that precisely the same kind of ability was being measured by the psychophysical tests of Seashore as by the musical tests of Wing. Furthermore, the same factor was also present in the Oregon tests of musical discrimination. McLeish concluded that this general factor of musical cognition could be defined as "the ability to recognise and understand the nature of changes in musical and quasi-musical tests". He also showed that in the structure of this ability musical memory, pitch discrimination and ability to analyse chords have greater weight than the ability to discriminate differences in rhythm, time and intensity.

The unitary theory of musical ability has, on the whole, been favoured by most psychologists (Shuter, 1968; Mursell, 1937; Schoen, 1940; Burt, 1940). On the other hand, the theories which postulate the existence of "specific abilities" have been the source of major criticisms. For example, Shuter (1968, p. 185) stated that "the results of trying to carve up musical ability have not always been too satisfactory, since clear and consistent divisions are rarely found".

## The nature of musical talent – clinical and experimental studies

However, the case for or against a unitary mechanism of musical talent remains open. Factorial studies have established that musical talents are not specific in their nature, that is to say there is a group factor of musical ability. On the other hand, clinical and experimental studies have suggested some specificity or dissociation of the components of musical ability. The data come from studies of patients with lesions of the brain as well as from normal subjects.

For a long time neuropsychologists have stressed the value of the studies of patients with cerebral lesions to unravel the mode of function of apparently unitary behaviours. Teuber (1952) pointed out that the analysis of the performance of such patients may be considered as a "biological alternative to factor analysis, suggesting what kinds of performance are impaired together or preserved together following a circumscribed lesion in a given region of the brain". Certainly, the intensive studies of the behavioural effects that follow brain damage have added to the understanding of the nature of intelligence, and have clarified to a great extent the dichotomy of general *versus* specific capacities (Piercy, 1969).

Furthermore, with the development of the dichotic listening technique (Broadbent, 1954) where the two ears receive simultaneous but different messages, it has been possible to obtain from normal subjects further evidence for the differential specialisation of the left and right hemispheres. This asymmetry of function is revealed because cortical response to stimulation of the contralateral ear is greater than to stimulation of the ipsilateral ear (Rosenzweig, 1951), and the effect is accentuated under simultaneous competitive stimulation (Kimura, 1967; Shankweiler, 1971).

Studies relating musical ability to cerebral specialisation are few. Also, the problem of general as opposed to specific abilities has been obscured by describing under the label of "musical task" a wide variety of tests, ranging from basic measurements of auditory perception to complex tasks requiring recognition and identification of musical passages.

However, in reviewing the available literature it is important to make a distinction between the studies of the elementary components of musical ability and those dealing with the perception and recognition of musical passages (e.g. melodies, tunes, musical phrases). The need for such separation stems from the fact that different conclusions — relative to hemispheric specialisation — have been reached for these two types of task. While there is basic agreement for the view that the right cerebral hemisphere is primarily concerned with perception of musical passages, no such accordant opinions exist in the case of the constituents of musical ability (e.g. timbre, pitch, intensity, etc.).

*Cerebral specialisation for the perception of musical passages*

(i) *Experimental studies.* Evidence for the dominance of the right hemisphere in the perception of musical passages has been largely provided by the use of the dichotic listening technique. The first study of this kind came from Kimura (1964), who presented to a group of normal subjects different portions of baroque melodies. The subjects were asked subsequently to recognise the musical passages. It was found that more selections were correctly identified when they were presented to the left than to the right ear. This was interpreted as a left ear advantage, and hence a right hemisphere superiority for the perception of melodies. Kimura's observation has been subsequently confirmed by various studies (Kimura, 1967; King and Kimura, 1972), as well as by Spellacy (1970), using passages of unfamiliar solo violin music, and by Spreen et al. (1970), using similar material. It is important to note that there are two conflicting reports regarding the above findings. Gordon (1970) presented dichotically four-bar motifs chosen from unfamiliar baroque dances. He found that neither the left nor the right ear exhibited a superior performance, and he ascribed this surprising result to the specific musical qualities of the test. The other discrepant observation came from Bever and Chiarello (1974) who found that musically experienced listeners recognise simple melodies better in the right ear than in the left, while the reverse was the case in non-musical subjects. These authors pointed out that it was significant that the study by Gordon, mentioned above, also used college musicians as subjects. However, right-ear superiority in experienced musicians has not been a consistent finding. Cook (1973) found in a group of musically sophisticated subjects a left-ear superiority for the recognition of musical passages. Furthermore, this study controlled for such variables as timbre, registration, tempo, intensity and musical style. Additional confirmation for right hemisphere dominance in normal subjects has been obtained with the use of other methods of investigation. For example, McKee et al. (1973) demonstrated a right hemisphere specialisation for the perception of music using an electroencephalographic technique. The authors recorded relative bilateral alpha activity in the temporo-parietal regions of the two hemispheres while the subjects were engaged in either a musical task or one of three linguistic tasks of varying difficulty. The records showed that the left/right ratios of alpha activity were highest for the musical task but tended to decrease progressively with the increasingly difficult linguistic tasks.

(ii) *Clinical studies.* Evidence of right cerebral dominance for the perception of melodies has also been derived from studies of patients with unilateral lesions of the brain. Shankweiler (1966), employing also the dichotic listening technique, presented data indicating impairment of the perception of orchestral melodies following removal of the right temporal lobe. Gordon and Bogen (1974) also showed evidence of right hemisphere dominance for singing with the use of the Wada technique. Investigating patients who had transient hemiplegia after carotid injection of sodium amylobarbitone, Gordon and Bogen found that after right carotid injection singing but not speech was markedly deficient. By contrast, singing was less disturbed than speech after left carotid injection.

## Cerebral specialisation for the components of musical talent

In contrast to the almost general agreement of the above findings, the evidence for cerebral specialisation of the constituents of musical ability is unclear and conflicting, and the following pages deal with this problem. The review covers studies bearing upon musical, as well as non-musical, sounds; however, it is concerned only with those reports which relate to the constituents of musical ability, especially to those which Seashore and Wing have used for the assessment of musical talent.

(i) *Clinical studies.* The pioneer work in this field was carried out by Milner (1962) with a study on the effects of temporal lobe excisions in auditory discrimination. Milner tested 27 patients with the six items of the Seashore Scale before and after unilateral temporal lobe removal for the relief of epilepsy. The findings indicated that after operation the right temporal group, but not the left, showed an increased number of errors in all tests. The increase was more marked for the subtests of tonal memory and timbre, although statistically significant changes were also seen for the scores of loudness and time. On the other hand, pitch and rhythm appeared to be unaffected by the removal of the right temporal lobes. These findings were the first to suggest a differential cerebral specialisation for the components of musical talent.

Subsequent studies of auditory discrimination in patients with cerebral lesions have supported some of Milner's earlier findings. For instance Schulhoff and Goodglass (1969), using a dichotic presentation of tonal sequences, tested a group of patients with unilateral brain lesions – mostly patients who had suffered cerebral vascular accidents – and a normal control group. Their results indicated a left-ear superiority – right hemisphere dominance – in the case of normal subjects, whilst patients with right hemisphere lesions showed a decrease – when compared with normal subjects – in both the left and the right ear. Schulhoff and Goodglass concluded that one would expect to find bilateral decreases in material for which the injured hemisphere is dominant. Moreover, the normal superiority of the left ear for tonal sequence-discrimination was maintained, with a small margin, by the patients with lesions of the right hemisphere.

Another of the components of musical talent that has been investigated in patients with cerebral lesions is intensity-discrimination; but the findings from the various studies have shown rather conflicting results.

The study by Milner (1962) indicated that there were no significant differences in intensity-discrimination before operation in patients with left- and right-sided lesions. Moreover, no change was seen after left temporal lobectomy; but there was a statistically significant change, although a small one, after right temporal lobe excision. This observation has not been substantiated by recent studies. Shankweiler (1966) obtained pure-tone audiograms in 45 patients with temporal lobectomies. When the patients were tested before operation he found that every subject had good hearing acuity. After operation there was no evidence of deficits in either ear in the patients with left- or right-sided excisions. Yet another discrepant finding has been reported by Peck Swisher (1967). In a study of the analysis of auditory intensity-discrimination in patients with temporal lobectomies it was shown that before operation there were no significant differences between patients with left- and right-sided lesions. However, after operation patients with left temporal lobectomies (which included the transverse gyri of Heschl) showed hypersensitivity to changes in intensity. The finding was an important one, as improvement rather than deterioration occurred after removal of the temporal lobe. This observation was explained by stressing the importance of the role of the transverse gyri of Heschl for intensity-discrimination; however, no clear explanation was given for the increase in sensitivity following a left temporal lobe excision. The lack of consistency in these reports is most significant as data in each study have been obtained from subjects with comparable pathological conditions.

(ii) *Experimental studies.* Turning now to the studies of the components of musical ability based on normal subjects, the findings are also conflicting and inconclusive. This partly stems from the lack of systematic investigations bearing upon the issue of cerebral specialisation for musical talent. None of the studies so far has assessed the same group of subjects with all the items that are generally considered basic components of musical ability. In fact, they have investigated only a few isolated elements of musical talent. Certainly there is a spate of work dealing with the performance of normal subjects in all the items of the musical test-batteries (*vide* Shuter, 1968); but most of these studies have aimed at the evaluation of musical aptitude for educational purposes.

The analysis of auditory discrimination of musical and non-musical sounds relative to the problem of cerebral dominance has been carried out using two different methods: the dichotic listening technique, and more recently the choice reaction time procedure (*vide* Fry, 1970). The dichotic technique takes into account the subject's correct report of what he has heard. The reaction time procedure measures rapidity of response. This latter method is based on the assumption that speed of reaction can be used as a measure of ear superiority and hence of cerebral dominance. The basic procedure consists of presenting stimuli monaurally or binaurally and asking the subject to press a button whenever he hears a particular target sound.

Recent studies bearing on the question of cerebral dominance for musical and non-musical sounds using the methods described above have been reported from Darwin (1969), Gordon (1970), Spellacy (1970), Spreen et al. (1970), Halperin et al. (1973), Nachshon (1973), Haydon and Spellacy (1973), Robinson and Solomon (1974) and Kallman and Corballis (1975). The relevant features of these investigations are summarised in Table 1.

*Table 1*   Ear differences in the discrimination of musical and non-musical sounds (normal subjects)

| Author | Left–ear superiority | Right–ear superiority | No difference | Method |
|---|---|---|---|---|
| Darwin (1969) | Simple pitch patterns | | | DLT |
| Gordon (1970) | Musical chords | | | DLT |
| Spellacy (1970) | | | Timbre Frequency patterns Temporal patterns | DLT |
| Spreen et al. (1970) | Tonal patterns (Pure tones) | | | DLT |
| Halperin et al. (1973) | Simple sequences varying in frequency and duration | Complex sequences varying in frequency and duration | | DLT |
| Nachshon (1973) | | | Pure tone discrimination | DLT |
| Haydon and Spellacy (1973) | | Pure tones (If uncertain as to side of presentation) | | DLT and RT |
| Robinson and Solomon (1974) | | Rhythmic pure-tone patterns | | DLT |
| Kallman and Corballis (1975) | Single musical notes | | | RT |

DLT: Dichotic Listening Technique.
RT: Reaction Time.

Studies dealing with the discrimination of frequency show clearly a lack of consistency. Darwin (1969) demonstrated a left ear superiority for simple pitch patterns. Also, Gordon (1970) showed that the left ear was more proficient than the right in recognising the pattern of pitches in a musical chord. Contrary to this, in a more recent study, Nachshon (1973) found no difference between the ears in a pure tone discrimination task. Moreover, three experimental variables have been shown to be crucial in determining ear superiority. First, the interval elapsing between the presentation of the dichotic stimuli and the presentation of the recognition stimuli: Spreen et al. (1970) showed a left ear superiority for tonal patterns if the interval between presentations was only one sec., while Spellacy (1970) demonstrated no ear difference for intervals of five and 12 secs. Another feature of experimental design that can change ear superiority is the complexity of the test material. Halperin et al. (1973) found a left ear advantage in the report of dichotic sound sets (three sounds in a set), provided that all the sounds were of equal frequency, that is to say, they were all high- or all low-frequency sounds. On the other hand, if the set was composed of sounds of varying frequencies (e.g. a high-frequency sound followed by one of low-frequency and then another high-frequency sound) there was a shift of ear superiority so that in the latter case the sequences were more accurately reported when presented to the right ear. Finally, another important variable is the subject's expectation as to the ear in which the stimulus is presented. Early in 1967, Simon, using a reaction time procedure, found a right ear advantage in the discrimination of pure tones when the subjects were uncertain as to the side of presentation, and this finding has been recently confirmed by the study of Haydon and Spellacy (1973) using also a reaction time procedure.

There are only a few studies dealing with the question of timbre and cerebral specialisation; even so, conflict between the different findings is apparent as in the case of pitch. The study by Gordon (1970) reported above suggests a left ear advantage for timbre as the musical chord tests used in his study contained mainly two musical qualities: pitch and timbre. Also a left ear superiority for timbre can be inferred from the study by Kallman and Corballis (1975). The tests in this study consisted in the dichotic presentation of pairs of the note A played on four different instruments: bassoon, viola, piano and cello. The subjects were asked to depress a button whenever they heard the note played on the cello (the target sound). The results showed a left ear advantage for the recognition of the notes presented; however, this superiority was only of limited duration, as the difference disappeared after repeated trials. On the other hand, Spellacy's study (1970) showed no significant differences between the ears. The stimuli in this experiment were simple notes played on a pipe organ, the fundamental frequency being the same for both members of the dichotic pair but the overtones differing according to the combination of pipes used. However, it is significant that in this study the interval between dichotic presentation and recognition stimuli was 5 and 12 sec., so it is possible that a different pattern of ear advantage can be elicited (with shorter intervals) as in the case of pitch.

Sense of time as defined by Seashore, i.e. the ability to discriminate between pairs of notes differing in duration, has been given little attention. Instead, interest has been directed to the analysis of temporal patterns. For example, Halperin et al. (1970) looked at ear superiority for temporal sequences of differing complexity; and Spellacy studied temporal patterns as a function of the interval between dichotic presentation and subsequent recognition. In the study by Halperin et al., the subjects were presented dichotically with simple sequences of sounds which were either all long or all short; also with complex sequences made up of notes of various duration, for example, a long sound followed by a short one and then another long sound. The results obtained were identical with those for sequences differing in frequency: namely, left ear superiority for simple sequences; right ear superiority for complex sequences; no differences between the ears when the intervals between dichotic presentation of temporal patterns and their subsequent recognition were five and 12 sec.

The problem of rhythmic perception and cerebral dominance has been largely neglected. Rhythm, in the present context, has been defined (*vide* Lovelock, 1964) as "the grouping of sounds according to their duration in time". Therefore, the temporal sequences used as stimuli by Halperin et al. (1970) and Spellacy (1970), mentioned above, contained too few signals (three and four) to qualify as rhythmic patterns. It is only recently that an attempt has been made to inquire into this question using adequate stimuli. Thus, Robinson and Solomon (1974) examined ear superiority for rhythms using a "refrain" repeated three times with a 50 msec interval. The refrain consisted of a random series of four to seven short and long pure tones. The results showed that the number of correct identifications for the right ear was significantly greater than that for the left ear. Robinson and Solomon concluded that rhythmic patterns were better processed by the left hemisphere, i.e. the hemisphere dominant for speech stimuli.

Summarising the findings of the experimental and clinical investigations cited above, it is apparent that the superiority which has been ascribed to the right hemisphere for the perception of musical and quasi-musical material is applicable only to "structured" musical passages; that is to say, to the perception of sounds built up into tuneful, melodic and harmonious combinations. On the other hand, the components of musical talent do not exhibit any distinct ear superiority, nor do they show any clear-cut pattern of impairment following cerebral lesions; therefore, there is no evidence at present to justify the view that the right hemisphere is dominant for *all* musical tasks. It is evident that neither the right nor the left hemisphere alone exhibits an unequivocal cerebral specialisation for the components of musical cognition.

The above observations, therefore, do not support the claim of the factor analysis studies which postulate the existence of a unitary mechanism of musical cognition; instead they favour the early views of Seashore, who proposed that musical talent depended on the combination of abilities which are independent of each other. This latter notion is strengthened by a recent study by Efron and Yund (1975). These authors demonstrated by means of a dichotic listening technique a dissociation in the processing of frequency and intensity information by the auditory system; they showed that the neural signals which represent the frequency of a sound presented to one ear and the neural signals which represent the intensity of the sound at that ear are separated at some point along the auditory pathway and are processed in different ways.

Moreover, the assertion of McLeish (1968) that the same ability is measured by psycho-physical as by musical tasks needs revision. A right hemisphere superiority has been demonstrated for the ability to recognise and understand the nature of changes in *musical* tests. On the other hand, there is no conclusive evidence that this superiority also applies to the perception and recognition of quasi-musical sounds. At present, cerebral specialisation for the components of musical talent do not show clearly that a distinction between musical and quasi-musical stimuli is a critical factor in determining laterality effects. However, the number of studies which are actually based on musical material is limited and therefore further research is needed to elucidate this point.

It is relevant to emphasise that a parallel can be drawn between the observations derived from the analysis of musical cognition and those which have been obtained from studies on the perception of language. Whilst there is an unquestionable superiority of the left hemisphere for the perception of verbal material, no such clear verbal lateralisation exists for the elements of speech. For example, it has been shown, using the dichotic listening technique, that vowel sounds can be identified equally well by both the left and the right ear (*vide* Shankweiler, 1971). Accordingly, the assumption (Darwin, 1971) that the type of stimulus-material (verbal or non-verbal) is the *only* index of which ear gives a better performance has recently been questioned. The controversy has arisen because an increasingly large number of experimental investigations has shown a right ear advantage for the perception of non-verbal material. Moreover, the studies of patients with severed interhemispheric connections (Sperry, 1974) have also provided evidence indicating that the differential functions of the right and left hemisphere are not based solely on a verbal *versus* non-verbal dichotomy.

At present, theoretical interpretations of the functional roles of the left and right hemispheres attempt to ascribe differences of control based on the modes in which information is processed by the two hemispheres (*vide* Eccles, 1973). The dominant hemisphere has been shown to deal with tasks which require sequential and analytical processing, whilst the right hemisphere is concerned with those tasks which demand synthetic and holistic organisation. Such a postulate is certainly more consistent with the experimental findings on the perception of musical passages, and with the observation concerning the perception of musical and quasi-musical sounds; but at this stage it is too early to reach any definite conclusions, especially as the research in the field of musical cognition and cerebral specialisation is at present still inadequate and fragmentary.

## II. *Cognitive abilities associated with musical talent*

The other important contribution of psychologists to the field of music has been the description of sensory, cognitive and performance capacities which are associated with musical talent. The majority of these studies has been concerned with the association of musical skills with other "general" cognitive abilities. For example, some studies have attempted to relate musical talent with intelligence and educational achievement, while others have looked at the connection with mathematical and other scientific abilities (*vide* Shuter, 1968). On the other hand, only a few studies on handedness, and others dealing with pattern perception, have been relevant to the problem of the respective roles of the dominant and non-dominant hemisphere in musically sophisticated subjects.

The questions raised by the studies of handedness in musicians have been twofold. First, they have asked whether there is a greater number of left-handers and ambidextrous subjects among this group; and second, whether there is a differential cerebral organisation in subjects whose competent musical performance demands highly specialised non-verbal skills.

Oldfield (1969, 1971) conducted an inquiry by means of a specially designed questionnaire into the prevalence of left-handedness among musicians. His results showed that the number of sinistrals among this group was equal to that of a comparable series of psychology undergraduates. These findings have since been corroborated by Byrne (1974), who found that left-handedness among instrumentalists did not exceed the number of sinistrals in an unselected group of students. However, Byrne, using the Oldfield questionnaire, showed that among the group of musicians there was a large proportion of mixed-handedness, a feature which was not present in Oldfield's finding. In view of the fact that competent musical performance demands highly developed skills and very refined neuro-muscular co-ordination of both hands, it is possible that a differential pattern of handedness can be elicited by using other measures, such as tests of the rapidity of hand movements as well as dexterity tests (Asso and Wyke).

The second question, i.e. the pattern of cerebral organisation related to musical ability, has been more difficult to answer. Byrne (1974) proposed that bilateral language representation, a pattern of cerebral dominance expected in mixed-handed subjects, may occur at the expense of certain musical as well as spatial abilities. In order to verify this notion, Byrne tested a group of right- and mixed-handed subjects with two subtests of the Seashore Scales (timbre and tonal memory) and with a verbal intelligence test. His results showed that both the right- and mixed-handed groups had comparable verbal abilities, and exhibited no difference in their performance on the Seashore subtests. Byrne suggested that his data supported the independence of musical ability and handedness. However, it is clear that further investigation is needed in order to provide an adequate answer to this problem. The chief point at issue, that is whether cerebral arrangements regarding handedness are related to those which have to do with musical execution, remains unanswered.

One further problem that has attracted attention is the relation of musical ability and visual pattern perception. Barrett and Barker (1973) investigated this question in a group of children whose ages ranged from eight to 12 years. The subjects were assessed with a musical performance test and with various tests of pattern perception. The results indicated a significant correlation between musical talent and three visual perceptual abilities: the ability to keep a configuration in mind despite distraction; the ability to combine apparently disconnected visual stimuli into a single percept; and the speed of symbolic discrimination. This investigation was not especially directed to answering questions concerning cerebral organisation in musically sophisticated subjects; but the authors' results suggested that musical skills are closely connected with perceptual abilities which are known to be primarily mediated by the right hemisphere. However, the test of perceptual speed, used in the study, required the subject to indicate in a list of words those words which contained the letter A; and therefore the verbal nature of this task would indicate a primary left hemisphere involvement.

One other study has investigated hemispheric differences in the perception of visually presented material. Oscar-Berman et al. (1974) tested a group of musically sophisticated subjects and a comparable group of musically naïve subjects. The test involved the tachistoscopic presentation – in the left and right visual fields – of a single musical note on a staff. The results obtained suggested that in the case of musically sophisticated subjects both cerebral hemispheres were actively involved in the analysis of the musical symbols. The findings in these two studies agree with the suggestion of Bever and Chiarello (1974) that increasingly greater sophistication of musical skill is likely to demand neural interactions which involve both the left and the right hemisphere. It is clear that the work in this field of inquiry is far too limited to attempt any valid conclusions. However, it is apparent that in selecting subjects for studies concerned with the perception of musical stimuli — whether this be in the auditory or visual modality — it is necessary to distinguish between musically sophisticated and musically naïve subjects.

*Conclusion*

The contributions of psychologists to the field of music described above have assisted in the elucidation of some aspects of inter-hemispheric differences in the localisation of musical talent. Two important points have so far emerged from this inquiry. First, the suggestion of a differential pattern of cerebral specialisation for the perception of musical passages and the perception of the components of musical talent; and secondly, the suggestion of a differential pattern of cerebral specialisation and hemispheric interaction for musically sophisticated and musically naïve subjects. At present many questions remain unanswered; but it is apparent that the study of individuals capable of highly complex modes of behaviour which demand close sensori-motor interactions will prove fruitful for a better understanding of the functional asymmetry of the cerebral hemispheres.

## REFERENCES

ASSO, D., and WYKE, M. Rapidity of hand movements in college musicians. (In preparation.)

BARRETT, C. H., and BARKER, H. R. (1973) Cognitive pattern perception and musical performance. *Percept. mot. Skills*, **36**, 1187–1193.

BENTLEY, A. (1966) *Musical Ability in Children and its Measurement*. London, Harrap.

BEVER, T. G., and CHIARELLO, R. J. (1974) Cerebral dominance in musicians and non-musicians. *Science*, **185**, 137–139.

BROADBENT, D. E. (1954) The role of auditory localization in attention and memory span. *J. exp. Psychol.*, **47**, 191–196.

BURT, C. (1940) *The Factors of the Mind*. London, University of London Press.

BYRNE, A. (1974) Handedness and musical ability. *Br. J. Psychol.*, **65**, 279–281.

COOK, R. B. (1973) Left-right differences in the perception of dichotically presented musical stimuli. *J. music Ther.*, **10**, 59–63.

DARWIN, C. J. (1969) Auditory perception and cerebral dominance. Unpublished Ph.D. thesis, University of Cambridge.

— (1971) Ear differences in the recall of fricatives and vowels. *Quart. J. exp. Psychol.*, **23**, 46–62.

ECCLES, J. C. (1973) *The Understanding of the Brain.* New York, McGraw-Hill Book Company.

EFRON, R., and YUND, E. W. (1975) Dichotic competition of simultaneous tone bursts of different frequency. III: The effect of stimulus parameters on suppression and ear dominance functions. *Neuropsychologia*, **13**, 151–161.

FRY, D. B. (1970) *Reaction-Time Experiments in the Study of Speech Processing.* Academia Publishing House of the Czechoslovak Academy of Sciences.

GORDON, H. W. (1970) Hemispheric asymmetries in the perception of musical chords. *Cortex*, **6**, 387–398.

GORDON, H. W., and BOGEN, J. E. (1974) Hemispheric lateralization of singing after intracarotid sodium amylobarbitone. *J. Neurol. Neurosurg. Psychiat.*, **37**, 727–738.

HALPERIN, Y., NACHSHON, I., and CARMON, A. (1973) Shift of ear superiority in dichotic listening to temporal patterned non-verbal stimuli. *J. acoust. Soc. Am.*, **53**, 46–50.

HAYDON, S. P., and SPELLACY, F. J. (1973) Monoaural reaction time asymmetries for speech and nonspeech sounds. *Cortex*, **9**, 288–294.

KALLMAN, H. J., and CORBALLIS, M. C. (1975) Ear asymmetry in reaction time to musical sounds. *Percept. Psychophys.*, **17**, 368–370.

KIMURA, D. (1964) Left-right differences in the perception of melodies. *Quart. J. exp. Psychol.*, **16**, 355–358.

— (1967) Functional asymmetries of the brain in dichotic listening. *Cortex*, **3**, 163–178.

KING, F. L., and KIMURA, D. (1972) Left-ear superiority in dichotic perception of vocal nonverbal sounds. *Can. J. Psychol.*, **26**, 111–115.

LEHMAN, P. R. (1968) *Tests and Measurements in Music.* Englewood Cliffs, New Jersey, Prentice-Hall Inc.

LOVELOCK, W. (1964) *A Student's Dictionary of Music.* London, G. Bell & Sons, Ltd.

LUNDIN, R. W. (1953) *An Objective Psychology of Music.* New York, The Ronald Press Co.

MILNER, B. (1962) Laterality effects in audition. In *Interhemispheric Relations and Cerebral Dominance*, ed. V. B. Mountcastle, Baltimore, Maryland, The Johns Hopkins Press.

MURSELL, J. L. (1937) *The Psychology of Music.* New York, Norton.

McKEE, G., HUMPHREY, B., and McADAM, D. W. (1973) Scaled lateralization of alpha activity during linguistic and musical tasks. *Psychophysiology*, **10**, 441–443.

McLEISH, J. (1950) The validation of Seashore's measures of musical talent by factorial methods. *Br. J. statist. Psychol.*, **3**, 129–140.

— (1968) *Musical Cognition*. London, Novello & Co. Ltd.

NACHSHON, I. (1973) Effects of cerebral dominance and attention on dichotic listening. *T.I.T. J. Life Sciences*, **3**, 107–114.

OLDFIELD, R. C. (1969) Handedness in musicians. *Br. J. Psychol.*, **60**, 91–99.

— (1971) The assessment and analysis of handedness: the Edinburgh Inventory. *Neuropsychologia*, **9**, 97–113.

OSCAR-BERMAN, M., BLUMSTEIN, S., and DeLUCA, D. Iconic recognition of musical symbols in lateral visual fields. Paper presented at the A.P.A., New Orleans, Louisiana, September 1974.

PECK SWISHER, L. (1967) Auditory intensity discrimination in patients with temporal lobe damage. *Cortex*, **3**, 179–193.

PIERCY, M. (1969) Neurological aspects of intelligence. Chapter 18 in *Handbook of Clinical Neurology*, Vol. 3, ed. P. J. Vinken and G. W. Bruyn. Amsterdam, North-Holland Publishing Company.

ROBINSON, G., and SOLOMON, D. J. (1974) Rhythm is processed by the speech hemisphere. *J. exp. Psychol.*, **102**, 508–511.

ROSENZWEIG, M. R. (1951) Representation of the two ears at the auditory cortex. *Am. J. Physiol.*, **67**, 147–158.

SAETVEIT, J. G., LEWIS, D. and SEASHORE, C. E. (1940) Revision of the Seashore measures of musical talents. University of Iowa Studies, Series on Aims and Progress Research, No. 65, University of Iowa Press.

SCHOEN, M. (1940) *The Psychology of Music*. New York, Roland Press.

SCHULHOFF, C., and GOODGLASS, H. (1969) Dichotic listening, site of brain injury and cerebral dominance. *Neuropsychologia*, **7**, 149–160.

SEASHORE, C. E. (1938) *Psychology of Music*. New York, McGraw-Hill.

SHANKWEILER, D. (1966) Effects of temporal lobe damage on perception of dichotically presented melodies. *J. comp. physiol. Psychol.*, **62**, 115–119.

— (1971) An analysis of laterality effects in speech perception. In: *Perception and Language*, ed. P. M. Kjeldergaard, D. L. Horton, and J. J. Jenkins. Columbus, Ohio, Charles E. Merrill Publishing Co.

SHUTER, R. (1968) *The Psychology of Music*. London, Methuen.

SIMON, R. J. (1967) Ear preference in a simple reaction time task. *J. exp. Psychol.*, **75**, 49–55.

SPELLACY, F. (1970) Lateral preferences in the identification of pattern stimuli. *J. acoust. Soc. Am.*, **47**, 574–578.

SPERRY, R. W. (1974) Lateral specialization in the surgically separated hemispheres. In: *The Neurosciences. Third Study Program*, ed. F. O. Schmitt and F. G. Worden. Cambridge, Massachusetts, The M.I.T. Press.

SPREEN, O., SPELLACY, F. J., and REID, J. R. (1970) The effect of interstimulus interval and intensity on ear asymmetry for non-verbal stimuli in dichotic listening. *Neuropsychologia*, **8**, 245–250.

TEUBER, H.-L. (1952) Some observations on the organization of higher function after penetrating brain injury in man. In: *Biology of Mental Health and Disease*. New York, Hoeber-Harper.

WING, H. D. (1941) A factorial study of musical tests. *Br. J. Psychol.*, **31**, 341–355.

— (1948) Test of musical ability and appreciation. *Br. J. Psychol.*, No. 27 (Monog. Suppl.).

DONALD SCOTT and
ADRIENNE MOFFETT

# 11

# The Development of Early Musical Talent in Famous Composers: a Biographical Review

Biographies of famous composers frequently note that exceptional musical ability occurs at a young age. In the present chapter an attempt is made to examine these observations in detail. Further, the many influences which mould development and lead to a successful adult career will be reported. In order to achieve success, a variety of attributes are required, and the so-called musical prodigies of Seashore, who show early musical ability but lack ordinary intelligence and do not develop, are not considered further. Apart from intelligence, the era in which the composer was born has an effect. His works at that particular time might be under-rated and lost wholly or in part to posterity. Later, the compositions may be re-discovered or his style and quality be appreciated. This presents problems for comparison between different individuals. There is another problem: biographies may embroider the facts and many accretions of apocryphal material result. This is also a difficulty which arises in attempts to make psychiatric diagnoses on historical personages (Scott, 1974). In spite of these difficulties, we feel that biographical material can reveal the ways that musical talent develops. It is a topic not just of interest but one, as will be shown, which has relevance to the education of gifted children today.

Composers vary greatly in their individual characteristics. So, as a starting point, the details of the early lives of four notable, but quite different, figures are given to show the development of their talent. Mozart, an example of one with exceptional early talent, the musical prodigy *par excellence*, is selected; then Beethoven, because of his ability to overcome adversity; Handel is of interest as there is a record of personality traits in early life, and Bach, as he represents the zenith of the achievement of a talented musical family, underlining the possible influence of heredity (see Chapter 2).

## Mozart

Mozart is of special interest not only because he is the outstanding example of a musical prodigy but also because there is a contemporary account of "psychological tests" given to him at the age of eight years. By that age Mozart was appearing frequently in public with his sister Maria Anna. Indeed, it was Mozart's interest in her music lessons which indicated his own early talent. Leopold, their father, at first taught them both, but by the age of eight in the case of his son, he realised that other instructors had to be found (Blom, 1974). Leopold also arranged extensive tours to many parts of Europe. It was on one of these that the family came to London, and Mozart was examined by the Hon. Daines Barrington before he knew that Mozart would become a mature musician of lasting importance. However, it is surprising in view of his conclusions, that Barrington waited six years before publishing his findings. Perhaps he was therefore not as confident as the report suggests.

Nevertheless, Barrington, a non-musician, is an intriguing character, as he had an enquiring mind for a variety of scientific subjects. Further, he had not only examined Mozart but also four other contemporary talented youngsters (see below). This type of study clearly yields considerable information on musical development so it is perhaps surprising that there have been few similar investigations.

As a result of his studies, Barrington communicated to the Royal Society in 1779 a paper "An Account of a very remarkable musician". He was obviously serious, taking the trouble to obtain documentary evidence of Mozart's age, confirming that in fact he was not older than was claimed, a trick used by Beethoven's father to make his son's performance seem the more remarkable.

The first task that Mozart was set concerned sight reading. The piece, which he could not have previously seen, was by an "English" gentleman. It was in five parts, two for violin, one for double bass and there were two vocal parts. Barrington recounted "the score was no sooner upon his (Mozart's) desk than he began to play the symphony in a most masterful manner as well as in the time and style which corresponded with the intention of the composer . . . the symphony ended Mozart took the upper part, leaving the under one for his father". Barrington indicated from the performance that followed that Mozart was better at sight reading than his father.

Barrington then tested Mozart's ability at extemporisation. Knowing that he was much taken notice of by Manzoli, a famous singer who had visited England in 1764, he asked Mozart to improvise a love song of the sort Manzoli might choose. This, according to Barrington, "was not amazingly capital, yet it was really above mediocrity, and showed most extraordinary readiness of invention". He was also then asked, unrehearsed, to play a "Song of Rage". During this Mozart worked himself up to such a frenzy that he rose from the chair and beat the harpsichord like a "person possessed".

Mozart was next requested to play one of his own compositions which he executed with amazing skill, "considering that his little fingers could scarcely reach a fifth on the harpsichord". His "astonishing readiness" did not apparently arise, in Barrington's view, through great practice, but by basic understanding of composition, since he could immediately write a bass when a treble was shown to him. Barrington noticed that Mozart had a particular ability at modulation and that his transition from one key to another was "excessively natural and judicious". At this stage of the testing a handkerchief was placed over the keys of the harpsichord so that Mozart was unable to watch his fingers as he played. Barrington concluded by emphasising that he himself set the tests and on the basis of these he regarded Mozart as a genius. Barrington suggested that this prodigious talent would in his view mature with age. He had access to Mainwaring's (1760) account of Handel's early musical abilities and concluded that there was a great similarity between the two in relation to their precocious musical ability.

Mozart's visit to London was in the middle of a grand tour of Europe. He was received by King George III and his performances and that of his sister delighted many of the nobility. There is no doubt, therefore, that he obtained great social reinforcement at an early age. Indeed, it is said he sat on the lap of a dowager Countess in Vienna at four years of age to play (Barrington, 1779). Mozart's father heightened the excitement of the sensation lovers by calling his children "prodigies of nature". Ecstatic reception cannot continue for ever so it was necessary for them to move on.

The strain of extended tours had an adverse effect on Mozart, and this became more obvious on the return journey, which took 18 months. A break in travelling was marked by the production of his opera *Bastien and Bastienne*, but soon after this his father took him to Italy where one of Mozart's prodigious feats of memory occurred (see Chapter 1). He returned home with a commission to produce a work for the Milan opera house and in addition began composing string quartets.

By 18 years Mozart was moving into the period when, if he was merely an "infant prodigy" his talent would have waned, but it was just at this point that he burst forth into a brilliant career of great productivity and creativity.

His later years were marked by many compositions in a variety of genres. The works are so well known that they need not be catalogued here. In spite of the fact he survived a mere 34 years, he is a figure almost without equal, composing in his last weeks the *Requiem Mass*.

The life of Mozart shows certain features which we must bear in mind to see if they are displayed by others. He had a family background of music and possibly an inheritance of talent. His obvious ability at a young age was fostered by his father. Though Mozart is said to have written pieces at the age of four or five years, his early life was naturally mainly concerned with performing music, and from this he moved irrepressibly into the world of composition, where he has a lasting place. His character might have been distorted by the undue attention received as a child. It is said that he did not leave his father's side until 21 years of age (Sadie, 1970). Nevertheless, he was able to develop his abilities and continue until death. He was certainly a musical prodigy, which often implies first, elegance, economy and neatness of style, and second, lack of depth of emotion (Sullivan, 1972). Though Mozart's early years were clearly marked by the former, and some of these characteristics persisted and gave his late compositions their special quality, nevertheless, in adult life his works were certainly not lacking in depth of feeling.

## Beethoven

Beethoven, a contemporary of Mozart and Haydn, also displayed musical ability by his early teens, though it was not to reach fruition until later life. He was born into a family limited in material things but one which had members with musical ability. His grandfather had shown talent, and his father was a tenor singer in the chapel of the Elector of Cologne, a post which brought him a modest income, but he was not a man of distinction like Mozart's father, Leopold. Beethoven had a less systematic training than Mozart. His early life perhaps corresponded most closely to that of Haydn, who though born of impoverished parents was brought up in a home where there was great interest in music. It was a recreation for the family, and Haydn's brother Michael was a musician of significance in his own right. Haydn became a chorister in Vienna and when his voice broke life was one of hardship, as he gradually established himself in a more adult rôle (Redfern, 1970). He nearly became a victim of the barbarous practice of castration, which would almost certainly have robbed us of all the music he wrote.

Beethoven's musical instruction was started by his father at the age of four years and continued until he was nine years. At this time, Pfeiffer, a member of a theatrical company, found lodgings with the family and played with Beethoven to the amazement and delight of passers-by (Valentine, 1969). He learned piano, organ, violin and viola. When $11\frac{1}{2}$ years old he was left as chapel organist by Neefe, his teacher, who thus indicated confidence in his pupil. Beethoven excelled in sight reading and extemporary playing. He had already by the age of 11 years written a funeral cantata on the death of a friend, and at 13 years he composed songs and piano sonatas. A piano quartet written at 15 years is extant in the boy's own script (Valentine, 1958).

Beethoven's early life was marked not only by poverty but by another shadow. His father, like his grandfather, drank heavily and this probably accounts for his lack of proper training. Nevertheless, he certainly was made to practise, if at unorthodox times. It is said that his father returning from the local tavern, having consumed more wine than was good for him, would drag Beethoven from bed in the middle of the night and force him to play. He apparently wanted his son to develop the same reputation as Mozart. With this in mind he falsified his son's age so that the performance could seem the more remarkable. There is no doubt, however, that he did show unusual powers as this contemporary communication reveals, "Louis von Beethoven, son of the tenor singer mentioned, a boy of 11 years and of most promising talent. He plays the clavier very skilfully and with power, reads at sight very well and – to put it in a nutshell – he plays chiefly 'The well-tempered clavichord' of Sebastian Bach, which Herr Neefe puts in his hands. . . . This youthful genius is deserving of help to enable him to travel. He would surely become a second Wolfgang Amadeus Mozart, were he to continue as he began."

On his first visit to Vienna at the age of 17 years Mozart gave him instruction and observed that Beethoven would contribute something for the world to talk about.

Beethoven's determination and staying power are shown by his ability to continue a musical career even at 18 years of age, when he had to take over the responsibility of the family because of the dire financial straits due largely to father's drunkenness. At this time Beethoven had various posts as instrumentalist, conductor and organist but it was also a period marked by composition. This was done not with the fluency and confidence of Mozart but with steady persistence. Indeed, Beethoven's slowness was one of his characteristics which persisted throughout life. He was, however, absolutely dedicated to his music, rising at daybreak and working virtually non-stop until three in the afternoon.

At the age of 22 years he met Haydn who was travelling through Bonn and who encouraged him to go to Vienna. Like Mozart, Beethoven made his reputation there as a performer at gatherings of the nobility. In particular his piano improvisations were prized, because of their precision, perception and taste (Fischer, 1972). His personality was very different and less appealing than that of Mozart. There is no doubt that he was rude and difficult, and he showed earnestness and obstinacy, characteristics that were not endearing. They led to difficulties with Haydn, who Beethoven felt did not treat his composition with sufficient seriousness. Even though his early works do not have the originality of Haydn or the outstanding facility of Mozart, he was developing rapidly under his teacher of counterpoint, Albrechtsberger. Piano sonatas, trios, piano concertos were all early compositions, and before the age of 30 years he had written many trios for various groups of instruments. Beethoven made a great contribution to music, in particular his piano sonatas with the modifications of form that he wrought are superb, as are his magnificent series of symphonies and piano concertos, lasting evidence of his musical talent.

The outstanding point is that Beethoven continued to develop with increasing age against various odds such as his lack of money and loneliness, which was to some extent self-made because of his discordant personality. For example, he often failed to accept help when it was offered. His most remarkable achievement was the continuation of composition in spite of deafness which began in his early 30's and became total. It is difficult to appreciate this disorder because Beethoven surmounted it so effectively, but the idea of a blind painter brings home, by analogy, the crippling nature of his disability (Fischer, 1972). There is no doubt that it exaggerated his personality problems and led to increased isolation. Nevertheless he persisted, so that in his later years he wrote the string quartets which are among his greatest compositions. One might contrast his maturation with Bach who also worked until the end of his days but who seemed more and more to be concerned with pure technique. Bach was deeply religious and perhaps the impact of events on him was less direct. Beethoven is therefore the more remarkable for, in spite of a painful childhood, failure to realise his hope of romantic love, and deafness, he was able to remark on his deathbed "Plaudite, amici comedia finita est" — for the "comedy" had been striving until the very last moment (Sullivan, 1972).

Beethoven continued until his death and there is therefore no indication that he is an example of "early bloom, early fade" (Gardner, 1961). Indeed he probably did not show his best face until later in life. In fact, if he had died prematurely, say at the age of 20 years, we would perhaps not even remember his name. Nevertheless, he did show early ability, even if it was not exceptional, and he is significant because of his perseverance into old age.

Thus, in Beethoven we note the importance of family background of music, and possibly inheritance, a young person of considerable talent who worked hard and who surmounted many obstacles which might have prevented composition in less audacious individuals (Cooper, 1970). He persisted into adult life and made a major contribution to the sphere of music. In the view of Cooper, this is unique because the works from his death to the present time, 150 years later, are still part of the staple of the orchestra, the chamber group, or of whoever plays music. He showed remarkable tenacity in the face of deafness, which to a musician can be crippling, yet in spite of it he continued producing greater and greater works until he died. Beethoven was somewhat different from Mozart in that his early abilities were less striking, and his major works came later in life. He was a "late bloomer" and showed that though musical abilities may not always be as advanced or early as in the case of Mozart, talent is still well developed by the early teens.

## Handel

Handel showed an early interest and aptitude for music which, though not of the level that was displayed by Mozart, was of significance. He was torn between his desire to devote himself to it and his father's wish that he should study law. Handel seems to have made a considerable effort to follow both courses, even after his father's death. By the age of 18 years, however, when he left home for Hamburg, an important musical centre at the time, his face was clearly set for ever on a career of music.

Soon after his death, the *Memoirs of a Life of Handel* written by John Mainwaring were published in 1760. One of the early events Mainwaring related shows Handel's tenacity even at the age of seven years. He had a strong desire to pay a visit with his father to his half-brother (Handel's father had been married before), who was the valet of the Duke of Saxe-Weissensels. Handel's father had decided not to take him, but the young lad set out behind the chaise on foot, and because of the poor roads and other mishaps was able to overtake it. Father was of course displeased with his son's obstinacy but was persuaded, and Handel was taken into the chaise.

This incident is of importance for it shows how determined Handel was and this characteristic was to shape his future. Handel was playing the organ after service and the Duke heard. Something of the manner attracted his attention and he asked his valet who it was. The valet replied that it was his brother and the Duke demanded to see Handel. He then persuaded Handel's father to allow his son to follow a musical career. This seemed clearly the right course, for as Mainwaring wrote, "From his very early childhood Handel had discovered such a strong propensity to music that his father, who had always intended him for the study of the civil law, had reason to be alarmed. Perceiving that this inclination still increased, he took every method to oppose it. He strictly forbade him to meddle with any musical instrument," but, as the well-known story goes, he found means to get a small harpsichord conveyed to the top of the house and played assiduously while the family were asleep.

Handel's doctor father was not lacking in money but he regarded music as a lowly occupation to follow and was reluctant to agree. However, short of "cutting off the boy's hands" there was little he could do to stop Handel, who was given encouragement by the Duke on his departure from Saxe-Weissensels. At last father was persuaded, so on his return home Handel was provided with a teacher called Zackow, under whose direction he learned composition from the age of nine years and was soon composing church services for voices and instruments.

It was decided that he should go at the age of 14 years to a bigger centre. So in 1698 he went to Hamburg, a place where opera was flourishing and there his career blossomed. He then moved to London, where his talent developed the more, so securing him an important place as a figure in the musical world.

Handel therefore had a trait of importance in the developing musician at a remarkably young age, namely that of tenacity. He shows also how performing and composing could both appear even before the age of ten years, the one preceding the other.


## Bach, Johann Sebastian

Bach was born in 1685 in the same year as Handel and less than 100 miles away, but in quite different circumstances. As we have seen, Handel was strongly discouraged from a musical career, whereas music was a natural way of life for every member of the Bach family, perhaps the most remarkable musical family of all time. He received like Mozart, but unlike Beethoven, a thorough grounding in music from his father and brothers. However, his life was not without difficulty early on, and he therefore shows some similarities to Beethoven. By the age of ten years Bach had lost both his parents and he then lived with his elder brother, who was apparently strict. It is said that Bach, anxious to learn all about music, copied out by moonlight the contents of one of his brother's manuscripts. When this was discovered both the original and the copy were taken away.

Bach, like Handel, showed early musical talent, but neither began as early as Mozart, though they certainly indicated promise for the future. Bach came from an unusual family, for his forebears had made, and his sons were to make, significant contributions to music. This kinship is one which shows the inheritance of musical ability most strongly, and though important in the demonstration of early talent, it is by no means the only factor (Chapter 2).

At school Bach was given lessons in composition. He had an excellent singing voice and had written many pieces by his early teens, including chorale preludes. Bach entered the choir of St. Michael's Church at Lüneberg. He became particularly interested in the organ, and used to walk to Hamburg to hear Reinken, a famous organist of the day. Though Handel was actually in Hamburg at this time, Bach and he never met. The reason why is quite clear; Handel was already overwhelmingly attracted by opera and Bach was mainly, but not wholly, devoted to church and organ music. Bach, like all musicians of that time, had to play to make a living, as composition could not be financially rewarding.

Bach continued his musical career throughout his life. Apart from his choral and organ music he produced large numbers of works for harpsichord and clavichord as well as for various instrumental groups. In spite of the fact that Bach is often thought of as an extremely serious composer by many, he had a wide range of human feelings, moments of irrepressible gaiety, deep sorrow expressed in his Passion music, and magnificent splendour in the *B minor Mass*.

To summarise, Bach established his musical ability in his 20's and continued to work for the rest of his days. He inherited talent and had an intensive early musical education. In spite of living in Germany for the whole of that time he shows influences of a variety of contemporary composers. He displays another feature of composers, which is that though not excelling in fields outside music, at least they explore the possibilities of all types of music, ranging from that for the quiet clavichord to the reverberating sonority of full organ, and from the unaccompanied 'cello suites to the large scale magnificence of the *St. Matthew Passion*.

### Are there general trends emerging?

A point has been reached where some general trends appear to emerge from the four biographies selected. To begin with, all were well-known as showing musical talent by their early teens, and secondly, there was no doubt that they were, as adults, in the top rank of composers. However, some of the qualities they reveal must now be tested in a wider context. It is fortunate, therefore, that we have a psychological study based on the biographies of eminent people (Cox, 1926). This investigation came about at the time when Terman was setting up his study on "the gifted child". He selected a group of children of outstanding ability and over the years followed their progress. However, Terman was convinced that the biographies of outstanding people who had lived in the past could yield useful information. This he felt was not recognised by biographers as they had no way of collating details of many individuals and comparing them with those in other fields of endeavour.

Cox's study, entitled "The Early Mental Traits of 300 Geniuses", attempted to do just this. It was based on a selection from a list made by Cattell of a thousand eminent historical figures. The investigation was detailed, with a thorough search of the biographies of each of the individuals. Obviously biographies compiled 50 years ago take no account of the recent work of music scholars including the new discovery of scores, letters and manuscripts. Nevertheless, the details provided by Cox and her colleagues have the merit of a consistent method of collection which is often lacking in biographies. It is difficult to collate the information from these and, in any case, biographers often tend to emphasise or exaggerate the particular significance of the composers they wrote about. There is no doubt that the interest in or the value of a particular composer varies from age to age, but in this review we have tried to reduce such variation by using material which has no bias.

The details of the famous people in Cox's study were obtained by three separate researchers. They confined themselves to leading biographies in English, French and German, and the data were divided into development up to 17 years and between 17 and 26 years. It was systematised under particular headings — family standing, interests, education, school progress and evidence of precocity. Then three psychologists made assessment on this material of the Intelligence Quotients (IQ) of each person. They gave a rating on the individual's life up to the age of 17 years and a second for the period of 17 to 26 years. Of course this method of arriving at the IQ is to some extent suspect, but the fact that agreement was obtained between their assessments is of considerable significance. Further, there was generally a slight increase for the later age-period compared with the earlier, indicating that the influence of special gifts was leading to an increased performance with maturity. It also shows that there was some internal consistency in the method. Here, only the IQ for up to 17 years of age is given.

The group of Cox, apart from figures in the artistic world, included statesmen, scientists, soldiers, religious leaders and philosophers. Writers (poets, novelists and dramatists) were the largest single group, 18 per cent., while musicians were one of the smallest, 4 per cent., not dissimilar to artists, 5 per cent. The list in fact contained 11 notable composers. Their IQs ranged from 110 for Gluck to 155 for Mozart. Towards the lower end of the scale were Palestrina (110), Haydn (120) and Bach (125). At the upper was Handel (145) and Mendelssohn (150). Beethoven (135) was in the middle. It is of note that there are other non-musicians at the bottom of the range, for example Murillo (110), Goldsmith (115), Harvey (120) and Jenner (125). Mendelssohn, although the highest rated of the musicians, is well away from the top of the scale where both John Stuart Mill and Galton obtain values of 200.

In comparison with other groups the composers cited rated relatively lower on intellectual and physical activity as well as social traits, but they scored relatively higher on emotional behaviour than for the total group of eminent men. Musicians had a marked degree of aesthetic feeling, a desire to excel, belief in their own powers and originality of ideas. They had the ability to work towards a distant goal, tenacity in the face of obstacles and showed quiet determination. Like eminent men in general, they had a tendency to rate their own abilities correctly, although their average score in intellectual achievement was slightly below that for the total group of famous men. Their persistence was, however, about average for the whole series.

Of particular interest for us is the conclusion that composers showed greater eminence in their chosen field, in youth, than did any other group. Another point was that to achieve significance subsequently required not only intellectual ability, but also persistence of motive and effort, confidence in their abilities and great strength of character.

The biographies of Cox and her colleagues were re-assessed with a view to determining whether points which emerged from our initial four biographies had some common features. In nearly every case there was evidence of musical ability before 17 years of age and this had been encouraged by musical education. One of the latest to demonstrate his talent was Rossini. Wagner's interest was both in drama and in music. Palestrina, the only musician coming from the 16th century, presents some difficulty because his biographical details are thus less complete. Nevertheless there was some evidence of at least performing ability before the age of 17 years.

In most instances there was an indication not only of performing ability, but also a talent for composition, Gluck and Rossini are two people in whom there is little sign of original work before the age of 17, though they showed considerable talent as performers. There was a tendency for this to precede attempts at composition. However, it may be that the early works have not been preserved, as apart from displaying skill in musical notation they are of little interest, lacking the originality of more mature compositions. In half the instances there was evidence of a familial and possibly an inherited musical trait. Examples include Palestrina, Haydn, Bach, Beethoven, Mendelssohn and Mozart. The attitude of the family to the display of early talent, as has already been shown, was variable, and there are further examples here. Weber was under considerable family pressure. He was lame because of "a disease of the hip bone" and before he could use his legs he was taught to sing and play the clavier. This was at the age of six years before he could write. His father's firm intention was to make his son a musical genius, and if possible a second Mozart. His father's wishes were realised only in part, for though Weber became the founder of German romantic opera he did not reach the stature of Mozart.

Mendelssohn is of significance in two respects. First, he came from a rich and cultured background. His father was a man who did not have any particular musical ability, but his mother was a well educated woman who had remarkable accomplishments in music, art and languages. She gave her son piano lessons when he was very young, and distinguished musicians provided instruction even from the age of seven years. In other words, he had all the encouragement that was possible. This resulted in musical activity as remarkable as that of Mozart. By the age of 17 he had composed two important works, the *Octet for Strings* and the overture to *A Midsummer Night's Dream*, both of which have not only a youthful quality but a flair and originality which not even Mozart or Schubert achieved at the same age (Blunt, 1974). Mendelssohn is also interesting because of a wide range of activities outside the musical field (see below).

It appears therefore that at least some of the ideas that arose from our initial biographies are supported by the work of Cox and her colleagues. There also emerges a suggestion made by Seashore (1938), namely that musicians are "one-sided" in their development, a point now to be examined.

### Are composers one-sided?

If we just consider how varied composers are within the field of music itself we find that they are usually performers of considerable merit. Further, most composers have among their music works of all types. Mozart, Beethoven, Bach and Handel have already been quoted in this connection but there are many others. For example, Purcell, although notable in relation to opera, also wrote church music, arias and incidental music for plays as well as songs, solo works and those for small combinations of instruments. Schubert, in spite of his short life and his particular penchant for song writing, composed choral works and symphonies as well as piano sonatas and chamber works. More recent composers, including Bartok, Britten, Stravinsky and Tippett, have all produced many different types of composition and to this extent musicians, as Révész (1953) wrote, are not "one-sided".

The next point concerns whether or not musicians show ability in other art forms. Of those cited by Cox (1926) only one is noted as showing other "talents". This is Mendelssohn and it is probably of relevance that he is at the top of the suggested IQ ratings. Another contributing factor was his family background of both culture and wealth. He had access to a much wider range of activities than many other budding composers. In addition to music, he took part in physical pursuits such as gymnastics, riding, swimming and dancing as well as the unlikely hobby, at least for a musician, of billiards. He had skilled teachers for a variety of subjects, and he developed proficiency in Latin and Greek. As an amateur he attained a "high degree of perfection" in drawing, and he was a water-colourist of no mean talent. Mendelssohn is not the sole example. Schumann, who had exceptional musical skill, with compositions by the age of 12 years, had great literary ability in his early teens, writing plays and translating the Odes of Horace.

The restricted interest of musicians is partly related to history. It results for example, from the fact that in the 18th century he was a paid servant, not only as a performer and composer, but he was required to organise the groups to play his or other works. With the change in status of the composer, corresponding with the period of romanticism, musicians were liberated. Thus Wagner was both a composer and a master of theatre. Berlioz was a business man and a writer. This liberation has extended to the present day so that architects, painters, singers and even an Olympic athlete are found among the ranks of important musicians.

Why are musicians generally considered to be "one-sided"? Seashore (1938) believes that it relates to their musical education, aesthetic attitude, poetic intuition and life of feeling. For these reasons musicians, according to Seashore, are often impractical both in business and in pursuits which are of social significance, perhaps one of the penalties of specialisation. There is no doubt that long hours of daily practice are necessary if the talented individual is to continue developing. He must use his time most effectively, and this means to the exclusion of other interests. Terman (1926) observed that genius is characterised in children, apart from superior intelligence, by traits of interest, energy, will and character which foreshadow later successful performances in their chosen field. In this connection Gardner (1961) noted that "there is a tyranny of talent which tends to force the narrowing on any one with an extraordinary high ability in a specific line.

Once the talent is developed it is so highly rewarded that the individual is apt to neglect (or not to discover) his other talents, and society abets him in this neglect." Obviously, the low financial reward which many musicians receive, particularly composers, does not usually divert them from their chosen career, which necessitates long hours of devoted effort from an early age. This is well appreciated in any field of musical endeavour but is particularly important for ballet. Certainly it raises important questions in the educational sphere, as gifted young people should have assistance in exploring the whole range of their talents and not be exposed too early to the "tyranny" of one particular type, to the total exclusion of all others.

It is commonly said that genius, a term often applied to composers, is akin to madness. There is, however, little evidence supporting this view, though because of their "one-sided" interests musicians and particularly composers have often been labelled "eccentric". They appear limited to the outsider in their thinking and more mundane in their conversation. One could argue that the more varied the composer's social intercourse, the more varied would be his music. Such a generalisation is difficult to support or to refute. However, because of the nature of music itself, especially its non-verbal component, being articulate in a literary sense may add little. Indeed Schubert is an example of someone who was totally devoted to music, but in spite of this he was able to speak through his music, beguilingly in a varied and cultivated way, to the musician and the non-musician alike (Cooper, 1975). Perhaps then, the one-sidedness of composers is not a disadvantage and may allow them to develop in ways that would not be possible if their talent was dispersed in a variety of directions.

Musical talent is rather exceptional in that it manifests itself at a much younger age than abilities in other artistic fields, and this is one aspect of the "one-sided" development already mentioned. Though graphic artists may show early talent for drawing, only exceptionally do they produce works which go on public view before their early teens. One outstanding exception in art is Dürer, whose ability is revealed in a self-portrait done at 13 years. Picasso represents a contemporary example. Chatterton in the literary world and Pascal in the mathematical field are other examples, as are John Stuart Mill and Galton who could both read at an early age, the latter even before he could speak. It is of interest that Mainwaring (1760) made a comparison between Handel and Pascal. He wrote "just to remind him (the reader) of the minute and surprising resemblance between these passages in the early periods of Handel's life and some which are recorded in that of the celebrated Monsieur Pascal written by his sister. Nothing can equal the bias of the one to mathematics but the bias of the other to music."

These few examples contrast with the wealth of composers whose biographies are almost monotonous in citing outstanding early expression of talent. One other difference between musical prodigies compared with manifestation of ability in other fields is the fact that the former less often fade into oblivion and usually continue to flourish artistically until old age.

## An unselected group of musicians

Various points thus seem to emerge as to the early expression of musical talent. However, some further investigation is needed, because attention has so far been devoted to figures of outstanding importance, and no systematic attempt has been made to compare them with those in other fields of artistic activity. To do this we selected those in the musical sphere whose surnames began with the letter "B". It is known that many famous composers' names begin with "B", but there are many other less well-known composers as well. To keep the investigation to a manageable size, the index of a musical textbook was used (Colles, 1956). This was obviously an arbitrary choice and, in particular, the list ends at the beginning of the 20th century. This means that Bax, Berg, Bliss and Butterworth do not feature, but the assessment of recent and contemporary composers is in any case difficult. Thus we have concentrated on figures of former times and about whom there is less doubt of their overall place.

The details of the resulting series were then studied in the *Encyclopaedia Britannica* (1972 edition) with a view to determining facts concerning early ability, family background and other notable features of development in adult life. To compare the achievements of the musicians with those in other artistic areas, the next appropriate entry was examined, *i.e.* those relating to painters, sculptors and poets. As with other compendia the *Encyclopaedia Britannica* tends not to take account of the most recent data. However, it was chosen since presumably there is a consistency in the entries for musicians and non-musicians alike. The information is therefore comparable. The list obtained, of course, included Johann Sebastian Bach, three other members of the Bach family, Beethoven, Berlioz and Brahms, as well as figures of lesser rank such as Bellini, Bizet and Boccherini. English personages were Blow, Boyce and Byrd, while from the 19th century there were Balfe, Sterndale Bennett and Bishop. Clearly this type of study presents difficulties since information from earlier times may be incomplete, as in the case of John Bennet and Buxtehude. Nevertheless the method is not invalidated because the same argument presumably applies to the non-musical group.

The musicians show a marked tendency to have a family background of musical interest, and where this was the case, one of the parents was responsible for the early education. Apart from the Bachs, this holds true for Balakirev, Bellini, Boccherini and Brahms. For the earlier composers there is a fairly consistent pattern. They were choristers from an early age, and then they often became organists. Blow, Boyce, Bull and Byrd followed this pattern and so did Sterndale Bennett in the 19th century. Brahms is of interest for, though his father was a double-bass player, the family were improverished and it fell upon Brahms to play in his teens in order to earn money to supplement the family income (Dale, 1970). Bizet was the son of a hairdresser married to a singing teacher who was responsible for his early instruction. Berlioz's career bears some similarity to that of Handel, for he was under pressure from his parents to study medicine rather than music, and he made an attempt to do both. Von Bülow is a figure of note in late 19th century music. He was entirely interpretative in talent, being both a pianist and a conductor as well as being responsible for the first production of Wagner's *Tristan*.

Sterndale Bennett, though an Englishman, was a figure of international importance, both as a pianist and composer. By the age of 16 years he was producing several orchestral works each year. At 22 he started an arduous career as a teacher and, soon after, began to experience difficulty with completion of works. Not only was there a falling-off in quantity, but, for some unexplained reason, also in quality. Nevertheless he has not received due recognition for his diversity and originality, which included songs of considerable merit (Temperley, 1975). The composer Bishop, although remembered only for the song *Home, Sweet Home*, showed considerable talent in composition in his teens, writing music for theatrical productions at the age of 18 years and he was in this respect an important composer of his time. Balakirev, who emerged in the search, is one of an interesting group of five 19th century Russian musicians (the majority do not have "B" as the initial letter of their surname). Balakirev showed ability and received early musical education from his mother. He was the only one of the group who was intent upon a musical career. In contrast, Cui was an engineer, Moussorgsky an army officer, Rimsky-Korsakov a naval officer, and Borodin a chemist. This group was never associated with the contemporary Tchaikovsky, who is unusual in that his first intention was to become a lawyer, and he did not begin to study music seriously until later.

A pattern therefore emerges which is rather less homogeneous than has already been seen, but the striking feature of early demonstration of musical talent does continue to appear in a wide variety of individuals destined to become composers of note.

*Comparison with other artistic fields*

The non-musicians who came to light from the *Encyclopaedia Britannica* search consisted mainly of writers, novelists and poets, with smaller numbers of painters and sculptors. Though some of the figures are of a relatively unimportant nature, the group included the writers Arnold Bennett, Hilaire Belloc and Baudelaire, the painter Boccioni, and the sculptor Borromini. There are few mentions of artistic creative ability before the age of 20 years, with no particular family interest in the chosen field, with the exception of one novelist who was the son of a painter. Borromini was trained as a stone-cutter from the age of nine years and Boccioni worked from the age of 16 as an artist. On the whole the earliest works of such members of this group as Baudelaire and Belloc were published in their early 20's. However, like the musical group, having selected a particular career, they generally pursued it throughout the rest of their lives, and they did not show great diversity of interests in fields other than the one of their particular choice.

This study clearly supports the view that composers demonstrate evidence of musical ability as performers usually before puberty and in many instances even before the age of five years. Those in other fields develop their talents after puberty rather than before, and may not be in evidence until their early 20's. However, neither the musical nor the non-musical groups appear to be greatly diverse in their interests. That is neither is more "one-sided" than the other, a finding which is borne out by general observation. For example, there are very few individuals who are sufficiently skilled at both writing and painting to reach standards of excellence which render them of international repute.

*"The ripeness of time"*

The period of history in which the creative artist finds himself is of supreme importance, as Koestler (1967) remarked, not only in relation to art but also to science, there being a "ripeness of time" for a particular innovation. Obviously creative activity operates against the background of contemporary ideas and styles (Scott, 1970), a view which does not detract from the originality of the scientist or musician who makes a sudden discovery or perfects a new form of composition.

One particular musical example will suffice. Charles II returned to England from exile, which he had spent in France. He was there accustomed to gay dances, ballets and masquerades, while in England, as a result of puritanism, theatres had been forbidden and elaborate cathedral music suppressed. It was a dull place for him, so he re-opened the Chapel Royal and put the choir under Captain Henry Cooke. However, the music seemed uninteresting, and Charles sent one of his choristers, Pelham Humfrey, to France for study under Lully, for whom he had a high regard. Humfrey was only 17 years old at the time and was considered, on the basis of works he had already produced, as the most promising composer in the choir, where Wise, Blow and Turner were his contemporaries. Humfrey's life was brief. He died at the age of 27 years. However, in the meantime he had a great influence on music, establishing a distinctive English style. In addition, through teaching he perhaps exercised an even greater effect, as he succeeded Cooke as Master of the Chapel Royal. Among the choristers at that time was Purcell (Dennison, 1974). He, like Humfrey, was a young and talented musician, exposed to European influences in an environment in which change and innovation were prized. Purcell clutched at this opportunity and produced a great variety of music which was appreciated in his day, and though he was forgotten in the 18th and 19th centuries, the present century has seen a great revival of interest. He has even been considered as the musical equivalent of Shakespeare. Had he lived in another age with different influences one can only speculate on his possible potential.

*Performers and conductors*

It is helpful to divide musicians into those predominantly concerned with composing and those who represent the interpretative side of the art, either as performers or conductors. However, most musicians in earlier times had to perform to earn a living, as composition is something which produces monetary reward only in later life and initially must be produced by an inner drive, and with little social reinforcement. There were composers who wrote works in which they themselves could perform, and obtain not only the fee for the piece but also for their playing. Further, performing in most composers acted as part of their musical education and formed a spring-board for their subsequent development. So obviously access to an instrument is important, and it seems that the budding composer himself realises this, both Handel and Mahler early in life secretly finding something on which to play. Others have been denied this at an early age, for example, Leonard Bernstein, and it appears there that progress was hindered rather than blocked. On the other hand Berlioz, the outstanding orchestral virtuoso, played the flageolet and guitar and certainly not the piano, which is often regarded as the best compromise in the absence of an orchestra.

Some composers, like Bach, Bartok, Chopin and Mahler, first attracted attention through their interpretative rather than their composing abilities. Some remained important as performers throughout their lives, including Chopin and Liszt who were fêted in their time for this reason rather than their composition. Liszt had a prodigious talent, as though music was his native tongue. He found his way to the piano and could improvise long before he could read. His father was his first teacher (Walker, 1971).

Rubenstein is another example of someone who was to become an outstanding performer. He was taught the piano by his mother and gave his first public recital at the age of ten years. Later, he continued as a virtuoso performer and conductor as well as producing important compositions. Paganini is also notable. He was giving concerts at the age of 11 years and he remained a highly skilful violinist all his life. His music was rather limited in appeal but, nevertheless, his virtuoso playing widened the horizons of his instrument and created a style and method of playing that has never been surpassed (Wechsberg, 1973). In addition, his technique influenced piano and orchestral playing as a whole.

There are truly great musicians for whom performing is their métier. One such is Pablo Casals. He devoted himself exclusively to one instrument, the 'cello, and transformed the whole art of the way that it is played. Casals is of interest because he displayed early talent and in his teens rebelled against the teaching on the way the 'cello should be held, playing it with his arm away from the side (Kirk, 1975). About this time he discovered the Bach works for solo 'cello, sometimes regarded as difficult to appreciate, but he made them "live" in a remarkable manner. Casals showed great persistence, for he practised these Bach pieces daily and continued to do so until the end of his life at 97 years of age. He therefore persisted with his playing not only into maturity but also into extreme old age. He composed some works, but though he himself regarded them as being of importance, it seems likely that he will be remembered as a performer of excellence, one who transformed his chosen instrument.

Casals survived to old age and had the advantage, like most composers who live for a long time, of the opportunity to receive recognition. There are, however, some like Arriaga, Thomas Linley and George Frederick Pinto who showed prodigious talent and yet barely survived into their twenties. They might, had they lived, be remembered in the same way as Bach, Mozart or Beethoven, but it was not to be. On the other hand, Schubert is an example of an outstanding musical talent who not only started young (Einstein, 1971), in fact as young and as brilliantly as Mozart, but continued to develop. He died at 31 years before many in a non-musical field have really begun to flourish. Yet he is an outstanding musical figure remembered not just for his exceptional songs but for a wide range of solo, chamber and orchestral works.

Conducting as a separate musical profession is a relatively recent innovation, and it is this particular role which established Mahler on the musical scene. It is recounted that at the age of five years he could not be found. After a long search he was discovered strumming on an old piano. As a result he was encouraged by his father who arranged music lessons. He said of himself, cited by Blaukopf (1973), "From my 4th year on I had always made music, I was composing before I could play scales". Unfortunately, as with many composers, nothing remains of his early works and his first extant composition, *Das Klagend Lied* for choir and orchestra, dates from the age of 20 years. His conducting began when he was 21 years old with the opening performance at the Landestheater in Laibach, now Lubliana. His major compositions, though first appearing in his 20's, mainly appeared after he was 40 years old. However, the double role of composer-conductor continued throughout his life. He conducted many famous orchestras including the Vienna Philharmonic and, in his last years, the New York Philharmonic.

So far we have concentrated on "serious" music but it is quite evident that early musical talent appears also in the popular sphere. One of the most remarkable examples concerns the Viennese waltz composers (Wechsberg, 1973). Lanner, the son of a glovemaker, was the first in the line of Viennese composer-performers. He taught himself the violin by observing others playing and joined an orchestra in his early teens. Composition he learned from books, in fact the total *Autodiktat*. His waltzes were melodious and sentimental, in contrast to the fire, life and boisterous movement of the Strauss family, who raised this popular art form to one of its highest peaks. Johann Strauss senior, like Lanner, was self-taught. His tavern-keeping father wanted Johann to be a bookbinder. However, following his father's suicide, he was at last able to get hold of an instrument, begged from his step-father. He practised hard and, in spite of an unhappy time as an apprentice bookbinder, by 15 years of age he had joined the Pamar Orchestra, in which Lanner had also played. Strauss, a contemporary of Paganini, ran a large organisation as well as composing new pieces for each grand occasion. He toured widely, at home and abroad, so that his sons Johann, Josef and Eduard rarely had much contact with him. All were eventually to become musicians, playing the violin, conducting and composing.

There was always a sound of music in the house and father's instruments were available. Yet father Johann actually attempted to keep music away from the boys. His desire was for Johann junior, who is now the member of the Strauss family regarded most highly, to be a banker, and Josef an architect and engineer. Frau Strauss recognised the young Johann's talent and she wrote a tune *First Thoughts* which the boy played on a table piano at the age of six years. She arranged secretly for violin lessons from Franz Amon who taught Johann, it is said, to practise in front of the mirror so that an elegant posture and movement could be obtained. The father discovered his son playing and took away the instrument, which was returned surreptitiously by his mother. Johann the younger had two years of instruction in book-keeping and banking, but by the time his father moved out of the family home, after the marriage was over, Johann junior had decided firmly on a musical career. Here we again see obstinacy and persistence shown by someone who displayed early musical talent. It was not long before he had formed his own orchestra and begun a career writing waltzes and, later, operettas including *Die Fledermaus*. There was great rivalry between father and son, each running his own orchestra. The father was never reconciled to this, but the son always had a deep feeling of respect for his father and played his compositions at concerts. When his father died, Johann junior took over the Strauss family orchestra, continuing his career as the "Waltz Emperor".

The tradition of Viennese light music still continues. Robert Stolz, who died in 1975, was a child prodigy and played the piano at the age of ten years to Brahms. At 19 years he heard the music of Johann Strauss junior. This particularly appealed to him, and he remained faithful to that tradition throughout his life, his most famous operetta being *White Horse Inn*.

### The "success rate" in the talented

From what has gone before it is clear that early display of talent in famous composers is the rule rather than the exception. However, in some it reaches an exceptional level and emerges at a very early age. To these individuals the term prodigy is then applied. Mozart obviously falls into this category. We are fortunate in having some historical evidence about the "success rate" in this group, because Barrington (1781) published an account not only of Mozart but also of four other children who were exceptionally talented musically. They were the Wesley brothers, Charles and Samuel, W. H. Crotch and Lord Mornington, thus making a series of five in all.

The Wesley brothers came from a distinguished family. Their father was the Rev. Charles Wesley, the hymn-writer, and their uncle the Rev. John Wesley, the founder of Methodism. Charles Wesley picked out tunes on the harpsichord before three years of age and continued to increase in ability, composing pieces by six years. Barrington reported that when a stranger arrived at the house Charles would ask "Is he a *Musiker*?" If the answer was "yes" then he was willing to play. Both Stanley and Boyce, well-known musicians of the day, were impressed by his ability, but as he grew older, though attaining a certain degree of excellence as an organist, he failed to live up to his early promise. His compositions were of little lasting interest.

Charles' younger brother Samuel was somewhat later in displaying ability. He listened to his brother playing the violin and would beat out the rhythm. He was composing almost as soon as he could read. This he learned by studying the scores of Handel's oratorios. He played the organ by the age of six or seven and soon gave public performances. Boyce said that he was an English Mozart and was impressed not only by his improvisation but by his oratorio *Ruth*, completed by the age of eight years. Barrington witnessed Samuel's ability at just under ten. His sight reading was not only accurate and neat but in true taste. When given "lessons", which according to a publisher friend of Barrington were unplayable, the boy boggled but made a good try, which was completely accurate on the second attempt. He later said that the pieces were "queer and awkward". Samuel was also taken to an organ with quarter tones and soon mastered the unusual qualities. His first composition, *Lessons for Harpsichord*, was published when he was 12. Unfortunately he suffered a head injury in his youth which may have impaired creativity. Certainly, his later years were marked by periods of illness which were probably of a depressive type. Nevertheless, he wrote a magnificent choral work, *In Exile Israel*, and pioneered the symphony in England. He also composed much church music and was regarded as one of the great organists of his day, his extemporary playing being especially prized. Nonetheless, one must say that his achievements did not match his promise, though some musicologists today consider his works as being of considerable interest and that his significance has been under-rated.

Crotch was a remarkable youngster who picked out the tune *God Save Great George Our King* at the age of $2\frac{1}{4}$ years on an organ his father made. Both Burney and Barrington examined him, the latter when he was $3\frac{1}{2}$ years. His fingers could barely cover a fifth and yet he was able to play with agility. He had considerable aural ability in that he could identify wrong notes deliberately played in chords. Crotch was introduced to Samuel Wesley who was some seven years his elder and he was asked to play a piece composed by Wesley. At first, out of pique, he refused. However, later when requested to play the treble he not only did so but also added the bass. Crotch continued his musical career as an organist and composer to a limited extent, but his life was mainly academic. He became Professor of Music at Oxford at 21 years and first Principal of the Royal Academy of Music. In addition, he was a water-colourist of no mean ability (Chapter 14).

Rennert (1975) has recently reassessed the place of Crotch and compared him with Mozart, his contemporary. It is at once clear that, "though both performed astonishing feats when very young, their later childhoods and their adult lives differed radically. Mozart composed music which has survived two centuries of popularity, though he died young and a pauper. Crotch settled down into a comfortable academic life, honoured by his contemporaries, dying in old age, but leaving to posterity only a comparatively small number of musical compositions, most of them containing both fine craftsmanship and much originality – but little that could be called genius."

The last prodigy to be reported by Barrington was Mornington. He showed an early interest in music. He was delighted by the sound of a violin playing while in his nurse's arms and would beat time before he could speak. He became a respected academic, his compositions were mainly glees which were successful in their day. Even now he is still known for the chant, *Mornington in E flat*. However, he must be thought of as an unsuccessful composer.

These five all showed remarkable early musical ability and in their various ways all continued in a musical career. There is no doubt that only one could be regarded as highly accomplished as a composer – Mozart. We can therefore have a broad estimate of "success-rate", with one in five reaching an exceptional standard in adult life.

At a later date, some children with exceptional musical ability have been studied in detail, for example Pepito Areola (Richet, 1900). He is of interest because his ability arose apparently without any direct influence by parents, though his mother had played the piano at the age of five years. At about $2\frac{1}{2}$ years of age Pepito picked out tunes on the piano, perhaps those he had heard his mother singing though some were apparently original. Richet found that at $3\frac{1}{2}$ years he was able to execute 20 pieces with appropriate harmonies in spite of his small hands. He had a feeling for improvisation but hated correction and refused to play on any instrument other than his mother's piano. Pepito's ability continued to develop as he grew older, but though reaching professional status he did not fulfil his early promise.

Révész (1925) had the opportunity of studying a gifted child over a period of some six years. The child, Erwin Nyiregyhazy, came from a musical family, his father and grandfather both having been singers in the chorus of the Royal Opera in Budapest. His mother also possessed musical talent and his younger brother had a feeling for rhythm and a good musical memory. Erwin could sing tunes correctly in his second year and was composing melodies in his third year. By the age of four he had begun to play everything he heard on the piano. He also had the ability to improvise. Piano lessons began in his fifth year and on a regular basis at the age of six years, when he entered the Academy of Music. Révész tested him at the age of seven years and found he had absolute pitch, and was thus able to name notes whether played to him on a piano or a stringed instrument, and he could sing a particular note on request. He could analyse chord sequences. Further, he had a remarkable facility for transposition. Erwin was given a fairly complex five bar passage which he was asked to read but not play until he had memorised it. This took 6½ minutes and then he was able to reproduce it on the piano without a mistake. His excellent musical memory is illustrated by the fact that he played it two years later faultlessly. An original work was composed at the age of eight years, similar in style to that which Mozart wrote at about the same age. Nevertheless, Révész concludes that Erwin, though gifted, was not in the category of genius. Indeed, like Areola, also a professional, he did not mature to become a musician of great stature (Shuter, 1968).

There are other comments on the success-rate of child prodigies. For example, Nicholas Slonimsky (1948) reported on their outcome, observations which are of particular interest since he had been a gifted child musician himself. He estimated that only ten per cent. of prodigies became adult virtuosi. On the other hand Drake (1957) estimated that 70 per cent. of great violinists showed exceptional early ability. Clearly then, there are difficulties of definition both of what constitutes exceptional talent in a child, and what can be regarded as a "successful" adult career. Nevertheless from the biographies already cited it can be seen that children with precocious musical ability often mature into adult musicians of importance. Thus it is a talent which should be encouraged in the young (see below).

### The stages of development of talent

At this point we are now able to trace the sequence of events which occurs in the development of young, musically talented individuals. The basic features are either the inheritance of this talent or its spontaneous appearance. Whether he is the first or a later child in the family is not significant, but if the child is a male he seems more more likely to be successful. An important requirement is early access to a musical instrument. Obviously if one is not available this lack may retard rather than block progress. The young musician then begins to practise, and as his ability develops it is appreciated by both family and friends. This usually leads to even more active encouragement and arrangements for musical education, often undertaken initially by the parents or an older brother. Of course, as we have seen, strong discouragement may ensue, although in some instances this reinforces rather than dissuades the young musician. Clearly if maturation of the talents is to take place, parallel development of the personality is important, particularly confidence, tenacity and zeal. He must possess determination to succeed and be capable of sustained effort. Performing skills precede those of composition, and exposure to the rigours of public performance occurs at a much earlier age than is usual in most other creative spheres. He must be capable of facing an audience without undue nervousness, besides the intense practice which is required. Soon the cost of failure will become apparent. Most virtuoso performers have appeared in public in their early teens, that is before puberty, at a time when it is rare for musical ability to display itself for the first time.

At this point two curious features must be mentioned. First, the predominance of males in the musical world, certainly in the past. However, the number of female orchestral players has been steadily increasing. There are also now notable women composers. The other point concerns the reason why musical talent often emerges so early in life and shows rapid development. Though there is no true explanation some answers can be suggested. In part it relates to how psychologists view mental ability. On the whole emphasis has been placed on general intelligence. However, it seems unlikely that any single global concept can account for the extremely varied development found (Vernon, 1962). Consequently special factors have been advanced to explain the appearance of certain faculties. We may contrast, for example, music and the classics. In the former, special factors are important, while in the latter general intelligence is of greater significance. It may also account for the observation that at a time when a child is just beginning to develop language, he may be exhibiting musical ability at an advanced level. The second explanation to some extent follows. Music, by its abstract and formal nature, creates its own material, material not so dependent on words as in some of the other artistic spheres. Neither does it spring from the experience of life and the interaction with others. On the emotional side, the young musician has free rein within the musical world. In contrast, writing a play or a novel requires an intimate knowledge of a wide range of human emotion and experience, not as a rule available to the young.

The late teens bring the crucial phase. It is essential at this time that he displays a marked development of talent. Such transition from the precocious youngster to the adult musician was even more difficult in the past than today; for talented individuals were often choristers, and they were suddenly faced with the "adult" world when their voices broke. This period of transition is frequently associated with leaving home and a move to a musical centre. There he is exposed to the pressures of intensive instruction, without the support of a close family circle, and for the first time he submits to the wider public and greater competition. It is no longer the question of tasteful, neat performances. Instead there is the awesome emptiness of the concert platform, where a very different scale of ability is expected.

A flurry of works usually emerges from the composer's pen. Though they may have produced numerous works by this stage of their lives, these *juvenilia*, as in other art fields, are of little lasting import. Nevertheless, by the early 20's, major compositions begin to emerge.

As to the outcome of those who have displayed ability early, there are three varieties. First, one in which failure is almost complete. Here music may become just a hobby and a livelihood is achieved by some other means. At the other extreme, there are those whose early success continues not only into maturity but, in spite of adversity, often to the final days of life. Between these two extremes there are many possibilities. Perhaps a life devoted mainly to teaching, writing and academic pursuits, or one principally as a performer of greater or lesser merit, with little or no composing ability, so that works which may reach public performance are of relatively minor significance in the overall world of music. The chances of reaching the status of a Bach or Mozart are small, but of becoming a successful orchestral performer greater; hence the need for encouragement in the young who show obvious talent.

## Conclusion

In this account of those who show musical ability early in life we have merely hinted at some of the interesting facets and have used but a fraction of the information available. The material has tended to imply that early display of talent occurred in previous centuries. However, late 19th-century composers like Saint Saëns, Richard Strauss and Hindemith were all figures of importance who were precocious in displaying exceptional talent. In the present century Barber, Britten, Shostakovitch and Walton all displayed outstanding ability early in life and later became composers of international repute. Yehudi Menuhin showed exceptional aptitude for the violin before school age and soon performed in public, continuing to do so throughout his life. Further, though this account has concentrated largely on serious music, jazz musicians also show precocity (Chilton, 1970). For example, Earl Hines played the cornet from an early age and began a study of piano seriously at the age of nine years. Jelly Roll Morton played before his feet could reach the pedals. Duke Ellington began serious piano studies at the age of seven, but was attracted to ragtime in his late teens and elected to pursue the role of a popular musician.

Musical ability is therefore not just something in the past; it is, as Révész (1953) noted, a common phenomenon in children of today. Many who show exceptional musical talent could thus make a significant contribution to the overall world of music and creative art in general. They are of importance both for the enrichment of cultural life and the intellectual enjoyment of all.

What then should be the attitude towards these talented children? It is clear that they must be given instruction early on if they are to develop, and nowadays they are referred to by the educationalists as "gifted" children who require special attention. There are sophisticated tests of musical ability, for example those of Wing (1970), which can be applied, but their precise validity at predicting success is less certain. Both the professional musician Cortot (1935) and the psychologist Terman (1926) have noted that interest and devotion appear to be of greater importance for success than actual ability. The gifted child requires something over and above the ordinary school curriculum, otherwise he may become bored if not totally disillusioned (*Brit. med. J.* (Editorial) 1975). It seems that only with constant encouragement, expert tuition and the right atmosphere can development take place. Then many will, at least, have the opportunity to be successful. If appropriate educational facilities are not provided they may well not mature. Nevertheless, in spite of everything it seems likely that the outstanding children of today will, as hitherto, take care of themselves and become important composers and performers in the future.

## REFERENCES

*General*

*Encyclopaedia Britannica* (1972) London, William Benton.
GROVE, G. (1954) *Dictionary of Music and Musicians*, 5th edition, ed. Eric Blom. London, Macmillan.

*Specific*

BARRINGTON, DAINES (1779) Account of a very remarkable musician. *Philosophical Transactions*, **60**, 54.
— (1781) *Miscellanies*. London, Nichols.
BLAUKOPF, K. (1973) *Gustav Mahler*. London, Futura.
BLOM, ERIC (1974) *Mozart* (revised edition). London, Dent.
BLUNT, W. (1974) *On Wings of Song: a biography of Felix Mendelssohn*. London, Hamish Hamilton.
CHILTON, J. (1970) *Who's Who of Jazz*. London, Bloomsbury Book Shop.
COLLES, H. C. (1956) *The Growth of Music*. Oxford, Clarendon Press.
COOPER, MARTIN (1970) *Beethoven, The Last Decade*. London, Oxford University Press.
— (1975) In a world of their own. *Daily Telegraph*, Saturday, August 30th.

CORTOT, A. (1935) Do infant prodigies become great musicians? *Music and Letters*, **16**, 124.

COX, C. M. (1926) *Genetic Studies of Genius*, Vol. 11, *The Early Mental Traits of Three Hundred Geniuses*. Stanford, California and London, Stanford University Press.

DENNISON, PETER (1974) Pelham Humfrey, 1647–74, A tercentenary survey. *Musical Times*, **115**, 553.

DALE, KATHLEEN (1970) *Brahms*. Bingley, London.

DRAKE, R. M. (1957) *Manual for the Drake Musical Aptitude Tests*. Chicago, Science Research Associates.

Editorial (1975) Gifted children. *Brit. med. J.*, **3**, 394.

EINSTEIN, A. (1971) *Schubert*. London, Panther.

FISCHER, H. C. (1972) *Beethoven*. London, Macmillan.

GARDNER, J. W. (1961) *Excellence*. New York, Harper.

HARDING, R. E. M. (1967) *An Anatomy of Inspiration*. London, Frank Cass.

KIRK, H. L. (1975) *Pablo Casals*. London, Hutchinson.

KOESTLER, A. (1967) *The Act of Creation*. London, Heinemann.

MAINWARING, J. (1760) *Memoirs of the Life of the Late George Frederick Handel*. London, Bodeley.

REDFERN, BRIAN (1970) *Haydn*, London, Bingley.

RENNERT, J. (1975) *William Crotch (1775–1847) Composer, Artist, Teacher*. Dalton, Lavenham, Suffolk.

RÉVÉSZ, G. (1925) *The psychology of a musical prodigy*, New York, Harcourt Brace.

—— (1953) *Introduction to the Psychology of Music*. London, Longmans Green.

RICHET, G. (1900) Note sur un cas remarquable de précocité musicale. IV Congrés Internationale de Psychologie.

SADIE, STANLEY (1970) *Mozart*. London, Calder and Boyars.

SCOTT, DONALD (1970) *The Psychology of Work*. London, Duckworth.

—— (1974) *Fire and Fire Raisers*. London, Duckworth.

SEASHORE, C. E. (1938) *The Psychology of Music*. London, McGraw-Hill.

SHUTER, ROSAMUND (1968) *The Psychology of Musical Ability*. London. Methuen.

SLONIMSKY, N. (1948) Musical children: prodigies or monsters? *Étude*, **66**, 591.

SULLIVAN, J. W. N. (1972) *Beethoven. His Spiritual Development*. London, Unwin.

TEMPERLEY, N. (1975) Sterndale Bennett and the Lied I, *Musical Times*, **116**, 958.

TERMAN, L. M. (1926) Foreword to Cox, C. M. (q.v.).

VALENTINE, E. (1958) *Beethoven*. London, Thames and Hudson.

—— (1969) *Beethoven and His World*. London, Thames and Hudson.

WALKER, ALAN (1971) *Liszt*. London, Faber and Faber.

VERNON, P. E. (1962) *Intelligence and Cultural Environment*. London, Methuen.

WECHSBERG, J. (1973) *The Waltz Emperors*. London, Weidenfeld and Nicolson.

WING. H. (1970) *Tests of Musical Ability and Appreciation*. Cambridge, The University Press.

# 12

G. HARRER and
H. HARRER

## *Music, Emotion and Autonomic Function*

It has been known for many years that perceptual and emotional musical experiences lead to changes in blood pressure, pulse rate, respiration, the psycho-galvanic reflex and other autonomic functions. These autonomic changes represent the vegetative reflections of psychological processes. The nature and extent of such somatic changes, as well as the determining factors, have been accurately analysed by the use of modern recording techniques.

Our extensive and detailed investigations have led us to the following conclusions.

1. The autonomic response depends on (a) its reactivity, that is the lability or stability of the autonomic regulatory processes. This in turn is influenced by constitution (predisposition), age, sex, mode of life, physical fitness, general state of health, or such temporary factors as fatigue, drinking alcohol or coffee, and so on; (b) emotional reactivity; and (c) attitudes toward music, the importance of music in the subject's life, and also upon his immediate attitude towards the piece of music presented in the test situation.

The subject's current attitude can be disturbed by the setting of the test (the laboratory and the use of apparatus), but individual associative ties with the piece of music may also lead to spurious results. In this case such changes as are observed may be due to an event which the subject associates with the music rather than to the music itself. For these reasons subjects must be familiar with the laboratory setting and, furthermore, pieces of music unknown to them should preferably be presented with subsequent exploration of their attitudes, personal impressions resulting from the music and associations with other events.

Figure 1a shows the marked autonomic changes which occurred when the subject was completely involved in the piece of music which was being presented. When the same piece of music is critically analysed by the same subject, that is, without emotional involvement, these autonomic changes are not demonstrable (Figure 1b). Nevertheless, the enjoyment of music may be just as profound. In individuals with a musical background and

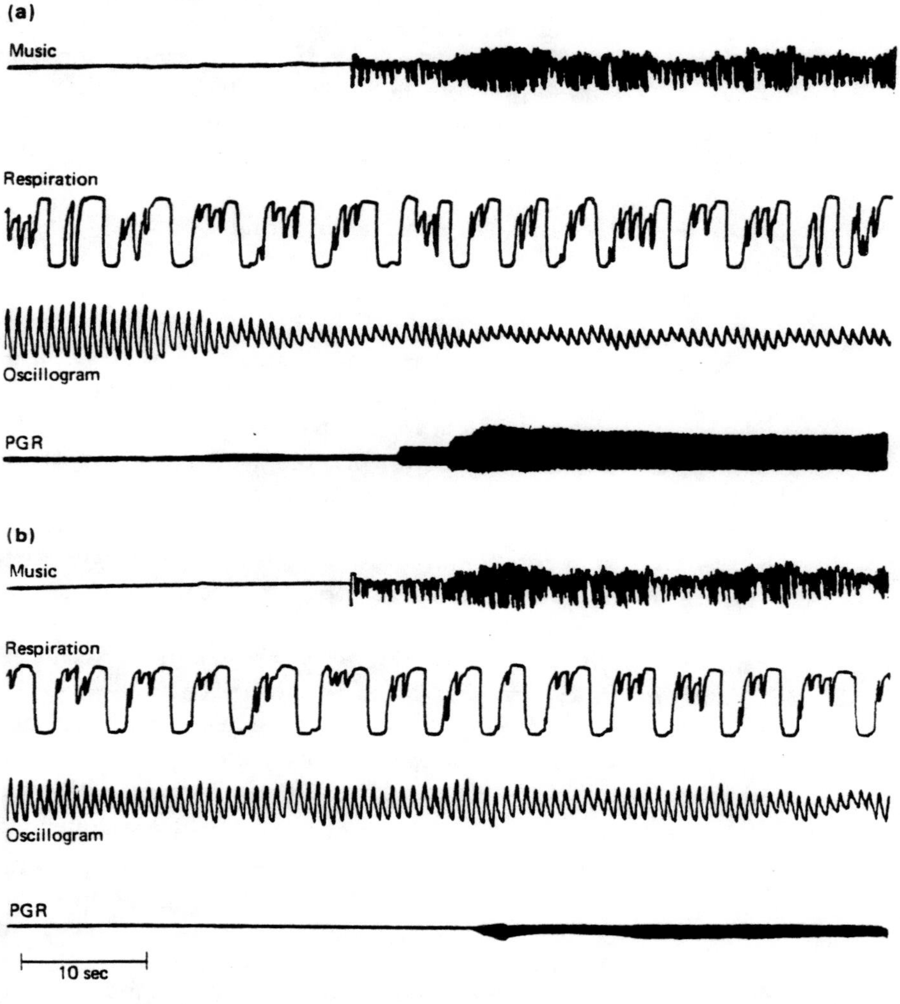

**(a)**

Music

Respiration

Oscillogram

PGR

**(b)**

Music

Respiration

Oscillogram

PGR

├─── 10 sec ───┤

Figure 1 Vegetative Diagram. (a) with and (b) without emotional involvement.

education the aesthetics of a piece of music may be experienced even more pleasurably by an objective rather than a subjective approach.

Music may lead to an autonomic reaction although the sounds are not consciously perceived, for example, in sleep, with "background" music such as incidental music for plays and films, and "functional" music which is provided in places like factories, elevators and milking parlours.

The nature and extent of the autonomic changes also depend upon (d) the kind of music which is presented. The nature of a subject's perception of music depends upon his prevailing attitude, indifferent or emotional, towards the music, his manner of listening and on his current mood, *inter alia*. The reproduction of music should be technically impeccable and the sound volume must be adjusted for each subject. Arbitrary changes in the sound volume made by the person who is testing may change the autonomic diagram.

2. The system of maximal response (comparing cardiovascular with respiratory and galvanic skin responses) depends mainly on (a) the character of the subject's individual autonomic response. In some persons psychological stimuli such as stress give rise to respiratory changes predominantly, whereas in others marked circulatory or galvanic skin response alterations are elicited by the same type of stimuli; (b) the type of music which is being played. There are pieces of music such as dance music or orchestral marches which produce predominantly motor responses, while other types of music are more liable to elicit respiratory or cardiovascular responses. The resulting autonomic diagram is based upon the effectiveness of factors (a) and (b) and reflects both the reactivity of a certain system of organs and the "organotropism" of the piece of music which has been presented.

3. There are marked differences in reactivity between the performer and listener. As to the former, reactions due to physical strain must be separated from those which reflect the emotional accompaniment. The extent of the emotionally induced changes is often surprisingly great. During the act of conducting, for instance, the highest pulse frequencies are not reached at moments of greatest physical effort but occur at passages producing the greatest emotional response. Thus, the maximum increase of pulse frequency telemetrically recorded from Herbert von Karajan while conducting the Leonora Overture No. 3 was obtained during those passages with the greatest emotional impact upon the conductor. These were the same passages which the conductor singled out in a subsequent conversation as being the ones he found most profoundly touching. At these moments the pulse rate increased for a short while to twice the level of the initial value (Figure 2a). When shortly afterwards the tape of the performance was played back to von Karajan and a further pulse record made there was evidence of considerable qualitative parallelism between both tracings, but the changes were much greater while he was conducting.

Our data suggest that the artist's emotional concomitants may be even more important than artistic perfection as far as success and acceptance by the public are concerned.

In this context it might be interesting to present further data on von

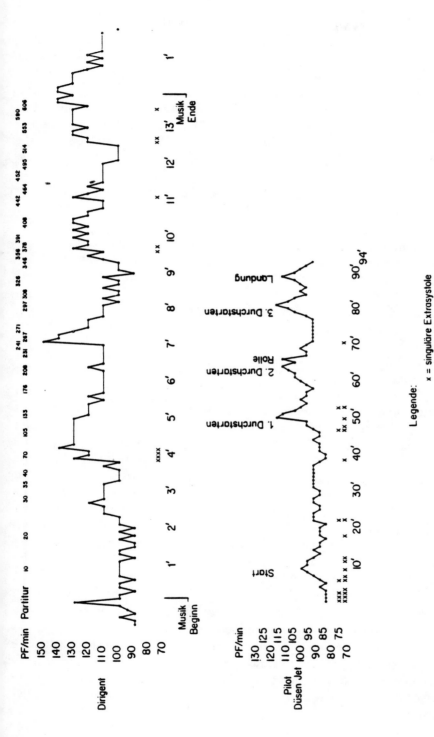

Figure 2 Pulse rate (Herbert von Karajan). (a) while conducting (b) while piloting a jet aircraft.

Karajan's pulse rate in a variety of situations and in special circumstances. Yoga exercises have enabled him to reduce his pulse rate by 10 to 15 beats a minute within a very short time. We also had the opportunity of recording his pulse rate while he was piloting his own jet aircraft. He had been asked to carry out several special tasks: three times he had to execute a landing manoeuvre consisting of almost touching the runway and then making an immediate steep ascent. This was associated with an increase of pulse rate during the approach to the runway, but the response was clearly smaller than the music-induced effects (Figure 2b). It is interesting to note that the tachycardic response is marked whenever this response-type seems to be desirable but small when it could affect the required task adversely.

As already mentioned, active performance of music gives rise to stronger autonomic responses. In contrast with the responses to music heard, these powerful reactions cannot be suppressed by deliberate detachment.

4. Autonomic reactions impinging on various systems: (a) Cardiovascular system. The pulse rate is technically easy to record among the various parameters and it is also quite a sensitive indicator. In general increases occur in response to music, and even in short lasting tests a decrease of pulse rate below the initial level is seldom detected. An increase of pulse rate may be an expression of pleasure and approval, but also of displeasure and disapproval.

Pulse tracings are fairly consistent when the same piece of music is played several times to the same subject. There may be repeated episodes of premature beats at one or two special points. Syncopated rhythms are particularly capable of producing such extra-systoles, as might be expected. It is sometimes possible to "drive" the pulse rate by dynamic changes in volume such as the crescendo and decrescendo of a rolling drum beat. The same phenomenon can be obtained by a change in rhythm. Hence an acceleration may lead to tachycardic responses and a deceleration of rhythm to a slowdown of the pulse rate (Figure 3). In some subjects synchrony of activity between external "pacemaker" and pulse rate are noted within certain limits.

Relaxing and pleasure-charged passages, and sometimes the ending of a piece of music, may give rise to changes in pulse rate synchronously with the respiratory rhythm. Third order fluctuations are also noted, probably due to changes in the central vasomotor tone.

In subjects with some degree of cardiac disease marked qualitative electrocardiographic changes may occur as the result of music, like those seen with physical stress. In cases of purely functional cardiac disturbances such changes may be seen with music only and not as the result of muscular stress.

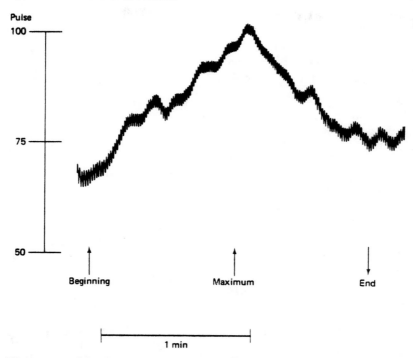

Figure 3   Pulse rate at crescendo and decrescendo of a rolling drum beat.

Oscillographic and plethysmographic changes may also occur which suggest an increase or, in certain circumstances, a decrease in the vasoconstrictor tone. It is worth-while mentioning in this context the noise induced peripheral vasoconstrictor response.

In these investigations no recordings of the blood pressure were carried out during the presentation of music.

(b) Respiration. Recordings of respiratory movements during the playing of music are very informative. Not only do changes in frequency and depth of respiration occur, but the relation between inhalation and exhalation may also be changed and this may be true of other respiratory characteristics. These include tendencies towards rhythmical or arrhythmical respiratory activity.

Figure 4 illustrates the pneumograms of five different subjects (A–E) while listening to the same piece of music (negro drumming from Uganda). Subject A exhibits a gradual adjustment of the respiratory rate to the gradually accelerating and temporarily slowing beat. The same mode of reaction is shown by subject B except that the respiratory rate is much slower. The subjective experience of fatigue manifests itself by a sighing

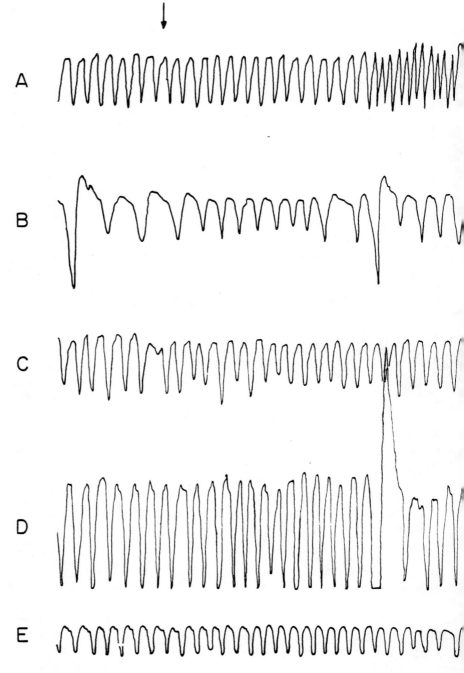

Figure 4  Pneumogram of five different subjects (A–E) listening to the same piece of music (negro drumming by natives of Uganda).

1 min

respiration. While subject A shows an equal length of the inspiratory and expiratory phase, the expiratory period is clearly lengthened in B, while the tracing of subject C occupies an intermediate position. The tracing of D is characterised by a slowing of the respiration at the period of the fastest drum beat; this type of response is found when an intrinsic biorhythm is unable to follow the extrinsic pacemaker any further, and a shift is made to a different subharmonic relation between intrinsic and extrinsic rhythms, for instance to a rate of 1 : 2 or 1 : 3. Subject E is characterised by consistency in the amplitudes; changes of rate are also smaller than those seen in the other subjects. These individual modes of response were widely reproducible whenever the tests were repeated with the same piece of music. Such pronounced inter-individual differences in the respiratory response, associated with marked intra-individual consistency, correspond with considerable differences of individual attitudes towards the presentations. These attitudes are clearly greater in younger subjects than in older ones; the latter regarded the bush drum music as disagreeable and not to be rated as "music". In conventional or "classical" music the inter-individual respiratory differences were less significant, and certain pieces of music elicited responses in all subjects.

In reaction to pieces of music with a prominent acceleration or deceleration of the rhythm, some of the subjects show a tendency towards a primary pulse synchronisation, others tend to exhibit synchronisation of the respiratory rhythm. This suggests that it might be possible to differentiate "primary circulatory reactors" and "primary respiratory reactors".

(c) Psychogalvanic reflex (PGR). This proved to be the most sensitive indicator in our investigations. Its disadvantage lies in the difficulties of signal calibration and also in a certain fatigue of the response in the course of a lengthy test. Here again, strong responses may be the expression of either pleasure or displeasure. Any sort of mental distraction, a person entering the room, or a noise, can lead to responses which may be misinterpreted.

(d) Motor activity. Simple observation of a concert audience with their different types of motor responses is an interesting experience. Under laboratory conditions it is possible to assess muscular activity electromyographically (EMG) during the perception of music. Figure 5 shows increased muscular activity during the process of listening to music (also noticeable in other states of mental and emotional tension) as evidenced by an increase in the number and amplitude of muscle action potentials. There are also quantitative as well as qualitative differences between various muscular segments; for instance, between cranial muscles

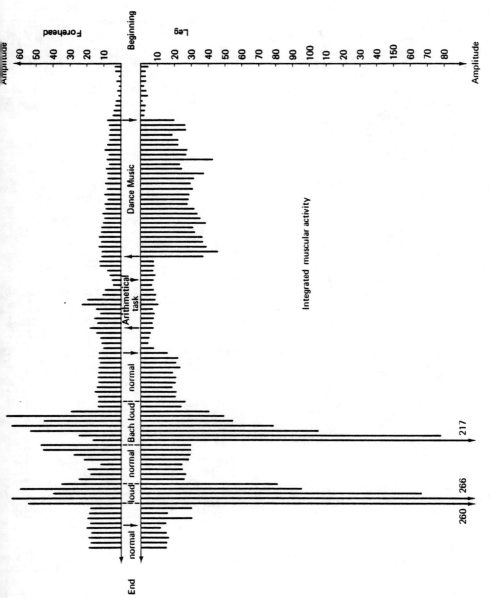

Figure 5 Integrated muscular activity shown electromyographically. Differences between the region of the forehead and of the legs while the subject is listening to dance music, during an arithmetical task; and listening to Bach's Brandenburg Concerto No. 6.

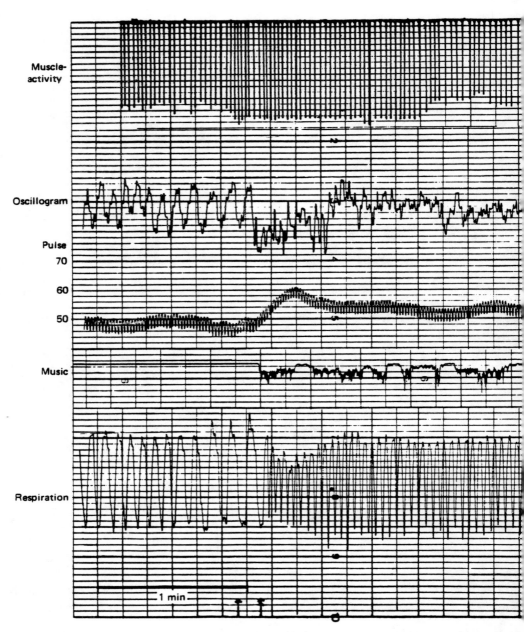

Figure 6    Polygraphy taken while the subject was listening to a performance of Bach's Brandenburg Concerto No. 1.

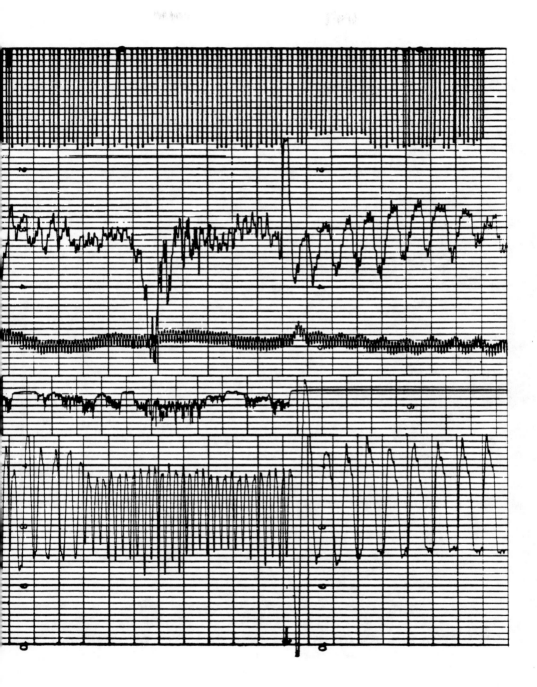

and those of the extremities. At rest only minor differences occur between muscular activity in the forehead region and in the legs. While the subject listens to a record of dance music the effect of the music goes, so to speak, "into the legs"; muscle action potentials increase sharply in the legs and relatively slightly in the frontalis muscles. A reverse effect is found during a silent arithmetical task, when there is a greater increase of muscular activity in the region of the brow than in the legs. Listening to Bach's Brandenburg Concerto No. 6 enhances crural and, to a somewhat lesser degree, frontalis muscular activity. With temporary marked augmentation of the sound volume a very pronounced increase of muscle action potentials in both leg and forehead was noted. The subject had been asked not to move during the test and there was no muscular movement as far as one could judge from observation, even at the height of the EMG discharges. A simultaneous recording of body movements showed no response.

Simultaneous recordings of muscle activity and of other autonomic parameters have proved informative. Even shortly before the presentation of music some increase of muscular activity can be detected (as shown in Figure 6). While the subject was listening to a performance of Bach's Brandenburg Concerto No. 1 fluctuations of muscle activity were recorded; these changes were reproducible by repeat performances and they occurred at the same passages. The pulse rate increased at the beginning of the presentation and continued at a raised level. At the end of the performance oscillations of the pulse rate occurred synchronously with the respiration and presumably indicated an alteration in the respiratory regulation. The respiratory rates accelerated at the beginning, temporarily coupled with a decreasing respiratory volume, the latter, however, subsequently showed an increase. At a certain passage bradypnoea was noted temporarily; repeat performances showed the reproducible nature of this response at exactly the same passage. At the end of the performance the respiratory rate fell to levels which were less than half those at the peak. The increase of muscle activity, pulse and respiratory rates which occur at the beginning of the musical presentation are the expression of a generally raised level of activation.

Figure 7 shows the changes of pulse rate and integrated muscular activity during the playing of various pieces of music and other acoustic stimuli of symbolic nature.

The recording of the ankle jerk represents an indication of muscle tone and its changes. This test is carried out with the use of an apparatus permitting the elicitation of the reflex with stimuli of equal strength delivered at regular intervals. Figure 8 shows music-induced changes in the reflex caused by changes in muscle tone.

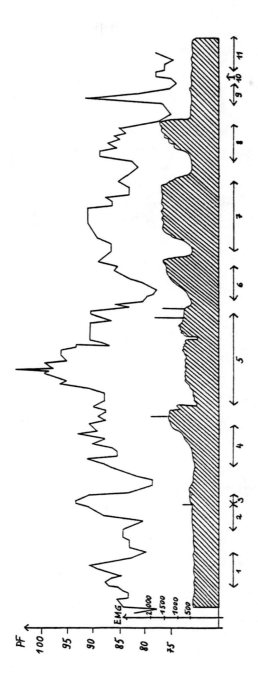

Figure 7 Pulse rate and integrated muscular activity while the subject was listening to: (1) Brahms' "Wiegenlied", (2) the hooting of sirens (firefighting vehicles), (3) the grating of a saw, (4) Concertino No. III in A flat, G. B. Pergolesi, (5) Kalinka, (6) Telemusic, K. Stockhausen, (7) Bach's Toccata in D minor, (8) Dixieland music, and (9) during an arithmetical task, (10) associated with a cough, (11) during relaxation.

When a subject is asked to squeeze an ergometer, an instrument to measure the strength of the handgrasp at regular intervals and with equal effort he will be unable to carry out the test properly while music is being played. Lullabies invariably decrease and march songs increase muscular strength.

5. Finally, the effect of tranquillisers is noteworthy. We observed an almost complete suppression of music-induced autonomic responses after the administration of tranquillisers within the limits of certain dosages. The suppressive effect was obtained without any concomitant reduction or alteration in the emotional musical experience. This dichotomy appears to be important with regard to the frequently expressed view that the physical and autonomic components of affect constitute an inseparable entity. When larger doses are administered both the autonomic and the emotional responses are suppressed. There is reason to believe that some individuals

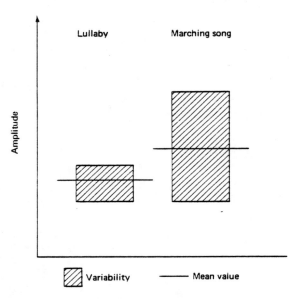

Figure 8    Music-induced changes of the ankle jerk.

will thus be able to give themselves up to the aesthetic pleasures of music in an undisturbed manner.

This work does not merely pertain to the experience of music and the set of accompanying autonomic processes, it may also serve as a contribution to basic research in the domain of the therapeutic use of music and, furthermore, as a contribution to the problem of mind-body relationships.

# 13

MACDONALD CRITCHLEY

# Ecstatic and Synaesthetic Experiences during Musical Perception

"Music is a strange thing," Heinrich Heine wrote. "I would almost say it is a miracle. For it stands half way between thought and phenomenon, between spirit and matter, a sort of nebulous mediator, like and unlike each of the things it mediates — spirit that requires manifestation in time and matter that can do without space . . . we do not know what music is."

These words bring up two of the most baffling aspects in the psychology of music, namely the cognitive and expressive elements. What sort of mental mechanism is activated when one thinks and talks about what goes on in the sensorium during musical experiences. Music can bring about a veritable perceptual spectrum ranging from the simple reception of auditory sense-data to impressions which in sensitive subjects well-nigh baffle description. So evocative, overwhelming and transcendental may these be as to defy description. Many listeners, indeed, do not attempt to force their sensory experiences into the Procrustean bed of ineffectual articulate usage. Others, compelled perhaps by materialistic circumstances, endeavour to do so by a process of juggling, fumbling, struggling, wrestling with verbal counters in a vain effort to exteriorise their emotions.

Whether there really exists a true "language of music" has long been debated. Someone has said that music belongs where language ends. To quote the late Sir Jack Westrup, Professor of Music at Oxford: "Strictly speaking you cannot write about music; music expresses what it has to say in its own terms, and you cannot translate these into language any more than you can translate a picture. Mindful of the perplexities, Aldous Huxley also proclaimed that music comes nearest to expressing the inexpressible — after silence, that is. Weber proclaimed "*Musik ist die Währe allgemeine Menschensprache*". In similar vein L. Newman (1919) asserted that we cannot phrase a musical idea in words; nevertheless the fact remains that it *is* an idea, addressing us in its own language, with a force and a logic as great as any that words can command.

At the same time it is often needful to refer in verbal terms to musical experience, even though words may not be the essential tools in this type of cognition. Like some other highly abstract processes of thought, music is not necessarily tied to thinking-in-words. When indeed words become inaccessible, as after a brain-lesion, musical thinking may well remain as intact as ever it was. Langer had much to say upon the ineffability of music, and referred to "those subtle complexes of feeling that language cannot even name, let alone set forth". Discussing music as an aspect of symbolism, she spoke of its untranslatability. "Music at its highest, although clearly a symbolic form, is an unconsummated symbol. Articulation is its life, but not assertion: expressiveness, not expression."

To some musicologists, poetry is regarded as occupying a niche somewhere between language and music. For example Aaron Copland said that as he matured he came gradually to see that music and poetry were perhaps closer kin than he had first realised, and that "beyond the music of both arts there is an essence that joins them – an area where the meaning behind the notes and the meaning beyond the words spring from a common source". This prescient conception is of great importance to neurologists, and if literally true may prove disturbing to those brain-anatomists who seek to relegate speech and song to opposite cerebral hemispheres.

Commonsense teaches us that some kind of linkage can and does exist between verbalisation and music, but that the nexus is neither binding nor obligatory. Although discussion of this problem lies properly within the province of the philosopher of music, nevertheless the idea is of considerable neurological interest.

This is where one is tempted to refer to transitory states of ecstasy or near-ecstasy in relation to music. Strictly speaking, that mystical change in self-awareness which is known as ecstasy* or "cosmic consciousness" falls properly within the province of the theologian. Such a statement is not mandatory for in some rare circumstances this unusual phenomenon may attract the attention of psychiatrists. So far, however, no satisfactory technical definition has been achieved, but rather a descriptive epitome. In states of ecstasy, there develops a curious sense of "merging" whereby the subject becomes identified with external reality which itself is endowed with a feeling of complete personal significance. William James spoke of its four factors of transiency, passivity, ineffability, and noetic quality (see also Anderson, 1938).

Psychiatrists are furthermore aware that ecstasy is not necessarily a manifestation of psychopathology. States of near-ecstasy may be drug-induced even in normal subjects. They may also arise under the impact of

* The definition posed by Dr. Johnson in his dictionary is difficult to better. "Any passion by which the thoughts are absorbed, and in which the mind is for a time lost."

musical stimuli with their powerful evocative properties. A listener who is specifically perceptive may become temporarily overwhelmed by the sounds of music.* Copland said that to the ideal listener "there is something about music that keeps its distance even at the moment that it engulfs us. It is at the same time outside and away from us and inside and part of us. In one sense it dwarfs us, and in another we master it." These are experiences which possibly do not apply to the professional critic nor to instrumentalists who remain detached. However, this peculiar transcendental state of cosmic consciousness may at times sweep over an orchestral conductor, and occasionally a singer. The ecstatic or near-ecstatic feeling is compounded of several factors beyond the four criteria mentioned by James. They may also include loss of time-sense, de-realisation, depersonalisation, heautoscopy (or specular illusions), and also subjective aberrations in corporeal awareness. One operatic soprano confessed that she would become so entranced as finally to be oblivious of her audience. A conductor of international repute once admitted to me that when caught up in the web of sound while at work, he would imagine himself released as it were from his own body and transported to the rafters of the theatre. From that lofty vantage point he would visualise himself in miniature, confronting yet dominating his orchestra.

Statements like these are but rarely divulged, maybe because the appropriate questions are not always posed. To the musical aesthete, such bodily illusions may be so familiar as not to warrant comment; or perhaps they cut a figure so odd as to ordain a discreet reticence.

To a neuropsychologist, however, the phenomena are familiar enough. Illusory distortions in the size, shape, weight and appearance of one's anatomy are well recognised as common anomalies of the body-image or body-scheme. A more acceptable term is "corporeal awareness", for the phenomenon is something which lies midway between a percept and a concept, lurking on the fringe of awareness, especially in introspective intellectuals.

## Synaesthetics in music

The neurology of music also raises for discussion the interesting problem of perceptual synaesthesia or secondary sensations. As long ago as the 17th century, Kircher spoke of sound as the "ape of light" (*le singe de la lumière*),

* The musicians of the ancient Arabian culture were well aware that revelation could be achieved by way of music. In his treatise *Music and Ecstasy* Al-Ghazāli (d. 791) gave seven reasons why singing was more powerful in this respect than the Qaran itself (*vide* H. G. Farmer in Guillaume's *Legacy of Islam*).

saying that everything visible can be made audible, just as everything which the ear perceives can also be perceived by the eye. Behind these words seemingly so absurd lies a glimmer of psychological truth.

For well over a century it has been known that some individuals, otherwise unremarkable from a clinical standpoint, have the capacity or rather the compulsion to associate sounds with a visual imagery of colours or shapes. An early reference to this phenomenon as occurring in the brothers Nüssbaumer was made by Professor Brühl in 1873. Many descriptive terms have since been suggested, such as *oratio colorata*, *Farbenhören*, *Farbighören*, *audition colorée*, colour-hearing, psycho-chromasthesia. The precise incidence of this intermodal endowment is not known, but from Bleuler and Lehmann's questionnaire (1881), 76 out of 596 persons in Zürich gave affirmative replies, thus giving an incidence of 12·7 per cent. This figure accords closely with Colman's estimation of 12 per cent. (1898). Either sex may be involved and it seems to be the endowment of those with artistic, sensitive or aesthetic personalities, especially musicians. Sokolov (1910) described synaesthetics as possessing a lively imagination, deep sensitivity, a predominant visual imagery, and an inability to cope with pure abstractions. Earlier, Binet (1889) had said much the same. Synaesthetics, he observed, were characterised by their love both for colours and for nature; for their innate culture; their literacy and their artistic vocations. Synaesthesia seems thus to be a perquisite of sophisticates. It is safe to assert that synaesthesia is a phenomenon which is more vivid in childhood and which gradually fades with advancing years.

In all probability, sonogenic synaesthesia constitutes just one aspect of a more fundamental endowment whereby colours or forms are associated with concepts which entail serial order, as for example the letters of the alphabet, numerals, days of the week, months of the year. This particular phenomenon will not be pursued for it lies outside the scope of this article. The literature is extensive, but attention should be particularly directed to the monographs of Maria Bos (1929), Flournoy (1893), Suarez de Mendoza (1890), A. Weller (1931) and Kloos (1931).

The topic of colour-music association has been treated in a serious and scholarly fashion in Scholes' "Dictionary of Music". An undertone of scepticism permeates this important essay, implying that synaesthesia is a purely subjective experience which constitutes a problem belonging not so much to the science of physics as to the realm of psychology. But it is precisely for this reason that neurologists are concerned.

In those possessed of the faculty of *audition colorée* the provoking stimulus is usually not confined to music. It can also apply to non-melodic sounds like the beating of a gong, the ticking of a clock, a whistle, and so on. The resulting "secondary" sensation" or "photism" has been interpreted in divers ways. Sometimes it seems to be a matter of a pure visual image: at other times it constitutes a veritable hallucination. Yet again the subjective experience may seem to lie midway between the two. Colman (1894) believed that four degrees of secondary sensations evoked by music can be distinguished: (1) photisms located somewhere behind the eyes or within the skull; (2) a background of colour appearing behind actual objects in the environment, though not obscuring them; (3) photisms projected spatially in the direction of the source of the auditory stimulus; and (4) those visual impressions which are so brilliant as actually to obliterate the environment, or else to blend with its colours and thus engender a totally different hue.

In some subjects the colours evoked are merely tints forming an unobtrusive part of more brilliant optical patterns whether simple or complicated. For example, Ayala (1909) visualised in a lively fashion elaborate architectural shapes, the pattern of which changed according to the nature of the music. So vivid were these photisms that he could sketch them, their contours appearing more important than their hues. The same applied to the case reported by Dudycha and Dudycha (1935).

A secondary sensation may vary in shape and colour according to such physical parameters as loudness; the source of the musical stimulus, i.e. whether the human voice or an instrument; the key or pitch of a single note; and the tempo of the sound-track. Furthermore, the musical composition in its entirety may be charged with its own over-riding colour-association. A loud noise in the vicinity of a sleeper may also bring about synaesthetic dream-states without waking him.

Examples taken from personal observations of composers may be quoted to illustrate some of these points.

*Intensity*

Scriabin would experience no more than a "feeling" of colours when the musical intensity around him was subdued, but with louder music the secondary sensation would constitute an "image". To Helène Stilzner, full-tone speech engendered a coloured picture, whereas whispering, with its attenuated resonance, would conjure up the idea of a copperplate engraving.

*Human voices*

According to Lumley (1864), Mario's singing was golden; that of Sims

Reeves a rich brown; while Grisi's voice was a primrose yellow. Myers (1911) associated Clara Butt's powerful contralto with violet, male voices varying from pink to reddish brown. Parodus commented that to him some voices were red; others blue, black, tan or slate. Some handsome women had voices "like buttermilk".

*Timbre: harmonic composition: overtone-structure*

Secondary sensations may also depend upon the mechanical origin of the musical sounds. Specific differences arise according to whether the notes emanate from a single instrument, a small chamber music *ensemble*, or from a full orchestra. According to Donath (1923), sounds proceeding from a piano, 'cello, harp, violin, flute and oboe evoked photisms which were violet, orange, wine-red, chrome yellow, blue and olive-green respectively. However, in Myers' subject, the colour-linkages were quite different. Thus, a 'cello, bassoon, horn, trombone, violin, and fife were related in a specific manner to brownish pink, brownish yellow, brownish rose, red, pink merging into blue, pale blue, or green.

In some other subjects it is not the individual notes, nor their overtonal structure, nor yet the factor of volume which produce the most explicit synaesthesia, but rather music in its role as a complete and coordinated entity. A personally observed patient with a right frontal meningioma, associated the sound of any military band with an image of "nasty red", and dance-music "of the nice quiet sort" with a misty blue. Scriabin, listening to a theme in D major, became aware of a photism of yellow, while to Rimsky-Korsakov, seated beside him, the same sound evoked a tint which was more golden. According to Myers (1914) Chopin inspired "translucent colours like green leaves in Spring" while the works of Schumann conjured up an opaque purple. Schubert's Third Impromptu was wine-red, while Beethoven's *Laube Sonata* Opus 27 No. 2 was blue (Donath). Of a more contrived character was the linkage of one of Schubert's *Arias* with "so sunny a warmth and so delicate a green" that Myers seemed to become aware of the scent of fir trees. Gounod (quoted by Fraser-Harris (1905)) went further, by implicating the language employed by the singer. To him French was not so colourful as Italian, though finer in hue. Pedrono and Ughetti observed a polyglot synaesthetic whose colour-associations varied according to the particular language employed.

In anecdotal vein it can be said that when Liszt was appointed to Weimar as *Kapellmeister*, he bewildered his players at rehearsals by urging . . . "more pink here, if you please"; or by declaring "that is too black"; or, "here I want it all azure".

The same melodic phrase may possess secondary sensations which change according to the key selected by the instrumentalist. That major and minor keys should differ in this context is not surprising. Some have spoken of minor keys being associated with grey or black photisms, major ones being green, blue, pink, or red. To some subjects, major chords are "brighter" than minor. But to those gifted with a more elaborate faculty of synaesthesia, highly specific differences may result according to the particular key chosen, whether it be major or minor.

As already stated, the simple frequency of the sound-waves may be an important and decisive determinant in colour-associations. In some persons the matter appears to go deeper. For example, middle C heard in acoustic isolation might bring about a certain colour-association; but were this same note to be sounded immediately after another note, say F sharp, then the colour-association would be different. Thus a note of 500 Hz following 1200 has been known to evoke a rosy brown, while after 600 the brown was much softer; the photism of 500 Hz alone was blue.

The deeper one delves into this problem, the richer the treasures that are salvaged. For example, a phenomenon of perceptual perseveration may be detected in some cases, or alternatively, an imagery which is astonishing in its accuracy. A musician might strike a single note on a piano, and then, back at home, he would later be able to tune his violin with absolute precision by the simple device of matching the colour-photism (Colman).

In aphasic subjects something similar may occur. A life-long synaesthetic became afflicted after a stroke with a marked anomia, and would be at a loss to put a name to an article presented to him. In his efforts he might utter various sounds which were phonemically analogous to the elusive term, but not quite accurate. That the utterance was wrong was obvious to the aphasiac, because to him its secondary colour-association was also wrong. In his search for the *mot juste* he was greatly assisted by his more rapid power of discovering the appropriate photism.

A case has been described of a couple of synaesthetics, both of whom associated a note with the pitch of G with the colour red. Neither subject, however, could identify this note when it was sounded alone. Both these individuals also happened to be afflicted with a red-green colour-blindness. Albertoni (1889), referring to these two persons, spoke of an "auditory Daltonism".

Then there is the unusual phenomenon which may be referred to as "sporadic synaesthesia". Bowers (1969) is an instance in point when he wrote "on two occasions I have seen radiant flashes of blinding colours and lights during performances of Scriabin's music. I was neither prepared for them, nor was I able to repeat them at any other time. They happened; I saw light unexpectedly and for no explicable or useful purpose. The experiences lasted for not more than a few seconds and were gone. They were quite different from a thrill of sensation, tears of pleasure, or usual emotions associated with beautiful music. I was more surprised than pleased. They have not recurred. But I have not forgotten them."

Chromatic sensations secondary to music seem to be independent of the deliberate conjuring up of colour-imagery. Thus, while a synaesthetic subject is directed to concentrate on a mental concept of redness, and then a note is struck on a pianoforte carrying with it some other type of colour-hearing, the two colours do not blend, but remain distant and apart. Schultze, on the other hand (1912) described a phenomenon of "reciprocal conditioning", whereby the subject, when surrounded by an environment of red, would modify his piano-playing almost insensibly so as to produce that type of music which was evocative of a secondary sensation of identical tint. Should, however, he feel himself to be in a mood of "blackness" he could deliberately "play himself out of that particular feeling-tone" into one of, say, redness.

At least one instance has been reported, again by Schultze, of *tertiary* sensations coupled with music. A man of 30 years had been aware of his synaesthesia since the age of ten, but his personal colour-hearing was also closely linked with gustatory associations. Thus, instrumental music would produce an imagery first of taste and then of colour, as if the stimulus "went from the ear through the mouth to the eye". Minor chords would in his experience give origin to a hard and bitter taste, and major chords one which was sweet and pleasurable. The distinction was so clear-cut that the subject could accurately identify the keys concerned. After listening for a time, he would feel "full up". He used to refer to "a mouthful of music" ("*Mund voll Musik*"). Perseveration would also occur, and when the music ceased, after-associations of taste and colour would linger on. The subject spoke of "digesting" the music ("*die Musik verdaut*"). One of the subjects described by Myers (1911) proclaimed that of a particular musical note . . . "I call it lilac . . . it rather suggests the taste of thick soup." In this same connection one is reminded, too, of Proust who spoke of clear sounds evoking blazing colours . . . something comparable to the perfumed silkiness of a geranium ("*La soierie embaumée d'un géranium*").

That decadent eccentric J.-K. Huysmans in his "À Rebours" afforded us a long description of the search for unusual sensory experiences by the voluptuary Des Esseintes. An elaborate assemblage of liqueurs constituted his *orgue à bouche*. Tasting now here, now there, he played "internal symphonies" which produced on his palate a series of sensations analogous to those with which music gratifies the ear. Each liqueur corresponded in taste with the sound of a particular instrument. Curaçao, for instance, was like the clarinet with its shrill, velvety note; kümmel like the oboe, whose timbre is sonorous and nasal; crème de menthe and anisette, the flute, at one and the same time sweet and poignant, whining and soft. Kirsch blew a wild trumpet blast; gin and whisky deafening the palate with their harsh blare of cornets and trombones; *marc de bourgogne* matched the tuba with its deafening din; whilst "roulent les coups de tonnerre de la cymbale et de la caisse frappés à tour de bras, dans la peau de la bouche, par les rakis de Chio et les mastics!"

Des Esseintes went further: the music of liqueurs had its specific scheme of interrelated tones. On his tongue he became able to perform voiceless melodies and mute funeral marches solemn and stately. At times he would compose melodies of his own, executing pastorals with the gentle blackcurrant ratafia that set his throat resounding with the mellow notes of warbling nightingales. . . .

The phenomenon of colour-hearing can be provoked or facilitated with particular liveliness in two very different circumstances. First, there are the states of intoxication from such hallucinatory drugs as marihuana, mescal and lysergic acid. References to pharmaco-phantastica go back many years. Thus, Gautier (1843), after experimenting with hashish, wrote "*J'entendais le bruit des couleurs. Des sons verts, rouges, bleus, jaunes, m'arrivaient par ondes parfaitement distinctes.*"

Lewin (1924), an early writer upon such drugs, asserted that he could see, as well as hear, musical stimuli . . . "From the far distance came tones, spherical sounds."

The literature dealing with acute mescal intoxication is considerable. According to Mayer-Gross and Stein (1926), the beating of a metronome kindled in one of their subjects a synchronous play of form and colours. The note C conjured up a red, and F an orange-yellow, higher tones bringing about tints which were lighter and less defined. The beating of chimes induced an hallucination of purple. When the window-frame was struck by an iron bar, the green of the trees outside seemed to become rhythmically lighter in strict unison with each impact. The mescal-intoxicated subject was astonished. In his own words "*Da haben wir die Magie*". K. Behringer described in his monograph *Der Meskalinrausch* (1927) examples of *Mitempfindungen* evoked by this drug. "Unter Musikeinwirkung nahm diese Erscheinung mehr Bandform an, worauf die höhen Töne lebhafte grelle Farben und die tiefen Töne mehr stumpfe, matte Farben und mehr eintönige hervorriefen . . .".

The other condition which promotes synaesthesia is blindness. Many have quoted — though not always accurately — Locke's account of a congenitally blind man who, asked to explain what was his conception of the colour "red", likened it to the note of a trumpet.* It is well known that individuals who have been sightless for many years often become afflicted by obtrusive visual hallucinations specific in colour and constant in shape, though often strongly influenced by auditory stimuli. This topic was exhaustively dealt with by Wilhelm Voss of Kiel in his monograph *Das Farbenhören bei Erblindeten* (1930). The association of musical talent with blindness must surely be more than fortuitous, and synaesthesia may well constitute an important link, suggesting a type of compensation. The late Thomas Wood (1936), a blind musician of my acquaintance, once described to me his own life-long faculty of colour-association. "It brings a definite colour to single notes, to notes in groups, to movements; it changes the colour according to height or depth, scoring, key; over all this it lays a colour that goes with the work as a whole, and at times a shape is added which is just as fortuitous as the colours themselves." Different patterns and colour-qualities of these phenomena could be evoked by playing Mendelssohn's Spring Song in this key or that. In his autobiography the author stressed that colour-association is something which transcends mere metaphor or linguistic juggling.

This last point is important, for it is easy for one devoid of the gift of *audition colorée* to dismiss the whole matter as a mere literary contrivance stemming from a vocabulary which is either superabundant but poorly controlled, or on the other hand one which suffers from sheer verbal inadequacy. The metaphorical use of chromatic terms to describe auditory experiences is a literary commonplace, sometimes grossly overplayed. Oscar Wilde, for example, wrote that "her voice was exquisite . . . but it was wrong in colour". Elsewhere he referred to the vermilion lips of Salome . . . "like the scarlet blast of trumpets". Proust spoke of the "red and mysterious" appeal of the Vinteuil septet, and in another place he mentioned the "geranium scent" of the music. Still more strained is the following passage from Myro Brinig in *The Copper City*. "He was a brass band of a man and his voice packed with all the colours and sounds and thrills of all the instruments in Sousa's band. He spoke, and his voice soared, dived, flew, swam, crashed, and thundered. His voice was a brush that painted a drab canvas into a conflagration of colours galore, but his voice could be soft too and sweet and win women and soothe babies."

---

* Locke's precise words deserve quotation:
  ". . . a studious blind man who had mightily beat his head about visible objects, and made use of the explications of his books and friends, to understand those names of light and colours, which often came in his way, betrayed one day that he now understood what *scarlet* signified. Upon which, his friend demanded what scarlet was? The blind man answered, it was like the sound of a trumpet."

Much may be forgiven those masterly writers whose creative upsurges and whose quest for revealing associations – even if far-fetched – resort to such stylistic tricks as strained but arresting metaphors, evocations of imagery or memory which are barely tangible, and illusions ranging from a *déjà vu* through a *presque vu* to a thrilling *pas encore vu*. But with many musical critics the problem is different. Their writings are not necessarily endowed with any conspicuous literary merit. Perforce they are compelled to draw upon the language of one art-form to describe the qualities of another. To the sensitive reader who happens to be musically deprived, such licence may become distasteful. All too often a veritable jargon results, as irritating as any other trade-language. Just as art critics borrow such musical terms as "tone", "scale", "loud", "soft", so journalists of music have not hesitated to refer to "brilliance", "form-hues", "tone-colour", and, of course, the fundamental term "chromatic".

Three other matters arising out of colour-hearing associations may be briefly touched upon.

The first refers to the occasional attempts by professional composers to interpolate within their orchestral works some other special sense modalities – most commonly visual, but olfactory too. That eccentric innovator, Scriabin – musician, mystic and theosophist – introduced within his *Prometheus, the Poem of Fire*, a special colour-scale and notation, which he described as a *Clavier à lumières* or *Tastiera per luce*. This work, conducted first by Koussevitsky, later by Altschuler, has been rendered but rarely and with very mixed reactions except in the U.S.S.R. The critics in America were unimpressed and disapproving. Undismayed, yet not content, Scriabin had the further ambition to compose a work which combined musical sounds not only with a play of light, but also with a medley of olfactory titillation. This was the basis of his elaborate work *Prefatory Action and Mysterium*, which has never yet been performed, for its completion was prevented by the composer's death. As a matter of fact, Scriabin had been anticipated in 1891, when a piece called *The Song of Solomon* was played in Paris giving "simultaneous appeal to the eyes, ears, and nose" (Philip Hales). The book was by Paul Rionard, the musical adaptations by Flamen de Labrely. The following year, New York witnessed an "experimental perfume concert" entitled *A Trip to Japan in Sixteen Movements*.

Arising naturally from the foregoing is the second consideration. I refer to that deliberate contrivance whereby sound and light are artificially combined in such a way as to form a novel art-form. This topic is not without intrinsic interest, and has been admirably documented by Adrian Klein in his classic *Colour Music, the Art of Light* (1926). The story

3
Prométhée.
A. Scriabine, Op. 60.
Lento. Brumeux. M. M. 𝅗𝅥 = 60.
più lento
a tempo
avec mystere
Luce.
Flauto Piccolo.
Flauti I. II.
Flauto III.
Oboi I. II.
Oboe III.
Corno inglese.
3 Clarinetti in B
Clarinetto Basso in B.
Fagotti I. II.
Fagotto III.
Contrafagotto.
con sord. calme, recueilli
8 Corni in F.
5 Trombe in B.
3 Tromboni e Tuba.
Timpani.
Cassa.
Piatti.
Tam-Tam.
Piano.
Violino I.
Violino II.
Viola.
Violoncello.
Contrabasso.
sur la touche
div.
I. Solo
Russischer Musikverlag, Berlin-Moskau.
R. M. V. 85
Eigentum des Verlags.

begins with Arcimboldo's "calorific music" in 1591, followed in 1720 by the invention of the Jesuit Louis Castel of a *clavessin oculaire*. Next in time came the works of D. Jameson, 1844, and H. R. Haweis, 1875. In 1893, A. W. Rimington constructed a colour-organ. In 1900 appeared Louis Favre's monograph *La musique des couleurs et des musique de l'avenir*. Then came the clavilux designed by Thomas Wilfrid in 1916. Nor must one overlook the contributions of Mrs. Greenewalt (1918) in New York, A. B. Hector (1922) in Sydney, Mr. Luckiesh of the American General Electric Company, and more recently the painter Kandinsky.

In the opinion of Ernest Newman, the claims – or perhaps it should be the hopes – that colour and music can be "translated" into each other, or that an art of "mobile colour" can be created as the visual equivalent of an art of mobile sound, rest on nothing but a pathetic fallacy.

However quaint or intriguing, this topic of artificial colour-music signifies but little within the province of the psychology of music and still less its neurology.

In the context of synaesthesia, it is not enough merely to describe, for it is necessary to venture beyond mere reportage and to ponder over the possible origins of this phenomenon.

Two main hypotheses exist. The first, coupled with the name of Peillaube (1904), is relatively simple. It subsumes that colour-synaesthesia is the product of a chain of mental associations, some of the intermediate links having dropped out of awareness. Thus the familiar story of trumpet-blasts provoking a photism of red, may stem from the fact that such a sound immediately culls up in some persons an imagery of soldiers on parade. Ordinarily they will be in dress-uniform. This evokes a mental picture of scarlet. Should the middle part of this notion eventually become submerged, there will remain a synaesthetic linkage of trumpet-calls with redness.

An alternative theory regards colour-hearing – and for that matter colour-taste – as a perpetuation of some primitive perceptual experience, a sort of amorphous *Urempfindung*, which later in evolution becomes elaborated, differentiated and dissociated along the channels of the various special senses (Myers; Wundt). This idea implies a basic unity of these special senses, and when it comes to communication, a poverty either of cognition, or of vocabulary, or of both. Thus, in the French language, the verb "*sentir*" means not only to feel but also to smell and touch, while in German, the adjective "*hell*" (bright) was originally an auditory attribute, but its usage has spread so as to apply to vision. At least one African tongue utilises a special word for "seeing", but in addition, only one other term to stand for "hearing", "touching", "smelling", and "tasting".

The intriguing doctrine of the unity of the senses probably took origin in an arresting albeit obscurely written work by E. M. von Hornbostel which first appeared in *Melos, Zeitschrift für Musik*, Berlin (1925). The author envisaged that a sensuous state exists which is not limited to one single sense – a super-sensuous sense-perception as he called it. The essential component of the "sensuous-perceptible" is not that which separates the senses from one another, but that which unites them; "unites them among themselves; unites them with the entire (even with the non-sensuous) experience in ourselves; and with all the external world that there is to be experienced".

The same idea was discussed by H. Kleint of Luxembourg (1940) and by E. G. Boring (1942), and by E. A. Hayek in 1952 in depth. Hans Werner also examined critically this conception in his volume on the *Comparative Psychology of Mental Development* (1948). Hayek's contribution was of particular value. He observed that these intersensory and intermodal relations are relatively inconspicuous, and that with the development of conceptual thought, and the weighty influence of sensualism in scientific thought, these phenomena tend to be suppressed. Contrary to the view of Max Planck that intermodal associations are the product of our reflective powers of imagination, Hayek believed that the opposite was the case. It is sophistication which makes us overlook that which is obvious to naïve experience. Synaesthesia is not a linguistic matter of metaphor, but is the outcome of genuine intersensory attributes, which may at times be so dynamic as to lead to phenomena such as colour-hearing. Hayek believed that the employment of transmodal metaphors in speech is something more than a turn of phrase, being the product of veritable perceptual attributes of an intersensory kind. These may occasionally be so strong that sensations belonging to one modality may regularly be accompanied by others which belong to some other modality, as in the case of colour-music. Synaesthesia of this sort is especially vivid during the earlier stages of mental development. Although hesitant to go all the way with Boring, Hayek asserted that all mental qualities – directly or indirectly – are so interrelated that any attempt to give an exhaustive description of any one of them would make it necessary to describe the relations existing between all of them.

## REFERENCES

ALBERTONI (1889) Quoted by Fraser-Harris, 1905.

ANDERSON, E. W. (1938) A clinical study of states of ecstasy occurring in affective disorders. *J. Neur. Psych.*, N.S. 1, 80–99.

AYALA, G. (1909) Riv. speriment. di Freniat. 35, 229.

ARCIMBOLDO (1591) *Il Figino, overo del Fine della Pittura.* Mantua, p. 249.

BEHRINGER, K. (1927) *Der Meskalinrausch.* Berlin, Springer.

BINET, A. (1893) L'Application de la psychométrie a l'étude de l'audition colorée. *Rec. philos.*, 36.

BLEULER, E. and LEHMANN, K. (1881) *Zwangsmässige Lichtempfindungen durch Schall und verwandte Erscheinungen.* Leipzig, Fues Verlag (R. Reisland).

BORING, E. G. (1942) *Sensation and Perception in the History of Experimental Psychology.* Appleton & Co., New York, p. 27.

BOS, M. C. (1929) Uber echte und unechte Audition Coloree. *Zeit. Psychol.*, III, 321–401.

BOWERS, F. (1969) *Scriabin.* Kodanska Internat. Ltd., Tokyo. 2 vols.

BRINIG, M. *The Copper City*, pp. 20, 44, 49.

BRUHL (1873) Quoted by Lewis, *Problems of Life and Mind*, p. 280.

CASTEL, L. B. (1720) *La Musique des Couleurs.*

— (1734) Nouvelles Expériences d'Optique et d'Acoustique. In: *Esprits; Sailles et Singularities du père Castel.* 1763.

COLMAN, W. S. (1894) Further remarks on colour-hearing. *Lancet*, I, 22.

— (1898) On so-called colour-hearing. *Lancet*, I, 795.

DONATH, J. (1923) Uber Farbririechen (Oratorio colorata). *Jour. Psych. u. Neur.*, 29, 112.

DUDYCHA, G. J. and DUDYCHA, M. M. (1935) A case of synesthesia: visual-pain and visual-audition. *J. Abn. Soc. Psychol.*, 30, 57.

FAURE, L. (1900) *La musique des couleurs et des musique de l'avenir.*

FLOURNOY, TH. (1893) *Des Phenomènes de Synopsie*, pp. 98 et seq. Paris, Alcon.

FRASER-HARRIS, D. (1905) *Colour-thinking and Allied Conditions.* Dalhousie University, Halifax.

— (1905) On psychochromaesthesia and certain synaesthesiae. *Edin. M. J.*, 18, 529.

— (1928) *Coloured Thinking.* Routledge, London.

GAUTIER, TH. (1843) Le Club des Haschischiens. *La Presse*, July 10th.

GREENEWALT, M. H. (1918) Light; Fine Art the 6th. *Tr. Ill. Eng. Soc.*, 13, October 10th.

HALE, P. Quoted by H. E. Krehbiel. *New York Tribune*, Quoted by Klein, pp. 240 *et seq.*, 1915, March 21st.

HAWEIS, REV. H. R. (1875) *Music and Morals*, pp. 30–34.

HAYEK, E. A. (1952) *The Sensory Order.* Routledge & Kegan Paul, London, pp. 19 et seq.

HECTOR, A. B. (1922) Colour-music. *Sydney Morning Herald*, February 18th and 25th.

HUYSMANS, J.-K. (1884) *À Rebours.* Paris.

JAMES, W. (1902) *Varieties of Religious Experience.*

JAMESON, D. D. (1844) *Colour-Music*, Smith Elder & Co., London.

JOHNSON, S. (1755) *Dictionary.*

KIRCHER, A. (1657)*Iter extaticum secundum*.

KLEIN, A. B. (1926) *Colour Music, the Art of Light*. Crosby Lockwood & Son, London.

KLEINT, H. (1940) Versüche über die Wahrnehmung. *Zeit. Psychol.*, **149**, 31–82.

KLOOS, G. (1931) Synästhesien bei psychisch Abnormen Auch. *Psych. u. Neur.*, **94**, 417–469.

LANGER, S. (1948) *Philosophy in a New Key*, Chap. VIII. Harvard University Press, Boston, Mass.

LEWIN, L. (1924) *Phantastica*. Stilke, Berlin, p. 146.

LOCKE, J. (1690) *Essay Concerning Human Understanding*.

LUCKIESH, M. (1918) *The Language of Colour*, pp. 262–281.

MAYER-GROSS, W. and STEIN, H. (1926) Ueber einige Abänderungen der Sinnestätigkeit im Meskalinrausch. *Zeit. d. ges. Neur. u. Psych.*, **101**, 354.

MYERS, C. S. (1911) A case of synaesthesia. *B. J. Psychol.*, **4**, 228–238. Quoted by E. G. Lind, *The Music of Color and the Number Seven*.

NEWMAN, E. (1919) A note on colour-music. *Observer*, London, September 21st.

NUSSBAUMER, J. A. (1873) *Wiener med. Woch.*, January, pp. 4, 28 and 52.

PARODUS (1914) Two cases of synaesthesia. *B. J. Psychol.*, **7**, 112–117.

PEDRONO (1882) *J. de Méd de l'Ouest.*, p. 294.

— (1882) *Ann. d'Oculistique*, p. 224.

PEILLAUBE (1904) *Rev. Phil.*, November, p. 675. Int. Congr. Physiol. (Brussels), 1904, September.

PROUST, M. H. *À la Recherche du Temps Perdu*, 1927, XII, 224; 1924, X, 223–234.

RIMINGTON, A. W. (1911) *Colour-Music: the Art of Mobile Colour*. London and New York.

SCHOLES, P. A. (1938) Colour and Music. *The Oxford Companion to Music*. Oxford University Press, London, pp. 181–189.

SCHULTZE (1912) Krankhafter Wandertrieb, räumlich beschrankte Taubheit fur bestimmte Töne und "tertiare" Empfingdungen bei einem Psychopathen. *Zeit. d.g. N.u.P.*, **10**, 399.

SOKOLOV, P. (1901) L'individuation colorée. *Rec-philos.*, 51.

SUAREZ DE MENDOZA, F. (1890) *L'Audition colorée*, Doin, Paris.

VON HORNBOSTEL, E. M. (1926) Unity of the senses. *Psyche.*, **7**, 83–89.

VOSS, W. (1930) Das Farbenhören bei Erblindeten. *Psychol.-Asthat. Forschungsgesellschaft*, Hamburg.

WELLER, A. (1931) Zur Geschichte und Kritik der Synästhesia – Forschung. *Arch. d. ges. Psychol.*, **79**, 325–384.

WERNER, H. (1948) *Comparative Psychology of Mental Development*. Follet Publ., Chicago.

WILDE, O. (1891) *The Picture of Dorian Gray*.

— (1893) *Salome*.

WOOD, T. (1936) *True Thomas*. Cape, London.

# The Language of Music

The term *language* has been defined as "the whole body of words and methods of combining them used by a nation", but other meanings include "method of expression, otherwise than by words", "manner or style of expression" and "the style of a composition" (*Shorter Oxford English Dictionary*, 1959). There is a continuing debate whether music can be properly described as a language, but semantically there is no objection to the statement for music is a "method of expression otherwise than by words" or "a manner or style of expression". The words *meaning* and *language* are sometimes used interchangeably in relation to music, and this is permissible where meaning implies intended sense. Commentators on composers use the word *language* to denote style of composition and again this is a correct use of the term.

The real ground for debate is not whether music is a language but what it conveys to the listener. There is a large literature on the subject and Strunk's (1950) *Source Readings in Musical History* contains, among other things, a valuable collection of Greek and early Christian views. Isidore of Seville was Archbishop of the city and died in A.D. 636. Writing on *What Music Can Do* between 622 and 633 he said, "Thus without music no discipline can be perfect, for there is nothing without it. For the very universe, it is said, is held together by a certain harmony of sounds, and the heavens themselves are made to revolve by the modulation of harmony. Music moves the feelings and changes the emotions. In battles, moreover, the sound of the trumpet rouses the combatants, and the more furious the trumpeting the more valorous their spirit . . . music soothes the mind to endure toil, and the modulation of the voice consoles the weariness of each labour. Music also composes distraught minds, as may be read of David, who freed Saul from the unclean spirit by the art of melody. . . . But every word we speak, every pulsation of our veins, is related by musical rhythm to the powers of harmony." This passage contains ideas on the emotional and therapeutic effects of music which are still held today, though the idiom is strange to modern ears and we no longer discuss the harmony or music of the spheres. Music was treated symbolically in mediaeval art, the artist sought to establish links between heavenly and earthly or human music, the concept of universal harmony. Matisse took these ideas as recently as 1910 and translated them into his work *La Musique*, now in the Hermitage at Leningrad (Kostenevich, 1974).

Many composers have recorded their views on what they express when they write music, and their letters are particularly useful and revealing. It is important for any writer on this subject, including the neurologist, to take account of what the creative musician has to say about his work. Serious Western music will be considered here, as in Chapter 1.

## The languages of man and their relationship to music

Man uses several languages or methods of expression and communication, speech and writing, gesture and mime, and visual forms such as drawing and painting, sculpture and architecture. The first step in exploring the language of music is to see how these other languages relate to it or if they do so at all.

Gesture and mime constitute an international language for it is a commonplace observation that satisfactory communication can be achieved by these means without the use of words. The best example is the sign language employed by the deaf and dumb, a language capable of conveying complex ideas and sentiments. In a different context artists like Marcel Marceau are able to communicate a wealth of meaning to a hearing audience by mime alone. As described in Chapter 1, gesture and mime play a part in musical experience. An elegant harpist adds to her performance by beautiful hand movements which can delight the audience of themselves. Additionally, a musical idea can be conveyed by gesture, for devices such as the Guidonian hand (after Guido D'Arrezzo, c. 905–1050) of earlier days and the tonic solfa hand signs can be used to communicate a tune. However, gesture and mime are more commonly involved with speech. Dance is used as a means of expression and communication in more primitive communities and is closely related to music as an art form, indeed, both serious and popular music have strong antecedents in the dance.

Music is often described in terms of the visual arts. We speak of the structure or architecture of a piece. Havergal Brian named one of his works the *Gothic Symphony*; he was concerned with the immensity, grandeur, and sometimes fantastic nature of Gothic architecture (Simpson, 1975). Xenakis provides a further link between architecture and music. Terms applicable to general art movements, such as impressionism and expressionism, are commonly used in describing the work of composers or individual compositions, and words indicating shading or colours, like chromaticism, are similarly employed. Thus, authors write of orchestral colour, the orchestral palette and light and shade. Rogers' *The Art of Orchestration* (1951) is sub-titled "Principles of Tone Colour in Modern Scoring", and he is concerned with the "kinship between painting and music . . ." These approaches stem from at least two points; firstly, from synaesthetic experiences, though a minority of people have this faculty; secondly, words are needed to describe music, and it is natural to use terms deriving from other arts, indeed practitioners in these fields sometimes use musical terms in description. Words such as architecture and structure are employed widely in description, for example, in subjects as diverse as anatomy and verse. There is no obvious relation between painting and music. Music is a temporal or time governed art form, like poetry, which no picture can ever be, but there are frequent points in history when artists in words, music and painting have pursued common artistic ideals and have influenced each other's thinking through the mutual effects of work and conversation.

## Speech and music

Speech and music have been frequently compared by neurologists and they possess certain points in common. Both are expressive and receptive, including among their several functions composition or invention, performance, and reception and comprehension. Vocally music is expressed in song, while speech has its own melody, melody which can be lost from focal brain disease, as Monrad-Krohn (1947) has described. Speech and song are linked in *Sprechgesang* (speech song) and *Sprechstimme* (speech voice). Scholes (1955) defines *Sprechgesang*, the older term, as "properly singing tinged with a speaking quality", whereas "*Sprechstimme* is rather speech tinged with a singing quality". Perhaps the best known examples of *Sprechstimme* are Schoenberg's *Pierrot Lunaire* and *Ode to Napoleon*. There are affinities between poetry, with its rhythm and melody, and music; both are linear, but music unlike poetry is linear in both horizontal and vertical planes, as a glance at almost any score will show. Speech and music combine in song, and for the majority of the population music is song, melody with words, or dance. Most popular music is written for dancing or singing.

In order to compare speech and music further it will be helpful to examine the language of words. Speech like music consists of sounds. The smallest isolable sound made in the course of speech is the phone, but the basic linguistic unit is the phoneme. Phonemes are derived by abstraction from connected speech (Gimson, 1962) and are transcribed more or less precisely by the letters of the alphabet, alone or in combination. English has forty-two phonemes, twenty-four being consonantal. Phonemes are not meaningful; the smallest meaningful unit of speech is the morpheme, which is the conjunction of particular phonemes in sequence. This minimal semantic unit should not be identified with a word, which may contain more than one morpheme. The most constant context of a word is with other words in a sentence, the purpose of which is to communicate something (Brain, 1961). Are there musical parallels to these speech components? The smallest units in music are single notes or chords which may be compared with phonemes; it is more difficult to think of a musical parallel for a word but a cell or unit of notes is a fair approximation; a sentence can consist of two words or many, similarly a musical statement can be brief or long, containing a succession of musical ideas; cadences can be likened to punctuation marks though they are far more than this.

The meaning of a word can vary according to the context in which it is employed. Brain frequently used the term "chair" as an example. "Will you take the chair?" can mean, "Will you preside at this meeting?", "Will you take this university appointment?" or simply, "Will you take this chair (away)?" Music can pose similar problems of differences in meaning according to the context and the capacity and experience of the perceiver.

If we consider this note we find it evokes differing responses from different musicians, for the individual with absolute pitch it means 440 Hz when heard, but for the violinist it is an open string; the tenor regards it as a note towards the top of his range, while the pianist sees it as a lever near the middle of the keyboard. More complex examples are easily found. When composers use similar or identical material in different works recognition of a piece is difficult or impossible, particularly if it is played out of context. A pianist asked, "What is this?" as he played the opening notes of Bach's C major organ prelude (BWV547) and received the immediate answer, "The first chorus of Cantata 65, *Sie werden aus Saba alle kommen*." There is only one difference in the first eight notes of the two works, both are in C major, but the organ prelude is in 9/8 time while the cantata is 12/8. Encouraged by his success the pianist challenged his friends with the opening of the G major organ fugue (BWV541), and they were wrong again with the suggestion, "The first chorus of Cantata 21, *Ich hatte viel Bekümmernis*." The pattern of notes is again very similar, though not identical, both works are in 4/4 time, and although the cantata is in C minor the fugal choral entry is in the major; the listeners failed to appreciate the differences in pitch and sequence of notes. Their mistakes in both tests were a reflection of their interests, musicality and memory. In the proper setting of organ, instrumental sinfonia or chorus no difficulty would arise.

Authors as diverse as Hindemith the composer (1961a) and Ustvedt the Norwegian neurologist (1937) regard speech as precise and music as necessarily imprecise, though Mendelssohn, a classical scholar, took the opposite view when he remarked that music is more precise than words. In fact, while speech can be beautifully precise it can also be imprecise, as in people who express themselves poorly or are suffering from an emotional disturbance. Imprecision may be deliberate, as in the civil servant's "We reserve our position on that one", which may mean "No", "Perhaps", "We will think about it" or "We are going to do nothing". On its own terms music can be extremely precise when the composer is a master, for example, any chorale prelude or organ fugue by J. S. Bach, a Haydn quartet or a serial piece by Webern. Lesser composers may be imprecise or the master may not be at his best. Musical precision implies exact musical grammar, including faithful observance of the form employed. Speech can be precise or imprecise according to the emotional state of the speaker, his verbal capacity, or the demands of the moment. Music can only be regarded as essentially imprecise in the sense that it cannot convey information and ideas in the way that words do but that is all.

The next question is whether composers use musical units in any universal or general way in order to achieve meaning, that is to say whether there is a vocabulary of music. Hindemith (1961b) said there is no evidence that composers have ever agreed that any group of notes or chords represents a certain meaning or communicates the same thought, though he conceded that "certain patterns of tone setting correspond with certain emotional reactions on the listener's part". Cooke (1959) argued forcefully that composers use similar material to express similar meanings or to depict similar situations, and he provided a wealth of examples to support his contention. Meaning in words, however, can be misunderstood or interpreted in different ways, and the same must be true of music for in both cases the ultimate interpretation is the prerogative of the listener.

There are similarities between the languages of speech and music in the use of anticipation. In speech we are often able to anticipate the words which are to come and sometimes a whole paragraph or even an entire speech. Delight comes when the cue proves false and an unexpected meaning emerges. This is the basis of some of the best verbal humour. In music auditory cues may lead to correct anticipation, which can be intellectually satisfying, or to an unexpected further sequence of notes and chords, which provides a new experience; for example, the finale of Mozart's *Haffner Symphony*. The performer can also contribute in this way, as happened at a performance of the *St. Matthew Passion* of J. S. Bach before an informed audience, many of whom were armed with scores. In one of the soprano arias a foreign singer produced an unexpected and unusual ornament. Many heads were raised, smiles exchanged, and a brief but new musical experience was shared. The perceptual situation is comparable to that of a batsman in a cricket match facing a spin bowler who produces an ostensible leg-break, but the ball is in fact a well concealed top-spinner or a googly; of course, the response of the misled batsman is not one of pleasure though it includes appreciation of a false cue.

The ultimate difference between music and speech is that music is always an art, though sometimes debased, whereas speech is the language of common people who employ it as a practical means of communication. Art in words, drama, verse and literature, forms a rather small proportion of the total output of spoken or written speech.

This incomplete comparison of speech and music may be concluded with the thought that they are different languages employing different symbols, words and notes; the subject will arise again when score reading is discussed. We must now look more closely at the language of music, which can be conveniently defined as the way in which musical sounds are employed to convey musical ideas.

## Direct representation in music

The capacity of musical language to represent exactly is extremely limited in contrast with speech. Certain sounds can be reproduced approximately, for example, the sounds of water or of a storm, and the noises of insects and calls of birds and animals. Familiar examples of exact representation are the use of the cuckoo's call by Beethoven in his sixth symphony and Mahler in his first, and by Delius in *On Hearing the First Cuckoo in Spring*. Bach imitates the sounds of the turtle dove with recorders in the sixth movement of Cantata 71, *Gott ist mein König*. Insect sounds can be approximately represented, as in Bartok's "night music", for example the third movement of the music for *Strings, Percussion and Celesta*, while Ravel depicts cats and frogs in *L'Enfant et les Sortilèges*. These onomatopoeic effects are often of secondary importance to the melodic, harmonic and rhythmic material which they accompany or of which they form a part; they provide appropriate backgrounds and incidental sounds which help to create an atmosphere or a scene, as in the piano accompaniments of many of Schubert's songs. However, there are exceptions to this generalisation, like Ravel's *Jeux d'Eau*, where water sounds echo throughout the piece; the composer wrote of *Jeux d'Eau*, "This piece, inspired by the sound of water and the music of fountains, waterfalls and streams. . . ." (Ravel, 1972a.) Messaien employs and imitates birdsong extensively in many works, but it seems unlikely that anyone listens to the *Catalogue d'Oiseaux* in order to learn the calls and songs of different birds, it is more helpful to buy recordings made in the field. Enjoyment stems from the music which Messaien has composed on the basis of birdsong he heard and recorded.

It is not possible to represent a word or sentence in musical terms, although a text influences or determines the structure of a musical work. Word painting has formed an important part of the composer's equipment from the earliest times until the present day. Dallapiccola (1964) spoke feelingly on the subject of word painting and serial composition. Richard Barnfield (1574–1627) wrote in verse on the agreement of music and "sweet poetry". The idea of music and poetry as sister and brother is contained both in this poem and the writings of others. The successful union of words and music provides memorable experiences in musical life, but there can be no word painting without words.

Music is concerned with the communication of musical ideas, and this notion needs some further consideration. Unless music is accompanied by words, either in song, an inscribed score, or a written programme, or is heard in a particular environment or set of circumstances, no ideas other than musical will pass from composer to listener, except in so far as the latter is informed so that his knowledge and expectation compound the experience. Admittedly such situations are rare in practice but the basic idea contained in this statement appears sound. Busoni (1941) wrote, "Music in whatever shape and place and however paired remains music and nothing else . . . it may . . . become part of a given genre . . . through imagination, by means of a title or motto, or of a text, or by reason of the situation in which it is placed. No music bears the indelible imprint of church music and is recognisable as such. . . ." This point is also made by Westrup (1966) who remarked that the structure, style and instrumental writing of Bach's sacred and secular cantatas are similar, indeed Bach sometimes uses the same music in both contexts. It is particularly difficult to identify the sacred and secular in the case of Bach, and only a well informed listener could assuredly distinguish a secular aria or recitative from a sacred version, assuming that the words could not be clearly heard. This does not imply that composer, performer or hearer may not enjoy a valid religious experience. A known melody may give a context to the music, for example, a chorale tune in an organ prelude announces that the work has religious significance. Other musical styles may be regarded as characteristically ecclesiastical by the informed listener, for example, plainsong, melismatic organum, the verse anthems of Gibbons and Purcell, or Victorian and Edwardian services and anthems with robust organ accompaniment, say Stanford's *Magnificat* and *Nunc Dimittis* in B flat; but it would be unwise to state the point more firmly than that.

Musical ignorance in an audience can lead to misinterpretation. In one home Handel's *Largo* in G was considered appropriate music for a Sunday afternoon. Family and visitors would sit with rapt attention, quite unaware that they were listening to a piano transcription of an operatic aria in which the singer apostrophises the shade in which he sits.

## The composer

Music begins with the composer and there would be none without him. The terms composer and composition have the sanctity of long usage, though inventor and invention convey the sense of original musical thought and creation more correctly. A musical work may have its beginning in a musical idea conceived in the composer's mind. Ravel said, "I think and feel in sounds" and, "I am a musical hydrant, music flows from me like water." Schoenberg (1947a) wrote, "A real composer is not one who plays first on the piano and writes down what he has played. A real composer conceives his ideas, his entire music in his mind, in his imagination, and he does not need an instrument"; the point made here is partly technical, while Schoenberg affirmed that music is conceived in the mind he was also deprecating the use of instruments in composition. Sessions (1971a) described how the first idea for a piano sonata came in the form of a complex chord preceded by a sharp but heavy up beat, "this chord rang through my ear almost obsessively one day as I was walking in Pisa".

At this point we must digress briefly to consider when a musical idea becomes music. Presumably this should be at the time of conception, but in practice the transformation can only be seen to take place when the idea is exteriorised by performance or notational recording. This definition is an important matter for some music is never written down. A composer who is a good performer may extemporise fluently and not all the music invented in this way will be recorded. C. P. E. Bach said that some of his father's finest inspirations in organ music were never committed to paper. If J. S. Bach was pleased with an extemporisation and had sufficient leisure immediately after the performance he would write out the work directly; both the *Fantasia and Fugue in G Minor* and the three part *Ricercare* from the *Musical Offering* were preserved in this way. This method of composition is essentially one for keyboard music. The practice of exploring or strumming a keyboard instrument in a search for musical ideas was deplored by Bach, he dubbed pupils indulging in it "keyboard cavaliers". However, Stravinsky admitted that he worked in this fashion and the technical and intellectual objections of Bach and Schoenberg are hard to sustain if the music thus produced is of a high standard.

According to some composers the idea of a whole work can come as a sudden inspiration so that the general structure of a symphony or other major invention is imagined; Mozart wrote that his best works appeared to him all at once. However, the creative musician usually has many hurdles to overcome before realisation is complete (Hindemith, 1961c); Brahms wrote, "What is properly called invention, or a real musical idea, is . . . a gift, an inspiration which I cannot encourage in any way . . . but ultimately I have to make it my own by incessant labour. And that will not be quickly accomplished" (Fuller-Maitland, 1911), an experience confirmed by Debussy who said that he might require weeks to decide on one harmonious chord in preference to another (Lockspeiser, 1936).

Even the unskilled musical person can have an apparently new melodic or rhythmic idea, just as he may imagine visually or mathematically. The material is not necessarily novel, it may derive from conscious or subconscious memories of folk tunes, other men's work or natural sounds.

While musical ideas are often spontaneous they can be evoked by various experiences, religious, literary, or poetic, pastoral or emotional. The provocative emotional experience may be happiness or sorrow, for example, Wagner's *Siegfried Idyll* and the last movement of Mahler's *Das Lied von der Erde* respectively. The stimulus may be a picture or collection of pictures, as in Moussorgsky's *Pictures from an Exhibition*, Martinu's *The Frescoes of Piero della Francesca*, Granados' *Goyescas* and McCabe's *The Chagall Windows*. The composer may write for himself, for a group of people, or for an individual artist. Schoenberg (1974b) wrote of his variations Op. 43B, "It is one of those compositions which one writes in order to enjoy one's own virtuosity, and . . . to give a certain group of music lovers . . . something better to play . . . technically this is a masterwork . . . it is also original, and I know it is inspired." Many compositions have been written for individual performers because the composer has admired their musicianship.

It is not unusual for creative artists and other less gifted persons to undergo peculiar experiences in hypnagogic states, that is states of near sleep. Musical ideas arising in these states must be written down immediately for they are evanescent and once forgotten do not return. In practice these notions, musical or otherwise, are rarely recorded and the value the individual accords them may be erroneous. Berlioz (Cairns, 1969) wrote, "I dreamed one night that I was composing a symphony and heard it in my dreams. On waking next morning I could recall nearly the whole of the movement, which was an allegro in A minor in two-four time (that is all I can remember about it)." He went on to describe how the prospect of additional work and attendant financial problems at a difficult time caused him to reject his idea so that he did not write out what he had heard. The next night "the symphony appeared and rang obstinately in my head. I heard the allegro in A minor distinctly. More, I seemed to see it written. . . ." Again he resisted the temptation to rise and write, "clinging to the hope I would forget. At last I fell asleep, and when I next awoke all recollections of it had vanished for ever." It is a matter for speculation whether a major work was lost to posterity; on the whole this seems unlikely, hypnagogic and dream ideas commonly appear more remarkable at the time than the light of day proves them to be.

The amateur should not take too romantic a view of the sources of inspiration. The composer is a professional creative artist, a thinker in music, and he invents music because he must. Once known a proportion of his work will come from commissions. He may be asked to provide a ceremonial piece for a state occasion, a setting of some part of the liturgy for the Church, an opera or a string quartet. The occasion, the text or thoughts of an individual patron may influence subsequent invention but they cannot provide it. A commission to compose certainly channels the composer's ideas and compels him to concentrate on one particular problem (Bush, 1954). The nature of the commissioned work stimulates appropriate musical ideas for the instruments or voices involved in its performance.

Reading can be helpful; describing his method in writing *The Apostles* Elgar said, "When I propose such a work as this I first of all read everything I can lay my hands on which bears on the subject either directly or indirectly, meditating on all that I have sifted out as likely to serve my purpose, and blending it with my musical conceptions. Every personality appears to me in a musical dress"; he concluded, "I never sit down and say 'Now I will compose'. The thing is inconceivable to me. What comes, comes of itself; of course I am often thinking in music." (Buckley, 1905.)

Once the musical idea or ideas have been conceived by introspection or in response to some external stimulus creation depends on the composer's professional artistic skill. His technical expertise derives from detailed study of his subject, including the works of the masters, as in other artistic and scientific disciplines; the music he has heard in the past provides a constant store of auditory experience from which both old and new ideas may grow.

The belief that originality stems from general breadth of knowledge has been widely canvassed in the past, an individual so endowed has been said to have a greater capacity for original ideas. There is certainly truth in this notion but it is questionable how far or how often wide ranging knowledge contributes to originality in musical composition. Some distinguished composers have proved highly accomplished in artistic or intellectual fields other than music; Berlioz and Schumann were able literary men; Mendelssohn possessed many gifts including classical scholarship and a pleasing skill with watercolour; Crotch was a modest composer but his drawings are so competent that some have been attributed to Constable. Against this group must be set the majority whose talents have been solely musical (Chapter 11). Musical originality derives from originality of musical thought, which in turn springs from the inherent capacity and acquired experience of the individual. Realisation of musical ideas depends ideally on a degree of technical skill which allows their easy translation into notation.

In practice the process of invention may be swift or slow, easy or laboured. Mozart, that great creative artist, wrote his three last symphonies (in E flat, K543, G minor, K550, and C major, K551) in three months during the summer of 1788 and both Bach and Mendelssohn had the facility of rapid composition. Mahler composed his huge eighth symphony over a period of eight weeks in the summer of 1906 despite the interruption caused by an engagement to conduct *The Marriage of Figaro* at Salzburg (Mahler, 1968). On the other hand, Beethoven's great music evolved more slowly; his sketchbooks show the way in which his original ideas were revised over months or years.

At the end of the creative process stands the completed score, constructed from musical ideas, melodies and fragments of melody, chords and rhythmic figures, which are worked out in a musical train of thought according to an appreciable plan (Sessions, 1971b). During invention the composer is aware that certain patterns of notes are likely to cause predictable emotional responses in those who listen, but he will not expect all to share the same experience. Boulez (1975) took an extreme view on this question, "I am convinced that however perceptive the composer he cannot imagine the consequences, immediate or ultimate, of what he has written. . . ."

In writing the composer uses his own style of musical language, though this may be partly or largely shared with his contemporaries; an individual or unique style is the mark of originality and sometimes of innovatory genius. Styles change with the years, as do styles of speech, and these changes become incorporated or embodied in the whole language of music if they prove acceptable; in some cases acceptance and incorporation may be delayed for many years, in others there may be later rejection. While musical language transcends national barriers more easily than spoken language, and the baroque provided a general European style for several decades, individual composers and groups adopt dissimilar styles so that there are different dialects or languages, which may be international, within the whole language at any point in time.

The score provides performers with indications of what notes to play and how to play them. Some modern composers restrict their notation and instructions to broad indications of what they require, for example, the performer is allowed freedom of choice of notes within prescribed limits. Successful score reading requires a considerable gift of auditory imagery. While it is possible to comprehend the meaning and imagery of a piece of prose, and more arguably verse, by the simple act of reading to oneself, reading music is an incomplete experience unless the music is heard within the reader's private perceptual world. This demands the addition of instrumental timbre to the written notes of the score and timbre is weakly represented in musical notation. If the score reader has no memory of the nominated timbres at his disposal his experience is substantially diminished. Tovey once remarked, "To me, the music of Palestrina was a mass of grammatical constructions until I heard a choir singing in the apse of a cathedral"; presumably he had not heard the music of Palestrina before this event, or he had not heard it in the traditional context of the Church. The late Ernest Newman wrote that he would rather experience a silent ideal performance sitting at home with his scores than attend a concert performance with all its imperfections and physical limitations. Score reading at this level is a minority accomplishment, and there must be doubt whether it is achieved by ordinary mortals unless the work read has been heard at least once.

Schoenberg (1974c) drew attention to the importance of score reading in assessing a composition; defending Mahler he wrote that by reading the students "would see all those strokes of genius which are never to be found in lesser masters. He would discover them on every page . . . in every bar, in every succession of notes and harmonies."

The score becomes fully alive only when translated by performance into music heard. Nevertheless, it is apparent that the language of music is conveyed by reading to those who are sufficiently educated and more fully to individuals who possess considerable powers of auditory memory and imagery.

What is the composer communicating as he writes and thereafter when his work is played or read? We have argued previously that the ideas conveyed can only be musical though their conception may have derived from non-musical stimuli or experience. As an artist the composer creates to fulfil and please himself and to communicate his musical thoughts to potential audiences. His only method of communication is the structure of his composition, both he and his audience are dependent on his skill in transforming ideas into an acceptable comprehensible whole.

Does the completed work express anything more than the composer's technical capacity and inventive powers? While many composers have been in no doubt that they express their feelings or affirm their beliefs in their work, some modern composers, notably Stravinsky and Hindemith, have taken a contrary, anti-Romantic view. Hindemith (1961d) stated his position when he wrote, "If the composer himself thinks he is expressing his own feelings we must accuse him of lack of observation." This attitude may reflect both a philosophical view and a predominant concern with technical ideas. It is difficult for the neurologist to accept that the creative intellectual activity concerned in musical composition can be divorced from the artist's emotional life and temperament. The division of thought and experience into the cognitive or intellectual and emotional or affective aspects may be a convenient convention for neurologists and psychologists to adopt, but it has no sound foundation in neurophysiology and neuropsychology. We can all think of situations in which emotion appears to exclude intellect and *vice versa*, but these episodes are generally passing in normal persons and the two elements combine in virtually all experience. There seems no reason to suppose that musical composition is not associated with parallel neural activity in the several parts of the brain which are particularly concerned with the emotional or intellectual aspects of experience, though one may dominate the other.

The idea that emotion and intellect, that is to say the whole person, combine in composition does not imply that creation is necessarily affected by the feelings of the moment, by socio-economic problems or by the environment, in normal individuals, though this may be the case. Creative thought and work demand intense concentration, and successful conception and delivery require the capacity to inhibit all mental activity which is not concerned with the task on hand. A composer's work is a reflection of himself, but the image may be different from that which others commonly see in him. It follows that we cannot expect to learn about the artist's non-musical thoughts and experiences from his music; we can expect to encounter and explore his musical mind through the medium of his work. However, the composer is not limited to musical symbols in communicating his ideas, for he can provide clues to meaning by inscriptions on scores or by writing verbal accounts of what he is trying to convey. Naturally the scope of communication is broadened when words and music combine in composition.

## The performer

The composer's work has been completed in the score and the performer is the essential intermediary who should fulfil the composer's ideas by reproducing the written symbols in sound with technical precision and faithful interpretative skill. This paragraph refers to more recent and modern times, for much early music such as madrigals was written for performers only. Performers constitute part of the audience in a peculiar way, as the composer may do, but their objective is communication to a group of hearers and they are popularly divorced from the listeners. The performance is all important to players and singers and their audience, but in the context of this argument adequate realisation is taken for granted. The important question of interpretation, over which the composer commonly has no control because he is absent from the scene, cannot be pursued here, although it is apparent that dissimilar interpretations of the same work will evoke differing perceptual responses among listeners.

## The listener

We must now turn to the audience and examine the receptive aspects of musical language. It is easy to be too solemn in discussing the role of the listener in a musical event; music is written and played for people to hear, enjoy and hopefully understand. Before examining the listener's part we will look briefly at the problems of musical semantics, development of musical appreciation and other factors involved in audience response.

We have noticed that words are necessary to describe music or to talk about it; these words can be employed objectively or subjectively. Words are used objectively in analysis of a piece, and persons of comparable musical education can be expected to produce similar, if not identical, verbal analyses of the same work under test conditions. Words are used subjectively to describe affective or emotional responses, and here we are on far less certain ground, as a study of different interpretative commentaries on many major works will show; Sessions (1971c) quoted the different descriptions of Beethoven's *Seventh Symphony* by Berlioz and Wagner as an example of the difficulty of defining the emotions aroused by a specific composition. Imberty (1970) examined the problem experimentally by recording individual subjective verbal responses to Debussy's *Preludes for Piano*; responses were different and even contradictory for the same musical extract. Imberty concluded that music is semantically ambiguous. These observations support the view that musical experience, that is, reception, perception and interpretation, is a matter for the individual listener. Persons of similar musical education and verbal capacity cannot be expected to have identical experiences, or if they do they are unlikely to formulate these experiences in the same terms, though we may all be socially guilty of using descriptive terms deriving from what we have read or learned about a composition.

French psychologists in particular have investigated musical perception over the last twenty years, for example, Francés (1958). Imberty (1968, 1969) and Zenatti (1969, 1970) studied the development of musical perception in children and university students. They found that melody is the most important factor for children; appreciation of tonal structure is progressively acquired with increasing age. The question whether consonance is socially or biologically determined was examined by Imberty (1970). He concluded that evolution of the sensation of consonance and development of musical language run along parallel paths. The acceptance of chords as consonant is not simply a matter of hearing, education and familiarity are influential in persons of all ages. Adults accept certain chords as consonant, in contrast to children, because they recognise them as a functional element in a language in addition to simple auditory acceptance. Consonance is an individual attainment influenced by biological and "acculturation" factors. This interesting work shows how the receptive aspects of musical language are enlarged over the years.

Any concert or radio audience consists of a heterogeneous group of people with differing standards of musical knowledge, variously developed musical vocabulary or language, and differing capacities for discussing what they have heard. They come in different states of preparedness, some are well informed about the programme and have studied the works to be played or sung, while others have come unprepared except for the intention of enjoying the music. However, virtually all are conditioned towards what they are about to hear because they know the names of the composers and the works to be played. The composer's name raises mental pictures of the person and his style, and these notions, whether true or false, modify expectation; knowledge of the programme raises memories of previously heard performances and of things read or otherwise learned about the compositions included there. Anticipation also stems from knowing the names of the performers, especially if the conductor, soloist and orchestra or choir are familiar.

There are also non-musical factors which influence or modify a musical occasion, and some of these have been mentioned in Chapter 1. The environment is important, the concert hall or opera house may appear beautiful or ugly and the acoustics good or poor, or it may be unacceptably hot or cold; listening may take place at home against a benign, familiar background. Pre-performance expectation can be heightened by knowing one will meet friends beforehand. The audience may prove acceptable or unacceptable; their dress and manners may be alien or they may applaud too long and too loudly. There are sensitive individuals who only fully enjoy music heard alone or in the presence of carefully chosen companions. Some listeners who are themselves performers are not fully satisfied musically unless they are actively engaged in performance.

Apart from all these musical and non-musical influences which modify audience response there are other individual factors to be considered. The listener can attend different events in different frames of mind. He may go in an analytical mood and listen carefully to the structure of the items performed, or he may decide quite voluntarily that he will listen in a relaxed way and simply enjoy himself; ideally he will combine these types of approach. His mental state will also affect perceptual experience so that the fatigue, anxiety or depression of daily life can alter his responses. Modification of responses in persons with emotional disorder can be extreme; a highly competent amateur brass player noticed no tendency to sadness on hearing or playing pieces in a minor key until he suffered a depressive illness following a head injury; thereafter he wept unrestrainedly whenever he heard music in the minor. The effects of organic brain disease on the listener's emotional responses cannot be discussed here, but the selective results of thalamic damage have been mentioned in Chapter 1 and may be usefully recalled at this point.

What is the listener's role in a musical event? He is an essential member of the group for he has the privilege of ultimate interpretation whether he comes in knowledge or ignorance, enthusiasm or boredom. The one element in the event which is permanent and unchanging is the score, for although the performance can be expected to accord generally with the composer's ideas this cannot be guaranteed, and executants may hold genuinely different opinions on the manner of performance. Each listener is free to reach his own conclusions, both on the music and the composer's intentions, but these individual notions about meaning all derive from the musical structure embodied in the score, with the reservation that early scores are generally in a rather fluid state, for example the figured base.

We have argued that intellect and temperament or emotional state are indivisibly linked in musical invention. This idea is also true of performance, at least in general terms. Similarly, the listener's responses are both intellectual, that is to say cognitive and objective, and emotional or affective, though the proportions vary from one person to the next. If a composition is technically faultless or approximately so and the listener is sufficiently educated to understand the ways in which the composer is using musical language, that is to say his style, then hearing and comprehension may go hand in hand. However, this intellectual approach is clearly insufficient, for emotion can never be excluded from artistic experience, even a didactic work like *The Art of Fugue* brings a sense of satisfaction and completeness as Bach proceeds to solve the problems in counterpoint he has set himself. Admittedly the work of some composers speaks more to the intellect and that of others predominantly to the emotions, but the man who appeals equally and unitedly to the twin horsemen of mind and affect gains the wider response. It has been implied that a proportion of any audience is insufficiently educated musically to appreciate the composer's skills and subtleties to the full; insofar as such persons enjoy the performance they will do so in more subjective than objective ways, but their experience is not necessarily less valid or perceptively acute than that of the more informed.

In contrast to the score a musical performance is a transient evanescent thing; it can never be exactly repeated, there are too many variables involved in the environment, performers, and audience, but the effects of a performance can be long lasting granted good musical memory and auditory imagination; admittedly as time passes certain passages or aspects tend to stand out in memory so that the long term picture is to some extent a caricature of the original.

Listening to music is not always planned in the ways we have been discussing, unexpected or accidental exposure is a common experience which deserves attention. Events of this sort may enlarge or enhance the whole perceptual experience because of the unusual or pleasing surroundings in which the music is heard; personal examples include a Bach violin *partita* floating across an English meadow from one cottage to another, and perhaps more predictably a Buxtehude organ fugue suddenly sounding through the cloisters at Heiligenkreuz Abbey near Vienna.

The B.B.C. have recently broadcast a few musical programmes without giving the composers' names and it would be interesting to know the audience's responses. One celebrated example of the consequences of concealing the composer's name concerns Ravel's *Valses Nobles et Sentimentales*. These "were first performed to the accompaniment of hoots and catcalls at the Société Musicale Indepéndente, where the music was all anonymous. The audience voted for the authorship of each piece. By a minute majority the paternity of the *Valses* was ascribed to me" (Ravel, 1972b). "So many votes wandered in unexpected directions: Zoltan Kodály and Erik Satie for instance . . . such howlers are surprising" (Roland-Manuel, 1972). To the prepared or unprepared listener the music is the important element in any musical occasion, nevertheless the experience is incomplete for some people unless they know at least who wrote the music and preferably details of the work.

## Musical symbolism

The difficulties and disagreements which arise when listeners describe their emotional responses or try to discover non-musical meanings in a work have been briefly explored above. Composers may aim deliberately at an emotional effect or series of effects, and many have written about the methods used to reach this goal; moreover, some have recorded details of the emotions they sought to evoke together with the technique employed, for example, Monteverdi's preface to his eighth book of madrigals (*Madrigali Guerrieri e Amorosi*, 1638). This can be described as conscious symbolism. Both Morley and Weelkes were conscious symbolists, and Weelkes' madrigal *As Vesta was from Latmos hill descending* is an apt illustration of this approach. In the baroque period an ascending major passage symbolised the Ascent to Heaven.

There have been times in musical history when conventions such as the use of certain intervals, *tempi* or rhythms, conveyed definite meanings to the audiences, or different instruments were employed in a stylised way to depict defined situations or human and supernatural characters.

On the other hand there is unconscious symbolism, much of which is conjectural. Cooke (1959) has explored the whole subject of musical symbolism, and a brief note must suffice here. The ascending notes of the major triad (1.3.5) have been used to express joy or triumph, for example, the beginning of the last movement of Beethoven's fifth symphony; variations on this pattern of notes, like Byrd's *Sing Joyfully* (1.5.3) and the *Gloria* from Bach's *B minor Mass* (5.1.2.3) convey similar, though not identical, feelings of joy. The notes of the minor triad and minor keys generally have been used to convey a sense of sorrow, discomfort or pain; the descending minor progression (5.3.1) in the *Qui Tollis* of the *B minor Mass* reflects the words of the text. For many years composers were expected to complete a piece in the minor by a modulation to the major, the *Tierce de Picardie*, so that the end was a perfect consonance. The tritone or augmented fourth was forbidden by the Church for centuries because it was the *diabolus in musica* and therefore associated with the Devil and other demonic forces. Later both remote and modern composers have used the tritone to symbolise Satan, similar inimical agencies and horrific or sinister events; Elgar did this in the *Dream of Gerontius* and *For the Fallen*. Usages of this sort have naturally declined or disappeared with the widespread abandonment of tonality. Modulation, that is passing from one key to another, changes the mood of the music and through this the feelings of the listener. The modulation from the tonic (D major) to the subdominant (G major) at the words *Et in terra pax* in the *Gloria* of *Bach's B minor Mass* provides a striking example which even the inattentive ignorant hearer is unlikely to miss. More generally, plainsong melodies, such as those used in the *Credo* and *Confiteor* of the Mass and the *Dies Irae* of the *Mass for the Dead*, have sounded messages of faith to the Christian believer over the centuries.

The intermedii of Schütz's *Historia von der Geburt Jesu Christi* (The Christmas Story, 1664) contain several examples of the ways in which different instruments can assist in characterisation, viols for the angel, recorders for the shepherds, trombones for the high priests and clarini (small bore trumpets for use in the high register) for Herod the King. Trombones were employed traditionally to suggest the supernatural in seventeenth and eighteenth century opera. Mozart used these instruments to indicate deep religious feeling in the choruses of the priests in *The Magic Flute* and to paint the supernatural in another sense in the Cemetery Scene and descent of the Don into Hell in *Don Giovanni*. Trumpets and drums have long signified civil or military power and continue to do so, but they may also celebrate divine power, as in the Masses of Bach and Haydn. Bach used *pizzicato* strings, sometimes with "tender and mournful oboes" (Whittaker, 1959), in cantata movements treating the subject of death, for instance, BWV8 No. 1, *Beloved God when shall I die?* and BWV95 No. 5, *Strike soon blessed hour of death* (Whittaker, 1959; Steinitz, 1975).

Naturally it is hard to know what proportion of contemporary populations was aware of the musical conventions and what they implied at different points in history, but even today there are social or cultural groups who share an emotional response to a musical interval or phrase, for example, the falling sound of the priestly intonation at the beginning of the *Credo* or the ascent of the bugler's reveille. Generally or widely agreed responses of this sort probably account for only a small proportion of musical happenings; the subject is one which is susceptible to more detailed objective study than it has been afforded to date.

Mutual agreement about the referential aspects of a piece, as distinct from its strictly musical content, is most likely to be achieved in specialist groups of listeners who are well informed about the works performed, though even here total agreement cannot be expected. When the composer attempts to express philosophical or political notions in his work the references will only be accurately identified by those who have read or have been told what he has tried to do, although some composers have conveyed such thoughts by judicious quotations, like John Ireland, who used the *Internationale* in *These Things Shall be*, and Charles Ives, *The Unanswered Question* and other pieces.

When one compounds all the factors concerned in a musical occasion, place, standard of performance, and an audience comprising many conditions of people in all varieties of mood, it appears unlikely that any consistent message or meaning can flow from the composer to the individual listener. In fact, musical language is precise and given adequate performance the messages in sound come through unmistakably to those who know the language and more remarkably to many whose acquaintance with it is scanty. As we have seen, each listener is on his own perceptually, both experience and interpretation or assignment of meaning are his alone. One of the charms of music lies in the capacity of the relatively uninformed listener to penetrate the musical thought of the composer as the fruit of his own concentration and open mind; he may have, on the day, a richer artistic experience than his more learned companion.

### Conclusion

We have seen that music can properly be defined as a language. While there are similarities between speech and music there are also important differences between them. Music is concerned with the expression and communication of musical ideas and it is an unsatisfactory medium for conveying non-musical notions; speech deals in words and the suggestion that it is more precise than music probably stems from universally greater familiarity with words. Music is always an art but speech is only sometimes so. Speech and music are alike in that both are living languages which change with the passing years. Words are necessary to music, both in song and in reading or conversation about the art, but words cannot describe music to someone who has never heard it. Reading is essential for study of the composer's life and the age in which he lived, two important considerations for those who are interested in the whole man and his work.

Are there always meanings beyond musical ideas which the listener should seek in musical works? The answer to this question is a matter for the individual to decide. Judgment of the worth of a composition rests, however, on its musical value, the composer's skilful and original use of musical language. With great works the audience is so impressed by the fruits of the composer's invention and art that questions of non-musical meaning take second place.

Intellect and emotion are inseparably bound up in expressive and receptive musical experience, but although a good deal is known about the neuroanatomical and neurophysiological substrate of emotion we do not know why music moves us as it does. Proust (1913) wrote of "keys of tenderness, of passion, of courage, of serenity" which awaken in us the emotion corresponding to the theme; music is then the image of these emotions, but that thought is only a partial answer to our problem. In the absence of any expectation of an immediate solution we turn to the poets, and in this case to Addison, "Music the greatest good that mortals know and all of heaven we have below."

# REFERENCES

BARNFIELD, R. (1574–1627) *Poems in Divers Humors*. Sonnet 1.

BOULEZ, P. (1975) *Boulez on Music To-day*. Trans. S. Bradshaw and R. R. Bennett, London, Faber & Faber, p. 18.

BRAIN, LORD (1961) *Speech Disorders*. London, Butterworths, pp. 9–12.

BUCKLEY, R. J. (1905) *Sir Edward Elgar*. London, John Lane: Bodley Head, pp. 75, 76.

BUSH, G. (1954) *Musical Creation and the Listener*. London, Fdk. Muller Ltd.

BUSONI, F. (1941) *The Unity of Music*. Scritti a pensieri sulla Musica. Ed. L. Dallapiccola and G. M. Gatti, Florence, pp. 70, 71. Quoted by J. Barzun (ed.) in *Pleasures of Music*, 1954, London, Readers Union, Michael Joseph.

CAIRNS, D. (ed.) (1969) *Memoirs of Hector Berlioz*. London, Gollancz, p. 470.

COOKE, D. (1959) *The Language of Music*. London, Oxford University Press.

DALLAPICCOLA, L. (1964) Personal communication.

FRANCÉS, R. (1958) *La Perception de la Musique*. Paris, Vrin.

FULLER-MAITLAND, J. A. (1911) *Brahms*. London, Methuen & Co., pp. 69, 70.

GIMSON, A. C. (1962) *An Introduction to the Pronunciation of English*. Reprinted 1970. London, Edward Arnold, pp. 42 et seq.

HINDEMITH, P. (1961a) *A Composer's World*. New York, Doubleday & Co., p. 40.

— (1961b) Ibid., p. 41.

— (1961c) Ibid., p. 70.

— (1961d) Ibid., pp. 42–44.

IMBERTY, M. (1968) Recherche sur la genèse du sentiment de consonance. From *Sciences de l'Art*, vol. 5, p. 29.

— (1969) L'acquisition des structures tonales chez l'enfant. From *Sciences de l'Art*, vol. 6, p. 59.

— (1970) Polysémie et coherence semantique du langage musical: I. La polysémie dans les réponses verbales associées à la musique, et la construction d'une échelle circulaire des expressivités musicales. From *Sciences de l'Art*, vol. 7, p. 77.

KOSTENEVICH, A. (1974) La Danse et La Musique by Henri Matisse: A New Interpretation. *Apollo*, vol. C. 154, 504–513.

LOCKSPEISER, E. (1936) *Debussy*. London, J. M. Dent & Sons, p. 108.

MAHLER, A. (1968) *Gustav Mahler, Memories and Letters*. Ed. D. Mitchell, London, J. Murray, p. 102.

MONRAD-KROHN, G. H. (1947) Dysprosody or altered "melody of language". *Brain*, **70**, 405–415.

PROUST, M. (1913) *À la Recherche du Temps Perdu*. vol. 2, Du côté de chez Swann. Translated 1924 by C. K. Scott Moncrieff, London, Chatto & Windus.

RAVEL, M. (1972a) *Biographic Sketch*. Quoted by Roland-Manuel, 1972, p. 31.

— (1972b) Ibid., pp. 58–60.

ROGERS, B. (1951) *The Art of Orchestration* (Principles of Tone Color in Modern Scoring). New York, Appelton-Century-Crofts Inc.

ROLAND-MANUEL (1972) *Maurice Ravel*. New York, Dover Publications.

SCHOENBERG, A. (1974a) *Letters*. Ed. Erwin Stein, London, Faber & Faber, p. 218.

— (1974b) Ibid., p. 222.

— (1974c) Ibid., p. 260.

SCHOLES, P. (1955) *Oxford Musical Companion*. Oxford University Press, p. 972.

SESSIONS, R. (1971a) *The Musical Experience of Composer, Performer, Listener*. Princeton, New Jersey, Princeton University Press, p. 52.

— (1971b) Ibid., pp. 46, 47.

— (1971c) Ibid., p. 23.

SIMPSON, R. (1975) Personal communication.

STEINITZ, P. (1975) *New Oxford History of Music. Opera and Church Music 1630–1750*. Oxford University Press, vol. 5, p. 763.

STRUNK, O. (1950) *Source Readings in Musical History*. New York, W. W. Norton & Co. Inc., p. 94.

USTVEDT, H. J. (1937) Über die Untersuchung der musikalischen Funktionen bei Patienten mit Gehirnleiden, besonders bei Patienten mit Aphasie. *Acta med. Scand.*, Suppl. 86.

WESTRUP, J. A. (1966) *Bach Cantatas*. London, B.B.C. Publications, pp. 7, 17, 18.

WHITTAKER, W. G. (1959) *The Cantatas of Johann Sebastian Bach*. 2 vols. Oxford University Press.

ZENATTI, A. (1969) Le développement génétique de la perception musicale. Monographies françaises de psychologie, 17. From *Sciences de l'Art*, vol. 6, p. 60.

— (1970) Perception melodique et acculturation tonale. Étude experimentale de l'influence du sexe sur les performances d'enfants ages de 5 à 10 ans. From *Sciences de l'Art*, vol. 7, p. 71.

# The Search for a Morphological Substrate in the Brains of Eminent Persons including Musicians: a Historical Review

## Introduction

To Rudolf Wagner (1860–1862) belongs the credit for having opened the discussion on the brains of eminent persons. He gave macroscopic descriptions of the brains of five scholars, including the illustrious mathematician Karl Friedrich Gauss. From this beginning, a large literature has arisen, particularly in the French and German languages and with a concentration around the turn of the century. It is associated mainly with the names of Rüdinger (1882a and b), Duval and his associates (including Chudszinski, Hervé, Manouvrier and Papillault, almost all published in the Bulletin of the Society of Anthropology at Paris), Retzius (1898–1905) and in English, of Spitzka (1901–1907).

Of these, the investigations by Retzius on the brains of Scandinavian scientists, scholars and of an unnamed statesman were the most influential. His work was almost contemporary with that of Spitzka of the United States who examined the brains of eminent physicians, scientists and other scholars. In addition, there have been investigations of smaller series or of individual brains; they include studies by Bastian (1880), by Sperino (1901), Hansemann (1899, 1907, 1908), Stieda (1908), Bechterev and Weinberg (1909), Horsley (1909), Maurer (1922, 1924), Donaldson (1928), Anthony (1935) and by Riese and Goldstein (1950). All these contributions dealt mainly with the brains of scholars; they will be discussed in some detail presently.

On the brains of eminent *musicians*, Auerbach (1906–1913) made the most outstanding contributions; we owe another investigation of a musician's brain to Klose (1920) who in addition provided a comprehensive review (in German) of previous work.

All these investigations were confined to *macroscopic* description. Only three histological (cytoarchitectonic) studies are known to me: in a preliminary communication (to my knowledge not yet elaborated),* Vogt (1929) described abnormally large nerve cells mainly in the 3rd layer of the cerebral cortex in Lenin's brain, which was damaged by arteriosclerosis. Somogyi (1930) counted nerve cells and studied the cytoarchitecture of relevant temporal areas in the brains of the violin prodigy Nagy and of the tenor Pogány. Economo (1929, 1930) gave full instructions on the investigation of "élite brains", but died before he could start work on the subject. Maximilian Rose (1938) described and illustrated the brain of Pilsudski. (This work could only be quoted from a review by Minkowski (1939) and the description and illustration by Schaffer (1939).)† Vogt spoke of a collection of 13 "élite brains" of Soviet scientists which were under investigation. These apparently are the same brains to which Blinkov and Poliakov briefly referred in 1938 and which include those of Pavlov, the writers Gorky and Mavakovsky and the musician Souk. The Russian authors spoke of important preliminary results without disclosing any detail.

Since the early studies by Bastian, Marshall and Horsley, there has been virtually no discussion on the subject in this country. Lord Brain (1960), in his *Reflections on Genius*, made only some general remarks which indicated that he was familiar with the literature. He appeared to be sceptical of morphological abnormalities in the brains of eminent personalities. Genius, he pointed out, is not necessarily more richly endowed with nerve cells. What is important, in his opinion, is their higher organization in functional units – which he called "schemata". I have failed to find any appreciable discussion of the subject in volumes 2 and 4 of the *Handbook of Clinical Neurology* which deal with localization of cortical function.

### Findings in the brains of outstanding scientists and other scholars:

Wagner investigating the brains of five scholars found a more complex and richer convolutional pattern than usual and an increase of brain-weight in most of them; he was, however, restrained in his conclusions, being well aware of the great variability of the brain in normal persons. Figure 1 reproduces Wagner's drawing of Gauss' frontal lobe compared with that

---

* Crome (1972) also did not know of any further publication on Lenin's brain. He was rightly critical of Vogt's far-reaching conclusions from findings in a heavily damaged brain.

† Of Rose's publication Minkowski said that both text and atlas are the work of a master, and that the excellent illustrations form a model for the investigation of brains of talented persons.

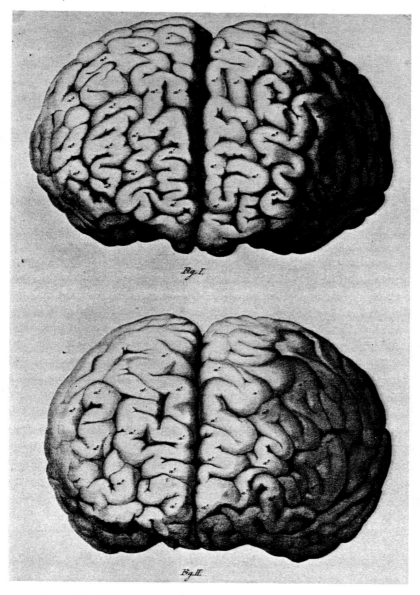

Figure 1    Reproduced from Wagner (1860), table 3, showing the frontal lobe of the brain of Gauss (Figure I) compared with that of a worker aged 57 (Figure II). There is a difference, but part of it is explained by the "stenogyrencephalic" (numerous, narrow gyri) pattern in the former and an "eurygyrencephalic" (fewer, but broader gyri) pattern in the latter. Both Retzius' types may occur in well developed brains.

of an ordinary workman aged 57. When Gauss died at the age of 78 from heart disease, there had been no appreciable mental deterioration.*

In Britain, Bastian (1880) described the brain of the mathematician de Morgan, in which he found a development of the frontal lobes, similar to that observed by Wagner in the brain of Gauss. Marshall (1892), investigating the brain of the distinguished historian, George Grote, was impressed by the great breadth, distinctness and volume of the convolutions generally, but particularly marked in the frontal lobe. Horsley (1909), investigating the brain of the mathematician Charles Babbage, described marked macroscopic development of the regions concerned with "locutory" and "graphic" function: i.e. in frontal and occipito-temporo-parietal regions of both hemispheres.

To Retzius and Spitzka we owe more concerted investigations. The former described in 1898 the brain of the Swedish astronomer Hugo Gyldén which he followed up with that of the mathematician Sonia Kovalevski (1900a), the physicist Adam Siljeström (1902) and the histologist Christian Lovén (1905). All these brains, despite age and terminal disease, showed a marked development of the cerebral cortex, especially in the frontal and parietal association areas. Retzius was particularly impressed by the prominence of the gyrus supramarginalis which, in the case of Hugo Gyldén for example, was "in the right hemisphere extraordinarily developed so that the upper posterior branch of the (Sylvian) fissure is much extended both posteriorly and superiorly". On the left side, the supramarginal gyrus was also well developed, though to a slightly lesser degree (Figure 2). He spoke of an "overhanging" of the gyrus within the Sylvian fissure, a phenomenon which he regarded as a genuine "opercularisation" of the fissure, comparable with that commonly seen in the simian sulcus lunatus. This prominence of the supramarginal gyrus Retzius found, in varying degrees, in the brains of Gyldén, Kovalevski and Siljeström, all of whom were distinguished mathematicians. He was, therefore, inclined to correlate mathematical talent with the conspicuous development of the supramarginal region in contrast to the prevailing opinion (Wagner, Bastian, Möbius (1900), Horsley) which regarded the frontal lobe as the mathematical "centre".

The extraordinary development of the supramarginal cortex is apparent not only in its posterior aspects, but Retzius found it conspicuous also in the

---

* Spitzka (1903, 1907), who also reproduced Wagner's drawing of Gauss' brain, compared it (undoubtedly more effectively) with the brain of a bushwoman (originally described by Marshall (1864)).

adjacent parts of the first temporal and supratemporal convolutions which include the anterior transverse temporal convolution and its adjacent associational areas. He wrote that he would not be surprised if mathematical and musical talent should to some extent be parallel. As will be seen presently, Auerbach's findings and conclusions moved in the same direction.

Christian Lovén and Adam Siljeström had shown outstanding oratorical qualities: Retzius found in their brains an especially developed inferior frontal convolution − in Lovén's brain the operculum frontale intermedium was particularly marked in the left hemisphere. In Siljeström this area was well developed on the right side, while the posterior operculum was larger on the left. I was unable to find clear indications of handedness in any of the four cases of Retzius.

Marked differences in the convolutional and fissural pattern in the two hemispheres were described by Retzius in all four brains, but − from his experience of his large normal series − he considered these to be within the normal ranges; in contrast, the *weight* of the two hemispheres was the same on both sides in all comparable cases (see Retzius 1896, pp. 156 and 158). Slight asymmetries (not exceeding *circa* 5 g) had been reported by Boyd (1861) in favour of the left hemisphere, while Wagner (1862, pp. 87 *et seq.*), Thurnam (1866) and Broca (1875), had found the right hemisphere slightly heavier. Wagner believed it "impossible to conduct section in the midline with such a degree of accuracy as to ensure total equality of the two halves . . ." However, the figures of Retzius clearly show that skill and experience may go far in achieving accuracy of sectioning.

Brains of outstanding physicians and of members of the American Anthropological Association were described by Spitzka who found, overall, a more complex and richer convolutional pattern than usual. However, although among his material were a few mathematicians, Spitzka did not emphasise the prominence of the supramarginal gyrus. Spitzka was especially interested in the weight of the brain: he compared the weights of "élite" brains (over 100 selected cases, including his personal observations) with the allegedly "normal" series of Topinard (1878), Bischoff (1880), Retzius (1900b) and Marchand (1902) − a total of 1334 cases (see Spitzka 1903, Fig. 32). He found that at all age periods, the brain weights of eminent men exceeded that of the so-called normals by more than 100 g. He considered this difference to be significant despite the fact that several of his eminent men (for example the comparative anatomist Döllinger, the statesman Gambetta and Franz Josef Gall) had brains of distinctly light weight. The brain of Gall, however, showed marked atrophy, and since a weight of 1198 is not congruous with his internal skull capacity of 1692, Spitzka calculated a weight of *circa* 1500 g. Similar corrections were made by Bischoff for the brain weights of Tiedemann and Liebig.

Spitzka (1907) was well aware of our ignorance of the conditions influencing brain weight. He acknowledged that factors such as stature, body-weight and body-build had to be considered, but these were impossible to ascertain. Therefore, in his tables, he made no attempt at correction. He believed, however, that the figures in the list of his notable men were too low rather than too high.

Spitzka also made measurements of internal skull capacity, of "encephalization" (as indicated by the changing body-brain-weight relationship), of the corpus callosum, of the relative size of frontal and occipital regions in different categories of eminence and of the cerebello-cerebral ratio. Although in all these measurements he obtained some interesting figures in favour of eminence, he was nevertheless well aware of the small number of relevant cases and of the differences in methods employed in the control material.

Like Wagner and Rüdinger (1882a and b), Spitzka was interested in the asymmetry of the convolutional pattern in the two hemispheres which he believed was inherited (Spitzka, 1904). Comparing the brains of his 11 eminent men with those of healthy normal persons, he also found relatively large differences in the weight of the two hemispheres. In two neurologists (Séguin, father and son), he found (1901) in the most anterior part of the left Sylvian fossa a special feature of asymmetry, namely an exposure of what he named "preinsula" in the dominant hemisphere. Hitherto, he pointed out, it was only in the brains of deaf-mutes or of mental defectives that the insula had been found visible. In such cases the opercula were usually atrophic, in contrast to the present cases in which otherwise normal opercula were virtually thrust apart by the excessive growth of the most anterior part of the insula – obviously an example of true operculation in the sense of Retzius.

Of subsequent publications, the papers of Stieda, Hansemann, Maurer, Donaldson, Anthony and Riese and Goldstein will be singled out because all described the brains of scientists and linguistically gifted personalities, and they all raised points for discussion which follow from Retzius' and Spitzka's observations.

Stieda (1908) described the brain of the outstanding polyglot Georg Sauerwein who died at the age of 74. The right hemisphere, particularly, but not exclusively, in its frontal portion, showed a more complex sulcal and gyral structure than the left. (S. may have been lefthanded, although, to my knowledge, this is not expressly stated in the paper.) Of the pars opercularis of the third frontal convolution Stieda (*loc. cit.*, pp. 96 ff) said "that, on the right side, it is especially developed, whereas, on the left, it shows a far more simple structure . . . its breadth is about 1 cm on the left, whilst on the right, it measures more than 2–2·5 cm". However, in the photographs, this difference appears to me to be less conspicuous than in the description. Like Retzius, Stieda denied any significance to this difference, since he believed that the substrate of mental phenomena could only be accessible to histological investigation.

Stieda was not the first to describe abnormalities in the brains of linguistically outstanding persons; he had been anticipated by several publications emanating from the school of Duval between 1883 and 1903. Of these the best known is the description of the brain of Gambetta by Chudszinski and Duval (1886) who found Broca's "cap" larger on the left than on the right side. "On the left, it was doubled", i.e., it was subdivided into a larger anterior and smaller posterior part by an accessory branch of the Sylvian fissure from below and a superficial branch of the medial (probably our inferior) frontal sulcus from above. However, both the dorsal and ventral subdividing sulci seem to correspond with what Eberstaller, in 1890, described as the sulcus radiatus which is present in about one-third of apparently normal brains. Moreover, Broca's cap corresponds with the gyrus triangularis (not necessarily involved in speech activity) and not to the pars opercularis (area 44).

Although Rüdinger (1887) fully accepted the findings of Chudszinski and Duval, doubts were expressed in the discussion by Hervé who saw little difference in the size of the caps of Broca in the two hemispheres. I share Hervé's doubts. Although the cap appeared to me slightly larger on the left, it is difficult to be certain because of the small size and often indistinctly marked subdivisions in the diagrams of Chudszinski and Duval.

In 1899 and more fully in 1908, Hansemann described the brain of Helmholtz who, after two strokes, died at the age of 73 from cerebral haemorrhage which largely destroyed the white matter and basal ganglia of the right hemisphere. The weight of the unfixed brain was 1700 g from which at least 160 g accounted for the haemorrhage. The brain was discarded after a cast of the left hemisphere had been made. The cerebral gyri (mainly in the frontal lobe, the first temporal convolution in its posterior aspect and in the parietal region) seemed to be more numerous and tortuous than usual: this appearance was caused by an increased number of "sinuous deep sulci which confused the convolutional pattern." The size of the precuneus was striking. It is of interest that a particular development of the precuneus was also recorded in the brains of

Mendelejev (Bechterev and Weinberg 1909) and, partially, of Edinger (Riese and Goldstein 1950).*

In 1922 Maurer briefly described his findings in the brain of Ernst Häckel, the eminent German zoologist, who died at the age of 86; he had remained mentally alert until his death. The preliminary report was later (1924) elaborated by the author. The weight of the fresh brain was 1575 g. After fixation, the left hemisphere weighed 632 g against 619 g of the right. (Häckel was righthanded.) The convolutional pattern was unusually developed especially in the occipital regions (not including the precuneus), the inferior parietal and superior temporal convolutions and the superior and medial frontal gyri. The last ones showed an unusual fissural and gyral configuration, especially on the left side.

Donaldson (1928) compared the brains of three scholars (including that of Sir William Osler) with the three brains of an "ordinary" family. His paper is important because of the careful measurements he made of the convolutions and sulci in both hemispheres. Although his measurements showed a superiority, particularly marked in the frontal region of the scholars' group over the ordinary family, he was sceptical in his conclusions: "The brain after death is . . . but the crude machine lacking power and controls. . . . Unknown are the individual chemistry of the nerve tissue in each brain, the intimate connections between the neurons and the blood in all of its relations" (p. 83).†

Anthony (1935) described the brains of Professor "N" (according to Riese and Goldstein, Constantin von Monakov) and of his brother. N had died at the age of 77, his brother at 88. Brain weight of N was 1270 (after formalin fixation). The most conspicuous feature was the sulcal complexity of the neopallium which was more marked in the left than in the right hemisphere; the left hemisphere was also more voluminous than the right. Adding the data of Monakov's brain to the list of 11 outstanding scientists which Spitzka (1907) had collected, Anthony found that in five the left hemisphere was heavier than the right; in three the right exceeded the left hemisphere in weight. Only in four cases were the hemispheres of equal

---

* Edinger (1904, p. 323) independently investigated the brain of Helmholtz and confirmed Hansemann's findings, especially the abnormal size of the precuneus and gyrus angularis. Flechsig also appears to have accepted Hansemann's observations (Hansemann, 1907).

† Donaldson referred to work by Hindze (1926) of Moscow who had shown that in brains of persons of outstanding ability the arterial supply is more elaborate than in brains from persons of mediocre ability. However, Hindze's material, and especially his controls, was too small to permit of definitive conclusions. Hindze's paper was a preliminary communication which may have been amplified in his publication (in Polish) of 1927. I am not aware of any later work by this author.

weight. The differences varied between 4 and 81 g (average *circa* 26 g): i.e. appreciably above the figures obtained in the series of Boyd, Wagner, Thurnam and Broca (see p. 259).

As another feature of asymmetry, Anthony found in the left hemisphere of Monakov's brain "une petite partie de l'insula antérieure reste extérieurement visible – elle est due à une complication extrême de cet opercule". Like Spitzka (1901) he interpreted the phenomenon as a true operculation of the "preinsula". He also agreed with Spitzka that it was an uncommon manifestation; but no statistical data of its frequency were available to either. It was found only in Constantin v. Monakov's brain, and not in that of his brother.

Anthony had arrived at the general conclusion that marked hemispherical asymmetry may be a sign of outstanding ability: the same conclusion was reached by Riese and Goldstein (1950) from the investigation of the brain of Ludwig Edinger. Edinger died at the age of 63 from coronary thrombosis after an operation. In the last phase of his life his mental ability and creative energy, despite illness, had been unimpaired. The weight of his brain was 1223 g; the convolutions (of the eurygyrencephalic type) showed no atrophy. The right hemisphere was 5 g heavier than the left; Edinger had been left-handed.

The authors were impressed by a remarkable asymmetry of both convolutions and fissures. In the left hemisphere the pattern was "simpler and more schematic"; the fissures and sulci on the left took a straighter course, while on the right they were sinuous and interrupted by bridging convolutions. These differences were most marked in the frontal, precentral, parietal and occipital regions; the temporal lobe was less prominent and the Heschl gyri were of normal size. In the right frontal lobe, it was the medial and the triangular part of the inferior convolutions that were increased in size. The precentral gyrus of the same hemisphere was broader in its lower third. The whole right parietal cortex was more complex in its fissural and convolutional pattern than the left, and so was the right occipital cortex; both showed supernumerary opercular formations. The authors were particularly impressed by the similarity of the gyral and fissural pattern of the right frontal lobe in Edinger's brain with that of the left frontal lobe in the brain of Häckel (described by Maurer 1922) and with the right frontal lobe of (left-handed) painter Menzel (as described by Hansemann in 1907). In the right frontal and parieto-occipital regions formations were encountered which were completely absent on the left side. The whole right cuneus and the posterior part of the precuneus were prominently developed. Only the insula was larger in the left than in the right hemisphere. Some of these differences can be recognized in the illustrations but, as in the case of Stieda, they are not nearly as impressive as one would expect from the description. Perhaps higher magnification might have disclosed more detail.

Riese and Goldstein tentatively suggested that the complexity of the right occipital lobe might have been indicative of Edinger's pronounced visual gifts, the broadening of the precentral gyrus having been instrumental for his manual skill; but, as one would expect from these authors, focal morphological preferences may, at best, provide a "potential". It requires, in the authors's opinion, "a wealth of experiences affecting the whole brain in order to convert these potentialities into actual achievements. In some individuals such conditions may not be present and their potentialities will then remain fallow."

## The brains of eminent musicians

Auerbach (1906, 1908, 1911a, 1913) was the pioneer and at the same time the most important contributor. His material included the brains of the conductors Felix Mottl and Hans von Bülow, the teacher of music Naret Koning, the singer Julius Stockhausen, and Bernhard Cossmann, the "Joachim of the violoncello". Retzius was primarily interested in the "localization" of outstanding talent in mathematics, astronomy and natural science; but Hugo Gyldén and Christian Lovén happened to have been also musically gifted. Considering the two cases of Retzius, his own observations, and adding the violinist Rudolf Lenz (whose brain had been investigated by Guszmann in 1901), Auerbach concluded that in all cases so far investigated, the middle and posterior thirds of the superior temporal gyrus were strongly developed and showed great width; they were intimately connected with the equally well developed gyrus supramarginalis. Auerbach was particularly impressed by the characteristic curved course of the middle portion of the superior temporal gyrus which was caused by blood vessels pushing in from above and below. He had never seen a similarly striking formation, either in his own experience or in the series of 100 "ordinary" brains which Retzius had described and illustrated in 1896. Auerbach was right about the majority of the brains in Retzius' atlas which show a simple though variable pattern, but there are a few (for example in tables 61, 66, 70 and 75) in which the configuration of the gyrus is more complex, approaching that which has been described in musicians.

Auerbach's illustration (Figure 3, case Koning) corresponds with his description, as do those of Stockhausen and Bülow. In Cossmann, however, the curving of the middle third is not nearly as impressive, and, in Mottl's brain even less so, though Auerbach believed that its absence was compensated by a greater length of the superior temporal gyrus. In Retzius' cases Gyldén (Figure 2) and Lovén (Figure 4) the appearance is comparable with that in Auerbach's case Koning. Retzius, in discussing the case of Lovén emphasised, however, that all his suggestions for the localisation of special talents should be regarded as tentative; much greater experience would be required before they could be accepted as established facts.

In the brain of the singer Stockhausen, Auerbach observed a striking development of the left second frontal convolution which had been previously recognised by Probst and Henschen as a place where a lesion may give rise to expressive amusia. The same striking size, but in this case on the right

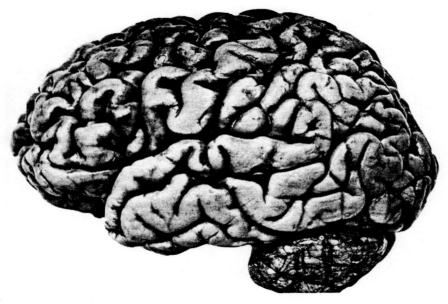

Figure 2   Reproduced from Retzius (1898), table 4, Figure 1. Left hemisphere of Hugo Gyldén. Description in text.

side, Auerbach described in the second frontal gyrus of Cossmann who, as a child, had possessed a fine voice. In Cossmann, he also found an unusual development of the left precentral and right postcentral gyri – possibly connected with his outstanding technical accomplishments as a cellist.

A tendency for bilateral representation in the brain of musical expression and to a lesser degree of musical reception had already been discussed by Probst. It has received recent support by cases of Luria et al. (1965),

Critchley (1970, p. 256) and Assal (1973). Critchley observed a composer, who developed a Wernicke-type of aphasia due to the presence of a left-sided parietal meningioma. While aphasic he was unable to compose, but after removal of the tumour both speech and musical creativity rapidly returned. On the other hand, in the case of Luria and associates, the composer continued to create successfully during sensory aphasia caused by a vascular lesion in the left hemisphere. Assal's case, a pianist aged 61, suffered from Wernicke's aphasia and profound word deafness following a probably embolic lesion in the left temporo-parietal region. His defect did

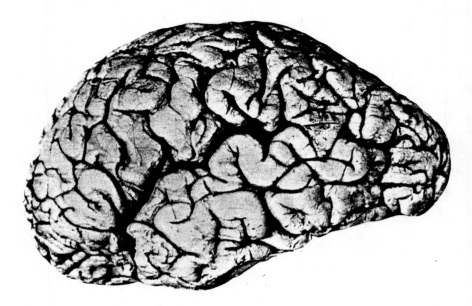

Figure 3    Reproduced from Auerbach (1906), case Koning. Description in text.

not impair his musical ability in any way. The author thought of "une représentation croisée pour la musique". The observation in Assal's case was clinical but supported by endarterectomy which revealed arteriosclerotic thrombosis of the left interior carotid artery. Alajouanine (1948) has also pointed out that the presence of aphasia need not necessarily abolish creativity. In the case of Ravel, who after being affected by a Wernicke-type aphasia with ideomotor apraxia completely stopped composing, the author was able to observe (during ten years) that Ravel's internal musical invention, affectivity and aesthetic sensibility were undisturbed. It was difficulty in playing the piano and in using musical signs which hindered his production. Alajouanine saw the same phenomenon in a writer suffering from motor aphasia and agrammatism. On the other hand, a painter also afflicted by aphasia was able to continue undisturbed with his artistic creation.

Experimental investigations support a greater participation of the non-dominant hemisphere in the perception (and expression) of music. Using dichotic listening Milner (1958) and Kimura (1963, 1967) demonstrated

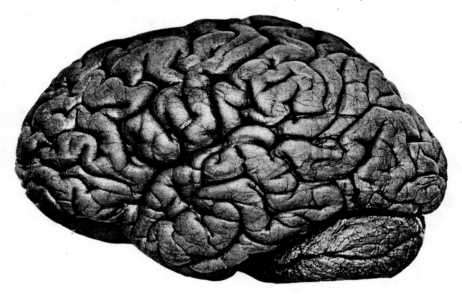

Figure 4    Reproduced from Retzius (1905) table 2, Figure 2. Left hemisphere of Christian Lovén. Description in text.

that, in left dominance, the right ear was superior in recognition of words, while the left was better in identifying melodies and melody pattern. However, Bever and Chiarello (1974) reported that, in contrast to untrained listeners, musically experienced persons recognise simple melodies better in the right than in the left ear: in other words "articulate" musical experience, like language, may be a task for the analysing dominant hemisphere.

To the material reviewed by Auerbach, Klose (1920) added the prodigy pianist Goswin Sökeland who died at the age of 33 and in whose brain Klose was able to confirm, to a large extent, Auerbach's findings. So did Somogyi (1930), but the illustrations of neither author always show this similarity clearly. In one of Somogyi's cases (Pogány) nerve cell counts in relevant temporal areas corresponded with the average values found by Economo and Koskinas (1925). In his other case, Somogyi illustrated larger cytoplasm of nerve cells in layer 3–6 of Heschl's first transverse convolution, as compared with an illustration of the same area by Economo and Koskinas. In the writer's opinion, however, differences in the quality of staining cannot be entirely excluded.

To this main group but few cases have been added. Among these was Helmholtz who, besides his eminence in physics, was a highly gifted musician. Hansemann showed that, on the left side, the posterior half of the first temporal convolution and the inferior parietal region were prominently developed. Rose (1938, quoted by Minkowski 1939) observed in the brain of Professor Trzebinski (who was a gifted polyglot linguist but entirely unmusical) that the anterior two-thirds of the superior temporal convolutions were relatively little developed, while – macroscopically and cytoarchitecturally – the posterior third of this gyrus was highly differentiated. On the other hand, an underdevelopment of the most anterior part of the left superior temporal convolution has been described by Verriest (1910, quoted by Lose 1920) in the brain of the Dutch composer Peter Benoit.

### Flechsig's acoustic cortex

Interesting observations have been reported by Auerbach and other earlier investigators concerning an unusual size of the first transverse temporal convolution in eminent musicians.

Heschl had described the transverse convolution in 1878, but did not connect it with the sense of hearing. This was left to Flechsig (1896, 1905, 1908) who, confirmed by his pupils Pfeifer (1921, 1936), Mayendorf (1909) and Polyak (1927), established that the auditory radiation, arising from the medial geniculate body ended in Heschl's first transverse gyrus. Using his myelogenetic method in the brains of newborns, Flechsig discovered that while myelination occurred early, the auditory fibres acquired their myelin sheath later than all other sensory pathways. He also found that the auditory cortex was more or less confined to the first of Heschl's (temporal) transverse gyri, and that, as a rule, there is only one Heschl convolution in the left hemisphere. Campbell also described an auditory-sensory cortex in approximately the same localisation, but this was in 1905, after Flechsig's first publication in 1896.

Pfeifer (1921) showed that the auditory radiation enters the first transverse gyrus in a fanlike manner and that the fibres arrange themselves in thin lamellae, and in phalanx-like order throughout almost the length of the transverse convolution. In man, he suggested, the fibres conveying high tones lie medially, those for low tones laterally. This arrangement has been confirmed in the homologous cortices of carnivores, monkeys and apes by later physiological investigations chiefly of workers in the U.S.A. (Woolsey and Walzl, 1942; Galambos and Davis, 1943; Bailey et al., 1943; Tunturi, 1944, 1950; see also Whitfield, 1967, who fully reviewed the not always clear-cut results of recent experimental tonotopical research).

The first attempts at a cytoarchitectonic investigation of the auditory cortex were carried out by Campbell (1905) and Rosenberg (1907); they were carried further by Brodmann (1909) who identified it with his area 41. Brodmann, however, largely missed its most characteristic feature, which it shares with all other "sensory" cortices – the "granulation" which Economo and Koskinas (1925) first described. In 1930, Economo (with Horn) reported cytoarchitectonic investigation of the auditory cortex in seven adult and two juvenile cases. The authors were impressed by the striking variations in size between individuals and between the two hemispheres. They suggested that these might be due to handedness and to differences in musicality. A decision could only be reached by statistically valid material becoming available. Economo and Horn emphasised that the region was easily accessible to encephalometric measurements, but had to admit occasional difficulties in defining its anterior border even with the help of cytoarchitectonics. The sulcus transversus primus which is supposed to mark the frontal border of Heschl's anterior convolution is well developed only in its medial portion, becoming less distinct lateralwards and occasionally bending towards the temporal pole before reaching the lateral fissure. Mayendorf's sulcus acusticus at the fissural end of Heschl's convolution is inconstant. Similar difficulties were encountered by Witelson and Pallie (1973) when they confirmed and amplified the observations of Geschwind and Levitzky (1968). As they kindly informed me (1974), they therefore decided not to attempt measurements of the anterior Heschl convolution. Nevertheless, if the differences in size between left and right are as conspicuous as they appeared to Economo and Horn and also to others, the hope remains that future measurements, even approximate, may yet yield significant results.

Auerbach, in 1911a and 1913, described and illustrated what he thought to be an abnormally large anterior Heschl convolution in the brains of the cellist Cossmann and the conductor Mottl (Figure 5). To these, Klose (1920) was able to add an even more striking example, in the brain of the prodigy pianist Sökeland (Figure 6). The following is his verbatim description (p. 79):

In the left hemisphere, the auditory convolution of Flechsig is enormously developed and vaulted . . . a long transverse convolution, coursing in steep oblique descent from its medial origin at the upper margin of the insula to its antero-lateral termination. Its length is 52 mm: this is enormously long. The distance of the point where the (transverse) convolution joins the anterior part of the superior temporal gyrus to the caudal end of the fossa Sylvii (measured along the convexity) is 72 mm, also abnormally long. The transverse convolution almost reaches the temporal pole. Wernicke's field, behind it, is also abnormally large.

In the right hemisphere, the gyrus temporalis superior is also well developed although not as complex as on the left side. Flechsig's auditory convolution is less steep and less vaulted. Its length is 38 mm (i.e. 14 mm less than left); the distance from caudal end of the Sylvian fossa is 47 mm (i.e. 25 mm less). . . .

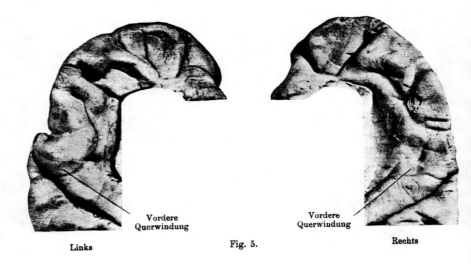

Vordere Querwindung    Vordere Querwindung

Links                Fig. 5.                Rechts

Figure 5    Reproduced from Auerbach (1913), Figure 5, showing from above the auditory cortices in the brain of conductor Felix Mottl. Both are larger than average, in the left hemisphere more than in the right one. Note, on the left side, the clear anterior demarcation of the convolution by the first transverse fissure which is deep in its postero-medial portion becoming shallow in its middle part to bend finally towards the lateral (Sylvian) fissures. On the right side, the middle portion of the fissure is not clearly identifiable in the photograph.

In the brain of Koning (1906) Auerbach noticed that the place where the primary auditory cortex joined the superior temporal gyrus corresponded exactly with the especially developed middle third of this gyrus. In Klose's case Sökeland, the junction would have been even more anterior: thus, it is possible to reconcile the earlier views of Edgren (1895) and Probst (1899) with those of Auerbach.

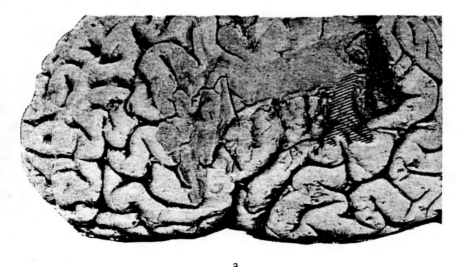

a

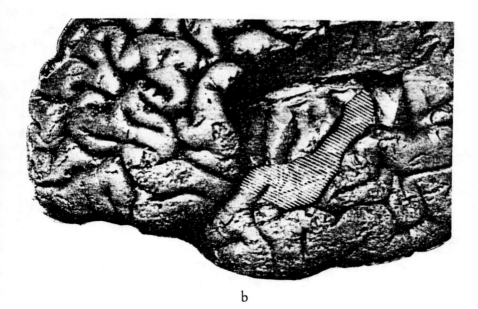

b

Figure 6   Reproduced from Pfeifer (1921) showing parts of his Figures 4 and 7, with the permission of S. Karger, Publishers, Basel. Figure 6a shows an auditory cortex of average size; Figure 6b the extraordinary size and steeply descending course of the auditory cortex in case Sökeland of Klose (1920). The extent of the cortices is cross-lined.

*Lower auditory pathways*

In an annotation of his essay of 1895, His reported an observation of Politzer, who found in the skull of Johann Sebastian Bach an abnormally large fossa cochlearis, which would point to an enlarged cochlear ganglion.

From Schaaffhausen (1886) we learn that in Schumann's brain, Richarz (who carried out the postmortem examination) was impressed by the number and delicacy of the striae acusticae on the floor of the 4th ventricle. Richarz also noted that both temporal fossae of the skull were more capacious than the frontal fossae and showed deep impressions of the temporal convolutions which were considered unlikely to be due to Schumann's fatal illness. Schaaffhausen also studied the incus, malleus and stapes which he compared with an average human specimen and with available illustrations of the ossicula in oran-utan: he concluded that they were large in Schumann's skull (especially incus and stapes) and that the malleus showed a far more elaborate concavity.

In the skull of Johann Sebastian Bach, His (1895) described an enormous *capacity*, especially in the temporal region; its width was greater than that of the frontal region. Schaaffhausen gave figures of two casts of the skull of Ludwig van Beethoven: one was made during life, when the composer was 42 years old; the other after his death. In the former, the distance between the two temporal regions (measured above the ear) was 160 mm, while, in the frontal region, the distance between the outer end of the upper lid was 124 mm. The measurements after death seem to have been similar. Auerbach (1911a and b) added that "vaulting" temporal bones were seen in the skulls of Koning, Bülow and Cossmann (investigated by himself) and in those of Haydn, Helmholtz, Brahms, Bruckner and Mahler.

## Comments

A critical analysis of the findings reported in the literature must begin with acknowledging that most of the investigators of "élite" brains were neuroanatomists of eminence and experience: their list contains names of enduring fame – Duval, Horsley, Retzius, Bechterev, Auerbach, Spitzka and Goldstein.

Most investigators were also well aware of the difficulties of interpretation and of mistaking as significant findings that were in reality haphazard individual variations of the gyral and sulcal pattern. "Who becomes involved in such studies", Auerbach (1906, p. 198) pointed out, "will soon recognize the difficulty of drawing conclusions from the appearance and size of convolutions, because brains of average persons show numerous variations in this respect." Similar reservations were voiced by Wagner, Retzius, Stieda, Hansemann, Klose and Maurer. Riese and Goldstein were the most confident in their conclusions; perhaps because they were almost the last to tackle the problem and thus could match their own findings against a material larger than had been at the disposal of earlier investigators. Riese was especially qualified by his previous studies on the asymmetry of the convolutional pattern in the two hemispheres.

That morphology is not the whole story and that functional factors such as affectivity, aesthetic sensitivity, education and general opportunity must play a major role, has been emphasised by several authorities such as Hansemann, Maurer and most eloquently by Riese and Goldstein. I have already quoted the relevant passages of Riese and Goldstein, but Hansemann also emphasised that "it does not suffice that the associational regions are there, they must also function. In order to effect this, some stimulus in the widest sense must be operative in these especially well developed regions" (1899, p. 8). Hansemann attributed some significance to an early mild hydrocephalus which later subsides, thus providing potential space for cortical development – a possibility for which he and Mingazzini (1914) adduce some evidence in the cases of Helmholtz and other famous men. However, this explanation does not seem to have found general acceptance: the major post-uterine development of the cerebral cortex probably occurs before the hydrocephalus regresses. The hydrocephalus theory goes back to Edinger who elaborated ideas introduced by his late friend Perls (Edinger 1904, p. 324).

The fact that most of the observations were made in persons dying from diseases of old age, particularly from cerebral arteriosclerosis, adds another cause of uncertainty. None of the brains on which Retzius and Auerbach reported had been submitted to histological examination. At the turn of the century macroscopic and histological study of brain pathology was still in its early stages; cerebral arteriosclerosis in its varying manifestations, oedema and brain swelling were as yet little known. In Retzius' (1898) case of Gyldén, the deepening of the sulci and the comb-like and, in places, puckered appearance of the gyri could have been, in part at least, a sequel of cerebral arteriosclerosis. Unfortunately illustrations offer no conclusive support to differential diagnosis.

Whether histological and cytoarchitectonic investigation will be more successful than macroscopic description is still an open question. So far we have only Rose's (1938) findings in the brain of a linguistically gifted, but unmusical person of greater cytoarchitectonic differentiation in the posterior one-third of the first temporal convolution than in more anterior parts of this gyrus. In a musical genius Somogyi described nerve cells with larger cytoplasm within the cortical acoustic centre. However, these are only isolated findings.* Rose himself (according to Minkowski's review) was well aware of the considerable variability of cytoarchitectonic areas between the two hemispheres of the same brain and between different brains. In this respect the cytoarchitectonic pattern shows no greater stability than the macroscopic pattern. This variability has been confirmed by Kononova (1938) and other Soviet workers. Conel (1939–1967) described the growth and the increasing organisation of cortical nerve cells and nerve fibres during post-uterine development up to the age of six years. Although the centres for the control of language and of hand movements participate in this development, Conel was unable to discover significant differences of their organisation in the two hemispheres. As far as accuracy and comprehensiveness goes, Conel's work comes very near to present-day limits of histological and architectonic achievements. We may have to wait for new methods of a histochemical or molecular histological nature before further progress can be expected.

The absence of specific anatomical features in language areas or of differences in the two hemispheres induced Mayendorf (1930) and Leischner (1957, see also Critchley 1970, p. 18) to deny the existence of preformed "language areas". According to Leischner, language is a secondary accessory or even parasitic cerebral function which develops after the essential design of the brain has been completed. The parallel to the localisation of special talents is obvious: the presence of centres differentiated by specific anatomical features is by no means a foregone conclusion.

*Statistical weakness*, however, is the central shortcoming of all macroscopic and microscopic findings, so far available in the literature. Large-scaled statistical figures have been provided (by Spitzka) for brain weight only. He was confident that the increase in weight by 100 g in all age-periods in the brains of 115 eminent persons compared with 1334 normal persons was significant. Bailey and Bonin (1951), however, computed the standard error in several so-called normal series which included Bischoff's and Marchand's figures used by Spitzka. They found it high, varying between ± 20 and ± 45 at different age-periods. Moreover,

---

* There may well have been other publications since Vogt (1929) and Blinkov and Poliakov (1938) referred to "important preliminary results" in "elite" brains, but, despite careful search, none seems to have penetrated into the Western literature – which may indicate that no breakthrough has been achieved. Regrettably, personal inquiries have been unsuccessful so far.

hospital populations on which these series were based are known to favour lower social strata. Again the weight of the brain depends on numerous factors such as the variable weight of meninges and cerebrospinal fluid, interval between death and removal of the brain, terminal disease, temperature, postmortem chemical changes, sampling process, etc. — factors difficult to correct.

Bailey and Bonin's conclusions were based on the work of Pearl (1905, 1934), Wendt (1909), Pearson (1925/26) and Appel and Appel (1942). Pearl, in his careful correlative study of 1905 found that brain weight correlated positively with skull capacity, stature and body weight, but there was no correlation with intellectual ability. Nor was any correlation with mental ability recorded by Pearson, who studied Cambridge undergraduates. Neither author, however, seemed to deal with special talent. The Appels found that after death the weight of the unfixed brain may appreciably increase for hours and often for days.

Donaldson (1895) and Edinger (1904, p. 323) were among the early critics of the significance of the weight of the brain for intellectual ability. Donaldson expressed doubts as to the accuracy of figures such as those for the brain of Cromwell (2231 g), Byron (2238 g) and Turgenjev (2012 g). Such exorbitant weights would have resulted in skull sizes not seen in extant portraits. Donaldson also pointed out that among the 59 cases of Bischoff's series with brain weights above 1500 g, there were found one learned man, 13 criminals, one mechanic and one labourer. Edinger doubted that the weight of the whole brain could be significant since intellectual or artistic eminence was likely to depend on the development of relatively circumscribed cortical areas.

To obtain statistically valid findings would require new comprehensive research. Such a project might be applicable in strictly limited and manageable aspects of the problem, as, for example, the asymmetry of the hemispheres and the size of the cortical and subcortical auditory centres in musically gifted persons. As a general approach to the problem of special talent, it would prove to be of immense scope and expense, since it would imply the collection of an adequate number of suitable cases and controls, control of the early treatment of the brains and finally investigations by all modern histological and encephalometric methods including computing devices for quantitative assessment. There is a distinct danger that such a vast programme, although theoretically desirable, might turn out to be a white elephant: almost all older investigators who described highly developed brains (at least in relevant regions), at the same time expressed doubts whether brains of a similar degree of development might not be found also in ordinary people. There are probably no sharp delineations and it would be unreasonable to expect new research to arrive at different conclusions. As many of the older investigators (Donaldson and Riese and Goldstein perhaps most eloquently) have emphasised, a morphologically highly developed brain is only one – though a necessary – condition of eminence, there being other prerequisites of crucial importance. Donaldson, as we have seen, referred to the brain as a crude machine which must be brought into intimate contact with the blood. Ingvar (1974a and b) and his associates at Lund have just given an impressive example of what may be achieved by investigating during life the regional cerebral blood flow, in a field not unrelated to our theme, of speech and reading, and of schizophrenia.

## REFERENCES

ALAJOUANINE, TH. (1948) Aphasia and artistic realization. *Brain*, **71**, 229–241.

ANTHONY, R. (1935) Étude du cerveau d'un savant biologiste et médecin. *Schweizer Arch. Neurol. Psychiat.*, **36**, 1–16.

APPEL, F. W. and APPEL, E. M. (1942) Intracranial variation in the weight of the human brain. *Human Biol.*, **14**, 48–68, 235–250.

ASSAL, G. (1973) Aphasie de Wernicke sans amusie chez un pianiste. *Revue Neurol.*, **129**, 251–256.

AUERBACH, S. (1906–1913) Beitrag zur Lokalisation des musikalischen Talentes im Gehirn und am Schädel. *Archs. Anat. Physiol. (Anat. Abt.)*, 1906, 197–230; 1908, 31–38; 1911a, 1–10; 1913 (Suppl.), 89–96.

— (1911b) Photographien von Gehirnen hervorragender Musiker. *Neurol. Zentbl.*, **30**, 1213–1214.

BAILEY, P., BONIN, G. v., GAROL, H. W. and McCULLOCH, W. S. (1943) Functional organization of temporal lobe of monkey (Macaca Mullatta) and chimpanzee (Pan satyrus). *J. Neurophysiol.*, **6**, 121–128.

—— (1951) *The Isocortex of Man.* Urbana, University of Illinois Press.

BASTIAN, H. C. (1880) *The Brain as an Organ of Mind.* London, Kegan Paul.

BECHTEREV, V. and WEINBERG, R. (1909) Das Gehirn des Chemikers D. J. Mendelejev. *Anat. Entwicklg.* Monographs, Leipzig, Engelmann. (Quoted from R. Klose, 1920.)

BEVER, T. G. and CHIARELLO, R. J. (1974) Cerebral dominance in musicians and non-musicians. *Science* N.Y. **185**, 537–539.

BISCHOFF, T. L. W. v. (1880) Das Hirngewicht des Menschen. Bonn: Neusser.

BLINKOV, S. and POLIAKOV, G. (1938) The activities of the Moscow Brain Institute. *Acta Med. U.S.S.R.*, **1**, 674–679.

BOYD, R. (1861) Tables of the weights of the human body and internal organs in the sane and insane of both sexes at various ages, arranged from 2614 post-mortem examinations (communicated by Dr. Sharpey), *Phil. Trans. R. Soc.* **151**, 241–262.

BRAIN, LORD (1960) Some Reflections on Genius. London: Pitman Medical Publishing Co.

BROCA, P. (1875) Sur le poids relatif des deux hémisphères cérébraux et de leurs lobes frontaux. *Bull. Soc. Anthrop.* (Paris) (2nd sér.) **10**, 534–535.

BRODMANN, K. (1909) Vergleichende Lokalisationslehre der Grosshirnrinde (quoted from 2nd edition 1925), Leipzig: Barth.

CAMPBELL, A. W. (1905) Histological Studies on the Localisation of Cerebral Function. Cambridge University Press.

CHUDZINSKI and DUVAL, M. (1886) Description morphologique du cerveau de Gambetta. *Bull. Soc. Anthrop.* (Paris), **9**, 129–152.

CONEL, LE ROY, J. (1939–1967) *The Postnatal Development of the Human Cerebral Cortex* 8 vols., Cambridge, Mass., Harvard University Press.

CRITCHLEY, M. (1970) *Aphasiology and other Aspects of Language.* London, Arnold.

CROME, L. (1972) The medical history of V. I. Lenin. *History of Medicine* (Lond.) **4**, 3–9, 20–22.

DONALDSON, H. H. (1895) *The Growth of the Brain.* London, Scott.

— (1928, with the assistance of M. M. Canavan) A study of the brains of three scholars. *J. Comp. Neurol.*, **46**, 1–95.

EBERSTALLER, O. (1890) *Das Stirnhirn.* Leipzig and Vienna, Urban and Schwarzenberg.

ECONOMO, C. v. (1929) Wie sollen wir Élitegehirne bearbeiten? *Z. ges. Neurol. Psychiat.*, **121**, 323–409.

— (1930) Some new methods of studying the brains of exceptional persons (encephalometry and brain casts). *J. Nerv. Ment. Dis.*, **71**, 300–302.

ECONOMO, C. v. and HORN, L. (1930) Über Windungsrelief, Masse und Rindenarchitektonik der Supratemporalfläche, ihre individuellen und ihre Seitenunterschiede. *Z. ges. Neurol. Psychiat.*, **130**, 678–757.

ECONOMO, C. v. and KOSKINAS, G. N. (1925) *Die Cytoarchitektonik der Hirnrinde des erwachsenen Menschen.* Vienna, Springer.

EDINGER, L. (1904) *Vorlesungen über den Bau der nervösen Zentralorgane des Menschen und der Thiere.* 7th edition, vol. 1, Leipzig, Vogel.

EDGREN, I. G. (1895) Amusie (musikalische Aphasie). *Dt. Z. Nervneilk.*, **6**, 1–64.

FLECHSIG, P. E. (1896) *Gehirn und Seele.* Leipzig, Veit.

— (1905) Einige Bemerkungen über die Untersuchungsmethoden der Grosshirnrinde, insbesondere des Menschen. *Arch. Anat. Physiol.* (*Anat. Abt.*), 337–444.

— (1908) Bemerkungen über die Hörsphäre des menschlichen Gehirns. *Neurol. Zentbl.*, **27**, 2–7, 50–57.

GALAMBOS, R. and DAVIS, H. (1943) The response of single auditory nerve fibres to acoustic stimulation. *J. Neurophysiol.*, **6**, 39–57.

GESCHWIND, N. and LEVITZKY, W. (1968) Human brain: left-right asymmetries in temporal speech region. *Science N.Y.*, **161**, 186–187.

GUSZMANN, J. (1901) Beitrag zur Morphologie der Gehirnoberfläche. *Anat. Anz.*, **19**, 239–249.

HANSEMANN, D. v. (1899) Über das Gehirn von Hermann v. Helmholtz. *Z. Psychol. Physiol. Sinnesorg.*, **20**, 1–12 (2 tables).

— (1907) *Über die Gehirne von Th. Mommsen, H. W. Bunsen und Ad. von Menzel.* Stuttgart, Schweizerbarthsche Verlagsbuchh.

— (1908) *Über das Gehirn von Hermann v. Helmholtz.* Leipzig. (Quoted from R. Klose, 1920.)

HESCHL, R. L. (1878) *Über die vordere quere Schläfenwindung des menschlichen Grosshirns.* Vienna, Braumüller.

HINDZE, B. (1926) Die Hirnarterien einiger hervorragender Persönlichkeiten. (Preliminary communication). *Anat. Anz.*, **62**, 1–24.

HIS, W. (THE ELDER) (1895) *J. S. Bach. Forschungen über dessen Grabstätte, Gebeine und Antlitz.* Leipzig, Vogel.

HORSLEY, V. (1909) Description of the brain of C.B., F.R.S. *Phil. Trans. R. Soc.*, **200**, 117–131.

INGVAR, D. H. and FRANZÉN, G. (1974b) Abnormalities of cerebral blood flow distribution in patients with chronic schizophrenia. *Act. psychiat. scand.*, **50**, 425–462.

INGVAR, D. H. and SCHWARTZ, M. S. (1974a) Blood flow patterns induced in the dominant hemisphere by speech and reading. *Brain*, **97**, 273–288.

KIMURA, D. (1963) Right temporal lobe damage. *Arch. Neurol.* (Chicago), **8**, 264–271.

— (1967) Functional asymmetry of the brain in dichotic listening. *Cortex*, **3**, 163–178.

KLOSE, R. (1920) Das Gehirn eines Wunderkindes (des Pianisten Goswin Sökeland). *Mschr. Psychiat. Neurol.*, **48**, 63–102.

KONONOVA, E. (1938) La variabilité de la structure de l'écorce cérébrale. La région frontale de l'homme. *Trav. Instit. du Cerveau, Moskow*, **3–4**, 213–274. (French Abstr. 271–273, quoted from Bailey and Bonin, 1951.)

LEISCHNER, A. (1957) *Die Störungen der Schriftsprache (Agraphie und Alexie).* Stuttgart, Thieme. (Quoted from abstract in *Zentbl. ges. Neurol. Psychiat.*, 1958, **143**, 207).

LURIA, A. R., TSVETKOVA, L. S. and FUTER, J. C., (1965) Aphasia in a composer, *J. Neurol. Sci.*, **2**, 288–292.

MARCHAND, F. (1902) Über das Gehirngewicht des Menschen. *Abh. K. Sächs. Ges. Wiss. (Math.-Physic. Kl.)*, **27**, 393–482.

MARSHALL, J. (1864) On the brain of a bushwoman; and on the brains of two idiots of European descent. *Phil. Trans. R. Soc.*, **154**, 501–558.

— (1892) The brain of the late George Grote, F.R.S., *J. Anat. Physiol. (Lond.)*, **27**, 21–65.

MAURER, F. (1922) Kurzer Bericht über die Untersuchung des Gehirns Ernst Häckels. *Dt. Med. Wschr. 48*, **2**, 1080–1081.

— (1924) *Das Gehirn Ernst Häckels.* Jena, Fischer (Quoted from W. Riese and K. Goldstein 1950.)

MAYENDORF, NIESSL v. E. G. I. (1909) Über die physiologische Bedeutung der Hörwindung. *Mschr. Psychiat. Neurol.*, **25**, 97—110.

— (1930) *Vom Lokalisationsproblem der artikulierten Sprache.* Leipzig, Barth.

MILNER, B. (1958) Psychological defects produced by temporal lobe excision. *Res. Publs. Ass. nerv. ment. Dis.*, **36**, 244—257.

MINGAZZINI, G. (1914) Der geniale Mensch und die Entwicklung des Hirnmantels. *Neurol. Zentbl.*, **33**, 1116—1124.

MINKOWSKI, M. (1939) Review of M. Rose, Le Cerveau de Joseph Pilsudski. *Schweizer Arch. Psychiat. Neurol.*, **44**, 406—409.

MÖBIUS, P. J. (1900) *Über die Anlage zur Mathematik.* Leipzig, Barth. Quoted from: Lange-Eichbaum, W. (1956) *Genie, Irrsinn und Ruhm.* 5th edition 1961 (ed. W. Kurth), München, Basel, Reinhardt.

PEARL, R. (1905) Biometrical Studies on Man. I. Variation and correlation in Brain weight. *Biometrica*, **4**, 13—104.

— (1934) The weight of the Negro brain. *Science N.Y.*, **80**, 431—434.

PEARSON, K. (1925—6) On our present knowledge of the relationship of mind and body. *Ann. Eugen.*, **1**, 382—406.

PFEIFER, R. A. (1921) Die Lokalisation der Tonskala innerhalb der kortikalen Hörsphäre des Menschen. *Mschr. Psychiat. Neurol.*, **50**, 7—48, 99—108.

— (1936) Pathologie der Hörstrahlung und der corticalen Hörsphäre. In: *Handbuch der Neurologie.* (Eds. O. Bumke and O. Foerster), Berlin, Springer, vol. 6, 533—626.

POLYAK, S. (1927) Über den allgemeinen Bauplan des Gehörsystems und über seine Bedeutung für die Physiologie, für die Klinik und für die Psychologie. *Z. ges. Neurol. Psychiat.*, **110**, 1—49.

PROBST, M. (1899) Über die Lokalisation des Tonvermögens. *Arch. Psychiat. Nervkrankh.*, **32**, 387—446.

RETZIUS, G. (1896) *Das Menschenhirn.* Stockholm, Norstedt and Söner.

— (1898) Das Gehirn des Astronomen Hugo Gyldén. *Biol. Unters.* (*Copenh.*), **8**, 1—22.

— (1900a) Das Gehirn der Mathematikerin Sonja Kovaleski. *Biol. Unters.*, **9**, 1—16.

— (1900b) Über das Hirngewicht der Schweden. *Biol. Unters.*, **9**, 51—68.

— (1902) Das Gehirn des Physiker und Paedagogen Per Adam Siljeström. *Biol. Unters.*, **10**, 1—14.

— (1904) Das Gehirn eines Staatsmannes. *Biol. Unters.*, **11**, 89—102.

— (1905) Das Gehirn des Histologen und Physiologen Christian Lovén. *Biol. Unters.*, **12**, 33—48.

RIESE, W. and GOLDSTEIN, K. (1950) The brain of Ludwig Edinger. *J. Comp. Neurol.*, **92**, 133—168.

ROSE, M. (1938) *Mozg. Józefa Pilsudskiego. Le cerveau de Joseph Pilsudski. Première partie.* Wilno, Zawadski. (Quoted from M. Minkowski 1939 and K. Schaffer 1939.)

ROSENBERG (1907) Histologische Untersuchung über die Cytoarchitektonik der Heschlschen Windungen. *Neurol. Zentbl.*, **14**, 685–686.

RÜDINGER, N. (1882a) Ein Beitrag zur Anatomie des Sprachcentrums. In: *Beiträge zur Biologie*. Stuttgart, Cotta, 135–191.

— (1882b) Ein Beitrag zur Anatomie der Affenspalte und der Interparietalfürche beim Menschen nach Rasse, Geschlecht und Individualität. In: *Beiträge zur Anatomie und Embryologie* (in honour of Jacob Henle). Bonn, Cohen, pp. 186–198.

— (1887) Das Hirn Gambetta's. S.-B. (math.-physical Kl.) *Bayr. Akad. Wiss.*, **17**, 69–71.

SCHAAFFHAUSEN (1886) Einige Reliquien berühmter Männer. *Arch. Anthrop. (Brunswick)*, **16**, (Suppl.), 147–149.

SCHAFFER, K. (1939) Einiges über das Gehirn der Hochtalente. *Schweizer Arch. Neurol. Psychiat.*, **44**, 347–352.

SOMOGYI, J. (1930) Über das morphologische Korrelat der musikalischen Fähigkeiten. *Mschr. Psychiat. Neurol.*, **75**, 113–169.

SPERINO, G. (1901) L'encefalo dell' anatomico Carlo Giacomini. *Riv. sper. Freniat. Med. leg. Alien. ment.*, **27**, 146–171, 548–581.

SPITZKA, E. A. (1901) A preliminary communication of a study of the brains of two distinguished physicians, father and son. *The Philadelphia Med. J.*, **7**, 680–688.

— (1903) A study of the brain of the late Major J. W. Powell. *Am. Anthrop.*, **5**, 585–643.

— (1904) Hereditary resemblances in the brains of three brothers. *Am. Anthrop.*, **6**, 307–312.

— (1907) A study of the brains of 6 eminent scientists. *Trans. Am. Phil. Soc.* (part IV), **21**, 175–308.

STIEDA, L. (1908) Das Gehirn eines Sprachkundigen. *Z. Morph. Anthrop.*, **11**, 83–138.

THURNAM, J. (1866) On the weight of the brain and the circumstances affecting it. *J. Ment. Sci.*, **12**, 1–43.

TOPINARD, P. (1878) *Anthropology* (transl. from French). Reprinted 1894. London, Chapman and Hall (with a preface by P. Broca).

TUNTURI, A. R. (1944) Audio-frequency localization in the acoustic cortex of the dog. *Am. J. Physiol.*, **141**, 397–403.

— (1950) Physiological determination of the arrangement of the afferent connections to the middle ectosylvian auditory area in the dog. *Am. J. Physiol.*, **162**, 489–502.

VOGT, O. (1929) Bericht über die Arbeiten des Moskauer Staatsinstitutes für Hirnforschung. *J. Psychol. Neurol.* (*Lpz.*), **40**, 108–115.

WAGNER, R. (1860, 1862) *Vorstudien zu einer wissenschaftlichen Morphologie und Physiologie des menschlichen Gehirns als Seelenorgan* (two parts bound together). Göttingen, Dieterich'sche Buchhdl.

WENDT, W. W. (1909) *Alte und Neue Gehirnprobleme, nebst einer 1078 Fälle umfassenden*

*Gehirngewichts-Statistik an dem K. pathologisch anatomischen Institut zu München.* Munich, Gmelin. (Quoted from P. Bailey and G. von Bonin 1951.)

WHITFIELD, I. C. (1967) *The Auditory Pathway.* London, Arnold.

WITELSON, S. F. and PALLIE, W. (1973) Left hemisphere specialization for language in the newborn. *Brain,* **96,** 641–646.

—— (1974) (personal communication).

WOOLSEY, C. N. and WALZL, E. M. (1942) Topical projection of nerve fibers from local regions of the cochlea to the cerebral cortex of the cat. *Johns Hopkins Hosp. Bull.,* **71,** 315–344.

# Is there an Anatomical Localisation for Musical Faculties?

It will be useful to start the discussion of this difficult problem by a short survey of the development of scientific thought concerning the localisation of complex functions in the brain.

True scientific research in this area began with the work of Gall and Spurzheim. Although their 'phrenological' doctrine is unacceptable today, it was a starting point. These scientists were also the first to stress that explaining the cause of a phenomenon is not the same as indicating the necessary conditions for it to take place. This formulation, made more than 150 years ago, is in conformity with our modern views.

The communication by Broca at the Anthropological Society in Paris in 1861 relating motor aphasia to a lesion in the area of $F_3$ may be considered as the first basis for a localisation theory of cerebral activity.

The researches by Fritsch and Hitzig (1870) on dogs, using circumscribed destruction and local faradisation of the cortex, led to the discovery of the motor area, and brought fresh scientific support to the localisational view. The beginning of our century brought us the first cyto- and myeloarchitectonic maps of the cerebral cortex, with efforts to correlate each particular area with a specific function (Brodmann, Vogt, von Economo, and others). One of these maps was based on the study of a large series of cases of brain injury occurring in the First World War (Kleist).

Observation of more and more clinical cases shed doubt on the reliability of these maps and led to the search for new approaches based on developmental biology and anthropology. The evolutionary theory of Darwin had a considerable influence on the study of comparative neurology, leading to the classification of nervous structures according to their "ages". But it was the influence of Herbert Spencer's principle of evolution which led to the elaboration by Hughlings Jackson of a new concept of structure and function. Spencer's theory of "integration" as developed by Jackson completely changed the course of neurology. According to Jackson, the different "centres" are organised hierarchically and as one proceeds from lower to higher centres there is an increase in differentiation, specialisation, and integration. The concept of localisation is more functional than anatomical. Evolution is broadly understood as moving "from the most to the least organised, from the most simple to the most complex and from the most automatic to the most voluntary".* Jackson also classified neurological symptoms into negative (from loss of function) and positive (from the activity of disinhibited lower nervous structures). The word "centre" in Jackson's system is devoid of any precise anatomical equivalent, and the greatest English neurologist was well known for his sceptical attitude towards cerebral maps.

The same dynamic attitude in neurology expressed itself in the writings of Head, Pierre Marie, von Monakow and others. Among others, Goldstein criticised the frequent confusion between the localisation of a symptom and the localisation of the corresponding function. He indicated that clinical facts will permit only the localisation of a deficit but not of a function. The fact that Critchley found it necessary to stress this idea again, shows that the mistake continues in our time.† In Goldstein's opinion, within the brain are special areas with a motor or sensory somatotopy, which he called "peripheral" cerebral areas, while there are other "central" areas, connected by multiple paths with the "peripheral" areas. Function is possible only as a result of cooperation between the specific "peripheral" and the "central" areas. So it appears that there are no "centres" for any specific function and that each function has a large and diffuse cerebral substratum.

With the benefit of new techniques, more recent research has brought additional doubt as to any conception of localisation of nervous activity. The introduction of neuronographic methods by de Barenne and McCulloch furthered the study of projection areas and the discovery of multiple association pathways. Since these studies there has been a general tendency to agree that there are multiple relationships between different areas, some of which utilise cortico–cortical pathways while the majority use more complicated "vertical" pathways, constituting a cortico-subcortico–cortical association system. Anatomical researches by Bailey and Bonin (1951) led to the conclusion that the isocortex can be divided into several architectonic types, the transition between the neighbouring areas being smooth and gradual, with considerable overlap. Accordingly they established a new map of the brain, based on the additional information regarding the intercortical and corticothalamic conditions.

The discovery of the reticular formation and the diffuse thalamic system brought modern neurological thought closer to a more or less holistic

* Quoted from W. Riese, *Dynamic aspects in the History of Neurology*, p. 11.
† Critchley, M., *The Parietal Lobes*, London, 1953.

conception of brain function. However, numerous clinical, anatomical and neurophysiological studies have pointed to certain correlations between location of lesions and specific disturbance. Today we have adequate somatotopical maps of the brain for the motor and sensory functions, but the vast, heterogeneous group of the aphasias, apraxias and agnosias has so far defied any narrow localisation for each type of specific disturbance.

Against such a background let us now examine the difficult problem of cerebral localisation as applied to musical function.

Before embarking upon this task we obviously must try to define musical function in an attempt to avoid concepts which are too vague to be useful. For instance such definitions as that of J. J. Rousseau ("Music is the art of combining sounds in a manner pleasant to the ear"), or Boetius ("Music? Everyone who looks into himself will know what it is") are useless for our purpose. Musical perception and performance is an inborn capacity of the human brain. This ability is common among human beings and is independent of education or culture which can refine but not produce it. There are wide variations in the degree and development of the musical faculty but the anatomo-functional substratum is probably the same in a professional musician and a person lacking all musical training. According to Ustvedt (1937) musical function is in fact a complex of functions forming a psychological whole. In the opinion of the present writer (1969) musical function relies in fact on three basic abilities. In the absence of any one of these there can be no musical function. These three necessary abilities are:

(1) *The rhythmic sense*, probably of biological origin, is a function of superior integration, the limits of which are far wider than those of musical function: however, the latter cannot develop in the absence of a normal rhythmic sense.

(2) *The sense of sounds* is a special ability permitting one to perceive correctly the four elementary physical properties of a sound (intensity, duration, timbre and pitch). While perception of intensity, duration and timbre is necessary for the musician, the perception of pitch is also essential for normal musical function. Most musical people distinguish a difference of pitch less than a semitone, and this interval can be shortened by training.

A special refinement of the sense of sounds is "absolute pitch". It is not a necessary condition for good musical function.

Dependent upon the sense of sounds is also the sense of musical intervals (Riemann, 1926), which is the recognition of the tonal distance between different sounds in a melody or a chord. It generally develops through singing or practising a musical instrument, although musical training is not a prerequisite of "feeling" the interval.

(3) *The aptitude to convert musical perception into emotional or intellectual content.*

All the foregoing components are part of the *receptive* aspect of the musical function. The *expressive* aspect (musical interpretation, composition) is built up empirically, or through persistent study which permits the elaboration of a special praxic ability based upon the three receptive components mentioned. It must be said that the expressive aspect of the third element is the ability to turn emotion into some kind of musical production, either interpretative or creative.

Let us now examine the contribution of neuroanatomy and neurophysiology to the problem of localisation.

Since Flechsig's discovery that the auditory radiations terminate in the temporal lobe, this region has been recognised as the cerebral projection of acoustic stimuli. Later, scientists sought in this area the "centre of hearing". Experimentation based on destruction and electrical stimulation met with increasing difficulties, and results were often contradictory. Neuronographic methods brought a valuable contribution but many questions still await definitive answers.

Ferrier (1875) was the first to observe hearing-loss on the contralateral side due to a destruction of the temporosphenoidal gyrus in monkeys. Bilateral destruction of this area led to complete deafness. A few years later Munk published similar findings as the result of experimentation with dogs. Bilateral destruction of the posterior area of $T_2$ led to complete deafness. Such animals did not react to any sound or noise and their barking was abolished. Moreover he found in this same $T_2$ convolution a more circumscribed area, destruction of which would lead only to what Munk called "psychic deafness". The animal could hear, but the sounds had lost their specific significance. For instance, the operated dog reacted to its master's voice only as it would to any other sudden sound. Later, Munk expressed the conviction that different sound-frequencies had different fixed cortical representations. In his opinion, the higher the frequency, the more anterior was its cortical projection. Experiments with birds and dogs led Bechterew to support Munk's views. He used different sound-sources and among them a series of tuning forks covering a wide frequency-range $(A^1, A, c, g^1, b^1, h^1, c^2, c \text{ sharp}^2, a^2, c^3)$, musical wind instruments and so on. All the animals were examined before surgery and their reactions to the different sources of sound were recorded. According to the findings of Bechterew it appeared that even a very slight lesion of the temporal cortex would lead to complete deafness of the contralateral ear and a definite hearing loss on the same side. After a few days an almost complete recovery of hearing would come about, although the operated animal maintained a permanent contralateral deafness to certain frequencies, dependent upon the site of the lesion. There would also be a partial hearing-loss on the homolateral side for the same frequencies. This fact led Bechterew to envisage a partial crossing of the pathways for hearing. In his opinion, high frequencies ($c^2$–$c^3$) were projected into the area of the angular gyrus, while tones between c and $c^2$ were represented in the posterior area of $T_3$ and low tones in the $T_2$ convolution. If we recall that to Bechterew an ear-movement or a sudden turning of the animal's head towards the sound indicated "a perception of sound" it will appear that his conclusions are open to serious criticism. Moreover, it is impossible to admit that in those experiments other sensory stimuli were completely excluded.

Kalischer tried another approach. Using a conditioning process, he taught dogs to respond by feeding-behaviour to a specific sound-frequency. At the end of the conditioning period, whenever the sound was emitted by an organ pipe, the dogs would approach the meat and eat it. A sound differing by only a semitone from the conditioning sound would leave the animal indifferent, and it would not touch the meat. A musical chord containing the key-sound would elicit feeding behaviour, while another chord without that particular sound would be without effect. Kalischer was so enthusiastic about the sensitivity of his dogs, that he concluded that they must have absolute pitch, a sensory privilege enjoyed by only a small percentage of humans. Destruction of the cochlea and removal of the temporal cortex on the same side left the previously acquired conditioned responses undisturbed. The obvious significance of this fact was that auditory stimuli from each ear reached both hemispheres. Moreover, a few weeks after bilateral temporal lobe destruction, the animal appeared to have retained its previous conditioning, only the behaviour seemed more automatic. Conditioning to new tones was still possible after such an operation although there were signs of a severe global hearing-loss. The general behaviour of the operated dogs was altered, and they resembled Goltz's hemispherectomised dogs. The conclusion reached by Kalischer was that perception and differentiation of sound-frequencies must be subcortical. This idea has been subsequently criticised, and it has been stressed that there is no proof that in Kalischer's experiment the whole of the temporal cortex had been removed, and that the influence of vibration perceived by other sense had been excluded.

More recent research based on limited destruction has not yielded definite conclusions concerning the cortical representation of sound-frequencies, and results are contradictory, depending on the techniques or the animal species used for the experiments. In dogs, Lipman could not find a fixed correlation between any cortical temporal lesion and specific frequency hearing-loss. In cats, Meyer and Woolsey had to remove extensive temporal areas bilaterally in order to obtain a perceptible loss in sound-discrimination. Finally Evarts (1952) showed that sparing of ten per cent. of the temporal cortex is sufficient to enable operated apes to differentiate frequencies between 350 and 3500 Hz. The neuronographic study of evoked potentials led to considerable progress in research of the auditory cortical projection. Davis (1934) showed that auditory stimulation caused changes in the electrical rhythms of area 22 in the cat. By means of the electrocorticogram (ECG) Bremer and Dow (1939) outlined the auditory area in the cat, locating within it the gyrus sylviacus. Electrical stimulation of acoustic fibres and correlation with evoked potentials in the temporal cortex (Woolsey and Walzl) also led to the establishment of the auditory projection in the cat. Ades and Felder (1942) using ECG techniques drew an auditory cortical map in the ape. They found that this area is more sharply defined in this animal than in cats. Woolsey and Walzl also described a secondary auditory area architectonically different and reacting only to stronger stimulation. While in the primary area, the higher frequencies seem to be projected in its more caudal part, the same frequencies are projected more rostrally in the secondary auditory area. This area may be connected with complex integration of auditory stimuli.

Mention should be made of the excellent electrophysiological studies of Tunturi (1950, 1960) who worked on dogs using sound-stimuli and detecting responses on the ECG. By this elegant technique, the author was able to establish precise localisation within the ectosylvian area of the cortex. According to Tunturi the fibres for each frequency terminate in parallel bands, 2 mm wide per octave.

In man it has not so far proved possible to detect electro-encephalographic responses in the temporal region after auditory stimulation. This lack of reaction may be explained by an alteration through phylogenetic development of the area found in dogs by Tunturi (Poskanzer et al., 1962). Indeed, the ectosylvian gyrus in dogs becomes the gyrus transversus in man, which is enfolded over the insula (Kappers et al., 1960). One should not forget, however, that although this region may be the site of frequency-representation, musical function is far from being a mere perception of frequency.

To sum up the knowledge so far acquired on the basis of anatomical and physiological studies in animals, we may say that there is a relatively large primary auditory projection centre located in the areas 41 and 42 of the temporal lobes. These areas correspond with the two transverse convolutions of Heschl, the main part of which is hidden and can be exposed only by retracting the opercula. The neighbouring areas 52 and 22 represent the secondary auditory projection. Many studies point to a tono-topical projection inside these auditory areas in animals. Auditory stimuli are projected from the medial geniculate body to the appropriate areas via the auditory radiation which passes through the internal capsule. There are many nerve-fibres connecting the primary and secondary areas with the neighbouring temporal and parietal cortex, and the inside, as well as the frontal and occipital cortex. Most of these are two-way connections allowing complex association and feed-back circuits. Through these and other ways the temporal lobe is connected with almost all the brain.

Most of these conclusions are inferred as the result of studies in different animals. They will now be completed by a survey of studies in man.

Some interesting observations have been contributed by neurosurgeons. Applying faradic stimulation to different cortical areas during surgery under local anaesthesia, Foerster obtained in his patients auditory hallucinations of different types (whistles, bells, etc.) on stimulation of the $T_1$. Penfield and Rasmussen (1952), using a similar technique, obtained different types of auditory hallucination by means of stimulating the primary or the secondary auditory areas. Recollection of music was produced by stimulation along the right $T_1$ convolution. In a later paper Penfield and Perot evoked musical hallucinations by stimulation of $T_1$ more on the right side than the left (see Chapter 1). Often this stimulation would lead to temporary deafness, and this, like the elicited hallucinations, was experienced most often, though not always, on the contralateral side.

The various clinical pictures appearing as a result of vascular lesions of the temporal lobes have also contributed, as might be expected, to the understanding of the localisation problem. For a considerable time, localisation of musical function has occupied the minds of clinicians. The contributions up to the end of World War I have been summarised by Henschen (1922, 1926) and also by Ustvedt (1937). Willis believed the cerebellum to be the site of musical function, while Gall was the first to claim the existence of a "musical organ" within the human brain. The first case of musical dysfunction, with alexia for musical symbols, was published by Proust in 1866. The word "amusia" was coined by Steinhals in 1871, and Knoblauch definitely established its place within musical terminology. Oppenheim was responsible, in 1888, for a review of 18 cases of aphasia with musical disturbances. In a series of papers, Henschen (1918, 1920, 1926) summarised all the published cases of amusia and made an attempt to analyse the "musical sense", and to locate topographically the different musical functions. Kleist (1928) attempted a classification of musical faculties and tried to describe a particular localisation of every type of clinical picture. Feuchtwanger (1930) published an extensive psychological study of disorders of musical function, while Jellinek (1933) was the first to offer the clinician a practical method of investigating cases of amusia. The most comprehensive study on amusia was published by Ustvedt (1937). On the basis of 14 cases of amusia, of which 13 were of vascular origin, submitted by the author to a thorough clinical and psychological analysis, some important aspects were stressed. In a series of studies with Botez (1959, 1961) the present writer has also endeavoured to elucidate the problem of amusia.

The first attempt to locate the lesions producing amusia was made in connection with the publication of the pioneer anatomo-clinical cases. The case published in 1898 by Mann (quoted by Ustvedt, 1937) was of motor amusia without aphasia, and was associated with a cyst of the right $F_2$ in a right-handed patient. Edgren (1895) and Brodman (1914), after anatomical studies of various cases of amusia, concluded that a lesion of the anterior part of one or both temporal lobes produces musical agnosia. According to Henschen (1920–22, 1926) there are some centres associated with musical functions, all within the left hemisphere: a "centre of singing" (pars triangularis of $F_3$); a "centre of the musical sense" (anterior extremity of the temporal lobe); "instrumental centre" (foot of $F_2$). He was even tempted to describe specific centres for each musical instrument.

Kleist believed that the lesion responsible for musical deafness was located in the middle of $T_1$: the loss of the symbolic sense of music in the fields 20 and 37; vocal apraxia in the left field 6, and instrumental apraxia in the foot of $F_2$. The necessity for a lesion of the fields 20 and 37 to be bilateral would explain the relative rarity of musical agnosia (1928). In a more recent work (1959) the same author presented a case of cerebral contusion with receptive amusia. Analysis of the lesions led the author to conclude that the tonal and interval sense are located in the transverse convolutions of Heschl, whilst the *regio separans* (as shown in the myeloarchitectonic map of Hopf (1954) is the seat of "melody understanding" (*Melodienverstandis*) and the *subregio magna dorsalis* seemed to be the anatomical basis of what the author called *Sinnverstandis der Melodien*.

Head (1926) emphasised the connections between musical function and the thalamus, in that he described patients with thalamic lesions who had strange, intolerable sensations when certain pieces of music were played.

According to Feuchtwanger (1930) musical agnosia is linked with lesions in Wernicke's area in both hemispheres, an auditory image-sphere extending in musical persons through the middle part of $T_1$.

Ustvedt (1937) considered that the anatomo-physiological substratum of the emotional components of musical experience lies in a thalamohypothalamo-striopallidal complex, wherein the cortex plays only an associative role.

The experience of reflex epilepsy may perhaps serve to support the belief that there is indeed a musical cortical area which can assume the function of an epileptic focus, but the evidence for such a conclusion is by no means convincing.

It is thought that Ballet (quoted by Ustvedt, 1937) was the first to draw a parallel between aphasia and amusia (1888). He sought to apply to amusia the scheme proposed by Lichtheim, and described a series of hypothetical clinical forms. This attempt, subsequently made by others, is the result of the frequent co-existence of amusia and aphasia in the same patient. This association can also explain the all too sketchy descriptions of amusia occurring in various cases of aphasia in the standard handbooks of neurology. However, the report of many cases of motor amusia *without* aphasia allowed Henschen (1922) to assert for the first time that the cerebral substratum must be entirely different for the faculties of speech and music. After an extensive review of the literature the author also asserted that one may find cases of "musical deafness" without "word deafness" and vice versa. However the analysis of 34 cases of sensory amusia made by Feuchtwanger (1930) demonstrated dysphasic disturbances in every patient. According to this author it is impossible to find any major difference between amusia and aphasia on the basis of either motor or sensory disorders.

These controversial statements seem to throw but little light on the complex problem of localisation. We know that while speech expresses precise ideas, music is unlike speech because it can convey only emotional experiences. There is an analogy, perhaps even a resemblance, between the two functions in the following aspects: both speech and music have expressive and receptive aspects; both of them use written or printed symbols which serve the purpose of recording and reproduction. It appears that although not exactly a language, music depends upon a morpho-functional substratum, the general pattern of which is perhaps analogous with that of speech. It is possible to analyse disturbances of the musical faculty by tests similar to those used in the study of aphasia.

Luria et al. (1965) showed that amusia does not necessarily accompany aphasia. They described the case of a composer and conservatoire director (Shebalin) who continued to compose and supervise the work of his pupils in spite of a severe dysphasia. The comment by Shostakovitch may give an idea of the quality of Shebalin's composing after he developed his impairment in the sphere of language: ". . . . Shebalin's Fifth Symphony is a brilliant creative work filled with highest emotions, optimistic and full of life. This Symphony, composed during his illness, is a creation of a great master".* Such a study leads us to think that faculties of both music and language use a different cerebral substratum although it does not permit us to reach any positive conclusions about the location of these complex functions.

Of special interest are the papers published by Monrad-Krohn (1947, 1963) which seem to provide a link between speech and music. This author showed that in addition to vocabulary and grammar one has to consider also a prosodic quality of human speech, which gives it various shades by means of variations in stress, pitch and rhythm. There is an *intrinsic* prosody which consists of "standard prosodic patterns inherent in the language", a *propositional* prosody which "serves the need of expressing various subtle shades of meaning" and an *emotional* prosody which may convey the various emotions. The corresponding disturbances were described by the author as hyperprosody, hypoprosody and dysprosody. In the presence of these impairments, the patient's speech may sound inexpressive and monotonous and his mother-tongue may sound like a foreign language. Monrad-Krohn considered the dysprosodies as an after-effect of aphasia, appearing during the stage of recovery. They seem, therefore, to be associated more with the functions of language than with the musical faculty. However, in a case published by Botez and Wertheim (1959), the patient developed expressive amusia without any sign of aphasia but with dysprosody.

In fact, the present state of our knowledge does not allow us to draw any definite conclusion concerning focal localisation without the risk of commiting grave errors. It seems, however, that most cases of receptive amusia correspond with a lesion of the anterior temporal area in the dominant hemisphere, while lesions of $F_2$ in the minor hemisphere may be related to some forms of expressive, mainly instrumental, amusia. Vocal expressive amusia seems to be associated with a lesion of the *pars triangularis*, also in the minor hemisphere. The location in the minor hemisphere of lesions causing expressive amusia may perhaps explain the total absence of receptive disorders in the published cases.

These observations are certainly not sufficient to allow any inference as to the location of musical function, unless we expose ourselves to the error of confounding localisation of lesions with the site of normal function.

During the last decades there has been increasing interest in the role of each of the cerebral hemispheres in different forms of higher nervous activity, as well as in the problem of hemispheric hierarchy or dominance.

* Quoted from M. Critchley, *Aphasiology and other Aspects of Language*, London, 1970, p. 261.

There have been statistical studies of handedness, reports of patients functioning with only one hemisphere (after surgical or temporary "chemical" hemispherectomy) as well as the recent studies of Sperry et al. (1969) on patients treated surgically by hemispheric disconnection for relief of intractable epileptic attacks. Although the musical faculties or their disturbance were not discussed in these studies, there seems to be a general trend nowadays to discard the idea of minor or subordinate hemisphere, in favour of the concept of hemispheric specialisation (Subirana, 1969). It appears that each of the two hemispheres may be specialised in certain functions while the other is specialised in other functions. This distribution may differ in different individuals. Certain complex functions seem to be represented in both hemispheres, and this representation may be complementary for different aspects of the same general function.

Often it has been said that music and mathematics are closely related. Leibniz wrote in 1712 that singers, instrumentalists and composers all use mathematics without being aware of it. Helmholtz (1879) wrote: "I have always been intrigued by the mysterious union of mathematics and music".* One can discern mathematics in the simple frequency relationships governing horizontal and vertical tonal combinations. It is reasonable to ask whether functions pertaining to mathematical thought and music are related. So far no cerebral site of mathematical function is known. However, disturbances are known as the acalculias and these have been extensively described. Grewel summarised the research in this field (1969). The fact that lesions causing acalculia may be situated in the occipital, temporal, parietal or frontal lobe – that is almost anywhere in the brain – makes futile any attempt to find a precise cortical localisation for mathematical functions. It appears that even if musical and mathematical functions were indeed correlated, this fact would not help us locate a musical faculty.

It is inconceivable to undertake any problem pertaining to the musical function including its localisation, without discussing the question of rhythm. Without rhythm there can be no music and, understandably, no musical function. Rhythm is the framework of music, it gives to melody its pattern, its emotional colour. The same piece of music played in different rhythms or time-patterns may have quite different emotional impacts. As already stated, music cannot exist without time. The pitch of sounds, their different duration, the development of melody, all rely on the element of time which is measured and divided into patterns by what we call rhythm. As Grey Walter (1968) put it: "any sound is an event in time". The vertical spatial arrangement of a musical chord is only symbolic. Simultaneity, also

* Quoted from P. Cossa, *De la gamme à l'intemporel*, Paris, 1965, p. 15.

a function of time, is the necessary condition for a number of different sounds to be perceived as a musical chord. Perception of a sound is also a function of its minimum duration. The lower the frequency, the longer the minimal duration necessary for perception. There is also a strong link between rhythm and movement as well as between rhythm and simple emotions. The music of primitive peoples is dominated by rhythm. Every tune having a marked rhythm provokes in the listener a tendency to rhythmical body-movements which are largely unconscious and which can be consciously inhibited. Dancing is an organised way of expressing these movements, and its refined form – the art of choreography – links rhythm with expression of a complex emotional sentiment.

A particular affinity of the brain exists towards rhythm. Listening to the regular ticking of a clock soon resolves itself into groups of two, three or four ticks although the sequence is unaccented (Grey Walter 1968). There is no meaning to a rhythm without a message and the impact upon the listener depends on this message carried by the rhythm, or else lent to it by the listener himself. A striking example can be found in "The Act of Creation" by A. Koestler:* "I can remember at least one ghastly (train) journey when I found myself in a predicament of my own making, and the wheels kept repeating, 'I *told* you so, I *told* you so, I *told* you so' with such hallucinatory clarity and insistence that I found it difficult to convince myself that the other passengers in the compartment did not hear it. Rhythm penetrates so deeply into the unconscious strata that it makes up suggestible even to self-addressed messages – from the yogic recitation of 'māntras' to Coué's 'every day in every way . . .'".

Some rhythms invigorate, others may diminish or even suspend the normal waking activity of the brain, lulling the listener to sleep. How can such a complex influence be understood? Perhaps our present knowledge about the reticular system could provide the beginnings of an answer. We know that this particular area of the brain-stem is concerned with a regulation of cortical electrical rhythms. We also know that there are abundant connections between the reticular formation and the auditory pathways. It may be that the rhythmical component of the auditory input has an impact on the whole cerebral cortex and also on large subcortical areas, *via* the extensive connections of the reticular formation with all these regions. The precipitation of some musicogenic epileptic fits might possibly use the same mechanism.

A brief discussion of musical memory is appropriate. It is difficult to imagine any musical function, receptive or expressive, without a special memory pertaining to all the components of this complex ability.

* A. Koestler, *The Act of Creation*, New York, 1967, p. 313.

Somewhere in the brain must be stored patterns of frequencies, durations, amplitudes, rhythms as well as a vast number of associative combinations. In order to be remembered, a stimulus must be part of a pattern, distinguishing it from a random event. We know no more about the mechanism or substratum of musical memory than of other types of memory. The same current functional, biochemical or electrical theories apply equally to all types of memory. Do the experiments of Penfield suggest that he touched upon the "hidden box" where musical memories are kept in store? Or did he merely activate a complex reverberating circuit involving many different cerebral structures? We are far from knowing the answers to these questions. Memory is a very general attribute of every nerve-cell, so it is increasingly difficult to speak about a locus of memory and still harder to discuss any representation of musical memory.

Many other aspects of musical function still defy attempts to find a suitable anatomo-physiological substratum. Thus we know nothing about the relationship between such a substratum and what is commonly called musical talent. Is it related to cerebral dominance? Or to a special functional development of some cerebral areas? Or perhaps in talented persons, special neuronal circuits establish themselves quicker and more easily than in other persons. There is no explanation of the fact that some persons are able to express their emotions more easily by music than by verbal symbols. This expression is possible even without the sensory feedback which is a *sine qua non* in other forms of art. It is impossible to imagine a blind painter. There are, however, many composers who do not need a piano or any other musical instrument for their work and who usually compose while they sit at a desk like an author or playwright. They rely on their "inner hearing" which can suffice for the creation of extremely complex works even after the anatomical organ of hearing has been inactive for years. In this connection, the example of Beethoven is universally known.

Another puzzling problem is the reversibility of the figure-background relationship in music as seen in theme-accompaniment, subject-countersubject in fugue. What causes the decision as to what is figure and what is background at any given moment? Is it the reticular formation by activating some circuits while inhibiting others? Or perhaps the decision depends on spontaneous activation of particular associative connections and not of others.

It is obvious that any attempt to find a representation in the brain for musical faculty encounters considerable difficulties, and our present knowledge is far from sufficient to enable us to give definite answers to the many problems in the field.

Even if musical function were a simple sum of its components — and it is certainly more than that — and even if we could localise some of these components within the brain, many important aspects would still defy any attempt at localisation.

## REFERENCES

ADES, H. W. and FELDER, R. E. (1942). The acoustic area of the monkey. *J. Neurophysiol.*, **5,** 49.

AJURIAGUERRA, J. DE and HECAEN, H. (1964). *Le cortex cérébral.* Paris, Masson.

ARIENS KAPPERS, C. U., HUBER, G. C. and CROSBY, E. C. (1960). *The Comparative Anatomy of the Nervous System of Vertebrates including Man.* Vol III, New York, Hafner Publ. Co.

BAILEY, P. and BONIN, G. von (1951). *The Isocortex of Man.* University of Illinois Press, Urbana.

BOTEZ, M. I. and WERTHEIM, N. (1959). Expressive aphasia and amusia following right frontal lesion in a right-handed man. *Brain,* **82,** 186.

BREMER, F. and DOW, R. S. (1939). The cerebral acoustic area in cats. *J. Neurophysiol.,* **2,** 308.

BRODMANN, K. (1914) *Physiologie des Gehirns.* Stuttgart, Deutsche Verlagsgesellschaft.

COSSA, P. (1965). De la gamme a l'intemporel. *Médécine de France.,* **159.**

CRITCHLEY, M. (1937). Musicogenic epilepsy. *Brain,* **60,** 13.

— (1953). *The Parietal Lobes,* London, E. Arnold.

— (1970). *Aphasiology and other Aspects of Language.* London, E. Arnold.

DAVIS, H. (1934). *The physiological phenomena of audition.* In: Murchinson's *Handbook of Experimental Psychology,* Chicago.

EDGREN, J. G. (1895). Amusie (musikalische Aphasie). *Dtsch. Z. Nervenheilk.,* **6,** 1.

EVARTS, E. V. (1952). Effect of auditory cortex ablation on frequency discrimination in monkey. *J. Neurophysiol.,* **15,** 435.

FEUCHTWANGER, E. (1930). Amusie. Studien zur Psychologie der akustischen Wahrnehmung und Vorstellung und ihrer Strukturgebiete besonders in Musik und Sprache. Berlin, Springer.

FULTON, J. F. (1949). *Physiology of the Nervous System.* London, Oxford University Press. 3rd edition.

GOTTSCHICK, J. (1955). Die Leistungen des Nervensystems. Jena, Fischer Verlag.

GREWEL, F. (1969). The acalculias. In: *Handbook of Clinical Neurology,* vol. 4. Amsterdam, North Holland Publ. Comp.

GREY WALTER, W. (1968). *The Living Brain:* Harmondsworth, Middlesex. Penguin Books.

GROSSMAN, S. P. (1967). *A Textbook of Physiological Psychology.* New York, Wiley International Editions.

HEAD, H. (1926). *Aphasia and Kindred Disorders of Speech*. London, Cambridge University Press.

HENSCHEN, S. E. (1918) Uber die Hörsphäre. *J. Psychol. Neurol*, **22** (Suppl. 3).

— (1920–1922) *Klinische und anatomische Beitrage zur Pathologie des Gehirns*. Stockholm, Nordiska Bockhandeln.

— (1926) On the function of the right hemisphere of the brain in relation to the left in speech, music and calculation. *Brain*, **49,** 110.

HOPF, A. (1954). Die Myeloarchitektonik des Isocortex temporalis beim Menschen. *J. Hirnforsch.*, **1**.

JELLINEK, A. (1933) Zur Phänamenologie der Amusie. *Jahrb. f. Psychiat. u. Neurol.*, **50,** 115.

KLEIST, K. (1928) Gehirnpathologische und lokalisatorische Ergebnisse über Hörstörungen, Geräuschtaubheiten und Amusien. *Mschr. Psychiat. Neurol.*, **68,** 853.

— (1959) *Sensorische Aphasien und Amusien auf Myeloarchitektonischer Grundlage (drei Vorträge)*. Stuttgart, Thieme Verlag.

KOESTLER, A. (1967) *The Act of Creation. A study of the conscious and unconscious in science and art.* New York, Dell Pub.

LURIA, A. R., TSVETKOVA, L. S. and FUTER, D. S. (1965) Aphasia in a composer. *J. neurol. Sci.*, **2,** 288.

MONRAD-KROHN, G. H. (1947) Dysprosody or altered "melody of language". *Brain*, **70,** 405.

— (1963) The third element of speech. Prosody and its disorders. In: L. Halpern (ed.) *Problems of dynamic neurology*. Jerusalem, Jerus. Post Press.

PENFIELD, W. and RASMUSSEN, T. (1952) *The Cerebral Cortex of Man*. The Macmillan Company.

POSKANZER, D. C., BROWN, A. E. and MILLER, H. (1962). Musicogenic epilepsy caused only by a discrete frequency of church bells. *Brain*, **85,** 77.

RIESE, W. (1963) Dynamic aspects in the history of neurology. In: L. Halpern (ed.), *Problems of dynamic Neurology*. Jerusalem, Jerus. Post Press.

SCHAPER, G. (1967) Musikogene Epilepsie im Kindesalter. *Mschr. Kinderheilk.*, **115,** 1.

SPERRY, R. W., GAZZANIGA, M. S., and BOGEN, J. E. (1969) Interhemispheric relationships: the neocortical commissures: syndrome of hemispheric disconnection. In: *Handbook of Clinical Neurology*. Vol. 4, Amsterdam, North Holland Pub. Co.

STRANG, R. R. (1966) A case of musical epilepsy. *J. Irish Med. Assoc.*, **59,** 85.

SUBIRANA, A. (1969) Handedness and cerebral dominance. In: *Handbook of Clinical Neurology*. Vol. 4, Amsterdam, North Holland Publ. Comp.

TITECA, J. (1965) L'épilepsie musicogène. Revue générale à propos d'un cas personnel suivi pendant quatorze ans. *Acta Neurol. Belg.*, **65,** 8.

TUNTURI, A. R. (1950) Physiological determination of the boundary of the acoustic area in the cerebral cortex of the dog. *Amer. J. Physiol.*, **160,** 395.

— (1960) Anatomy and physiology of the auditory cortex. In: G. K. Rasmussen and W. F. Windle (eds.), *Neural Mechanisms of the Auditory and Vestibular Systems*. Springfield, Ill. Charles Thomas.

USTVEDT, H. I. (1937) Über die Untersuchungder musikalischen Funktionen bei Patienten mit Gehirnleiden, besonders bei Patienten mit Aphasie. *Acta Med. Scand. Suppl.*, **86**.

WERTHEIM, N. and BOTEZ, M. I. (1961) Receptive amusia, a clinical analysis. *Brain*, **84**, 19.

WERTHEIM, N. (1963) Disturbances of the musical functions. In: L. Halpern (ed.), *Problems of Dynamic Neurology*, Jerusalem, Jerus. Press.

— (1969) The amusias. In: *Handbook of Clinical Neurology*. Vol. 4, Amsterdam, North Holland Pub. Co.

# PART II

# 17

J. N. BLAU and
R. A. HENSON

# Neurological Disorders in Performing Musicians

The goal of many a young aspiring musician is to become a soloist, but the great majority fail to achieve their ambition. Some become performers in orchestras or smaller groups, others take up teaching, and some seek employment outside their profession. The physical attributes of soloists and orchestral players and teachers are patently different. The soloist requires extreme physical fitness and stamina and at all times the capacity for outstanding performances. The orchestral player needs different qualities, including the ability to contend with much travel, irregular meals, and rehearsal, performance or recording in difficult and often uncomfortable circumstances; nevertheless his or her playing must be reliable and never fall below a high professional standard. The demands on a music teacher are different – often older, his problems are in communication rather than performance and he is therefore more able to cope with the physical restrictions imposed by neurological or other disease. He is equally or more exposed to the effects of speech disorder and intellectual deterioration.

Both soloist and orchestral player share responsibilities and whereas those of the soloist are clearly greater, members of the orchestra are frequently called on to play technically difficult passages so that they are individually exposed during a performance, particularly in the brass and woodwind sections. Pre-performance tension is shared by executants in activities carried out before an audience or spectators and is regarded by many to be essential for the highest level of achievement. The degree of anxiety varies among players, although some deny that they are affected in this way unless the circumstances are unusual. Factors likely to provoke or heighten anxiety include a new or very difficult work in the programme, an unfamiliar conductor, an audience known to be highly critical, or fatigue, as, for example, at the end of a tour. When some or all of these factors combine the physical manifestations of anxiety are evident to the observer for some hours before, and more so immediately before, the performance; irritability, restlessness, tightly drawn expressions, trembling, overbreathing, excessive hand perspiration and complaints of various bodily symptoms are a few of the signs encountered. Management staff may have to urge some players to go on stage as they dally for a last adjustment of their instruments, trials of difficult passages and discussions over technical points of performance. In frank discussion the majority of performers say that they are affected by "nerves", but once on the platform they must appear outwardly calm and relaxed.

While no attempt can be made here to discuss the physical and mental requirements for a successful career as a professional musician, certain points must be mentioned. Firstly, technical capacity of a high level is mandatory. Secondly, orchestral players must be alert and quick in their responses, qualities which are evident in social contact with them. It would be a mistake to generalise about temperament or personality. Temperaments differ notoriously, or so professionals assert, between members of different sections of an orchestra. For example, brass players are well known for their ebullience, and to travel with the brass section on a coach during a tour brings back memories of similar excursions with rugger teams.

In this chapter we discuss the effects of various types of lesions at different sites in the nervous system on musical performance but the account would be incomplete without briefly recalling the way in which many performing musicians have triumphed over physical disability due to non-neurological disease. For example there have been several blind keyboard virtuosi from Landini (*c.* 1325–1397) onwards. Goossens described the encouragement he obtained when he recalled how Douglas Fox, a pianist, became a first class organist after losing an arm (Wynne, 1967). Paul Wittgenstein, the philosopher's brother, lost an arm in the First World War; the technical capacity of his left hand increased with unwearying practice, and he subsequently commissioned, and played, piano concertos for the left hand by Britten, Ravel and Strauss. Celebrated artists have continued to perform at top level while suffering from advanced malignant disease.

When generalised brain damage due to injury, inflammation, degeneration or vascular insufficiency gives rise to deterioration in intellectual skills and changes in temperament, the prognosis for useful work is bad. While intracranial tumour or stroke may have similar devastating effects there are outstanding exceptions among our musician patients as we shall show. Lesions of the spinal cord or peripheral nerves can be equally damaging in practical terms, but performance may continue unimpaired when the paralysed or weakened parts are not involved in the act of playing. We have seen public performances by apparently paraplegic musicians playing string, wind or percussion instruments. Here we speak as members of the audience because we have no direct medical knowledge of these cases.

## Diagnostic difficulties of illness in musicians

In the majority of patients consulting the neurologist diagnosis presents no great problem. In cases where disorder of function rests between a psychogenic and a mild organic disturbance the diagnosis can be inordinately difficult, and this applies particularly to musical executants.

Musicians are sensitive and imaginative individuals who at intervals are liable to anxieties and preoccupation over unemployment, health and, in later life, maintenance of technical skill. During these anxious periods mild physical disabilities may be magnified and serious illness imagined as their source. The fear of disease, rather than actual physical illness, provides 10 to 15 per cent. of neurological consultations among the population at large, and musicians, like doctors, are prone to unnatural and unnecessary fears. Furthermore, the professional musical population is a small one and when a member falls ill it is not surprising if a colleague presents with similar symptoms not based on an organic pathological process.

Conversely, early or mild neurological symptoms can produce disability too slight for the clinician to identify. The inability to trill, for example, may be the first and only manifestation of Parkinsonism or of a minimal cerebral lesion. We include an illustrative example by kind permission of the patient.

In a radio broadcast tribute to Solomon on his 70th birthday his wife described how this famous pianist at the age of 54 developed difficulty in controlling the ring and little finger of one hand. He began his "tour of doctors" but no one seemed able to reach a diagnosis. During the next few months Solomon practised desperately hard and even managed to record, during one week, two Beethoven, the Schumann and Grieg piano concertos. However, during the last recording session. in the finale of the Beethoven C minor concerto, a florid but for him not too difficult phrase could only be recorded after numerous repetitions. At last he succeeded, but two days later, after an aeroplane flight for a belated holiday, he awoke with a dense hemiplegia from which there has been little recovery.

A helpful measure to determine the nature of the underlying disorder is to see the patient play his instrument. The musician often brings his instrument to the initial consultation and may feel he has been inadequately examined unless invited to demonstrate his particular difficulty. This practice aids rapport, especially if the neurologist is himself a performer, albeit at a modest level.

The musician, like other patients, is liable to ascribe difficulties arising from organic disease to stress or other psychological problems, a viewpoint to which the physician may wrongly acquiesce if no physical signs are detectable. Even the most detailed neurological examination does not demand the degree of integration required by, say, Ševčik's finger exercises.

It is therefore apparent that the diagnosis of neurological or seemingly neurological problems in these patients with highly developed sensorimotor and artistic skills demands considerable patience in history taking and physical examination. Identification or exclusion of an organic lesion provides the neurologist with as difficult a task as he is likely to encounter. Laboratory and radiological investigations may not reveal the diagnosis in patients with incipient serious disease, and decisive hesitation may be required pending further reviews of the case. To maintain the confidence of the patient and manage his illness throughout this period constitute a severe test in the doctor-patient relationship.

## Medical disorders peculiar to musicians

### 1. Occupational palsies and cramps

This important topic is discussed in Chapter 21. We mention the subject here because of its relevance to differential diagnosis. Our clinical experience of these often incapacitating conditions is limited to woodwind, guitar and string players. Recognition of the true nature of the muscular spasm or apparent paralysis is clinically simple if the examination includes observing the patient playing his instrument. Special investigations should be avoided in our view because they are non-contributory and at times misleading.

### 2. Muscular and skeletal pains

String players commonly complain of neck and shoulder pains, older performers being more frequently affected. These pains derive from the joints, muscles and ligaments of the cervical spine and are due to the physical strain of performance and the posture adopted. For example the posture of the head and neck in orchestral players can be highly artificial as they read the score, play and watch the conductor simultaneously.

Low backache is common in all groups of instrumentalists, again more so in older players. The chairs provided for orchestras are often uncomfortable, affording inadequate support for the lumbar spine. Discussion with orchestral players indicates that individuals differ on the comfort provided by chairs in various rehearsal and concert halls. Even if a player does not sit back while performing, better lumbar support from the chair would be appreciated during rest periods, particularly during rehearsal and recording sessions. Harpists required to transport their instruments can suffer from backache from the physical strain involved. The tension of rehearsal, performance and recording can induce muscular spasm, especially in the neck, and this compounds the physical pain-producing factors.

Musicians are not exempt from the degenerative condition, spondylosis, involving the cervical and lumbar spines, a source of much disability in the general population. The physical stress of playing under the conditions described above uncovers symptoms in the middle-aged that might be disregarded or not experienced in persons whose work places less strain on the spine. Neck, shoulder or back pain can be complicated by nerve root symptoms in the upper or lower limbs, presenting as pain in the arm or sciatica.

The middle-aged are not only thus affected. The student working under pressure for an examination or trying to learn a concerto rapidly may develop tendinitis, an inflammation at the bony insertion of a muscle or tendon. The local inflammation, often a granuloma, can provoke intense pain accentuated by movement. In young people the shoulder, usually the supraspinatus muscle, or the elbow, the so-called "tennis elbow", is the commonly affected site. A hydrocortisone injection and total abstinence from playing for ten days are usually curative. This advice may be difficult to accept at a critical point in a career but it is reasonable to prevent the condition becoming chronic.

At all ages treatment of these painful syndromes consists of physiotherapeutic measures and occasionally local procedures such as injection of the painful area with steroids, as has been mentioned, or with local anaesthetics. Many musicians resort directly to physiotherapists or osteopathic practitioners privately, because they can obtain prompt treatment in this way at times of their own choosing to fit in with their rehearsal, performance and teaching commitments.

## Neurological illness in the performer

As one might expect, there are no specific diseases of the nervous system selectively affecting musicians. The neurological literature contains many accounts of the effects of brain disease on composition, performance and listening to music (Chapters 1, 22, 23), but attention has been mainly centred on the cognitive and emotional functions. Accounts of the results of neurological disease on executive professional musicians can be found in the earlier German literature but little has been published in English. Head (1926), however, included two professionals in his series of patients with musical defects following brain injury or stroke. A singer of "serious sentimental songs" on the music halls (Case 7) suffered a gunshot wound of the head which left him with an amnestic aphasia. Thereafter he was able to sing well without words, but once these were introduced he sang out of tune, the volume of his voice decreased and a bad tremolo appeared. The patient returned to his occupation but lost his engagements because of these defects. Case 22 played the double bass and cornet in a seaside orchestra during the summer. A stroke left him with amnestic aphasia, dyslexia and inability to read musical notation. He complained that he could not play either instrument, "I can't read music, I cannot tell an A from a B." Botez and Wertheim (1959) and Wertheim and Botez (1961) have given detailed accounts of the results of left and right cerebral hemisphere lesions on two performers, a violinist and a singer-accordionist.

In this account we write from experience of some fifty professional performers with different varieties of organic neurological disease. Keyboard and string players naturally predominate but woodwind, brass and percussion players as well as conductors are included. This experience is insufficient to permit us to generalise and we can only draw attention to certain points. Our series is strongly biassed towards serious musicians and we have little personal experience of singers, who in any case have special problems stemming from dependence on the respiratory and vocal apparatus (Chapters 5, 6) and the consequent need to avoid infection, local trauma and fatigue.

## Migraine

The role of mental stress and physical fatigue in provoking attacks of migraine is generally recognised, yet we have only two patients with this complaint under our care and limited enquiry has produced two other examples. However, there is no reason to suppose that musicians are less liable to migraine than other persons. The musicians we have encountered illustrate the determination of the professional.

A violoncellist was playing in a performance of Mahler's eighth symphony when a white veil or curtain "came down over my eyes, and I tried to peer through the cracks to see the music". The visual disturbance passed and was replaced by a severe throbbing headache, but he continued to play until the end of the concert, and a notably vigilant conductor noticed nothing amiss although the player was seated "on the first desk". This was the patient's first attack of migraine.

Another orchestral cellist had many attacks during rehearsals and performances, the aura being most difficult to cope with: for thirty minutes she had tunnel vision and could see only two to three bars of music clearly. Notes often looked double and bar lines jagged. By intense concentration she usually managed to continue playing in spite of seeing only a vague outline of the conductor's beat.

A visual aura, although classical, affects only 10 per cent. of patients with migraine; it is the headache which constitutes the major problem. Our other two cases, both orchestral string players, show how migraine influences but does not interfere with performing. This pattern is typical of members of other professions.

In one case attacks could be provoked by a difficult concert but her headache usually began after the concert. Occasionally, if a migraine was present before a performance then during play the pain was in abeyance, but afterwards the headache was more intense and prolonged.

In the other musician migraines were unrelated to performances, attacks coming on without reason soon after awakening and persisting for the remainder of that day. The migraine never interfered with performing although it made playing more difficult and gave rise to "many a miserable day".

Only a few words can be devoted to treatment. Avoiding attacks is possible in some cases if precipitating factors are recognised. Diet can play a role and avoiding cheese, chocolate, alcohol on an empty stomach or not missing a meal before a concert may prevent attacks. Sleeping too long or too little may each provoke a migraine. In women premenstrual attacks, if accompanied by fluid retention, can be counteracted by a diuretic. Excessive heat, cold, light or noise can at times be avoided. The next approach is early treatment to abort an attack. Three rather than two analgesic tablets or in some cases an ergot preparation can be effective, but it is essential that the relevant tablets are readily available. A small proportion of migraineurs need regular prophylactic treatment with clonidine, propranolol or methysergide, and then only during a bad phase.

We are not impressed with the personality association of migraine. All professional musicians must, in order to succeed, be striving, determined and conscientious. Only a proportion have migraine.

*Epilepsy*

Musicians who develop epilepsy before or during training at colleges or academies are unlikely to become established as professionals unless their attacks are confined to periods of sleep. The very conditions of training, rehearsal and performance are such that persons with a notable tendency to diurnal attacks, whether major or minor, are inevitably excluded from executant careers. However, we have seen six examples among performers whose attacks, infrequent in all, ranged from severe major convulsions to brief minor seizures in which consciousness was altered but not lost. Only one of the six had suffered a major convulsion before embarking on a course of professional study.

Neurologists recognise that occupation and intense concentration tend to inhibit epileptic seizures in many, though unfortunately not all, patients. This may partially explain why only one of our six personal patients had an attack while performing. This was a pianist who worked as an accompanist and became subject to episodes of altered consciousness, lasting a few seconds, in adult life. One attack occurred during a performance, and although she continued playing she missed a few notes. The experience undermined her confidence for playing in public at first but anticonvulsant medication helped to restore this, and she continues to perform professionally "as far as my family commitments permit". This artist had already attained substantial professional standing when her seizures first developed. In contrast, a pianist with temporal lobe epilepsy resorted to various devices to conceal the minor episodes that sometimes arose during teaching, yet she never had an attack when practising or performing throughout twenty-five years of observation.

Five of these patients suffered from idiopathic or constitutional epilepsy and one from long-standing temporal lobe attacks following pyogenic meningitis with transient left hemiparesis.

Epileptic musicians obviously require the maximum seizure control that can be achieved within the limits of drug tolerance. It would be an elementary error to make an orchestral player drowsy in pursuit of control if he was continuing in his profession. Patients should be given detailed information about possible toxic effects of the anticonvulsant drugs prescribed for them. In fact, seizure control has not proved difficult in our highly selected group.

*Cerebrovascular disease*

A stroke is a major disabling illness in any patient. For the musician an incident of this type can be disastrous in terms of future employment and performance. While medical knowledge remains insufficient to prevent all strokes, proper care and supervision of hypertension and diabetes mellitus, or prompt recognition of transient ischaemic attacks with subsequent appropriate treatment, can prevent a major catastrophe in some cases. It is therefore important that any patient with signs of a threatening stroke should be investigated and treated as early as possible by hypotensive agents, anticoagulants or vascular surgery as the individual case determines.

The factors that determine mortality and morbidity after strokes are well understood and will not be discussed here. We simply record our observations on a small group of patients, three violinists and two organists, but our experience has been enlarged by courtesy of our colleagues. We have referred earlier to the effect of a major stroke on one distinguished pianist and will quote another in this section. Our aim is simply to describe the various disabilities suffered by these patients and to draw attention to the remarkable way in which some have overcome the imposed handicaps.

In his autobiography *Duet for Three Hands*, Cyril Smith (1958) gave an account of his major right-sided cerebral infarction and consequent left hemiplegia that started when he was flying in an unpressurised aircraft over Russia. As soon as he recovered full awareness Cyril Smith began to explore ways in which he could continue his playing career in spite of his disability. Naturally a great deal of musical ingenuity was required to arrange duets for three hands previously played with four. His consultant neurologist urged him to "live as full a life as possible" and after two years he returned to the concert platform, performing with his intact right hand and his wife's two hands until his death eighteen years after the initial stroke. This history gives an indication of the determination with which many professional musicians face neurological disabilities and strive to make the most of remaining capacity. It is important to note that the patient's musicality was apparently unimpaired, although the non-dominant right hemisphere sustained major damage in the stroke.

A right-handed fifty-five year old orchestral violinist, highly distinguished in her profession, was seen in consultation immediately after the onset of a moderately severe right-sided hemiparesis with sensory loss mainly involving superficial aspects; there was no dysphasia and musicality remained unimpaired. The patient was normotensive and without signs of generalised vascular disease. After a brief period of hospital treatment she began to practise at home in spite of her disability. Shoulder weakness caused difficulty in bowing which she found "rather rough", and this was compounded by a problem of controlling the little finger. She practised assiduously and ultimately returned to work with a leading orchestra, although minor right-sided signs persisted when she was examined neurologically. Twelve years after the insult she plays without handicap in the same orchestra.

We know of a retired cellist who was still playing chamber music for his own enjoyment at the age of 73 when he developed a stroke. He recommenced practising a month later but several more months elapsed before the resultant weakness improved sufficiently to allow him to resume his place in trios and quartets. His powers of performance had not declined but he remarked that he had to think harder when playing fast passages. He continues his hobby at the age of 76.

Two other patients were violinists who directed small ensembles. The first suffered two episodes of cerebral infarction with right hemiplegia. He made a good recovery from the paralysis and can now play his instrument at or near his previous level. Unfortunately the strokes caused predominantly expressive dysphasia which has effectively prevented work to date, but the patient practises daily in the hope of playing in public again. The second patient had a right cerebral infarction with consequent sensorimotor deficit in the left upper limb. He also made a good recovery and played his violin and directed his small group successfully for several months, when a more severe stroke left him with greater left-sided disability, complicated by symptoms of generalised cerebral disorder due to vascular disease. Neither patient showed signs of amusia on testing.

Another example of determination is illustrated by a professional trumpeter who also played a clarinet in a military band. This man suffered a left hemiplegia from a stroke in his early fifties. Handicapped by residual partial paralysis, he persevered in playing the trumpet with his right hand alone until he obtained full control. Although unable to work thereafter as an instrumentalist he was fully employed in teaching at schools and evening classes.

The case of one of our organist patients has no happy ending, but it illustrates the value of musical activity in rehabilitation. This man developed a severe right hemiplegia with dysphasia from cerebral infarction. An enthusiastic cricketer, he was unable to read the scores in the newspaper and comprehension of spoken and written commands was grossly defective. Communication with this unfortunate man was difficult so he was taken to the hospital chapel and seated at the piano. He was able to read simple scores without difficulty and played expertly and enthusiastically with his intact left hand. This retention of musical faculties was a considerable help during rehabilitation.

When a stroke involves the brainstem the musician faces the risk of bilateral motor disorder. We have one patient, a keyboard player, in this category and here prompt hypotensive and anticoagulant therapy arrested advancing basilar occlusion with gratifying subsequent recovery. Musicians with brainstem infarction can be comforted by the knowledge that the intellectual aspects of speech and musicality are preserved.

Although our whole group of patients contains examples of slight, moderate and severe cerebral damage affecting right and left hemispheres, there are no cases of amusia among them; none was left-handed. In our admittedly limited experience dysphasia has proved a decisive factor in preventing return to professional work, in contrast to Luria et al.'s (1965) observations on a composer. Severe minor hemisphere infarctions may not prevent a return to work, though this is usually teaching, an activity obviously precluded by any notable degree of dysphasia.

## Cerebral tumours

Cerebral tumours may be benign with a good prognosis for continued working. An outstanding example is provided by Otto Klemperer (1964) who in his autobiographical "Minor Recollections" mentioned that he was treated for a cerebral tumour in Berlin in 1936. His recovery from this serious illness and subsequent successful career indicate that the lesion must have been benign, probably a meningioma. We shall cite two other examples later but our first patient had a malignant tumour.

A sixty-seven year old double bass player in a symphony orchestra had an attack of loss of consciousness at home. He was fully investigated at hospital with negative results. Two months later he had a major seizure during a recording session and reinvestigation showed a right parietal glioblastoma, to which he succumbed. The patient, a determined man, continued working after his first attack and was fully employed, in spite of ultimate left-sided sensorimotor disorder from the developing neoplasm, until the second event recorded above.

The second patient was a twenty-five year old right-handed professional counter-tenor who developed symptoms of intracranial hypertension due to a large cystic astrocytoma arising in the right temporal lobe. The tumour was not malignant. After surgical treatment his recovery from the consequent left hemiplegia and difficulty with speech was slow. His voice remained slurred and reduced in volume, he was unable to sustain a long phrase because of the need to take breath, and hiccoughing also interfered with voice production. A year later further surgical treatment was required. Since that time he has made remarkable improvement and is able to earn his living as a clerk. Unfortunately his singing has not returned to its previous level and although he can undertake minor professional engagements there has been no question of a return to his former high standard. The clinical features suggest that his technical problems stem largely from brainstem damage associated with intracranial hypertension rather than from his right-sided temporal mass.

The next patient had a benign lesion, a colloid cyst of the third ventricle, which was totally removed without brain damage. A member of a string quartet developed difficulty in playing spiccato and maintaining a long note. He was aged thirty-six at the time and wondered if he was becoming insane or whether he was not up to the standard of his colleagues and this was a psychological method of escape. The anticipation of a concert performance filled him with fear and caused sleepless nights. Two eminent neurologists were consulted; neither could elicit any abnormal physical signs or reach a diagnosis. Psychotherapy made him slightly less anxious but failed to improve his playing. Relaxation treatment also helped a little. His colleagues noted a slowing of all movements but considered that his condition was psychologically determined. Eighteen months after the onset of symptoms his vision became affected: one evening at the beginning of a concert the score looked as if covered by a heat haze. A few days later he saw double while driving a car and asked his wife to take over. He then consulted a third neurologist. By this time papilloedema was evident and investigation revealed a colloid cyst of the third ventricle. Pre-operatively he was asked by the neurosurgeon which arm he would prefer to remain intact if slight damage were to follow the operation. Clearly if major damage occurred then his career as a violin player would be at an end. He felt that the bowing arm was that "which people heard" hence the surgical approach was planned and carried out through the right frontal region. Six weeks post-operatively he went to convalesce and began to practise. Ten weeks after the operation he was back on the concert platform playing with considerable trepidation but better than he had for a long time. Gradually the fear of public performance left him but it took a full year before he felt entirely confident. Now, some fifteen years later, he remains on top form.

The fourth patient had a cerebral angioma but his case is included at this point for convenience. A music publisher and administrator was a competent pianist who accompanied singers for selection in operatic roles and also assessed new scores for publication. At the age of forty-three he developed a subarachnoid haemorrhage from a left temporal angioma. This haemorrhage produced dysphasia and clumsiness of the right hand. The vascular malformation was successfully removed and he rapidly regained speech, but it took six months' practice to enable him to accompany again. A further five years elapsed before his facility with musical notation was fully re-established. Now, eight years after the initial episode, his only difficulty is minimal dysphasia under stress and he is working full-time.

*Parkinsonism and other movement disorders*

Parkinsonism constitutes a severe threat to the livelihood of the performing musician. One of us had the task of caring for an orchestral conductor many years ago who was afflicted by this complaint. The inability to initiate rapid movement and consequently to communicate his requirements to the orchestra by gesture made him incapable of carrying out his work. This was before the days of the newer drugs for treating Parkinsonism and in particular L-dopa. The prognosis for a player afflicted with Parkinsonism has subsequently improved, though it remains a formidable obstacle to a continuing professional career. The rigidity and slowness of movement interfere with rapidly alternating movements such as playing a trill or any rapid passage. We know of one orchestral violinist whose Parkinsonism prevented him from playing but he was able to work as a conductor for a time because the disease was unilateral. The impairment of intellectual faculties which one encounters in some patients with Parkinsonism constitutes a further problem.

We continue with the case history of a patient with a peculiar, non-Parkinsonian, movement disorder.

A sixty year old violin player in an international symphony orchestra manifested a dystonic movement disorder in the right arm of three years' duration. He first noticed difficulty in sustaining a long note. The disturbance gradually increased and he had to move from the first to the last desk of his section. At this stage he found that a light touch on his elbow or placing the bow on the string would inhibit the involuntary movement. Thus, allowing the elbow to touch the side of the chair enabled him to play perfectly well during concerts and rehearsals. By the time he came to consult us lack of control of the right upper limb interfered with daily activities such as holding a cup and shaking hands. When we examined him the abnormal movement consisted of hyperpronation at the elbow and internal rotation with a little flexion at the shoulder. He played rapid passages extremely well when his elbow was tucked into his side, but in slow pieces or in the extended elbow position affairs were quite different. Slow staccato playing was poorly performed and included wrong notes. This violinist showed a form of dystonic movement that we have not previously encountered in any patient. However, the method of inhibition of the involuntary motor activity was comparable with that which patients with spasmodic torticollis employ. In this patient's case we have advised relaxation therapy and await the result of this approach.

It is important to remember that not all tremors are due to Parkinsonism, a mistake sometimes made by non-medical diagnosticians. Thus it has been widely believed among professionals that Joseph Szigeti, the world famous violinist, suffered from Parkinsonism, or alternatively that his tremor was caused by excessive nervousness and tension. One of us (J.N.B.) was present at a master class which Szigeti took in 1965, by which time his tremor prevented his playing in public. During the lesson Szigeti became impatient with a Japanese pupil and took her violin and bow in an attempt to illustrate his point, but the bow was quite out of control and he was unable to sustain a single note. His speech, facial and limb movements appeared normal. We have been permitted to examine his handwriting at that time and in later years, and this shows clear evidence of benign essential tremor. This condition is unrelated to psychological disorder and so far no neural damage has been shown to account for it. It may stem from an abnormality of neurotransmitter production. The complaint does not shorten life, but it is a nuisance and an embarrassment, only affecting the livelihood of persons who are dependent on skilled hand movements in their work. Treatment with propranolol may be beneficial, and stereotactic surgery can be considered in severe examples.

### Lesions of the cranial nerves

Wind instrumentalists require intact motor and sensory nerve supply to the lips, cheeks and tongue; the teeth must not be forgotten because they constitute an essential part of the embouchure. In this section we do not discuss the part played by the respiratory system or the upper limbs. We give two examples of fifth nerve lesions – both traumatic in origin, and some instances of facial palsy.

A professional trumpeter suffered a severe closed head injury from which he made a good recovery in terms of cerebral function; unfortunately the fifth cranial nerve was damaged so that he was left with impaired sensation over the left upper lip. The resultant hypoaesthesia caused difficulties with playing through a sense of loss of control in the affected part. Nevertheless he can still play first trumpet in such works as Bach's B minor Mass and Magnificat.

Altered sensation in the lower lip is much more serious. Such a lesion affected the world famous oboist, Leon Goossens (Wynne, 1967).

At the age of sixty-five Goossens sustained a head injury in a car accident and was rendered deeply unconscious. His lower lip was extensively cut and a number of teeth were either lost or loosened. Goossens realised the implications of a numb lower lip as soon as he regained consciousness and during convalescence he became despondent. A dental surgeon offered to start dental reconstruction but an area of $\frac{1}{4}$ inch of numbness in the middle of the lower lip remained a daunting problem. The patient had no idea where this portion of his lip was in space due to loss of cutaneous sensation. However, when he took up his instrument to attempt to play he found that by widening the reed a fraction and pursing his lips together he could just feel the edges of the reed, imagine what the lower lip was doing and so start to play again. At first practice was tiring but after an interval of a complete year he started playing in short film recording sessions with an orchestra and three years after the accident he returned to the international concert platform as a soloist.

Acute facial paralysis, Bell's palsy, makes work impossible for woodwind or brass players. A professional saxophonist presented with an almost complete right facial palsy and acute anxiety deriving from his fear that he would never play again. In fact the condition followed the common benign course and he was back at work in a dance band seven weeks from the onset. Any notable degree of permanent weakness in such a patient would be highly prejudicial to his career. On the other hand, a pianist with a facial palsy simply suffered the discomfort and embarrassment which the condition entails until recovery occurred. It appears that a degree of facial weakness does not prevent singers from pursuing their careers successfully, and we have observed such artists with unilateral facial weakness, presumably deriving from incomplete recovery of Bell's palsy, who have reached and maintained international standards of performance.

As with other neurological problems affecting patients, precise explanation of the expected course of the condition can do much to allay anxiety and enable the musician to await full recovery or possibly modify his technique.

## Neuralgia

A spasmodic painful affection may be expected to interfere with concentration required to perform in public. Three patients with neuralgia illustrate differing responses to their illnesses. One with post-herpetic neuralgia was forced to give up professional piano playing as an accompanist. Another had atypical facial pain that at no stage interfered with her piano playing, on the contrary, she said it took her mind off the pain and made her more relaxed. The third patient, a seventy-seven year old professional violinist, had trigeminal neuralgia that responded ·o carbamezapine. Her neuralgia in no way affected her playing.

## Motor neuron disease

When this condition runs its usual course with advancing paralysis the effect on performance is only too evident. We are aware of one example in a professional pianist whose first symptom was the inability to span an octave. He rapidly became incapacitated and eventually died of the complaint. With more chronic forms of spinal atrophy the picture is less gloomy. We have a patient, another pianist, with progressive weakness and wasting of the muscles of the shoulder girdles and proximal parts of the upper limbs, right more than left, of perhaps ten years' duration. Electrodiagnostic tests have indicated a lesion of the spinal motor neurons. At this late stage the patient is still able to direct his ensemble from the piano despite his handicap and he remains in full employment.

## Multiple sclerosis

The variable course of this complaint is well known. Some patients suffer rapid incapacity while others remain ambulant and gainfully employed for many years. We give an example of each type from patients known to us.

A thirty-eight year old trombonist in a dance band noticed that the fingers of the right hand were stiff and clumsy in depressing the plungers of his instrument while at work. This symptom appeared spontaneously and completely disappeared in the course of a fortnight. Four months later he developed double vision and left-sided facial numbness. These symptoms subsided but his hearing seemed to diminish and he noticed noises in both ears. He recovered from this episode but six months later became unsteady on his legs. Again he improved and following resolution of yet another episode, this time vertigo, he was able to return to work three years after the initial symptom. However, after an interval his legs became weak due to spasticity and this prevented his going to work. While the effects of treatment in this patient were beneficial at first, amelioration was purely temporary.

A twenty-two year old percussion player developed numbness and a tight sensation in one leg and a feeling of constriction round the waist. Within two days he found difficulty in control of hand movements and attributed his condition to psychosomatic causes because he had been sent down by his musical college for not studying adequately. His family practitioner recognised his condition to be organic and referred him to a neurologist. Injections of ACTH produced rapid improvement but he returned to work earlier than advised. He has since had a minor recurrence with complete recovery and leaving him without disability. He continues in full employment.

## Peripheral neuropathy

We have had four patients suffering from polyneuritis:

The first, a cellist in a symphony orchestra, developed a mild post-infective sensory neuropathy affecting the upper and lower extremities. Although weakness was minimal the sensory disorder caused major problems in fingering and bowing. Such was this man's technical reserve that he continued at work throughout his illness although he could not feel the strings of his instrument properly as he played.

The second patient had a more severe and protracted Guillain-Barré syndrome with limb and respiratory weakness so that at one stage assisted respiration was necessary. She spent a month in hospital and a further six weeks convalescing. At first she was afraid to start playing her violin because the right shoulder was weak. Six months after leaving hospital she could play for only half an hour at a time. Even now, eighteen months after this major illness, she still lacks energy and retains some weakness of her shoulder so that an hour or, at the most, one and a half hour's play is her maximum; previously three to four hours was normal for her.

In two other cases excess alcoholic intake was the major contributory factor to peripheral neuropathy. A pop-group drummer developed upper and lower limb weakness and as a result found difficulty in holding his drum sticks. His disability lasted a few weeks only, responding to vitamin B injections and abstention from alcohol. A more chronic neuropathy affected a Northumbrian pipe player who suffered from haemochromatosis, diabetes mellitus and excess alcohol taken "to steady his nerves". His first symptom was producing an abnormal quality of tone because he was unable to place his finger pads accurately and firmly on the holes of his instrument.

## Cervical spondylosis with myelopathy

This complaint tends to affect older patients though persons in the fifth decade are by no means immune. Excessive trauma incurred at work, by miners, for example, gives rise to increased cervical spondylotic X-ray changes. It is reasonable to hypothesize that violin players, beginning to play before the age of ten, should develop spondylotic changes earlier than the average person due to prolonged abnormal posture and muscular contraction. We do not have any evidence for or against this hypothesis and our experience is limited to one patient.

A violin player retired from a leading symphony orchestra in his late fifties because of difficulty in the use of his hands, back pain and early deafness. Several years later he came under our care with severe disabilities in the upper limbs. He was unable to use his hands for fine movements, such as playing the violin, cutting up his food and picking up small objects. Furthermore, he had persistent unpleasant burning dysaesthesiae in both hands. Examination showed a spastic quadriplegia with depression of all forms of sensation in both hands. Plain radiographs of the cervical spine showed a narrowed spinal canal, less than 10 mm. in the anterior-posterior diameter, and the myodil column was held up in the mid-cervical region at myelography. The patient felt he "improved by fifty per cent." after a decompressive laminectomy of the third to seventh cervical vertebrae. Objectively the power in his hands had increased and sensation partially returned. However, a stiff feeling remained in the fingers. There seems no doubt that the myelopathy secondary to spondylosis was at least partially responsible for his early retirement. It is not possible to say whether earlier radical treatment would have enabled him to continue his work.

## Lesions of cervical nerve roots and brachial plexus

From the musician's point of view pain, weakness or altered sensation — separately or in combination — in an arm can immediately impair his expectation of carrying out a full day's work. Neurological disturbances in the upper limbs may present considerable diagnostic problems for the clinician because similar symptoms arise when the nerve roots or brachial plexus are affected. Modern electrodiagnostic techniques can help considerably, but some patients will require myelography to exlude root compression from herniated disc or other cause, and even then a firm diagnosis may not be possible. The following table summarises the clinical features in five of our patients.

| Patient | Instrument | Diagnosis | Treatment | Recovery |
|---|---|---|---|---|
| 1 | Viola | Probably C5 root (Rt) | Physiotherapy | Complete in 5 months |
| 2 | Violin | Probably C5, 6, 7 roots (Lt) | Physiotherapy | Complete in 6 months |
| 3 | Drums | Bilateral C5 lesions (? Neuralgic amyotrophy) | Physiotherapy | No recovery |
| 4 | Violin | ? root ? brachial plexus | Physiotherapy Dexamethasone | Complete in 3 months |
| 5 | Violin | ? brachial neuritis (Lt) (slow onset) | Physiotherapy | Partial in 18 months (teaching only) |

We have little doubt that the chronic trauma associated with professional work, added to the incidental injury of everyday life, was responsible for the complaints stemming from cervical disc lesions and may also contribute to localisation in brachial neuritis.

## Lesions of individual peripheral nerves

While lesions of peripheral nerves form a significant part of the average neurologist's practice, we have only encountered one example in a musician and that was most unusual in type.

Following an injury a young violinist suffered damage to the terminal part of the right radial nerve with consequent sensory loss in the expected area on the back of the hand and at the base of the thumb and index finger. This caused him grave anxiety as he feared his playing would be affected. In fact it was evident from the history that the lesion of the nerve was in continuity, and he was reassured by electrodiagnostic tests which showed perfect function in both main divisions of the radial nerve. Recovery occurred over a period of a few weeks. This can be regarded as a trivial case but the method of investigation and management show how apprehension can be allayed.

We have read or heard of two cases where over zealous practice has given rise to pressure palsies:

A twenty-five year old female guitarist played with her left leg crossed over her right for three hours at a time. She often experienced numbness of the foot. However, on one occasion a foot drop developed and on examination weakness of the anterior and lateral muscles of the left leg was evident. The diagnosis of a lateral popliteal nerve palsy was confirmed by a nerve conduction study and denervation potentials were present in the affected muscles (Mladinich and De Witt, 1974).

A colleague has told us about this second case, also in a guitar player.

A twenty-two year old music student had been practising intensively to pass an examination. He played his guitar in the classical manner with the thumb in front of the fret board, a position that gives rise to considerable tension in the carpal tunnel. Examination showed wasting of the thenar eminence and sensory changes in the median nerve distribution; electrical conduction studies revealed moderate slowing in the median nerve. The condition was relieved by a local hydrocortisone injection and general advice about excessive practice.

## Head injury

Two case histories involving injury to the head have been given earlier. We have had two other patients under our care on account of significant head injury.

The first, a young violinist, suffered a severe head injury in a road traffic accident with a post-traumatic amnesia of some six weeks' duration. There were no physical indications of defective function in the cranial nerves or limbs. In spite of the extreme severity of the injury there was no detectable impairment of intellectual functions or alteration in temperament stemming from the undoubted brain damage sustained. The patient returned to playing in a symphony orchestra at an early date and had no difficulty in coping with the demands of an extensive repertoire.

The second patient was a drummer in a dance band, aged forty-five. His injury was much less severe, the post-traumatic amnesia was no more than eight hours, but he complained of persistent symptoms, many of which appeared to have no physical basis. However, after rehabilitation he complained that he was unable to play the drums because of loss of rhythmic sense, and we have no reason to believe this was not true. One would not expect a closed head injury, without objective evidence of brain damage, to interfere with the rhythmic sense, and there was some doubt as to how far post-traumatic psychological problems played a part in his disability. Unfortunately he was unwilling to attend for regular treatment and we do not know the end of the story.

## Diseases of muscle

We have not encountered a professional musician who has suffered from hereditary or acquired muscle disease, but we have treated a competent amateur pianist with myasthenia gravis. Her response to thymectomy and cholinergic drugs was highly satisfactory, although she was disappointed by her inability to perform at her previous level owing to fatigue of the left hand and fingers after playing for about twenty minutes. This disability persisted for three years after thymectomy and her repertoire was consequently limited.

## Autonomic disorders

The anxiety which afflicts performers has been mentioned in the introduction to this chapter. One important manifestation of anxiety is hyperidrosis or excessive sweating of the face and hands, commonly visible in soloists and orchestral players during performances. Much more rarely excessive perspiration stems from defective autonomic control of the sweating mechanisms, and disorder in this system can lead to excessive coldness of the hands which can be a considerable nuisance to performers and interfere with the quality of their work. No professional patient with hyperidrosis has consulted us but we know of a young schoolgirl learning to play the piano who was unable to continue after a few minutes of practice because her fingers were so drenched by perspiration that they would slide from the keyboard.

When hyperidrosis affects the axillae, hands and face, local applications are helpful in treatment and render the patient more socially acceptable.

When the condition affects the hands to a serious degree sympathectomy is an effective form of treatment. While this operation causes drooping of the eyelid and reduction in pupillary size on the side surgically treated, these abnormalities can be expected to disappear over the course of a year or two. In female patients it may be advisable to carry out the operation bilaterally for this results in symmetrical but acceptable temporary alteration in appearance. We conclude that proper treatment of hyperidrosis might make all the difference between success and failure to the young musician suffering from this complaint, either as a primary disturbance or as a severe and persistent manifestation of anxiety.

## Conclusions

From such a wide scatter of conditions affecting differing types of instrumentalists, few conclusions can be drawn, although there may be some useful lessons in patient care and some observations on one profession looking at another.

Physicians who care for these highly talented members of the community have a duty to detect the early signs of systemic or neurological disease and counter the effects of excessive anxiety and stress. The importance of early treatment of hypertension has been mentioned and we have also noted the need to identify minor strokes so that the best treatment can be provided at the earliest possible stage. The difficulty in diagnosing organic neurological complaints or in identifying those disturbances which are due to anxiety or frank psychiatric illness has been discussed. These difficulties are sufficient to tax the skills of the most experienced neurologist. We take the patients into our confidence from the outset and ensure that they understand the case as fully as those who care for them, or at the worst share our ignorance. The accounts we have given of the sufferings of our patients indicate the resilience, reserve and determination of professional players.

Understanding of the special needs of performing musicians is sometimes lacking. One of us was asked to see a concert pianist because of a disability in his fingers which was not neurologically determined. The reason for consultation was largely the fact that the patient, who had been excellently and skilfully cared for, had been told to continue with his work, though this was manifestly impossible because of his disability. Advice to take six weeks off work proved successful, for the complaint ran its natural course and resolved. The patient was relieved of the anxiety of practising and performing at far below his proper level because of his incapacity. We do not encourage patients to give up work if they feel able to perform adequately and if examination confirms that this is the case. The only regular exception we would make is in the cases of cervical nerve root and plexus lesions, though our advice to our patients in this group was not always followed. The physician has the responsibility of identifying the degree of disability and advising the patient on his conclusions, this means that his examination should include observation of the patient at work.

A physician who is consulted by a musician should take additional care to assess the social background in which many factors play a role. He must remember that the demands of work and fears of unemployment to which players are subject may lead them to take on numerous engagements, some of which could possibly be shed. Musicians are not alone in this attitude to work but their profession is so demanding and the required standards so high that guidance should be attempted when the opportunity permits.

We have referred briefly to some of the physical and mental pressures imposed on soloists and orchestral players by their work but there are further considerations. These talented individuals have generally shown their capabilities at an early age, though prodigies in the true sense are rare. It follows that they are subjected to admiration or even adulation at home, in school and by the community. A stable personality, or more simply a level head, is required to cope with this environment, particularly when early promise is not fulfilled or adversities are encountered. The professional musical life tends to be all-embracing so that there is little time for those extra-curricular activities which are important in all walks of life. Hours of performance, concerts away from home and tours impose profound restrictions on the normal pattern of domestic life.

We feel we must strike a note of caution about alcohol. The irregular life and hours of work, coupled with a good measure of anxiety, sometimes lead to excessive indulgence in alcohol; the opportunities for such indulgence are only too frequent. In our experience the long-term effects can be damaging, indeed this must be obvious to every reader.

Finally, a constructive suggestion about postural problems. In the course of our professional and social contacts with musicians we have been struck by recurrent complaints about aches and pains in the back or neck. Many chairs on which musicians have to sit are uncomfortable. Although musicians pay a great deal of attention to their music stands it is surprising how tolerant they become of bad seating. We know of two cellists who have designed chairs especially for themselves, and one London symphony orchestra had chairs constructed for each member of the cello section, but not for other strings or the wind. In the medical profession there has also been a surge of interest in the common problem of skeletal pains with the formation of societies for research into back pain and posture. The time seems opportune for interested participants to co-operate and design a suitable "musical chair". Such a chair would earn the gratitude of many senior members of the musical profession and could even delay the onset of postural problems in those starting their chosen career.

## REFERENCES

BOTEZ, M. I. and WERTHEIM, N. (1959) Expressive aphasia and amusia following right frontal lesion in a right-handed man. *Brain*, **82**, 186–202.

HEAD, H. (1926) *Aphasia and Kindred Disorders of Speech*. Oxford University Press. Reprinted 1963, Hafner Pub. Co., N.Y. & London, vol. 2, 89–107, 329–347.

KLEMPERER, O. (1964) *Minor Recollections*. London, Dobson.

LURIA, A. R., TSVETKOVA, L. S. and FUTER, D. S. (1965) Aphasia in a composer, *J. neurol. Sci.*, **2**, 288–292.

MLADINICH, E. K. and DE WITT, J. (1974) A newly recognised occupational palsy. *J. Amer. med. Assoc.*, **228**, 695.

SMITH, C. (1958) *Duet for Three Hands*. London, Angus and Robertson.

WERTHEIM, N. and BOTEZ, M. I. (1961) Receptive amusia: a clinical analysis. *Brain*, **84**, 19–30.

WYNNE, B. (1967) *Music in the Wind. The Story of Leon Goossens and his Triumph over a Shattering Accident*. London, Souvenir Press.

# 18

J. D. HOOD

# Deafness and Musical Appreciation

Man's supremacy over animals has resulted in very large measure from his ability to communicate with his fellow human beings. In fact, civilisation as we know it today is highly dependent upon communication in one form or another. Without the sense of hearing this could not have come about. Those of us with normal hearing tend to take all this for granted but for the deaf, matters are very different. They exist in a world of silence, cut off from and uncomprehending what goes on around them. In their isolation their affliction often becomes a source of irritation to others so that they tend to be either ignored or at best patronisingly tolerated. Their unresponsiveness is subconsciously equated with idiocy and we derive amusement from their discomfiture so frequently portrayed in the music hall joke or the cartoonist's pen.

According to the World Health Organisation, at least one in ten persons will at some time during their lives experience a significant hearing loss. There are, of course, degrees of disability associated with deafness extending from the milder impairments that come to most of us in old age at one end of the scale to total or profound deafness at the other. It has always been customary to attempt to quantify deafness in terms of some measure of the intensity of the faintest sounds that can just be heard. One particular measure with which all otologists are familiar is the whisper test. If after exhaling, one forces a whispered voice, its intensity is reasonably constant from one person to another and the distance one has to be from the deaf person for it to be heard and understood relates reasonably well to the degree of deafness.

Although the whisper test is still widely used, it is now more usual to express the deafness more precisely in terms of the pure tone audiogram. For this purpose an instrument called a pure tone audiometer is used. It consists essentially of an oscillator which delivers pure tones to a headphone. It carries two dials, one controls the intensity of the tones, the other their frequency. Most commonly the available frequencies range in octaves from 128 Hz to 8192 Hz. An interrupter switch completes the equipment, the purpose of which is to establish at each frequency the intensity of the tones which can only just be perceived by the listener, the so-called threshold of hearing. The intensity is calibrated in decibels the reference level being the intensity at each frequency (now standardised by international agreement) which corresponds to the average threshold of normal hearing persons within the age range 18–30. The convenience of this arrangement is that 0 db on the intensity dial refers to normal hearing *at all frequencies* and hearing loss in consequence can be specified in terms of departures from normality at each.

The results of such a test procedure are conventionally plotted on an audiogram form of the kind shown in Figure 1 in which increasing intensity levels are plotted from above downwards. Degrees of deafness, therefore, appear on this form as curves connecting the various points which fall below the 0 db line. The heavy shaded area inscribed on this chart corresponds to the frequency and intensity range of sounds which are of importance to the understanding of normal conversational speech. The

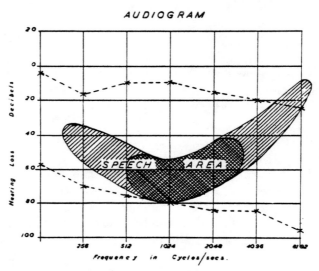

Figure 1   Pure tone audiogram. Degrees of shading indicate relative importance of frequencies necessary for the understanding of normal conversational speech.

upper audiogram is from a person with only mild hearing loss and since it does not intrude into the speech area such a person would normally be little incapacitated. The lower curve, by contrast, falls below even the louder sounds of conversational speech and in consequence a speaker would need to shout very loudly indeed to make himself heard.

Actually, this is an oversimplification of the problems facing the deaf because, as will be seen later, in certain varieties of deafness the pure tone audiogram provides less than the full picture of the patient's disability.

To understand why this is so it is necessary first to consider the various causes of deafness.

## TYPES OF DEAFNESS

By far the most common condition results from the accumulation of wax in the ears. This of course can easily be removed by syringing with complete restoration of hearing. Deafness can also result from a variety of conditions which affect the middle ear, the most frequent being the accumulation of fluid from one cause or another. This may clear up spontaneously or progress to a chronic condition which calls for surgical intervention. Otosclerosis is a middle ear condition which is hereditary and causes the formation of bone around the stapes footplate where it engages in the oval window thus impairing its free movement. All these conditions are collectively known as conductive deafness because they impair the conduction of sound from the outer ear to the inner ear. They result in a simple attenuation of sounds which can be rectified with a hearing aid given sufficient amplification to overcome the deafness. It has, however, to be admitted that although complete restoration of speech recognition can be accomplished in this way miniaturisation imposes severe restrictions on the frequency response of hearing aids so that the full spectrum of sounds so necessary for musical appreciation and enjoyment is lacking.

A feature of conductive deafness is that the bone conduction component of the speaker's own voice tends to be enhanced so that the deaf person hears his voice at a louder level than a normal hearing person and consequently speaks more softly (see page 28, Chapter 3). In addition, in noisy surroundings a normal hearing person reflexly raises his own voice above the level of the noise. This of course is to the advantage of the conductive deaf person who not only gains from being untroubled by the background noise, but also by the raised voices which surmount his hearing loss. The surprising result is that he appears to hear better in a noise.

Middle ear surgery has made considerable advances in recent years and future prospects for those with conductive deafness are reasonably optimistic. Unfortunately conductive deafness accounts for probably less than half the deaf population. Deafness in the remainder results from impairment of the hearing receptors of the inner ear itself or, more rarely, from a lesion of the nerve of hearing conveying neural information to the brain. This is collectively known as sensorineural hearing loss and for those with this particular affliction the outlook, except for a few, remains particularly gloomy.

Types of deafness which commonly fall into this category are the deafness which comes with old age, presbyacusis, and deafness resulting from over exposure to industrial noise, together with a wide variety of degenerative and disease processes which damage the delicate hair cells of the cochlea. Since the cochlea is closely linked anatomically with the vestibule which houses the balancing receptors it is not unusual to find deafness associated with disorders of balance, the classic example being Ménière's disease.

The functional characteristics of the hearing loss resulting from sensorineural loss are quite different from those of conductive deafness and give rise to a far more serious disability (the full implications of which are less well recognised than they ought to be even in certain authoritative circles).

The reason for this is that lesions of the cochlea (lesions of the nerve itself because of their rarity will not be considered here) without exception, give rise not only to an elevation of the threshold of hearing as revealed by the pure tone audiogram but also to certain particular forms of distortion so that simply amplifying a sound does not necessarily render it more meaningful in the case of music or intelligible in the case of speech. Pitch distortion is common and patients will report that they cannot distinguish the timbre of one instrument of an orchestra from another or certain notes in a scale may be displaced upwards in pitch, others downwards. Another form of distortion that is the consistent accompaniment of cochlear hearing loss is known as loudness recruitment.

## LOUDNESS RECRUITMENT

This is essentially a disorder of the loudness function whereby the deafness present at threshold intensities seems to disappear at higher sound intensities. The surprising result is that such patients, although deaf for all practical purposes, will complain bitterly about the irritating loudness of, say, pop music played too loudly, or the shouting of children at play.

Considerable insight into the characteristics of this phenomenon may be obtained from a consideration of patients with unilateral cochlear hearing loss in whom it is possible to make comparison of the hearing in the deaf ear with that in the good ear. The most convenient procedure for this purpose is the so-called alternate binaural loudness balance test. In this test the patient wears a pair of telephone receivers and the threshold of hearing for a tone of a particular frequency is first established at each ear separately. Thereafter the intensity of the tone applied to the good ear is increased by 20 db above threshold and alternated with a tone of variable intensity of the same frequency applied to the deaf ear, the object of the exercise being to adjust the latter until it sounds equal in loudness with the 20 db tone. The fixed intensity tone applied to the normal ear is then increased in steps of 20 db and further balancing intensities established at each. In this way we are able to determine how loudness at the deaf ear increases with intensity compared to the response of the normal ear over a wide range of intensities.

The results of this procedure are conventionally displayed on a chart of the form shown in Figure 2 in which the intensities of sound applied to the good ear are plotted on the vertical scale, those at the deaf ear on the horizontal scale. If the subject has normal hearing at both ears then clearly equal intensities at the two ears will evoke equal sensations of loudness and the result will be the 45 degree line AB. In the case of a subject with a unilateral conductive deafness of say 30 db then for all intensities applied to the good ear equality of loudness with tones in the deaf ear will only be

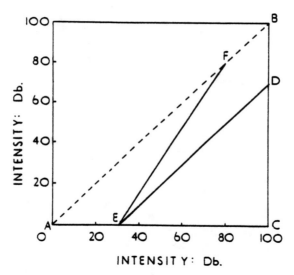

Figure 2   Loudness balance chart. The curve EF illustrates complete recruitment of loudness.

accomplished by raising their intensity by 30 db at each level. The result will be the curve ED simply displaced to the right of the normal curve AB by the amount of the deafness, 30 db. The curve EF is from a patient with a unilateral cochlear hearing loss of the same degree. By contrast it will be seen that it approaches and finally meets the normal curve at the point F. At this point equal intensities of 80 db at the two ears evoke equal sensations of loudness and the patient is said to have full recruitment of loudness. In other words the loudness change brought about in the good ear by an intensity change from 0 to 80 db is encompassed by an intensity change of only 50 db in the deaf ear and this is a measure of the compression of the loudness function which is such a feature of the phenomenon.

A particular attribute of loudness recruitment is the remarkably systematic manner in which its degree varies with hearing loss. The curves shown in Figure 3 are derived from a large number of subjects with unilateral hearing loss due to Ménière's disease and illustrate clearly how at the four main speech frequencies, 512, 1024, 2048 and 4096 Hz, the recruitment curves increase in steepness for particular degrees of hearing

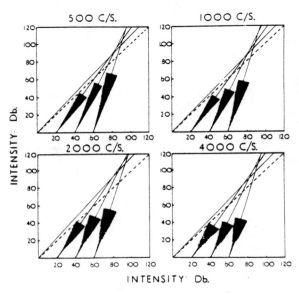

Figure 3   Average recruitment curves to be expected at the four main speech frequencies for varying degrees of deafness. The shaded area indicates twice the standard deviation. (Hallpike, C. S. and Hood, J. D. (1959). *Acta Oto-Laryng.* (*Stockh.*), 50, 472–486.)

loss from 0 to 60 db. Of special note is the fact that they all converge at higher intensities to a point at which an intensity of about 100 db in the good ear equates in loudness with one of 100 db in the deaf ear. It follows from this that irrespective of the magnitude of the deafness all the patients in this group will perceive a sound of about 100 db intensity with much the same loudness sensation. The fact that normally loudness continues to increase with intensity up to the threshold of pain at about 130 db makes it the more interesting that convergence should take place at the lower intensity of 100 db. However, it is now becoming increasingly clear that

this intensity has a particular physiological significance since a wide variety
of physiological and psychophysical phenomena appear to be critically
related to it and the inference is that it represents the upper physiological
limit of normal hearing. Among the psychophysical phenomena is the so-
called loudness discomfort level (L.D.L.) which has particular relevance to
loudness recruitment. If a normal hearing person is presented with a pulsed
sound of increasing intensity and asked to state when he finds it
unpleasantly (as distinct from painfully) loud, there is reasonably good
agreement that this occurs at an intensity of about 100 db. Now in view of
the convergence of the recruitment curves it may be concluded that all
subjects with loudness recruitment, however deaf they may be, will
likewise find a sound of 100 db unpleasantly loud. That this is in fact so can
be seen from Figure 4 which shows the distribution of L.D.L.s in 200
patients with varying degrees of cochlear deafness and 200 normal hearing
subjects. They are remarkably similar to each other. By contrast, of course,
the same test applied to a group of patients with conductive deafness would
produce an entirely different distribution with the L.D.L.s raised above
normal by the amount of the deafness in each case. We can, however, take
the matter further with interesting and more general conclusions. Normal
hearing is not precisely located at the 0 db level. Instead, there are wide
variations, some individuals possessing more acute hearing than others,
others less acute.

If now we divide the group of normal hearing subjects collectively
shown in Figure 4 into three ordered groups according to their hearing
acuity as revealed by the pure tone audiogram and display the distribution
of L.D.L.s in each group the result is as shown in Figure 5. The point of
importance which emerges is that despite the fact that the hearing acuity in
the three groups ranged over 20 db the L.D.L.s in each remained centred
around 100 db. Now if variations in hearing acuity in normal individuals
were the result of minor variations in the conductive efficiency of the
middle ear mechanism we would have expected the L.D.L.s in the three
groups to be displaced from each other by the same amount as the threshold
acuity. That this is not so means of course that in the normal subject hearing
acuity is by and large a function of cochlear sensitivity. Furthermore, we
arrive at the somewhat surprising conclusion that those subjects with less
acute hearing have loudness recruitment with respect to those with acute
hearing. This is exemplified in Figure 6 which summarises schematically
the findings both in normal hearing and deaf subjects.

The vertical bar at the right of the intensity scale denotes the L.D.L.
found to be constant as described above at 100 db in all subjects. The
hearing thresholds in db ranging from very acute normal hearing to severe

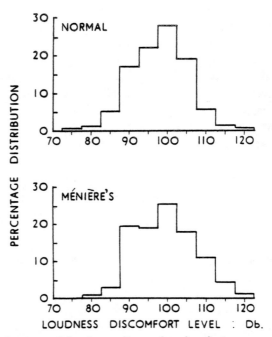

Figure 4 Distribution of loudness discomfort levels in 200 normal hearing subjects and 200 subjects with varying degrees of deafness due to Ménière's disease. Both distributions are centred around 100 db. (Hood, J. D. and Poole, J. P. (1966). *J. Acoust. Soc. Amer.*, **40**, 47–53.)

deafness are shown at the left. If now we make the not unreasonable assumption that all subjects base their experience of unpleasant loudness on much the same loudness sensation the horizontal bars connecting the various hearing levels all represent an identical loudness range from threshold to unpleasant loudness. In the case of those with a deafness of 70 db this is encompassed by an intensity range of only 30 db while the same loudness range in those with a hearing acuity of − 10 db involves an intensity change of 110 db. Upon this basis it is difficult to specify where normality ends and pathology begins. The fact of the matter is that loudness recruitment is a continuum closely linked to hearing acuity or to put it in another form, the rate at which we perceive loudness to increase with intensity is not uniform from one individual to another, instead it is itself a function of hearing sensitivity.

It might be concluded that since loudness recruitment seems to imply a restoration of hearing at high intensities, hearing disability should disappear with amplification. This, however, is not so. Instead this derangement of the loudness function introduces distortion which increases

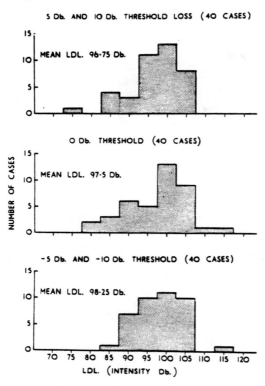

Figure 5   Distribution of loudness discomfort levels in three groups of normal hearing individuals graded according to their hearing acuity. (Hood, J. D. (1968). *J. Acoust. Soc. Amer.*, **44**, 959–964.)

in severity as the deafness increases and by analogy with sound reproduction those of us with normal hearing are only too well aware of the devastating effect a bad loudspeaker or well worn record can have on musical appreciation. It is, of course, not possible to give any kind of quantitative expression to the debasement of musical appreciation experienced by those with cochlear deafness. However, the following comments and reports volunteered by a number of patients with unilateral deafness who were able to make direct comparison with the hearing in their normal ears is particularly revealing. (The writer is indebted to Mr. E. Trinder of the M.R.C. Hearing and Balance Unit who collated the information.)

*E.A.   Unilateral Ménière's disease:*

With speech "Consonants are difficult to hear though the vowels are clear – sounds like Donald Duck." Music on the radio "sounded like tin cans

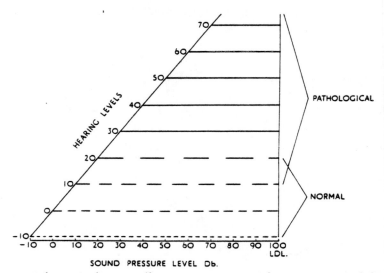

Figure 6   Schematic diagram illustrating variation of recruitment with hearing level. Each of the horizontal bars encompasses the same range of loudness. This, however, involves an intensity change from 110 db at one end of the scale to only 30 db at the other.

being dropped on to the ground". The notes of a piano "have no distinction of tone, they sound just like an anvil being struck by a hammer" and, in addition, "they appear to last longer in the deaf ear".

### M.S.   Unilateral Ménière's disease:

Loud sounds are "unpleasant in the deaf ear". He was unable to "distinguish a violin from a French horn". "A voice seems lower pitched in the deaf ear and is not so clear cut, there is a roughness." "A singer's voice sounds gravelly." Tone bursts of equal length sound longer in the deaf ear.

### A.P.   Unilateral Ménière's disease:

"Normal speech sounds harsh and chopped up" and "is difficult to hear in noisy surroundings". When listening to music in the deaf ear "the bass guitar disappears and the higher tones are harsh". He could not pick out a tune with the deaf ear "the loudness of the notes change but pitch doesn't". "The tones sounded a furry mess." Sudden noise gives him a start.

### A.H.   Displaced stapes prosthesis with cochlear damage:

"Cannot recognise a tune in the deaf ear, musical notes blur into each other." They are "not concise – no breaks" and he "gets no rhythm".

"Notes of different pitch played successively can be distinguished but they blur into each other."

Other patients commenting upon their perception of speech consistently use expressions such as "it comes in a blast"; "it is clipped" or "it seems like a belch in the ear." Attempts have been made to simulate electronically the distortion effects of loudness recruitment and to a normal hearing person the above descriptions would appear to be particularly apt.

## SPEECH AUDIOMETRY

Although we have to rely heavily on the patients' own descriptions to begin to appreciate how much has irretrievably been lost to them in terms of musical appreciation we are in a much better position to assess their disability for speech recognition.

For this purpose we make use of the speech audiometer. Basically this instrument consists as shown in Figure 7 of a gramophone turntable, an amplifier with a volume control or attenuator calibrated in decibels and a loudspeaker or headphone to deliver the sound to the patient. Recorded lists, each of identical order of difficulty of 25 words of the kind shown in table 1, are played at different intensity levels and the percentage number of

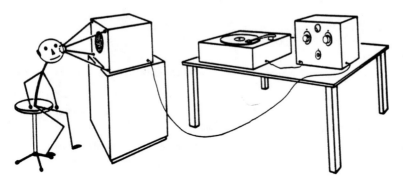

Figure 7   Diagram of equipment used in speech audiometry.

words correctly perceived by the patient scored at each level. Tests are usually carried out at five different attenuator settings within the patient's hearing range. The results are plotted on audiogram forms of the kind shown in Figure 8 with curves drawn through the successive articulation scores. The 0 db reference level is the intensity at which a normal hearing person would perceive 50% of the words without understanding them. The

*Table 1*  Phonetically balanced word lists.

| | | | |
|---|---|---|---|
| 1.  nose | earn | knob | face |
| 2.  browse | race | flick | range |
| 3.  shine | sketch | bog | roar |
| 4.  odds | pod | ode | by |
| 5.  base | how | gage | dwarf |
| 6.  hill | oil | eat | him |
| 7.  good | hot | leg | south |
| 8.  yawn | bee | prig | whiff |
| 9.  pass | dodge | raise | gasp |
| 10.  love | raw | thigh | siege |
| 11.  mast | shin | crib | gun |
| 12.  shove | beast | grope | grade |
| 13.  bed | rave | scan | cook |
| 14.  bronze | badge | prime | sniff |
| 15.  zone | eel | rooms | plod |
| 16.  thick | court | ray | rich |
| 17.  black | strap | sup | knit |
| 18.  curse | frown | as | though |
| 19.  gay | or | eyes | sag |
| 20.  cheat | barge | bag | dope |
| 21.  lend | heed | hitch | rash |
| 22.  flap | neat | deep | woo |
| 23.  puff | sour | cloth | but |
| 24.  grudge | move | badge | fake |
| 25.  find | touch | reap | woe |

full line curve to the left of each denotes the average normal response. As will be seen, about 10 per cent. of the words would be correctly perceived at a level of 10 db, 50 per cent. at 20 db, 85 per cent. at 30 db and so on with all the words being correctly heard at 40 db.

The curves to the right in the upper audiogram are from patients with conductive hearing loss. All the curves have the same form as the normal curve but are displaced from it by approximately the amount of the pure tone loss. In other words, given sufficient amplification, all these patients could attain 100 per cent. recognition of speech and this amplification can of course be provided by a hearing aid.

The curves shown below are typical curves from a number of patients with cochlear hearing loss. Their average pure tone thresholds at the main speech frequencies are given by the inset figures on each. By contrast to those in the conductive group it will be seen that as the hearing loss increases, the shape of the speech audiograms departs progressively from the normal. With increasing amplification a maximum score is obtained and beyond this, further amplification results only in a deterioration of speech recognition.

The maximum possible scores have been averaged for a large number of patients with cochlear hearing loss and related to their average pure tone loss in Figure 9 where it will be seen how systematically maximum discrimination score deteriorates with increasing deafness. Extrapolation of

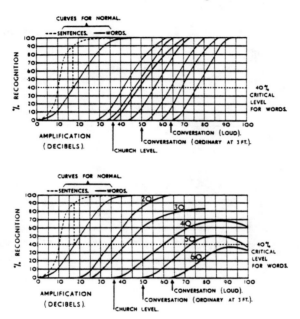

Figure 8   (a) Speech audiograms from patients with conductive deafness. (b) Speech audiograms from patients with cochlear deafness. The inset figures are the average pure tone losses at the main speech frequencies. (Hood, J. D. and Poole, J. P. (1971). *Sound*, **5**, 30–38.)

this curve indicates that total disability occurs with a hearing loss of about 90 db. In this context it is important to realise that in order to make speech audible to a patient with this degree of deafness, appreciably less amplification would be needed than might appear from the pure tone loss because of the presence of loudness recruitment. It would, however, be completely unintelligible.

This data has been obtained under ideal listening conditions and with ideal sound reproduction and therefore is likely to err on the optimistic side. The quality of amplification afforded by a hearing aid falls far short

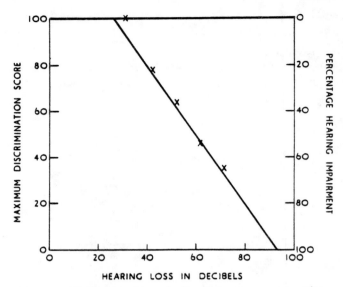

Figure 9   Variation of maximum speech discrimination score with average pure
tone hearing loss in patients with cochlear deafness. (Hood, J. D. and Poole, J. P.
(1971). *Sound*, **5**, 30–38.)

of this ideal. The sad fact remains that at present no hearing aid has
yet been devised with specially designed characteristics capable of
correcting this type of deafness, indeed in many instances a simple speaking
tube or ear trumpet can best provide what little assistance is available.

Since the neural transduction mechanism is damaged in cochlear
hearing loss, bone conducted sound is impaired to the same degree as air
conducted sound. It will be recalled that we rely heavily upon the
transmission of the sound of our own voices by bone conduction in order to
be able to hear and reflexly control its level. The cochlear impaired person,
however, remains as deaf to the sound of his own voice as he is to that of
others and in consequence tends to speak more loudly in order to hear and
modulate it. Most of us have, at some time or another, had experience of
such persons, sometimes with embarrassment when in quiet surroundings,
the uncontrolled raised voice draws the uncomprehending and unwanted
attention of others.

## DEAFNESS IN MUSICIANS

The onset of deafness, particularly cochlear deafness, is a tragedy to the
instrumentalist. As it progresses not only may he begin to lose control of
the tone of his instrument but he also loses the capacity to regulate the

volume of sound. If his deafness is predominantly confined to the higher tones, as it often is, then he will hear only a limited range of frequencies in the lower registers. This of course would be of considerably less importance to the tympanist than, say, the flautist.

The instrumentalists playing stringed and other instruments which call for some dexterity on the part of the player in order to create the notes have to rely critically upon their own hearing acuity for clarity and pitch of tone. Pianists, organists, harpists and so forth do not, of course, have this problem because, provided they strike the correct note the pitch is determined by the instrument. A professional organist of the author's acquaintance continues to give a credible performance despite the fact that he has an appreciable high tone hearing loss. How much his interpretation of a piece of music is coloured by what he himself hears is impossible to say. It could be that it possesses certain individual characteristics that the normal hearing listener finds aesthetically pleasing, if unusual. On the other hand the virtuosity of the keyboard instrumentalist acquired through long years of practice could well be retained after the advent of deafness. Smetana at the age of 56, by which time he was totally deaf, was persuaded to play the piano at an orchestral concert held in his honour. He played Chopin's *Nocturne in B* and his own *Polka in A minor*. A contemporary of the day wrote of his performance "Even though deaf he played with such originality, feeling and expression, that he clearly towered above all other pianists. Considering his state, he produced a rich range of dynamic nuances which were as astonishing as was his technical perfection. It was touching to see an artist whose performance so excited the public, especially when they realised that not one of the sounds which he charmed from the instrument could ever penetrate his soul. Many wept for Smetana's fate."

The effect of partial deafness upon conductors and composers is much less obvious, particularly in respect of presbyacusis. Beethoven attempted to conduct a revival of *Fidelio* in 1822 with disastrous consequences but his deafness at that time must have been so profound that he could have heard very little of the music. By contrast, Ralph Vaughan Williams, whose deafness did not become obvious until his seventies, continued conducting successfully until his 85th year culminating in a performance of the Bach *St. Matthew Passion*. His deafness was sufficiently severe to warrant the use of a hearing aid. He found an electronic aid of little assistance, however, and much preferred a form of ear trumpet which he referred to as "his coffee pot". The underlying pathology was clearly presbyacusis with a typical profound loss of high tone perception so that he no longer heard the sound of oboes and other high toned instruments. This made it difficult for him at times to judge orchestral balance so that in recording sessions of his own works with Sir Adrian Boult or Sir John Barbirolli he was obliged to consult them at times on this vital matter since he himself was often unsure of what he actually heard.

Of his deafness, his widow, Ursula Vaughan Williams, writes (personal communication) "I think it is difficult to estimate exactly how much deafness affected Ralph musically because he had a life-time knowledge of various works, of the scope of instruments, and of experience of both writing and conducting music. Looking back, I'd say that knowledge and expectation of what should be there filled gaps in music and imagination."

This form of deafness with advancing years of course affects all of us in varying degree beginning first at the high frequencies, extending to the middle frequencies and finally involving the low frequencies. This progression has been extensively studied by a number of investigators so that although wide variations do occur it is now possible to predict the average hearing to be expected within particular age groups. This is shown in Figure 10. Perhaps of even more serious consequences, however, from the point of view of musical appreciation, is the marked deterioration that occurs with age in our ability to discriminate tones of neighbouring frequency. This ability can be expressed as the so-called relative difference

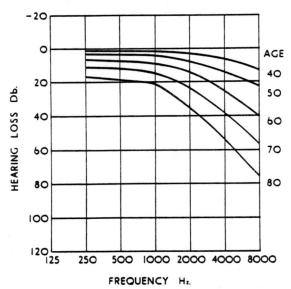

Figure 10  Deterioration of hearing level with age at different frequencies. (After Spoor, A. and Passchier-Vermeer, W. (1969). *International Audiology*, **8**, 328–336.)

limen DF/F where DF represents the smallest frequency change that can just be detected at a given frequency F.

Average values for relative difference limens for various age groups as a function of frequency are shown in Figure 11. It seems that our ability to detect small changes in frequency begins to decline at all frequencies as

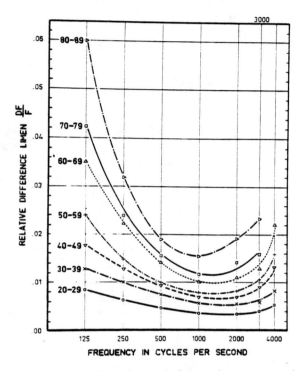

Figure 11   Average values of the relative difference limens DF/F for various age groups. (After König, E. (1957). *Acta Oto-Laryng.* (*Stockh.*), **48**, 475–489.)

early as our fourth decade of life while at the seventh decade the relative deteriorations are as much as 300 per cent. at the lower and higher frequency ranges and 200 per cent. in the middle frequencies.

Senile deafness, of course, has such an insidious progression that few of us notice its advance with time. We adapt to our changing hearing pattern so much so that many of the elderly stoutly deny that they have any problem even though this may clearly be demonstrated to them in the shape of the pure tone audiogram.

Longevity seems to be common amongst conductors and we are all familiar with the many distinguished octogenarian conductors whose services have been, and still are, much in demand. It would seem inconceivable that their hearing could have escaped the ravages of time which afflict the rest of us and in consequence one must presume that many, if not all of them, must be somewhat hard of hearing, particularly for high tones. It follows that they must have the greatest difficulty in hearing say the upper notes of a violin, a flute, or a piccolo, particularly in respect of the overtones which give to the notes their special quality. What they hear of a musical performance, therefore, must differ, perhaps appreciably, from what is heard by say the younger members of the audience. This, of course, raises questions of some interest. Does their interpretation change with their sensory degeneration? (This has certainly been shown to be the case with certain distinguished painters with failing eye sight whose work is no less revered because of this.) Are they perhaps through many years of experience so accomplished at their profession that good hearing is of less importance than a memory acquired over the years of what is called for during this or that passage of music? Do in fact the elderly with failing hearing derive any less enjoyment from a musical performance than the young?

What constitutes musical appreciation is so difficult to define that it is unlikely that satisfactory answers can ever be found for these questions. Both our behavioural and aesthetic responses to music are determined by cultural conditioning and ultimately these are dependent upon the characteristics of our own individual sensory systems. However, it will be apparent from what has been written concerning the loudness function in normal and pathological ears that very wide variations can occur. In its extreme pathological degree loudness recruitment certainly debases musical appreciation, but this applies in particular to adventitious deafness in those in whom their conditioning has been acquired during their normal hearing formative years. We are in no position to say that those born partially deaf with loudness recruitment derive any less enjoyment from music since the tonal attributes imparted by their deranged hearing mechanism could well take on a quality found to be aesthetically pleasing even though unique to themselves. After all, *musique concrète*, which many of us find cacophonous and incomprehensible, would be the rule in any musical repertoire rather than the exception if it was our only experience of music. This applies equally well, if to a lesser degree, within what can be considered the limits of normal hearing. Even if the brain processed the neural information it receives in an identical fashion from one person to another, which it clearly does not (tone deafness for example is central in origin) the peripheral transduction mechanism varies to such a degree in respect of the loudness function that this in itself might well account in part for our diversity of musical tastes.

No chapter on deafness as applied to music would be complete without some comment upon the deaf composers. Beethoven is, of course, the best known of these but it is perhaps less common knowledge that Fauré, Smetana and Franz were also deaf.

Beethoven first noticed his deafness at the age of 26 and it must have progressed rapidly because three years later his writings reveal that he was in very serious difficulty. Opinions as to its cause vary from syphilis, a typically sensorineural loss, to otosclerosis, a conductive loss. In fact it is unlikely to have been due to either. Acquired syphilitic deafness does not usually make its appearance until late middle age when, because it is frequently accompanied by attacks of vertigo, it is often confused with Ménière's disease.

In 1801, at the age of 30, Beethoven wrote in some desperation to his friend, Dr. Wegeler, a physician. "In order to give you some idea of this strange deafness, let me tell you that in the theatre I have to place myself close to the orchestra in order to understand what the actor is saying, and that at a distance I cannot hear the high notes of instruments or voices. As for the spoken voice it is surprising that some people have never noticed my deafness; but since I have always been liable to fits of absent mindedness, they attribute my hardness of hearing to that. Sometimes, too, I can scarcely hear a person who speaks softly; I can hear sounds, it is true, but cannot make out the words. *But if anyone shouts, I cannot bear it.* Heaven alone knows what is to become of me."

The reader will recognise in this an almost classic description of a recruiting sensorineural hearing loss. As to its pathology it was certainly not Ménière's disease because there is no evidence that Beethoven ever suffered from vertigo. There have, however, been suggestions that he survived an attack of typhus early in his life and in this event deafness could well have been one of the sequelae of this disease.

Smetana (1824–1884) did not become deaf until he was in his late forties and by the time he had reached the age of fifty his deafness was total. He was much troubled by tinnitus and gave expression to this in the finale of his autobiographical *Aus mein Leben* quartet by means of a high sustained violin note. Unlike Beethoven his deafness was accompanied by attacks of vertigo which plagued him for the rest of his life. He later developed hoarseness of the voice, acute stiffness, cramp and lapses of memory followed eventually by fits and a madness which necessitated his confinement to an asylum. There is a belief that Smetana suffered from neurosyphilis and this is certainly a possible diagnosis on the clinical evidence available.

Gabriel Fauré (1845–1924) first noticed his deafness at the age of 57. It progressed from then on and although it was never complete it must have been sensorineural in origin because he was considerably troubled by pitch distortion, high notes sounding flat and low notes sharp. He ultimately died of arterio-sclerosis, and this is likely to have been the cause of his deafness.

Robert Franz (1815–1892) became deaf at the age of 24 following a head injury. He was totally deaf in 1871 and in the intervening period much troubled by "a peculiar sort of irritability towards any sounds". This is clearly a reference to loudness recruitment.

A common feature of all these composers is that the deafness progressed fairly rapidly and on this account it was without exception regarded by each of them as a very considerable personal tragedy. Beethoven, for example, in the letter quoted above, proceeds "For almost two years I have ceased to attend any social functions just because I find it impossible to say to people: I am deaf. If I had any other profession I might be able to cope with my infirmity; but in my profession it is a terrible handicap. . . . Already I have often cursed my Creator and my existence. Plutarch has shown me the path of resignation. If it is at all possible I will bid defiance to my fate, although I feel that as long as I live there will be moments when I shall be God's most unhappy creature. I beg you not to say anything about my condition to anyone. . . . Resignation, what a wretched resource! Yet it is all that is left to me." Tragedy of course it undoubtedly was to all these composers but the truly remarkable fact is that far from having an adverse effect upon their work, their deafness marked the period of their greatest creativity. Smetana for example, some years after he became deaf, wrote "I have completed in these three years of deafness more than I had otherwise done in ten." It seems almost as if the isolation forced upon them by their deafness drove them to seek consolation and communion in their own work. How much, one wonders, would have been lost to our musical heritage had these composers not been deaf?

When we consider the world of discordant sounds and eventual silence in which they lived we can only marvel at their achievements. Perhaps, divorced from the competing sounds of everyday life, their powers of auditory imagery became more enhanced. Smetana certainly provides us with some evidence for this. Having completed a long series of orchestral and operatic works he wrote "I never heard a note of all these works and still they lived in me and through mental imagery alone moved me to tears and sheer ecstasy."

Various authorities have claimed to have been able to perceive an influence of the deafness upon the subsequent work of these compoers. For example, referring to the work of Fauré the *New Oxford History of Music* somewhat boldly states that "Total deafness accounts for the fact that as with Beethoven, his last works reveal a marked attitude of self communion and a tendency to explore to its furthest limits an esoteric and ascetic manner of expression." This may well be so. Indeed, in the case of Beethoven a discernible change is certainly apparent from the rather extrovert epic statements of the middle period symphonies to the inner contemplation and self discipline of the last quartets and sonatas. This, however, is pure speculation which can neither be proved nor disproved. Others may take the view that evolutionary developments of a similar kind are evident in the works of other great composers who were not deaf and moreover since Beethoven was deaf for much the greater part of his creative years any perceived change in his works could equally well be attributed to maturity rather than deafness. The supreme paradox is, that of all those afflicted with the catastrophe of deafness the composer is probably best equipped to bear it because he alone can revert to and find satisfaction and fulfillment in his own musical imagery. In his mind he can create perfection.

Experience suggests that he lacks little from having been denied the opportunity to hear the possibly indifferent interpretation of his work by others.

# *Musicogenic Epilepsy*

### *(1) The Beginnings*

The story of musicogenic epilepsy emerged in the early 30s of this century. In 1921, E. Rosenhaim had written a critical account of those rare forms of epilepsy where seizures appeared to be triggered off by some specific stimulus, varying in type from one patient to another. His concluding words were *und so wurde Reflex-Epilepsie in das Land der Schatten verbannt; möge diese Abhandlung mit dazu beitragen, ihr endgültig das Grab zu schaufein* ("so reflex epilepsy can be banished to the land of shadows; may this communication serve to dig its grave").

This nihilistic attitude was so alien to my experience of chronic epileptics, that I set out collecting cases in refutation. In 1933 I published a series of examples in which some specific stimulus would provoke an attack. This preliminary communication was expanded in 1935 in my paper *Ueber Reflex-Epilepsie*. Herein were described numerous instances — some personally observed, others collected from the literature — wherein divers external factors proved to be epileptogenic. One important group consisted in cases where fits were precipitated by noise, including at times music.

My introduction to this latter type of sonogenic or acoustico-motor epilepsy had dated from 1931. An epileptic hospital ward-maid periodically attended my Clinic to report progress and to collect her medicaments. On one of her regular visits she, as an afterthought, volunteered to me the throw-away remark that her attacks were exclusively connected with the hearing of music. This was an arresting observation, for neurologists as a body were quite unfamiliar with such a coincidence. The patient proceeded to specify that music of the "popular" type had no such effect, but only what she liked to term "classical" music, while confessing that she was aesthetically quite an ignoramus. The patient was admitted to hospital, and with her express permission, submitted herself to the hazards of musical influence. My then assistant (now Professor Denny-Brown) brought along his record player and several samples of danceband music were tried out. The patient assured us that none of these was of the sort likely to bring on an attack. Finally, Denny-Brown produced his most serious recording, which was Tschaikowsky's *Valse des Fleurs* played by the orchestra of the Berlin State Opera. Not many bars elapsed before the patient began to look distressed, and gradually she developed a seizure with generalised convulsive movements, frothing at the lips, and cyanosis. As the attack wore off, her plantar responses altered from being flexor to extensor in type. The patient subsequently told me "that's the sort of music which always brings on an attack".

My interest was aroused, and I was able to collect ten other cases, some of them already quoted in 1933.

For example, another patient of mine was a woman of 33 years who for four years had been subject to periodic seizures. Each attack was associated with the hearing of music. After a while an aura would appear in which she would suddenly "feel funny". Her voice then faltered; things would recede farther and farther and then go black. Consciousness would then be lost and she became convulsed. Her husband, witness of some of these episodes, observed that at the start his wife would suddenly become unaccountably frightened, and scream in terror. While unconscious she would distort her face to one side and draw up one leg.

While this woman was in hospital various records were played to her. None was effectual until Strauss's *Thousand and One Nights* was selected. While the music was being played the patient betrayed considerable unease. When the record was repeated she put her hands to her ears; screwed up her eyes; frowned and made other grimacing movements. Consciousness was not lost but when the music came to an end the patient showed obvious relief, and her facial movements relaxed. Questioned about her subjective experiences, she declared that she had not liked the music . . . "it sort of jarred . . . terribly". Had she been in control of the test, she would have stopped the record. The sensation had been identical with the aura of her attacks.

In 1936 I read a paper on this topic at a meeting of the Association of British Neurologists under the provisional title "musicolepsia". During the discussion that followed, Dr. Kinnier Wilson rightly took exception to the title on etymological grounds, and, as a result, I thereafter referred to "musicogenic epilepsy", a term at once universally accepted. The syndrome has now been secured a firm place within the corpus of neurological teaching.

Since 1936 other similar cases have been reported throughout the world. During the war indeed I met with two further examples which I published in 1942.

One of these concerned a naval rating aged 30 who had sustained a closed head injury nine years previously. Within a month of the accident he developed an epileptic attack and similar seizures thereafter recurred at weekly intervals. The patient had observed a very close association between music and the onset of a fit, though the connection was not invariable. "I might be listening to music on the radio when a certain note seems to catch me – or maybe it's the vibration – it gets into my head, and off I go". On this account he was careful to avoid music as far as was possible. The roaring noise of the blow-pipe he used in the course of his pre-war job as a decorator seemed also at times to induce an attack. As a boy the patient had been taught the piano, much to his distaste.

When one comes to the interesting yet rather futile task of assigning priority to the isolation of musicogenic epilepsy, it seems possible that credit belongs to Gowers. In a footnote contained in one of his works, he made a very brief mention of seizures being induced in some epileptics by the sound of music.*

In 1884, Merzheevsky had reported to a meeting of the St. Petersburg Psychiatric Society the case of a patient who had sustained three epileptic fits, each one brought on by the sound of music, always of an unfamiliar character. Some years later, Steinbrugge recorded another case of epilepsy precipitated by music. Another example, in a man of 31 in whom seizures came on when he heard pianoforte music, was published by Y. Y. Trutovsky (no date). H. Oppenheimer described one more such instance in 1905. In 1935, Nikitin published the case of a singer who developed epilepsy, the attacks at first being nocturnal. Later, fits would also occur by day, but only under the influence of a particular piece of music – the aria of Zaren Berendej from Rimsky-Korsakov's *Snow Maiden*. An attack would be induced when he sang this piece, or heard it played, or even if he merely imagined he was listening to it. This phenomenon happened on at least 30 occasions, and at a meeting of the Leningrad Neuropathological Society, the typical aura of an attack was precipitated, though not a complete convulsion.

The year 1913 is important in that von Bechterew demonstrated before a medical society in St. Petersburg two cases of reflex epilepsy induced by

* Perhaps, however, the story can be traced even further back, to 1660 in fact. Lord Cohen of Birkenhead brought to my attention Shakespeare's allusion in *The Merchant of Venice* to "some that are mad if they behold a cat, and others *when the bagpipe sing i'th'nose cannot contain their urine.*" Could this conceivably be an early reference to musicogenic epilepsy? If so, recognition must have come even earlier, for J. J. Scaliger (1540–1609) described the case of an individual similarly afflicted whenever he heard the music of the lyre. This observation was quoted in Le Loirier's *Treatise of Spectres* (1605).

music. Bechterew's second patient was specially significant, for he was musically experienced, indeed professionally so, for he was the well-known music critic, Nikonov.

So disturbed was he by his malady, and at the same time so interested in its workings, that he committed his experiences to print. He published a pamphlet which he entitled "Fear of Music". In this we read the circumstances of the first signs of his disorder. At the Imperial Opera House he was watching a performance of Meyerbeer's *The Prophet*. During the ice-skating ballet in the third act, he became tremulous, sweated profusely, and his left eye began to twitch. Then came a violent pain in his head, and consciousness was lost for a while. Thereafter Nikonov became a prey to similar attacks, each one brought on by music and by no other factor. Gradually his sensitivity seemed to increase, so that even distant, subdued music became epileptogenic. As a consequence, the victim was tormented by a veritable phobic dread of hearing music. If out of doors the sound of an approaching military band reached him, he would stop his ears, and seek refuge in a back street or any handy doorway or shop. Eventually, however, his attacks became more or less controlled under a regime of bromide of potassium.

The foregoing was the clinical situation prior to the routine use of electroencephalography in cases of epilepsy. In considering pathogenesis it was necessary first to determine the place of musicogenic epilepsy within the larger group of cases of *Lärmepilepsie*, i.e. acousticomotor or sonogenic epilepsy. In the one an unexpected, startling noise, frequently loud in decibel content, would culminate in a fit. In the other it was a stimulus of music, nothing startling, nothing abrupt, and not necessarily loud; and yet there were intermediate cases where not only music but also protracted monotonous sounds (ringing of a telephone bell, hissing of a kettle) were effective too.

The second question concerned the role of physical as opposed to emotional factors. Could musicogenic epilepsy, and for that matter, could other cases of acousticomotor epilepsy be the product of enhanced cerebral blood-flow, increased heart-rate, or tachypnoea, and be rated as the responsible stimulus? In Chapter 12 we read of the work of Harrer and Harrer who have demonstrated the considerable autonomic alterations which may result not so much from noise, as from the influence of music. Their studies suggest that the affective concomitants of music, rather than the physico-mechanical properties, are potent in bringing about the circulatory and respiratory changes.

This brings us to the question of wherein exactly does music differ from noise.

In discussing any neurological aspect of music it becomes imperative at the outset to be clear about the nomenclature we employ. For example, how does "music" differ from "noise", for it is notorious that a particular pattern of auditory stimuli may be regarded as musical to some persons, while to others the same sense-data merely constitute noise. Dr. Johnson admitted that he was not fond of music, but of all noises he regarded music as the least disagreeable. In extreme cases one may suspect the artistic sensitivity of the recipients, yet there surely must be an intermediate group where music and noise are difficult to differentiate. The obvious example concerns the decibel level of musical stimuli, which if augmented sufficiently, engenders noise even to those who are musically appreciative and informed. Apart from this purely mechanical consideration, there are types of music which pass over the heads of some hearers – not necessarily unsophisticated – and are written off as mere noise. Certain works of Stockhausen might be rated by some as acceptable musical compositions, but by others as sheer cacophony. From medical studies, it is found that noise and music at times evoke comparable effects, some of them purely physiological, others being far more subtle. The term "noise" usually carries with it the connotation of an unpleasant feeling, as opposed to music which is ordinarily regarded as an aesthetic or an intellectual experience. Both *noise* and *music* are products of a third element, namely *sound*, which in itself may carry an undertext of either an agreeable or a disagreeable quality.

Hence the importance of defining our terms.

*Sound* according to the O.E.D. is "the sensation produced in the organs of hearing when the surrounding air is set in vibration in such a way as to affect these". Although not explicitly stated, sounds may or may not carry with them some affective tone either of pleasure or of displeasure. Certain sounds in nature, like the rustling of leaves, the babbling of a stream, the breaking of waves on shingle are usually deemed pleasurable, in that as a rule they are subdued, non-obtrusive, evocative, and euphonious.

*Noise* may be defined as a loud or harsh sound of any kind (O.E.D.). Here we find simple physical parameters converting sound into noise. Other definitions of noise include "sound undesired by the recipient" (A. H. Davies), thus implicating the hearer's subjective response, his acceptance or rejection. To quote once more the O.E.D., the term "noise" may be applied to "any loud outcry, clamour, or shouting: din or disturbance". This attitude is far more involved, embracing factors which are communicative, if not purely psychological experiences.

*Music* is defined by the O.E.D. as "sounds in melodic or harmonic combination".

Obviously there exists a kind of three-way acoustic linkage between sounds and music, with noise constituting a third and associated factor.

Reference may be made at this point to the opinions of Diesserens and of Schoen who have asserted that music can produce: (1) increased bodily metabolism; (2) altered muscular energy; (3) acceleration and irregularity of the respiratory rate; (4) enhanced perception of other special senses; (5) exaggerated knee-jerks; (6) a lowered threshold for various sensory stimuli; and (7) a marked effect upon the blood pressure and also the peripheral and central circulations.

Each of the foregoing might equally well be the product of noise as opposed to music. For this reason, Stumpf deliberately tested a series of subjects who were notoriously non-musical, his findings implicating a *Tonpsychologie* rather than a *Musikpsychologie*.

The physiological data are also supported by a case published by Patrizi of a boy of 13 who sustained a severe head injury with a cranial defect over 12 cm in length. The pulsations of the underlying brain were consequently visible. Plethysmography demonstrated that the cerebral circulation increased under the influence of music, the brain-flow being augmented directly with the intensity of the stimulus, i.e. when it crossed the frontier between music and noise.

The clinical problem as it existed 30 years ago, might therefore have been expressed as follows:

(1) Musicogenic epilepsy is without doubt a clinical entity but a rare one. The naval rating whose case-record has been described above was the solitary example of musicogenic epilepsy among a series of 700 epileptics encountered in the Royal Navy between 1939 and 1942. I tentatively estimated the incidence of the musicogenic variety at least as low as 0·01 per cent. of the general epileptic population. That is to say, approximately one in ten million of the adult population is so affected. Or in other words, one might hazard the guess that in Great Britain five patients exist who are victims of musicogenic epilepsy.

(2) The syndrome of musicogenic epilepsy may develop at a comparatively late age; that is to say, after 20.

(3) Often the attacks appear without any obvious cause at first, music occurring as the precipitating factor only later.

(4) Many of the victims could be regarded as above average in their musical ability or in their aesthetic appreciation, but this certainly does not apply to all the patients.

(5) Typically, an attack of musicogenic epilepsy is preceded by increasing distress and agitation, along with tachycardia and rapid breathing; and yet simple deliberate hyperventilation in the absence of

music will not bring on an attack. At first it was difficult for neurologists to decide whether these autonomic features were primary, or whether they were the product of the affective state engendered by the music. The evidence of electroencephalography, when it became available, strongly suggested that the autonomic symptoms were emotionally determined.

(6) Although in some patients there have been factors which might raise the suspicion of a psychologically determined syndrome, musicogenic epileptic attacks are unquestionably organic, being often accompanied by tongue-biting, urinary incontinence, and extensor plantar responses.

(7) Electroencephalography clinches the organic nature of the disorder with its typical paroxysmal dysrrhythmia often preponderant in one or both temporal lobes.

(8) The musicogenic factors vary in nature from patient to patient. Sometimes any type of music may be provocative: in other cases, only one instrument whatever the tune, or perhaps just one specific melody whatever the instrument. In some patients the music needs to be continued for many minutes before a seizure results. There is reason to believe that the degree of loudness may be significant. Occasionally certain non-musical auditory stimuli may also prove sonogenic and act as precipitating factors, e.g. monotonous voices within earshot; the click-clack of tap dancing; the whirring of machinery; a whistling kettle; a ringing telephone. In one case not only was a diversity of sound-stimuli epileptogenic, but the patient was also liable to experience a seizure in certain non-auditory and emotionally charged circumstances, as when entering a lofty or awe-inspiring building like a cathedral, a conference hall, or even a lecture theatre. The lack of specificity in the musicogenic factors was emphasized by H. G. Sear (1939). In a contribution to *Music and Letters* he wrote "in the mass of material, although the observations essential to treatment are exact enough, the general survey is necessarily vague. The conclusion might also be reached that it is sound rather than music which causes epilepsy. Assuming the existence of a doctor whose knowledge of music is as complete as his neurological education, he would, at any rate in this country, where medicine is a private enterprise, hardly be able to spare the time to go through a whole range of musical works in order to ascertain what peculiar quality produces a certain group of symptoms. It seems to me that a musical analysis of considerable subtlety is demanded and that probably the question of rhythm would need to be answered before that of melody. First things first: a hammer tap; repeated hammer taps; an anvil stroke; anvils of varying pitch; repeated anvil strokes; the exploitation of the dominant as in the *Harmonious Blacksmith*; the anvil stroke in Bax's *Symphony*; Smetana's famous string Quartet; Cornelius's *Monotone*. The late Mr. Czerny would

be a study in himself. The thing could be developed to fantastic lengths".

Except for the correlation of medicine with private enterprise, these remarks still apply.

As mentioned earlier, under (5), "differentiation between effects purely physical and psychological effects is of great importance. The walls of Jericho may be accepted as a miracle by the faithful, as a symbol by the poetical and as a known effect by the scientist" (Sear).

(9) Repeated attacks of musicogenic epilepsy may eventually lead to a chronic state of apprehension, bound up with the hazard of being unwittingly and unwillingly subjected to the impact of provoking stimuli – a veritable "fear of music" as Nikonov described.

Reference has been made to the suspicion which sometimes arises that musicogenic epilepsy may – at times at least – be a wholly psychological aberration. We can recall the instances of mass hysteria in which music played a role, and where convulsive displays eventuated. Phenomena of this character were endemic throughout Europe during the Middle Ages. Bands of pious and peripatetic fanatics would hold religious assemblies and to the accompaniment of music would be moved to dance. As their antics became wilder, bystanders would be drawn in willy-nilly. Soon the dance would become an orgiastic frenzy in which participants would leap into the air uttering incoherent cries, or collapse in grotesque epileptic-like convulsions. This type of collective hysteria was spoken of as the "dancing mania", or, because of some fancied connection with a spider-bite, "tarantism". The mythical spider was a tarantula endemic to Taranto and hence the provoking music became known as a "tarantella", a term used even today in Italy.

With the Reformation the dancing mania waned, though here and there a single case might appear. Something comparable, however, may be encountered even today among the more fanatical sects in the Middle East (e.g. the dancing dervishes) or during the voodoo ceremonies of Haiti. In England perhaps one of the last cases to be reported was that described in 1790 by Lucas. A young man, convalescent from a fever, on hearing a fiddle played in the street, started from bed crying "Dance! Dance!" Thereafter, each day, he would insist on dressing himself, and to the accompaniment of a violin he would dance unrestrainedly in a "strange, frightful and seemingly involuntary fashion". First he would agitate his upper limbs; then his feet. Next he would nod and wag his head. Afterwards he would leap and make the most ridiculous and antic grimaces, shaking his extremities . . . "as if he was by design acting the part of a scaramouch or merry Andrew". Every day such performances would take place to the point of exhaustion. Later he became the victim of convulsive fits with loss of consciousness, tonic spasms, rolling of the eyeballs, jactitation and trismus. Such attacks, which lasted anything from 15 minutes to several hours, gradually abated, but were succeeded by a hectic fever to which he succumbed.

It is easy to dismiss such a case as one of *grande hysterie*, but the fatal termination seems to indicate some underlying organic delirium.

These cases of dancing mania bear but a superficial resemblance to musicogenic epilepsy, and the topic arises merely when differential diagnosis is discussed.

Today musicogenic epilepsy constitutes something of a neurological curiosity. To a medical scientist fortunate enough to be experienced furthermore as a musicologist, the syndrome should constitute a most worthwhile topic for research. To date, for example, it is difficult to discern the common factor pervading the manifold experiences of music, and which in certain individuals assume the unexpected property of provoking an epileptic reaction; but such a factor there must be.

## REFERENCES

BARRIOS DEL RISCO, P. and ESSLEN, E. (1958) Epilepsia musicogena. *Acta Neurol. Latinoamer.*, **4**, 130–144.

BASH, K. W. and BASH-LIECHTI, J. (1959) The psychotherapy of a case of musicogenic epilepsy. *Schweiz. Arch. Neur. Psych.*, **83**, 196–221.

CHRÁST, B., KALÁB, Z., and SKALNÍK, J. (1962) Observations on musicogenic epilepsy. *Csl. Neur.* **25**, 50–59.

CRITCHLEY, M. (1933) On reflex epilepsy. *Ann. Report Lond. County Counc.*, **4** (Part III), 133.

— (1935) Ueber Reflexepilepsie. *Schweiz. Arch. f. Psych. u. Neur.*, **35**, 256.

— (1937) Musicogenic epilepsy. *Brain*, **60**, 13–27.

— (1942) Musicogenic epilepsy: two cases. *J.R.N. Med. Serv.*, **28**, 182–184.

— (1975) Fear of music. Moscow Acad. Med., USSR., *Birthday volume in honour of Acad. Sarkisov*.

DALY, D. and BICKFORD, R. G. (1950) Sensory precipitation of epileptic seizures. *Tr. Am. Neur. Ass.*, **75**, 229–231.

DIESERENS, C. M. (1926) The influence of music on behaviour.

DOW, R. S. (1951) Electroencephalographic findings in a case of musicogenic epilepsy. *EEG. clin. Neurophysiol.*, **3**, 384.

FORSTER, F. M. (1967) Conditioning in musicogenic epilepsy. *Trans. Am. Neur. Ass.*, **92**, 236–237.

GOLDSTEIN, K. (1932) Auslösung epileptischen Anfälle durch Musik. *Berl. Ges. Psych. Nervenk* (1931) cit. *Zblat. Neur. Psych.*, **63**, 281.

HAMOIR and TITICA, J. (1948) Étude électroencéphalographique d'un cas d'epilepsie musicogènique. *Rev. Neur.*, **80**, 635.

INGEGNIEROS, J. (1907) La language musical et les troubles hysteriques. *Études de Psychol. Clin.*, Paris, 1907.

JOYNT, R. J., GREEN, D., and GREEN, R. (1962) Musicogenic epilepsy. *J. Am. Med. Ass.*, **179**, 501–504.

LUCAS, J. (1790) An account of the singular effects of music on a patient. *Lond. Med. J.*, **11**, 125–130.

MERZHEEVSKY, J. P. (1884) Sloochai epilepsi prepedki kotoroi vizibayootsya nekotopemi musikelmimi tonomi. *Minutes meeting St. Petersburg Soc. Psych.*

NIKITIN, M. P. (1935) Zur Psychogenese der epileptischen Anfälle. *Nervenarzt*, **8**, 66–69.

OPPENHEIMER, H. (1905–6) Psychasthenische Krampfe. *Jour. f. Psych. u. Neur.*, **6**, 257.

PIETROWSKI, A. (1959) A case of musicogenic epilepsy observed by clinical and bio-electrical methods. *Neur.; Neurochir.; Psychiat. Pol.*, **9**, 39–44.

ROSENHAIM, E. (1921) Ueber Reflexepilepsie. *Zeit. f.d.g. Neur. u. Psych.*, **64**, 99–110.

SCHÄFER, G. (1967) Musicogene Epilepsie im Kindersalter. *Mschr. Kinderhailk.*, **115**, (1), 47–50.

SCHOEN, M. (Ed). (1927) *The Effects of Music*, London, Kegan Paul.

SEAR, H. G. (1939) Music and medicine. *Music and Letters*, **20**, 43–54. London.

SHAW, D. and HILL, D. (1947) Case of musicogenic epilepsy. *J. Neur. Neurosurg. Psych.*, **10**, 107–117.

STEINBRUGGE Quoted by Trutovsky (*q.v.*)

STRANG, R. R. (1966) A case of musical epilepsy. *Irish Med. Ass.*, **59**, 351.

STUBBE TEGLBJAERG, H. P. (1949) On musicogenic epilepsy. *Acta psych. Neur.*, **24**, 679–688.

TAYLOR, S. (1942) Musicogenic epilepsy. *Jour. R.N. Med. Serv.*, **28**, 394–5.

TRUTOVSKY, Y. Y. (No date) Epilepsia, proyavlyayoskekayasya pod oliyaneem zvookovik razdrazheni. *Arch. Psych. Neur. i crimin. Psychopath.*

VERCELLATTO, P. (1953) A propos d'un cas de epilepsie musicogènique. *Rev. Neur.*, **88**, 379–382.

VON BECHTEREW, V. (1914–15) O reflektornoi epilepsi pod oliyaniem evyookovich razdrazheniye. *Obozrenie Psichiat.*, **19**, 513.

WEBER, R. (1956) Musikogene Epilepsie. *Nervenarzt.*, **27**, 340.

# Musicogenic Epilepsy

*(2) The Later Story: its relation to auditory hallucinatory phenomena*

Musicogenic epilepsy is a disorder where auditory features are important, and in particular those of musical type. They are encountered by neurologists and psychiatrists in a variety of conditions as diverse as alcoholic hallucinosis and temporal lobe epilepsy. Sometimes the sound may be ill-defined buzzings or hummings or it may have a clearer quality such as the ringing of alarm-clocks or guitar playing. Generally, the hallucinatory phenomena, sounds without external physical cause, are perceived inside the head as though heard by both ears, but rarely patients report that they seem to come from one ear only (Bergman, 1965). Disturbing hallucinations, though they may occur in anyone, may cause a particular problem for musicians. This was so in the case of Robert Schumann who suffered from subjective auditory phenomena in the last years of his life before his tragic death. Apparently the particular note "A" was constantly sounding in his head and made his life a misery (Révész, 1953). Such noises are not uncommon in degenerative processes of the inner ear associated with deafness and it is conceivable that Beethoven also suffered from them.

Auditory hallucinations are common in psychiatric practice. They often take the form of voices but this is not always the case, as patients with acute psychotic disorders hear confused noises and whistling as well as more organised sounds like the rattling of trains, the throbbing of a steamer or music at a concert. Sometimes these sounds are interpreted as speech, referring to the patient himself and having a special meaning for him (Jaspers, 1963). The auditory phenomena of the psychiatric disorder alcoholic hallucinosis are of particular interest (Victor and Hope, 1958). It is a psychosis associated with alcoholic withdrawal but in contrast to delirium tremens the patients with alcoholic hallucinosis have exclusively subjective auditory disturbances and report them in clear consciousness unlike the confused state of a patient with delirium tremens. Sometimes the disturbance begins with brief but intense rhythmical sounds such as tapping, or they take the form of short repeated phrases like "You are a fool" or "I'll get you" (Scott et al., 1967). Usually musical phenomena in this condition have been regarded as rare (Victor and Hope, 1958) but recently Robert Scott (1975) has observed that they may occur in as many as 63 per cent. of patients. These hallucinations are found in the early withdrawal phase preceding other types of subjective phenomena, they are often pleasant rather than frightening and are characterised by a chant-like quality.

The hallucinatory phenomena of temporal lobe epilepsy were examined by Currie et al. (1971) in the course of a detailed analysis of 666 patients with temporal lobe epilepsy. They found that though cephalic and abdominal sensations were reported in 40 per cent. of sufferers, special sensory phenomena affecting the auditory system were present in 16 per cent. These were of various types and often crude sensations were noted. They occurred five times more commonly than those of an elaborate type such as music. The quality of the sensation reported by the patients differed in different individuals but was always totally involving. It could be merely rhythmical; as one patient said "I am aware of a beating in my head and then I know I will usually have a fit." This is not merely a vague feeling of rhythm like someone tapping a pencil at the other end of the room but rather a commanding sensation as might be created by the whole of a brass section of the orchestra playing *fortissimo*. In other patients the sensations prior to, or incorporated in, the epileptic seizure have a melodic quality and much less often words are grafted onto a musical theme. These phenomena of temporal lobe epilepsy were separated into three categories by Hill and Mitchell (1953). Firstly, there were those in which a discrete cortical disturbance was thought to occur and simple auditory phenomena such as banging, ticking and whistling were found. Secondly, those in which the integrated cortex was involved and bell-ringing, repeated words and short phrases occurred. In a third category the disturbances were of a more complex type and the person indicated that there were not just auditory but also visual phenomena. In addition an emotional element was often present. One patient said, "A series of thoughts and scenes that I cannot remember, things and people seem strange and I seem as though I have been through this before."

From these examples it therefore appears that auditory phenomena reported in patients are diverse, and that rhythmical, melodic and verbal elements may be found either singly or in combination. These different elements may also be of importance in relation to cerebral localisation (Gordon and Bogen 1974), a topic covered in Chapters 9 and 16. For our purpose, however, music appears to be of particular importance in relation to temporal lobe epilepsy and musicogenic epilepsy and these two conditions will now be compared.

*Are musicogenic and temporal lobe epilepsy related?*

Musicogenic epilepsy is one form of reflex epilepsy, a disorder in which a seizure follows immediately after the patient is exposed to a particular stimulus (Daube, 1966). It is usually complex instrumental music in which many instruments are involved, a dance band or a full orchestra, music which can create an inner emotional response. Sometimes organ or piano music may be responsible and it may act as a stimulus only to the person who is playing the instrument. Simple sounds such as the ringing of bells very occasionally act as a precipitant. Patients with musicogenic epilepsy usually find that the appropriate provocative musical precipitant to their attacks produces unpleasant emotional changes. The observer notices apprehension and agitation, and in the test situation (see below) the patient may ask for the music to be turned off. In comparison the emotional concomitants of temporal lobe attacks with musical components are varied and may comprise for example, anger, fear or panic (Williams, 1956). The provocative stimulus of a seizure in individuals with musicogenic epilepsy usually has a variety of musical qualities, as noted above, but in the patient with temporal lobe epilepsy intense rhythmical qualities are prominent while melodic elements are much less often reported.

What sort of musical ability and experience has the person with musicogenic epilepsy compared with the individual who suffers from temporal lobe seizures? Here, there is a clear distinction.

Musicogenic epilepsy tends to occur more often in musically talented people. On the other hand, a person with temporal lobe epilepsy is no more likely to have been musically talented than any other member of the population at large. The patient with musicogenic epilepsy clearly remembers what has precipitated his attacks, for example a particular tune played in a special way, while the individual with temporal lobe epilepsy recalls only with difficulty both the warning and the seizure. It is a hazy memory like a film seen many years before.

These comparisons have been mentioned previously by Michaux et al. (1958). They noted that "musical perception" may often be distorted in cases of temporal dysfunction, temporal lobe epilepsy and musicogenic epilepsy being the two main examples. In the latter case the "perception" preceded the epileptic manifestation, whereas for temporal lobe epilepsy it could either precede or form part of a seizure.

Electroencephalographic (EEG) studies (see below) are of importance, as both patients with musicogenic and temporal lobe epilepsy show abnormality predominantly over the temporal lobes. However, in musicogenic epilepsy there is an equal chance that it will involve the right or the left hemisphere (Poskanzer et al., 1962), whereas in temporal lobe epilepsy the EEG disturbance occurs almost twice as often over the left side (Currie et al., 1971).

## The EEG in musicogenic epilepsy

Musicogenic epilepsy was first described by Critchley in 1937 at a time when electroencephalography was in its infancy and probably the first case to be studied electroencephalographically was reported by Shaw and Hill (1947). The technique is useful because changes are seen both during and between seizures. Further, it has permitted not only a clearer delineation of different types of epilepsy but has also made it possible to get rid finally of the notion that musicogenic epilepsy is some form of hysterical disorder.

Musicogenic epilepsy is one variety of reflex epilepsy, a disorder in which the specific stimulus can be auditory, visual or in other modalities of sensation. The reflex epilepsies are all rare types of seizure disorder. For example, I personally may see only one or two cases of these each year out of a thousand or more patients referred for investigation of epilepsy. It should be further emphasised that musicogenic epilepsy is perhaps the rarest form of reflex epilepsy. In my experience only one case in ten years has been seen, during which time three cases of reading epilepsy were diagnosed. Since the original description there has been a steady trickle of papers usually dealing with a single instance or a very small series of patients. Thus Titeca (1965) was able to make a detailed review of 65 published cases, but since that time relatively few further reports seem to have appeared.

The reflex epilepsies can be divided into two categories depending on whether the stimulus is simple or complex, a distinction which is particularly clear-cut in cases where visual stimuli act as precipitants for the seizures. There are firstly the patients who have a fit as a result of the unpatterned flashing light as delivered by a stroboscope, a "simple" stimulus. Secondly, there are other individuals who only respond to a more "complex" stimulus, for example patients with reading epilepsy (Critchley et al., 1960). Here not only light but pattern and possibly emotional factors are also essential for the stimulus to act as a specific trigger. The same general categorisation applies to auditory reflex epilepsy – the audiogenic or sonogenic epilepsy. In some instances loud startling noises lead to a seizure and in others music is responsible, nothing startling, nothing abrupt and not necessarily loud. There are however intermediate cases where a protracted monotonous sound of the ringing of a telephone bell, the hissing of a kettle or the whirring of machinery can trigger an attack. In the complex reflex epilepsies, i.e. both reading and musicogenic epilepsy, it is often necessary for the stimulus to be continued for relatively long periods before a seizure develops. The abnormal EEG patterns evoked by specific stimuli in cases of reflex epilepsy are of two main types, a discharge which appears in a widespread fashion over the hemispheres from the beginning as is seen with photogenic epilepsy, or, in contra-distinction a discharge seen to start in a localised fashion usually over one or other temporal lobe and then spread widely as the seizure progresses, as is the case in musicogenic epilepsy.

The EEG is of value in reflex epilepsies in general, and musicogenic epilepsy in particular, because detailed studies are possible during various forms of musical and auditory stimulation directed towards inducing seizures (Daly and Barry, 1957; Poskanzer et al., 1962). It is possible to test which aspects of the stimulus are important, that is to say its rhythmical, its melodic or other physical qualities and even emotional characteristics. However, laboratory attempts at precipitating attacks are not without difficulty. First, the artificial nature of the test situation, with attached electrodes as well as the presence of equipment and observers, often means that though the appropriate stimuli derived from the patient's own accounts, are used, no seizures result, a well known observation in a variety of types of reflex epilepsy (Scott, 1971). Secondly, the musical stimulus may need to be continued for many minutes in order to induce an attack (Bickford and Klass, 1969).

The latency between the presentation of the stimulus and the occurrence of a seizure may be one of the factors that account for the relative rarity of musicogenic epilepsy, in that the stimulus may not always be continued for a sufficiently long period to evoke a seizure, an important practical point in the investigation of all forms of reflex epilepsy. Perhaps the yield of cases of musicogenic epilepsy would be increased if auditory stimuli and in particular, musical passages were part of the routine EEG assessment. Gastaut and Pirovano (1949), attempted something of this sort when they examined 50 patients suffering from various types of epilepsy. They used high intensity sounds and found that it was only when these were inter-mittent that EEG changes and clinical attacks occurred.

These findings are of interest because they correspond with the observations of intermittent visual stimulation of the type provided by the stroboscope used in routine EEG work. However the seizures that Gastaut and Pirovano provoked were of the petit mal type and were probably some form of "startle" epilepsy in contrast to the complex psychomotor seizure which characterises most patients with musicogenic epilepsy.

What have EEG studies shown? Shaw and Hill (1947) investigated not only changes in cerebral potentials but also various other physiological parameters and noted increases in blood pressure, heart rate and respiration while the patient was listening to music. These were associated with overt signs of emotion, for example agitation and tearfulness. They observed that different types of music would elicit a fit after about five minutes, but that pure tones did not have this property. Furthermore, between seizures the EEG was abnormal and showed a disturbance in the form of high voltage irregular delta activity which tended to be more prominent over the left temporal region. When the seizure occurred there was a cortical discharge consisting of bilaterally sychronous elements of 6 cycles per second, steadily increasing in voltage and falling in frequency into the delta range as the attack proceeded. The investigation, however, was somewhat limited because electroencephalographic recordings at that time had only a few channels and spread of the attack was therefore difficult to assess. Nevertheless, in this complex case with many psychiatric features, Shaw and Hill proved that the attacks were occurring on an organic basis, but they were unable to establish the nature of the underlying process in spite of detailed neuroradiological investigations.

Three cases of musicogenic epilepsy with EEG investigations were reported by Daly and Barry (1957). In particular they noted that the temporal lobe was involved, the right hemisphere in two patients and the left in another. Furthermore, they introduced the idea that musicogenic epilepsy could be sub-divided into two categories, a primary type in which seizures occurred exclusively with music, and a secondary type in which seizures had occurred previously and were precipitated subsequently by exposure to music. This distinction is of value, since in their view the physical attributes of the stimulus appear to be of significance in the secondary type, whereas in the primary type the emotional changes aroused by the stimulus are of greater importance, a point which is relevant to possible therapy (see below).

Other authors have described EEG abnormalities in patients with musicogenic epilepsy. Teglbjaerg (1949) reported four such patients. One is of particular interest since there was evidence of a right hemisphere epileptic discharge and scarring of the temporal lobe. As a result of surgical excision of the scarred area the patient improved. Vercelletto (1953) noted a right temporal discharge during musical stimulation. More recently Joynt et al. (1962) observed a patient who had seizures induced by Bach organ music while the EEG was monitored. They were able to demonstrate that sharp wave activity was seen in the temporal areas when a seizure occurred; hillbilly music, which the patient felt might provoke an attack, did not do so in the test situation. Reifenberg (1958) reported a patient in whom music, as well as knocking and banging noises, led to seizures. In this instance during the attack a right fronto-temporal disturbance was seen but the EEG, between attacks, did not show any very specific changes. Perhaps the case of musicogenic epilepsy which has had the most detailed investigation is that of Poskanzer et al. (1962). They studied a 62 year old man who had psychomotor seizures for six years occurring only when he heard the sound of bells. The only possible relevant information in the history was that he had previously suffered a blow in the left temporal region which resulted in a brief period of unconsciousness. Routine and sleep EEGs showed no abnormality, but when a tracing was made during the playing of a record of church bells a left temporal disturbance appeared which progressed as a seizure ensued. To study further the physical characteristics of the trigger to this patient's attacks the frequency band of various bell recordings was investigated. It was found that if the cut-off point was one octave or more a seizure occurred, but sound of a smaller frequency range than this, wherever it lay in the whole frequency spectrum, was ineffectual. When the sequence was played in reverse order there was no effect. Pure tones which sounded like bells and an organ with a similar quality to the former were without effect on the patient as was white noise containing all frequencies presented with the same rhythmic effect. There did not appear to be any evidence of emotional change when the bells were played, though it seems that the initial impact of the sound was essential for producing a seizure.

The EEG changes in published reports on musicogenic epilepsy were also reviewed in detail by Poskanzer et al. (1962). The abnormalities were divided into those between attacks and those occurring during the actual seizure. In the former category information was available in 19 patients, seven showed focal abnormalities equally on both sides, the other seven showed non-focal disturbance, and in the remainder the tracing was regarded as normal. Adequate information about the EEG during seizures was available on 15 patients. Of these left-sided abnormality was reported in seven (four were temporally located, the remainder over the pre- and/or post-central areas) six showed right temporal disturbance and two generalised dysrhythmia. There are also isolated reports in which seizures occurred without convincing EEG change (Hamoir and Titeca, 1948) a feature which has been reported in some other forms of epilepsy. This happens mainly when the discharge arises and remains deeply placed and rather remote from scalp electrodes, for example in the amygdala. There are, however, no reported cases of musicogenic epilepsy in which attempts have been made to locate "remote" foci with depth electrodes.

These studies show beyond doubt that musicogenic epilepsy is a definite, if rare, clinical entity but difficulties remain in deciding just how the attacks are provoked. In some patients the seizures happen on occasions quite unrelated to music and indeed any known precipitant; in others they occur only with music and often specific types of music. Therefore the recognition of complex musical patterns is necessary for precipitation. It follows then that memory is important and indeed seizures can be precipitated in rare instances only by the recall of music (Critchley, 1937) without any external stimulus whatever. As music is such a potent trigger some patients always avoid it because of the effect it might have. Others, however, are aware of the times when they are sensitive to music and when they are not. This feeling is perhaps akin to that of a migrainous sufferer who is conscious that a certain precipitant, for example eating chocolate or cheese, will or will not at a particular time produce a headache. In some people with musicogenic epilepsy, as in the patient described by Poskanzer et al. (1962), it appears that the physical quality of the stimulus is all important, whereas in others not only is it necessary for the music to be played for sufficient time to provoke an attack but it seems to create an emotional state and then the seizure results. A personally observed patient became extremely alarmed at the prospect of EEG investigation in case music would be played during it. She had previously been thoroughly investigated and diagnosed as having musicogenic epilepsy; however, on this occasion quite a different problem was responsible for her referral.

It therefore appears that there is no unitary view of the mechanism of precipitation of musicogenic epilepsy and each case deserves to be investigated separately in this respect, a factor of importance in choosing the type of therapy to be adopted.

*The treatment of musicogenic epilepsy.* Most cases of musicogenic epilepsy, like the majority of the patients who have reflex epilepsies, do not present any serious therapeutic problem, as they respond to conventional anticonvulsant medication. However, there are two other possible methods that have been adopted in the treatment of musicogenic epilepsy in resistant cases. In the first, the patient is desensitised to music using a behaviour therapy technique, and in the second a psychotherapeutic approach is adopted for patients in whom there is a marked emotional element.

The behaviour therapy approach was employed by Forster and his colleagues for one patient with musicogenic epilepsy (Forster et al., 1965) as well as other cases of reflex epilepsy. The technique has two main bases. Firstly, the observation that a stimulus presented to one ear in the case of musicogenic epilepsy or one eye in the case of photically induced seizures, is less likely to induce an attack than stimuli presented to both ears or eyes. Further, unilateral presentations of noxious stimuli may lead to desensitisation of the patient. Secondly, a hierarchy of stimuli from the innocuous to the most noxious is established. In the case described by Forster et al. the latter kind elicited left temporal lobe spikes on the EEG. They found that innocuous music when listened to by the patient with both ears failed to reduce the sensitivity to subsequent presentations of the noxious variety. Similarly, when the patient listened to noxious music with only one ear, he was not desensitised to later binaural presentation. However, they found that a particular musical piece available commercially in many versions was innocuous in an organ or piano presentation, but noxious when played by the full orchestra. By gradual introduction of the provocative orchestral version into the innocuous version, desensitisation was achieved. Then it was possible to play music at increased speed or in a syncopated fashion, usually highly provocative stimuli, without any untoward effects. This study, admittedly carried out on only one patient, does imply that there are conditioning factors important in the genesis of musicogenic epilepsy.

The second line of treatment, the psycho-therapeutic approach, was adopted successfully by Daly and Barry (1957) in one of their patients. This 24 year old woman as a child "felt transported by loud swing music and discovered that by concentrating intensely she could see visions". Later some six months after a relatively minor head injury she had her first nocturnal generalised convulsion. Shortly thereafter visual hallucinations began to appear without conscious effort when music was heard. Later, loud dance band music engulfed her with "fear and a feeling of impending disaster. Her heart pounded, her breathing was rapid and her palms perspired. After a variable time, ordinarily a few minutes, an attack ensued with characteristic EEG abnormality." Anti-convulsant therapy was ineffective, so exploratory and interpretative therapy was commenced. This was continued for 120 hours over a period of seven months and revealed that music produced sado-masochistic sexual fantasies. As a result of therapy it took 15 minutes of music to produce an attack whereas previously this had been induced by as little as two minutes of the same record. Unfortunately treatment was interrupted because the patient moved to another part of the U.S.A. However, further progress was later achieved with another therapist. This case clearly reveals the somewhat complicated nature of the musical stimulus, although the physical attributes, the loudness of the music and the type were important, there was a strong emotional element. This is certainly borne out by another case (Fenton, 1975). The patient, again a woman, was married to a musician. Apart from seizures induced by music there was a marked fear of going out, amounting to a specific phobia. After the musicogenic epilepsy was treated successfully by desensitisation, the phobia remained.

## Conclusion

Musicogenic epilepsy constitutes even today something of a neurological curiosity, but like all rare disorders it is of interest because it can provide an impetus for detailed investigations which not only add to the knowledge about the particular condition under study, but in some respects to the understanding of the function of the nervous system itself. Musicogenic epilepsy, perhaps the rarest form of reflex epilepsy, is no exception. Whether there is some common factor pervading all the manifold experiences of music, remains uncertain, for to some patients it is essentially an emotional experience, to others a perceptual one and to yet others almost entirely intellectual. The nature of the provoking stimulus for musicogenic epilepsy is certainly not the same for each individual, or if it were, there would still be some elusive all-pervading aspect which has not so far been revealed.

## REFERENCES

BERGMAN, P. S. (1965) Unilateral auditory hallucinations. *Trans. Amer. Neurol. Assoc.*, **90**, 226.

BICKFORD, R. G. and KLASS, D. (1969) In: *Basic Mechanisms of the Epilepsies.* London, Little Brown & Co.

CRITCHLEY, MACDONALD (1937) Musicogenic epilepsy. *Brain*, **60**, 13.

CRITCHLEY, M., COBB, W. A. and SEARS, T. A. (1960) On reading epilepsy. *Epilepsia* (Amst.), **1**, 403.

CURRIE, S, HEATHFIELD, K. W. G., HENSON, R. A, and SCOTT, D. F (1971) Clinical course and prognosis of temporal lobe epilepsy. A survey of 666 patients. *Brain*, **94**, 173.

DALY, D. D., BARRY, M. J. (1957) Musicogenic epilepsy: Report of three cases. *Psychosomatic Medicine*, **19**, 399.

DAUBE, J. R. (1966) Sensory precipitated seizures: a review. *J. Nerv. Ment. Dis.*, **141**, 524.

FENTON, G. W. (1975) Personal communication.

FORSTER, F. M., HALLGRIM, K., PETERSON, W. G., BENGZON, A. R. A. (1965) Modification of musicogenic epilepsy by extinction technique. *Trans Amer. Neurol. Assoc.*, **90**, 179.

GASTAUT, H. and PIROVANO, E. (1949) Epilepssia indotta da stimolazione uditiva intermittente ritmica o epilepssia psofogenica. *Arch Psicol. Neurol. Psichiat.*, **10**, 297.

GORDON, H. W. and BOGEN, J. E. (1974) Hemispheric lateralisation of singing after intra-carotid sodium amylobarbitone. *J. Neurol. Neurosurg. Psychiat.*, **37**, 727.

HAMOIR and TITECA, J. (1948) Étude éléctro éncephalographique d'un cas d'épilepsie musicogénique. *Rev. neurol.*, **80**, 635.

HILL, D. and MITCHELL, W. R. (1953) Epileptic amnesia. *Folia Psychiat. Neerl.*, **56**, 718.

JASPERS, K. (1963) *General Psychopathology* (translated from German by J. Hoenig and M. W. Hamilton, Manchester). Manchester University Press.

JOYNT, R. J., GREEN, D. and GREEN, R. (1962) Musicogenic epilepsy. *J. Am. Med. Ass.*, **179**, 501.

MICHAUX, L., KOUPERNIK, C. and LABER, R. (1958) Des perceptions musicales pathologiques. Rôle du lobe temporal. À propos de trois observations. *Sem. Hôp. Paris.*, **34**, 9.

POSKANZER, D. C., BROWN, A. E. and MILLER, H. (1962) Musicogenic epilepsy caused only by a discrete frequency band of church bells. *Brain*, **85**, 77.

REIFENBERGE, E. (1958) Beitrag zur Kasuistik der musikogen Epilepsie. *Psychiat. Neurol. Med. Psychol.* (Lpz.), **10**, 80-91.

RÉVÉSZ, G. (1953) *Introduction to the Psychology of Music*. London, Longmans Green.

SCOTT, D. F. (1971) What triggers the individual fit? An Account of Sensory Precipitated Reflex Epilepsy. *Journal of British Epilepsy Association*, Spring issue, 3.

SCOTT, D. F., DAVIS, D. L. and MALHERBE, E. M. E. L. (1967) Alcoholic hallucinosis. *Int. J. Addict.*, **4**, 319.

SCOTT, ROBERT T. (1975) Hallucinations of music in alcohol withdrawal. *Neurology*, **24**, 362.

SHAW, D. and HILL, D. (1947) A case of musicogenic epilepsy. *J. Neurol. Neurosurg. Psychiat.*, **47**, 107.

TEGLBJAERG, H. P. S. (1949) On musicogenic epilepsy. *Acta Psychiat. et Neurol. Scandinav.*, **4**, 679.

TITECA, J. (1965) L'Épilepsie musicogénique. Revue générale à propos d'un cas personnel suivi pendant quartorze ans. *Acta Neurol. Belg.*, **65**, 598.

VERCELLETTO, P. (1953) À propos d'un d'épilepsie musicogénique. Presentation d'une crise temporal, discussion sur son point de départ. *Rev. neurol.*, **88**, 379.

VICTOR, M. and HOPE, J. N. (1958) The phenomena of auditory hallucinations in chronic alcoholism. *J. Nerv. Ment. Dis.*, **126**, 451.

WILLIAMS, D. (1956) The structure of emotions reflected in epileptic experiences. *Brain*, **79**, 29.

# Occupational Palsies in Musical Performers

Anaxagoras indeed asserts that it is in his possession of hands that makes man the most intelligent of the animals; but surely the reasonable point of view is that it is because he is the most intelligent animal that he has got hands. Hands are an instrument; and Nature, like a sensible human being, always assigns an organ to the animal that can use it.

Aristotle. *De partibus animalium.* IV. X

*Gweddw crefft heb ei dawn* (Without inspiration, technical skill is sterile).

University of Wales

The German expression *Beschäftigungsneurosen* is usually attached to what in the English medical literature are usually called craft or occupational palsies. These terms apply to maladies in which certain symptoms are excited by the attempt to perform an often-repeated muscular action, commonly one that is involved in the occupation of the sufferer. Such was the definition proffered by Gowers in his Manual, wherein he gave a masterly account of the most common of all the contemporary craft palsies, namely writer's cramp. He gave credit to Sir Charles Bell for the first description of what he called in 1844, scrivener's palsy. Gowers also referred to comparable disorders which might afflict professional musicians especially pianists, violinists and harpists.

The second classic contribution dates from 1897 with Vivian Poore's *Nervous Affections of the Hand.* By 1894 he had collected and studied at least 300 cases of writer's cramp.

The third brilliant account we owe to J. Collier and W. J. Adie in their contribution to the first edition of *Price's Textbook of Medicine*, 1922. Collier, having been afforded the opportunity of studying the neurological problems in the Central Post Office, was able to write a classic account of telegraphist's cramp, something which V. Poore had never encountered although it was known to him.

In many of the older medical textbooks the occupational palsies were relegated to a section lumping together a mishmash of ill-understood conditions such as tics, torticollis, stammering, and even Parkinson's disease, implying that such affections were mysterious in origin, and probably psychogenic.

Later, the attitude changed and it became realised that the "occupational neuroses" of the German neurologists display many common features of putative importance from an aetiological standpoint.

For example, the neurosis, palsy, or cramp usually arises in connection with the performance over a lengthy period of an exquisite motor skill which forms an integral element of the victim's work or profession. Thus solicitors' clerks who had to execute copperplate penmanship hour after hour, day after day, might eventually succumb to writer's cramp. Stenographers sometimes developed typist's cramp. Those operating a Morse key for inordinate periods of time were liable to telegraphist's cramp. Musical performers, professionals rather than amateurs, not unexpectedly are at risk as regards craft palsies.

In many cases fatigue from ill-health or emotional stress plays an additional background role.

Sometimes a further aetiological factor is operative, namely that of interruption. Thus, a post office telegraphist might have retired after years of successful keyboard transmission. After a break of five years or so he might be recalled to re-assume the duties of a telegraphist, only to find that not only has he lost his former technical skill, but early becomes a victim of cramp.

Of musical executants pianists are perhaps most often afflicted by occupational cramps or palsies. The extraordinary complexity of the manipulative skill of an accomplished pianoforte player is often taken for granted by physiologists.

The Victorian surgeon Sir James Paget once studied intently Mlle. Janotha as she played a *presto* by Mendelssohn: he estimated that in the course of 4 min 3 sec the pianist had sounded 5595 notes, executing 72 bimanual finger-movements per second. When one adds to these rapid motor activities the task of maintaining a correct seated posture, and perhaps also simultaneously reading and interpreting a difficult musical score, the fantastic complexity of the achievement can be realised.

The symptoms of pianist's cramp may implicate either hand, or both. An actual muscular weakness does not develop so much as a tonic spasm which mechanically impedes rapid and dextrous fingering. According to V. Poore the extensors of the wrist are the first muscles to be so involved. Sooner or later aching pains in the forearm are complained of and interfere still more with the player's expertise.

Unlike most occupational disorders pianist's palsy affects females more often than males.

Reference has been made to the importance of posture in piano-playing. A rather unexpected type of craft palsy has been seen in at least two professional performers of "light" music. Both victims would experience during their stage performance a steady, relentless spasm of one sterno-mastoid muscle causing the head and neck to twist to the right. In this way the pianist's gaze would stray from the keyboard so as to confront the audience.

Of considerable interest are the varieties of "cramp" which may afflict violinists. Some of them are so bizarre that at times it may be extremely difficult even with the help of electrical methods to decide whether the impaired skill is an occupational palsy, or the product of some subtle underlying disorder of quite a different type though wholly organic, e.g. incipient Parkinsonism, brachial mononeuritis, a cervical root affection, or even an apraxia. The same problem in differential diagnosis also applies to the disabilities affecting pianists.

There are craft palsies which involve the violinist's hand which is responsible for the fingering or – rather commoner – the right, or bowing hand.

If the motor skill entailed in piano-playing be conceded as exceptional, even more elaborate and in many ways artificial is the performance of a violinist. Quite apart from the wholly asymmetrical techniques of the two hands, there is the unfortunate posture which the player has to adopt whether he be seated or stands erect. The whole art of violin playing must be deemed in simple language excessively tiring.

According to Carl Flesch (whose monograph of 1930 is perhaps somewhat "dated") many of the defects to which violinists are prone late in their career result from incorrect techniques which stem from their days of apprenticeship. These faults will be enumerated later, for it is questionable whether Flesch was correct in making a sharp distinction between these errors and those that he called "purely psychic hindrances". The latter he divided into (a) hindrances due to general nervosity or stage-fright; (b) hindrances due to emotional paralysis; (c) hindrances due to overvaluation of the technical moment; (d) hindrances due to an exaggerated urge for perfection; and (e) hindrances due to coercive fixed ideas.

Regarding the last-named group, it was claimed that the power of imagination is usually the weak point of a violinist's artistic personality, and is emphasised by a certain inborn shyness, a want of expansiveness – in a word, by psychic bashfulness. Hindrances due to overvaluation of the technical factors comprise a diversity of phobias – dread of certain left-hand runs, of certain bow-strokes, and of trembling of the bow. Flesch referred to one of his pupils who was plagued by the fixed idea that before difficult passages he had a mental picture of an individual whom he hated and who had cursed the passage, with the result that he could not manage to play it. The pupil was advised to ban this "evil spirit" by conjuring up a "good spirit" – in point of fact, his fiancée. This simple psychotherapy proved efficacious.

Kato Havas, in her valuable monograph on the causes and treatment of nervous affections in violin-playing, posed the interesting question why it is that Hungarian gypsy-players appear to be immune to such disorders. She said that the reasons are manifold, but "first of all they are not burdened with the responsibilities of our social system. They do not have to do better than their fellows in order to succeed. In fact, they would be hard pressed to understand why anybody wants to succeed at all. Secondly, their sole interest is the pleasure of the listeners. They are free from all obligations, except the one and only obligation – to communicate."

The same author went on to enumerate and describe the various faults in technique attributable to sheer anxiety. She catalogued eight common phobias: the fear of dropping the violin; of the trembling bowing arm; of being out of tune; of high positions and shifts; of not being loud enough; of not being fast enough; of memory-lapses; and, finally, of not being good enough.

An occupational affection of the right arm in violinists is all the more troublesome because it cannot be concealed, being promptly detected by the sensitive ear of the orchestral conductor. What usually happens is a prolonging of either the adductive or abductive movement of the bowing arm, causing an audible and offensive extension of the note, upsetting the co-ordination of the whole orchestra. This is the affection which certain professionals dub "violinist's cancer".

Flesch was inclined, rightly or wrongly, to ascribe such a phenomenon to faulty teaching and inadequate practice. He did not speak of an occupational palsy – and indeed he seems almost to have ignored the subject – but he enumerated exaggerated movement of the wrist, of the finger-stroke in bow-shifts, unnatural movements of the fingers; a posture of the arm which is too high; an insufficient expenditure of bow; undue clinging to a point of contact; a continued inflexible bow pressure; or perhaps a superficial bow stroke with inadequate pressure. To Steinhausen belongs the credit for repudiating the idolatrous worship of the horizontal wrist movement.

Left-hand faults, which Flesch again put down to errors of technique (without mentioning craft-palsies), consist in exaggerated finger-pressure; undue flatness of the application of the fingers; inordinate rolling of the arm either to the left or to the right; pressure of the upper arm against the wall of the chest; over-hollowing of the hand so that the finger nails and not the pulps touch the strings; and increase or decrease of vibrato. These faults doubtless impede the progress of the learner but each one of these may also develop in a violinist of experience.

At this point one may discuss the question of ageing as affecting the skill of a professional violinist, and whether this "violinist's arteriosclerosis" as it has been called, is actually pathological or biological. The question ties up with the philosophical doubts as to whether the ageing process of the brain is a purely physiological operation of natural decay, or whether it is "pathological" and represents the product of a multiplicity of minimal lesions.

As far as violinists are concerned, technical deterioration seems to set in far earlier than in concert pianists. Typically it shows itself in what Flesch called "an atrophy of the *vibrato*". There are other characteristics, too, e.g. insecurity in change of position, unsteadiness in the sustained bow tones, and loss of digital elasticity. In his memoirs Flesch showed himself to be hypercritical if not captious, and he boldly stated that he was able to detect senile faults in many of his great predecessors. Thus Joachim was latterly heard to play shakily, out of tune, and without *vibrato*. His fingers had become stiff with gout, so that semitones in the higher positions came critically close to whole tones. As Sarasate grew old his art too began to show unpleasing features – he played sharp, and without *vibrato*. Rosé displayed a similar impairment in vibrato with advancing years. Ysaÿe remained in his prime until 1910 when he was 52 years of age, after which his bowing became tremulous. Ten years later he gave a disastrous performance in Vienna. At the age of 70 he became diabetic and could no longer play the violin, spending his last years first as a conductor and then as a composer. According to Flesch, the fundamental defect behind Ysaÿe's technical deterioration was that he never used the little finger of the right hand at the nut, but clasped the bow with three fingers only.

In 1911, Ysaÿe, Kreisler, Elman and Flesch lunched together and afterwards each played something of his choice, Ysaÿe played Vieuxtemps' *D minor concerto* and Flesch, Nardini's *D major sonata*. Whereupon Ysaÿe – already by this time a heavy drinker – sighed "Ah! si j'avais la tranquillité de votre archet!"

Achille Rivarde's violin-playing in private was superb but on the concert-platform he was disappointing. This was the result of an uncoordinated interplay of an overwhelming inner impulse with his mastery of the necessary technical resources.

It seems as though Flesch had something derogatory to say about all the great violinists with the exception of himself and Kreisler. Havas also referred to Kreisler, and explained his consistent brilliance by his ability to combine the ease of a gypsy with the music of Bach.

The role of spatial phobias in violinists was exemplified in one professional of my acquaintance who found himself unable to perform in Philharmonic concerts where he had to be seated high above ground-level. He developed a dread of heights and feared he would topple off his "riser" and crash. No such problem existed when he played in an orchestral pit, or on the stage at ground level.

Cellists, on the whole, are less prone to occupational palsies. Their posture on the concert platform is more relaxed than in the case of violinists. However, Lord Platt has isolated two or three specific affections. The first of these, "cellist's thigh", results from the performer being compelled to sit, sometimes for hours, on a hard unyielding stacking chair with two metal bars pressing against each thigh. Platt's second syndrome is cellist's osteo-arthritis of the second left interphalangeal joint, which is of course a structural lesion and not an occupational palsy. The third variety is a hyperpnoeic dystonia or "cellist's panic" which is due to hyperventilation tetany resulting from sheer stage-fright. Of the foregoing only the last can be regarded as falling within the ranks of a craft palsy.

Trumpeter's palsy is somewhat of a rarity. Again an elaborate synchronisation of numerous controlled movements combines to form the necessary embouchure in players of wind instruments. Peripheral defects such as lesions of the lips, teeth or jaws may render the correct playing of such instruments as the trumpet, the oboe, or the flute uncomfortable if not impossible. Quite apart from the effect of any oral or dental lesions, there are acquired disabilities which can be looked upon as true craft palsies. They are of special interest from the point of view of aetiology in that they concern motor mechanisms which are neither manual nor digital.

Drummer's palsy, though rare, has been described, as has harpist's cramp.

## NATURE AND PATHOPHYSIOLOGY OF OCCUPATIONAL PALSIES

No one today seriously ascribes the genuine cases of writer's cramp and the many other varieties of occupational palsy, to sheer nervosity. The cause of musician's cramp lies deeper than simple stage-fright, or even faulty learning techniques or senile deterioration. Gowers shrewdly visualised the pathology in all these diverse affections as being "central", but in using this term he was careful to warn us against allowing "mathematical conceptions to govern our physiological ideas".

Any discussion of aetiology must take into account the exact nature of volitional i.e. voluntary movements. There are degrees of voluntariness, and Hughlings Jackson stressed that some actions are "most voluntary" and others "least voluntary"; "most automatic" as well as "least automatic". Kinnier Wilson gave as an example the transit from highly volitional to simple automatic movements in the behaviour of a person who descends a flight of stairs in the dark. The first few steps constitute a cautious deliberate act and gradually this circumspection gives way to actions which gain increasingly in facility and speed, now becoming automatic. The last two or three steps are possibly managed with mounting caution and the resumption of highly voluntary movements.

Indeed Jackson was chary of using the word "voluntary" at all, pointing out that being a psychological term, it was not correct to apply it to physical processes.

The ontogenesis of a voluntary movement takes origin in the spontaneous motor activity of premature newborn infants. The mass movements of a baby are still scarcely to be regarded as volitional, for they are amorphous, uncoordinated and purposeless. Rather should they be regarded as the precursors of willed movements. Later in infancy, a process of steadily increasing economy and efficiency takes place: out of this disarray of movement fragments become isolated, and gradually achieve a measure of control (Critchley, 1954).

Gradually acts of volition lose their impulsive character and take on an aspect of deliberation.

Here then are the beginnings of a willed or volitional movement. All associated muscular activity becomes regulated, though not at a conscious level, so as to form a harmony of movement, of which the "prime movers" constitute the melody. From such a synergic unit the prime movers carry out the deliberate, volitional, conscious part of the act, the other components taking place at various levels of unawareness. Before acquiring such a simple motor achievement, the infant passes through many laborious stages, an apprenticeship of trial and error, with a gradual though uneven progress over a period of many weeks.

After the normal child has learned to carry out a modest repertoire of voluntary movements, he continues to acquire adroitness in certain more complex movements over the course of the next few decades, depending upon such opportunitites as are afforded by choice and vocation.

This stage is the one where the apprentice-musician begins to achieve his technical skills.

Briefly it can be said that by some process of training, combining both learning and practice, a particular set of movements, simple or complex, can eventually be effected with an unusually high degree of efficiency. A skilled motion is not necessarily a delicate one, though in musicianship most of the motor skills comprise delicate, small-range, complex and highly coordinated little movements.

What precisely are the criteria that distinguish a skilled from an unskilled movement, and what varying degrees of awareness are entailed?

(1) A skilled movement implies that the particular motor act has probably been performed on many previous occasions. In the case of the musician this entails long periods of learning and practice. The number of practice-efforts may bear an inverse ratio to the degree of "m" or the alleged factor of innate mechanical (musical) aptitude.

(2) A skilled movement eventually entails less deliberate effort than a simpler volitional motion. Thus a woman may be able to continue to knit while reading a book. A typist's thoughts may be miles away. The same dissociation between attention and motor skill may apply to a musician. A pianist may carry on an animated conversation while playing. Often indeed, skilled movements may become automatic, but the converse is not true: movements that are wholly automatic are rarely skilled movements. At the same time it must be stressed that some expert movements never become completely automatic, however often they are repeated. Thus the skills shown by jugglers and by acrobats always demand vigilance, perhaps because proximal muscles are concerned rather than digital manipulations. Perhaps, too, because the kinetic melody is not fixed or predetermined, but is impromptu, and depends upon a play of factors which are continually changing. Expressed otherwise, the movements belong to the "pursuit" type of motor adjustment.

In the case of a musical performer the factor of attention probably varies. Although it is true that a pianist can talk, sing, or whistle at the same time as he is at the piano, it is doubtful whether a virtuoso ever completely severs the silver cord connecting his attention with his manipulations. However skilled, however practised, the supreme artist is never wholly oblivious to the mechanism of his motor skill. A rapport continues despite the ecstatic experiences described in Chapter 13, experiences which incidentally belong more to the hearer than to the performer.

(3) Skilled movements are usually carried out with greater speed than unskilled voluntary movements.

(4) There is far more economy of movement in the case of the expert, the range of activity of the prime movers being more limited.

(5) Skilled movements tend to dispense with associated movements and also with movements of cooperation.

(6) Skilled movements are performed with a less forceful contraction of the prime movers than those which are unskilled: that is, with less expenditure of energy.

(7) Skilled movements – like involuntary movements – are less fatiguing, as was indeed noted by Aristotle.

Are special cerebral structures or coordinating centres concerned with the dextrous execution of complicated motor skills? Or are they "represented" – if that unfortunate term can be pardoned – in the motor cortex like other movements? There is no consensus upon this point. That cerebellar, striato-pallidal and proprioceptive influences operate in both skilled and unskilled movements cannot be gainsaid. But skilled volitional movements as opposed to unpractised volitional acts possibly entail a wider extent of cortical activity in "elaboration fields" lying both in front of and behind the motor cortex, and also perhaps in homologous but contralateral parts.

The last statement possibly does not apply to musical skills, but bi-hemispheric participation may be demonstrated by one striking motor skill of a non-musical sort. A Chinese masters the art of manipulating chopsticks. For cultural reasons only the right hand is used for this purpose. If, however, the Chinese can be persuaded to test his skill with his left hand, for the first time ever perhaps, he displays an adroitness which vastly transcends the efforts of an occidental, whichever hand he tries.

Another interesting question can be posed. Does skilfulness achieved with one complex act facilitate the learning of some other motor-skill? Does the ability to play the piano assist in the technique of typewriting or of embroidery? According to Thorndike (1931) this may well be so. Perhaps the answer depends upon the nature of the training which led up to the original skill. Should this have resulted mainly from practice, i.e. simple frequent repetition, it seems doubtful whether acquired dexterity can assist in the development of other skills. But if the dexterity has been the product of a process of learning, then it probably can be transferred to other complex movements, as industrial experience shows. Learning (in the strict sense) differs from practice in that it educates the apprentice in the fundamentals of motor efficiency, which stand in good stead whatever new task is concerned.

As is so often the case, the lesson of the pathological may throw light upon the nature of the processes underlying the normal. One musician in my experience, a lady of 55 years, developed a pianist's palsy. The disability also spread to the execution of two other instruments in which she had been skilled, namely the organ and the oboe.

This is on a par with our knowledge of the course of other craft palsies outside music. Collier (*loc. cit.*) cited a telegraphist who developed cramp after manipulating a Baudot instrument. He was rested and transferred to light duties involving the use of a Morse instrument, when too after a time he failed. Thereupon he was relegated to counter duties, involving the use of the pen, only to become incapacitated with writer's cramp. He was next put to the task of closing envelopes, and even then he developed cramp over that act, and ended his Post Office career as a messenger.

Neurologists are familiar with a dilapidation of movements as the result of some process of disease, e.g. apraxia. But apraxia is largely a phenomenon affecting unskilled movements. In contradistinction, the various craft palsies represent a specific disorder of certain motor skills. The disability cannot be wholly overcome either by an effort of deliberate concentration (i.e. by converting them into highly volitional movement); nor by downgrading them into "more automatic" movements. Such craft palsies exclusively involve – in the early stages at least – a particular complex movement which has achieved dexterity through controlled learning combined with tedious practice, and they spare all other willed movements whether skilled or unskilled, and furthermore, all movements belonging to the category of "least voluntary" and "most automatic". Later, as we have seen, the disability may extend to other skilled accomplishments.

The digital movements made by victims of writer's cramp have been recorded and analysed by the use of such techniques as cyclegrams, whereby photographs are taken in the dark of the movements of the fingers to which are attached tiny electric lamps (Critchley, *loc. cit.*). They show that the finger-movements in the craft palsy become so disorganised as to resemble the exuberant and uncoordinate movements of beginner. Such a technique of analysis can equally well be adapted so as to demonstrate the efforts in musicians with or without a craft palsy.

In occupational palsies, not only is the action of the prime mover disorganised in range and rate of movement, but a wide range of supportive muscles becomes active. This spread is obvious on close clinical scrutiny and it can also be easily demonstrated electromyographically (Critchley, *loc. cit.*) in cases of writer's cramp. It is reasonable to expect that such techniques would display similar findings in the various types of musician's palsy.

What then is the probable patho-physiology of any occupational palsy?

Why should an exquisite motor-skill built up by years of learning followed by assiduous practice deteriorate in efficiency, perhaps progressively so? Nowadays few neurologists would venture to invoke a psychogenesis: few again think in terms of a structural lesion of some hypothetical centre of coordination. Some neurologists regard fatigue as the all-important factor in determining the belated dissolution of the motor-skill, and yet evident debility, physical or mental, is not always conspicuous. One cannot venture as yet outside the confines of speculation except to implicate a breakdown occurring at a physiological level rather than at a particular anatomical site. We have not progressed far over the past century, when V. Poore expressed the situation, as referring to writer's cramp. "It is", he wrote "tolerably certain that, should one or more of the muscles which have been so laboriously educated exceed or fail in its work by an increased or diminished response to stimulation, the harmony of the complicated act of writing is interfered with, concord is converted into discord more or less marked, and that which had become a purely automatic act by dint of years of study relapses again into an act which requires a greater or less amount of attention."

The problem is no different when one considers the various musicians' palsies, and for that matter any other of the occupational cramps.

The prognosis of the disabilities due to the diverse types of cramp or palsy in musical executants is grave. In the very earliest stages a period of rest appears called for, and yet it would seem hazardous to lay aside the instrument too long lest a condition of unlearning should follow. Maybe the logical management varies according to the experience and bravura of the musician who is showing incipient symptoms. Should he belong to the second or third rank, it would be a commonsense counsel to enjoin a period of total rest, not too brief nor yet too long, followed later by a consultation with an eminent music-teacher who would critically appraise the fundamental pattern of the player's technique before embarking upon a cautious regime of rehabilitative practice.

The virtuoso who develops a craft palsy is probably incurable.

Psychotherapy, sedatives, tranquillisers, hypnosis, are unlikely to prove helpful in any case.

## MUSICIANS AS TICQUEURS

Flesch has written with scorn about the bizarre habit-spasms which some musicians display while at work. It seems as though the worst offenders are pianists. Their mannerisms are manifold.

In a recent monograph upon the subject of gesture (Critchley "Silent

Language", 1975) the topic was considered in musical executants while at work. Quoting freely from the observations of Flesch the author stated that professional pianists sometimes embellish their performances with animal-like vocalisations. They may pant, grunt, snore, groan, yodel, bawl, cry or even break into song in the highest and lowest registers. All these oddities fall within the genre of audible gestures.

Violinists, too, may indulge immoderately in habit-spasms and adopt ugly attitudinisings. Slow, spasmodic movements of the head and neck may be seen which are distracting and aesthetically ludicrous, "for they suggest the short, jerking, purposeless twitchings of a jumping-jack". Swaying of the body back and forth or from side to side are other unpleasing gimmicks, though deviation of the trunk backwards and to the left is deemed acceptable as a means of furthering expression. But inclination forwards and to the right smacks of the gypsy in a beer-hall. It constitutes a hindrance, not to be countenanced.

Tapping a foot is an intolerable habit while playing, for it does violence both to the time-beater himself and to his associates. Facial grimaces on the part of a violinist also provoked the disapproval of Flesch. However, he did not object to deliberate assumption of a rapt immobility of the face which he accepted as a temporary "spiritualised" pose; but, "the case is different when the facial movements take the form of a nervous tic, such as the raising or lowering of the eyebrows, a contraction or opening of the lips (fish-mouth), a convulsive clamping of upper and lower jaw, and gnashing of the teeth. . . . To these must be added the stereotype ballet-dancer smile, the sight of which puts the auditor out of humour, because, in most cases, it has no connection with a work's inner content, and hence makes an impression of artificiality."

Musicians' tics, like musicians' palsies, mar the aesthetic qualities of the executant, and would not be tolerated today. The former are largely unwitting, and the soloist probably has no idea of the extent to which he offends or distracts the audience confronting him. In other media the tic may pass unnoticed, for those who listen but cannot see may be as unaware of the mannerisms as the player himself. The situation is different in the case of the victim of a musician's cramp, for, though not necessarily visible, the effects are certainly audible. Moreover, the performer himself is all too alive to his technical difficulties. It is likely that florid mannerisms and tics such as Flesch described were commoner a generation or two ago, than at present. These remarks apply to musical instrumentalists rather than conductors.

How can this be reconciled with the fact that tics are unconscious and uncontrollable? Perhaps musicians' tics start as mere bad habits. In the early stage of learning these can be eradicated by a strict and critical teacher, and perhaps this is the current practice. Flamboyance is nowadays frowned upon as ridiculous, whether in acting, oratory, or musicianship.

# REFERENCES

BELL, CHARLES quoted by Gowers.

COLLIER, J. and ADIE, W. J. (1922) Craft palsy, *Price's Textbook of Medicine*. 1st edn., 1524–1528.

CRITCHLEY, M. (1954) Discussion of volitional movement. *Proc. Roy. Soc. Med.*, **47**, 593.

— (1975) *Silent Language*. Butterworth, London.

FLESCH, C. *Memoirs*.

— (1930) *The Art of Violin Playing*. Vol. II, trans. F. H. Marteus. Care Fischer Inc., New York.

GOWERS, W. R. *Manual of Diseases of the Nervous System*. Vol. II.

PLATT, LORD (1964) Cellist's panic and other rare diseases. *Hospital Life*. No. 6 20.

POORE, V. (1897) *Nervous Affections of the Hand*. Smith, Elder & Co., London. (Being the Bradshaw Lect., R.C.P., 1881.)

PORTER, M. PORTER (1973) The embouchure and dental hazards of wind instrumentalists. *Proc. Roy. Soc. Med.*, **66**, 1075–1078.

THORNDIKE, E. L. (1931) *Human learning*. N.Y.

WILSON, S. A. KINNIER (1928) *Modern Problems in Neurology*. Arnold, London.

# The Amusias

"Amusia" is a collective term denoting the loss or impairment of musical capacity that may occur as a consequence of brain disease. The impairment may take a variety of forms. It may be manifested in motor or expressive performances, for example, in loss of the ability to sing, whistle or hum a tune (oral-expressive amusia); loss of the ability to play an instrument (instrumental amusia or musical apraxia); or loss of the ability to write music (musical agraphia). By definition, the latter two disabilities can be sustained only by trained musicians. On the receptive side, the impairment may be manifested in noteworthy loss of the ability to discriminate between heard melodies (receptive or sensory amusia); loss of the ability to identify familiar melodies (amnesic amusia); or loss of the ability to read musical notation in a person who possessed this skill (musical alexia). Alteration of emotional response to music is still another form. Any of these disabilities may occur singly or in combination. They are encountered frequently in association with aphasic disorders but, as will be seen, this association is not at all obligatory.

## HISTORICAL SKETCH*

Disorders in musical appreciation and execution first engaged medical attention when systematic examination of aphasic patients disclosed that many of them had lost one or another musical skill along with their impairment in language. An early case report by Proust (1866) described loss of the ability to read music in an aphasic musician; however his capacity to recognize music remained intact and he could still sing, play, and even write music. Some years later, Proust (1872) described a different pattern of loss of musical ability in two aphasic patients. One could still read notes, play scales and recognize melodies but could no longer hum a tune. The other, an accomplished musician, could recognize melodies and not only read but also compose music; however, he was no longer capable of humming a tune. An early case report by Fischer (1867) described yet

* Detailed accounts of the historical development of our knowledge of amusic disorders may be found in Edgren (1895), Henschen (1920), Ustvedt (1937) and Dorgeuille (1966).

another type of impairment. His patient, who was a music teacher and a composer and who showed both motor and receptive aphasic defects, could discriminate between rhythmic patterns and recognize a melody which he himself had composed. He also handled a violin skilfully and could reproduce an appropriate tune if a scale were played to him. However, he could neither play nor sing a tune that had been sung to him and he had lost his ability to read and write music. In 1870 Finkelnburg described a most unusual case of a left-handed patient who presented with an amnesic aphasia in association with disease of the right hemisphere. This skilled musician could reproduce heard melodies on the violin with fair facility but was unable to do so on the piano.

The *sparing* of musical abilities in patients with congenital or acquired language defects was noted even earlier. Dalin (1745) described a 33 year old man who suffered a right hemiplegia and complete loss of expressive speech after a stroke but who nevertheless was able to sing the melody and words of hymns that were familiar to him. Bouillaud (1865) reported the case of an aphasic composer who could still play, compose and hum music, and even accompany singers on the piano. The retention of the ability to sing in an almost speechless aphasic patient of Gowers (1875) was disclosed only when he spontaneously joined another patient who was singing and then continued to sing the words and melody of the second verse by himself.

Conversely, instances of loss of musical skills in patients who were not aphasic were also described. Mann's (1898) patient was a good singer who lost the capacity to sing as well as to whistle after an injury to the right frontal lobe. However, recognition of melodies was well preserved. At no time did he show any signs of aphasic disorder. Jossmann (1926, 1927) described a patient who presented a very similar picture. This patient showed a transient left hemiparesis without aphasia following ligation of the right common carotid artery and removal of an aneurysm at its bifurcation. However, when he was examined some months later, this trained musician could neither sing nor whistle tunes to command and he could no longer read a score. Recognition of pitch and intensity remained intact and he was quite aware of his errors in expression.

Thus, once attention was directed to the question, a variety of distinctive types of impairment in musical capacity was observed and reported. By the close of the 19th century, every form of amusia that is currently recognized had been described and a number of systematic studies (Knoblauch, 1888; Oppenheim, 1888; Brazier, 1892; Edgren, 1895; Probst, 1899) had been devoted to the topic. The most comprehensive of these early studies was that of J. G. Edgren, Professor of Medicine in Stockholm, who presented a critical analysis of the literature with particular reference to those cases on whom autopsy findings were available. From this review and an analysis of his own exhaustively studied case, it seemed clear to Edgren that discrete forms of amusia did occur, that they were closely allied to comparably discrete aphasic disorders and that they had distinctive anatomical bases.

The first full scale monographic treatment of amusia was that of Henschen (1920) who made a detailed analysis of the published literature on the subject as well as of his own extensive case material. Although his primary interest was in questions of localization, Henschen did not neglect the theoretical and clinical aspects of the topic and he devoted considerable attention to the nature of the relationship between aphasic disorders and impairment in musical functions. His classification followed traditional lines in providing for two broad categories of impairment, motor and sensory, within which specific disabilities could be placed. However, he also recognized that a number of auditory capacities, such as pitch discrimination and tonal discrimination, underlay these musical skills and he viewed the central problem as the determination, on the basis of the available anatomo-clinical data, of the degree to which these more elementary capacities can be localized in the brain.

A second monograph on the subject, that of Feuchtwanger (1930), was quite different in character. Covering an extremely broad range of topics, he concluded that impairment in both integrative capacity and in differentiation constituted the fundamental deficits in "amusia". He emphasized the necessity for a thorough knowledge of the premorbid personality of the patient, a requirement that cannot often be satisfied in actual practice. Loosely organized and replete with speculation about the expressive, semantic and symbolic functions of music, the monograph covered all aspects of musical function in considerable detail; but Feuchtwanger's treatment was generally rather unclear, indeed at times mystifying, and his monumental treatise had no great impact on thinking in the field.

The comprehensive study of Ustvedt (1937) provided a more critical analysis of the problems associated with "amusia" than any work up to its time. Proceeding from a careful review of the literature, Ustvedt pointed out how little is actually known about disturbances in musical functions. He attributed this deficiency to a variety of factors, the primary ones being grossly inadequate techniques of examination, neglect of the premorbid musicality of the patient, and preoccupation with problems of localization without taking account of the complex clinical pictures shown by different patients. With respect to the last point, he emphasized the Jacksonian dictum that localizing the lesions producing amusic disabilities is not equivalent to identifying the neural mechanisms underlying musical functions. In addition, he sharply criticized the proclivity for erecting elaborate theoretical schemata (as reflected, for example, in the writing of Feuchtwanger) that were the product of pure speculation and without empirical foundation.

Ustvedt's own extremely detailed study of a group of patients, all of whom had had musical training and most of whom were also aphasic, led him to conclude that "amusia" is simply a shorthand term for "a heterogenous collection of rather complicated symptom-groups" about which very little is known. Specifically, both the neural mechanisms underlying these symptom pictures and the nature of their relationship to cognitive and linguistic function remain obscure. Nevertheless, he felt that it was of practical value to distinguish disorders of receptive functions and those of expressive functions and that, in the latter group, differentiation between productive as contrasted to merely reproductive activity was useful. The importance of both the emotional and structural aspects of music as potential areas of disturbances was emphasized. Problems of classification were discussed at length but left unresolved in view of the superficial nature of our understanding of these disorders. A major conclusion was that in this field "there has been much overemphasis of the intellectual, cortical factors, and in future research it will be necessary to devote much more attention to the subcortical driving forces of musical function". Ustvedt's monograph, over 700 pages in length, remains the most valuable single contribution to the field. Among more recent work, there is none that approaches it in breadth, detail and critical acumen.

## THE VARIETIES OF MUSICAL DISTURBANCE

Numerous classifications of types of amusia have been offered (cf. Henschen, 1920; Kleist, 1934; Wertheim, 1963, 1969; Dorgeuille, 1966; Grison, 1972). Many follow the lines of classical aphasia theory and divide musical disturbances into two broad types, motor and sensory. Thus, for example, Henschen (1920) adopted the following classification as a basis for his analysis.

I. Motor impairments
   A. Loss of the ability to sing (with or without words).
   B. Loss of the ability to write musical notation.
   C. Loss of the ability to play an instrument.
II. Sensory Impairments

A. "Musical deafness", including loss of recognition of familiar melodies.

B. Loss of the ability to read musical notation.

Kleist (1928, 1934) also accepted the dichotomy of motor and sensory categories of amusia and he identified specific types of disturbance in each category. Within the motor category, he distinguished between the inability to produce (i.e. sing or whistle) a single tune (*Tonstummheit*) and the inability to produce a melody (*Melodienstummheit; Motorische Amelodie*). Within the sensory category, he distinguished between the inability to discriminate single tones (*Tontaubheit; Perzeptive Sensorische Amusie*), the inability to discriminate melodies (*Melodientaubheit*) and the inability to identify a specific melody (*Musiksinntaubheit*).

Other classifications have been based on a hierarchical principle and have made a fundamental distinction between lower and higher levels of disturbance, contrasting relatively simple performances such as singing and recognizing familiar tunes with more complex functions such as the composing of music. A particular form of this classification differentiates impairment in comprehending music as a language or symbol system from impairment on the perceptual and motor levels. Still other classifications follow anatomical principles, distinguishing between disorders associated with disease of the left hemisphere and those that occur as a consequence of right hemisphere disease or identifying those types of disorder that appear to be associated specifically with lesions in different loci.

It can be said of all these classifications that they possess the merit of providing a framework within which empirical observations can be fitted. At the same time, it is clear that they are only of limited usefulness since none has been found to be capable of accommodating all the observed facts. Far more is known about the aphasic disorders than about disturbances in musical appreciation and expression. Yet classification in the field of aphasia is still a controversial question, testifying to a lack of certainty about the basic nature of these disorders. This uncertainty is even more pervasive with respect to the amusias and, as a consequence, attempts to develop rigorous classifications are often little more than logical exercises. Given this circumstance, it seems appropriate to acknowledge our present lack of understanding of the basic dimensions along with musical disturbances vary and to proceed on a purely descriptive basis. The forms of disturbance that have been identified by clinical observation will be sketched and their correlates noted without, however, attempting to fit them into a formal schema based on theoretical principles.

## Oral-expressive or vocal amusia

Loss of the capacity to sing, hum or whistle a tune is one of the more frequently described forms of amusia. The loss may be complete in the sense that the patient finds himself unable to produce either a single tone or a melody on verbal command or by imitation. The loss may be partial insofar as the patient may be able to produce a tone but not a melody. Conversely, he may be able to produce a familiar melody but be incapable of reproducing an isolated sound. The loss in oral-expressive capacity may also be partial in the sense that the patient may be able to carry a tune but his singing proves to be quite poor in terms of melody, intonation and rhythm.

Two case reports describing patients who showed oral-expressive amusia as their sole or most prominent disability, those of Mann (1898) and Jossman (1926, 1927), were mentioned earlier in the chapter. Neither patient was aphasic and both showed evidence of anterior right hemisphere disease.

The patient described by Botez and Wertheim (1959) presented a very similar picture. After removal of a calcified oligodendroglioma of the right frontal lobe, this 26 year old man who was an accomplished accordion player showed moderate articulatory disorder and dysprosody in speaking but no paraphasic speech, word-finding difficulties or impairment in the understanding of language. Reading, writing and calculation were intact. The slight motor and sensory impairments noted shortly after operation had disappeared. Receptive musical functions were not disturbed: he could discriminate pitch, recognize familiar melodies and identify intentionally made errors in the playing of a melody. In contrast, expressive musical performances were disturbed to a serious degree. While notes produced by voice were sung accurately, notes produced by an accordion were not. Reproduction of rhythmic patterns was faulty. He made gross errors in intonation when singing a familiar tune to verbal command. The capacity to whistle a familiar tune was even more severely compromised. Although he showed no evidence of generalized praxic difficulties, his ability to play the accordion was grossly impaired. Thus, in this case, the oral-expressive amusia appeared in combination with expressive speech disorder and instrumental amusia. However, the site of the crucial lesion, i.e. the anterior region of the right hemisphere, was the same as in the earlier reported cases.

In other cases, oral-expressive amusia occurs within the setting of pervasive impairment in sensory functions. The patient who was studied post mortem by Pötzl and Uiberall (1937) perceived musical notes as well as other sounds as unpleasant dissonant noises. Human voices, including his own, seemed to him to be too high in pitch. Aside from a very slight word-finding difficulty, he showed no signs of expressive or receptive aphasia. However, he had lost his previously well-developed capacity to sing and he was unable to reproduce auditory rhythmic patterns correctly. In contrast to the finding of frontal lobe disease in the previously mentioned cases, autopsy study of this patient disclosed bilateral lesions involving auditory cortex and its subjacent white matter.

A distinctive feature of the cases of oral-expressive amusia mentioned thus far is that none were aphasic although they might show articulatory difficulties in speaking, as was true of the patient of Botez and Wertheim. The intensively studied case of Jellinek (1933) provides an example of an aphasic patient who also showed motor amusia. Following removal of a left frontal glioma, this professional singer exhibited a non-fluent expressive speech disorder characterized by hesitations, blocking and repetition of words and syllables as well as impairment in reading, writing and understanding of oral speech. Calculation and design copying were also disturbed. He showed a partial vocal amusia in the sense that he would sing familiar melodies inaccurately and with uncertain intonation. Nor could he sing the notes of the scale accurately. His reproduction of rhythm patterns was also faulty. His perception of music was impaired and his ability to read music was completely lost.

Thus it is evident that loss of the capacity to sing can occur either in more or less isolated form or as part of a more general loss of musical capacity.

### Instrumental amnesia

Loss of the capacity to play an instrument has been the subject of only a few case reports. Moreover, in some instances it appears that the impairment may have been only a specific expression of a more pervasive motor disability. However, instrumental amnesia which is not attributable to general motor deficit has also been clearly described. An excellent example is provided by the patient of Botez and Wertheim (1959) mentioned above. Besides his vocal disabilities, this young man could no longer play the accordion, an instrument which he had practised continuously since he was nine years old. Motor deficits could not be made to account for the striking failure in performance which Wertheim (1963) designated a "bimanual instrumental apraxia".

### Musical agraphia

Two types of impairment in writing have been described under the rubric of "musical agraphia". The first is inability to write a series of heard notes. This can be elicited, of course, only in a trained musician. It typically occurs in combination with other defects in musical function. However, Dorgeuille (1966) has described a trumpeter who showed no noteworthy defects in either language or musical function after head trauma except for some difficulty and hesitation in writing down rhythmic patterns aurally presented to him. The second type of defect is impairment in copying musical notation. This may be simply an expression of visuoperceptive disability and may have no inherent connection with musicality.

## Musical amnesia

This term generally refers to failure to identify melodies which should be familiar to the patient. The patient may be unable to sing a familiar song when given its name although he can sing it after it has been played to him. Or he may be unable to give the name of a familiar melody when it is played to him. A trained musician may not be able to write the main theme of a piece, having been given its name. Thus, one of Dorgeuille's (1966) patients, an accomplished pianist, experienced no difficulty in copying musical notation, but wrote inaccurate notation when given the name of a familiar melody. She was a fluent aphasic who showed pronounced impairment in both naming and writing. However, failure to identify melodies by name is by no means necessarily associated with the presence of an aphasic disorder. Grison (1972) has described a number of non-aphasic patients with right hemisphere disease who showed this disability.

## Disorders of rhythm

Some writers (e.g. Jellinek, 1933; Döllken, 1935; Dorgeuille, 1966) have laid stress on impairment in the sense of rhythm as a basic component in disturbances in musical function. This impairment is expressed in failure to reproduce rhythmic patterns or to discriminate between them. The clinical literature suggests that disturbances in the recognition and execution of rhythmic patterns are frequently associated with both oral-expressive amusia and apraxic disorders.

## Receptive amusia

Defective perception of music as reflected in failure to discriminate between melodic patterns, timbre and pitch and in qualitative alterations of acoustic experience (e.g. hearing sounds as discordant or unpleasant) is a commonly reported type of amusia. In its most striking form, there is inability to discriminate between sounds of different timbre or pitch. An impairment that is so basic in nature necessarily results in grossly defective appreciation of music. However, its consequences extend beyond the field of music to all aspects of auditory experience. Thus most of the patients described in the literature as suffering from defective tonal discrimination were also "word deaf" to a greater or lesser degree, i.e. they suffered from a concomitant impairment in oral language understanding (cf. Vignolo, 1969). However, cases of "auditory agnosia" without receptive aphasic disorder have been observed. For example, the patient of Spreen et al. (1965) showed grossly defective recognition of non-verbal meaningful environmental sounds and performed on a chance level on an easy test of pitch discrimination. Yet a detailed aphasia examination did not disclose clinically significant defects. He showed no receptive or expressive difficulties in conversational speech, repetition, naming or object description. Nor were paraphasias, word-finding difficulties or agrammatism observed. His reading was slow but accurate and there were no disturbances in writing. However, verbal associative fluency, as measured by a word association test, was impoverished.

In other cases, there is retention of the capacity for tonal discrimination with impairment in melodic discrimination, i.e. in appreciating tonal sequences. It is natural to think of tonal discrimination as being the more basic capacity and to suppose that impairment in tonal discrimination necessarily implies defective appreciation of melodies which are essentially sequences of tones. However, exceptional cases in which the patient could discriminate between melodies and yet showed poor tonal appreciation have been described (cf. Kleist, 1934). But, as a rule, the two types of disability do occur together and in combination with disturbances in the appreciation of rhythm.

## Musical alexia

Loss of the ability to read music in a trained musician has been frequently described and is a clearly recognized type of amusia. It is seen very often in association with acquired verbal alexia. Thus the famous alexic patient of Déjèrine (1892), who was an accomplished singer, could no longer read a single musical note, although he could still sing well. Other cases of musical alexia have been described in association with receptive aphasia and receptive and expressive amusia (Dupré and Nathan, 1911; Jellinek, 1933; Dorgeuille, 1966). Convincing cases of isolated defect in the reading of music without other linguistic or musical disabilities have not been reported.

## ASSESSMENT OF MUSICAL CAPACITIES

The assessment of disturbances in musical function can pose formidable problems, particularly if the question of mild or subtle impairment is raised. There is an extremely wide variation in "musicality" in the population. Some people can read and write music but the majority are musically illiterate. Many people cannot "carry a tune". Others are essentially non-responsive to music and have difficulty in distinguishing one melody from another as well as in remembering tonal sequences. Thus there are no obvious normal standards against which the performances of a patient can be compared, as is usually the case with linguistic capacities. Consequently, in judging whether or not a change in musical capacities has occurred, it is necessary to consider each patient as his own control and make an evaluation of his premorbid musical capacity on the basis of his testimony or that of his relatives. However, one must be cautious about accepting such statements at face value for, as Ustvedt (1937) pointed out, there is a tendency for patients with brain disease to overestimate their endowment, musical or otherwise, and for relatives and friends to offer generalities such as "fairly musical" or "he liked music", which are not very informative. Thus the evaluation of premorbid musical capacity is valid only to the extent that it is based on specific information about how well the patient sang or played an instrument, how often he attended concerts, how critical he was, etc.

The desirability of utilizing a systematic examination schedule to ensure that all aspects of musical capacity are assessed and to make possible a meaningful comparison of the performances of different patients has long been recognized. A number of comprehensive batteries have been developed by specialists in the field such as Jellinek (1933) and Wertheim and Botez (1959). These test batteries, which are quite elaborate, provide for the assessment of virtually every aspect of musicality, including the reading and writing of music and instrumental performance. They are fully applicable only to patients who happen to have been trained musicians and only the more elementary parts assessing tonal discrimination, singing, and the recognition of familiar tunes can be used with the average patient. It must also be noted that none of these batteries has been standardized on the basis of performances of normal subjects, in the sense that mental ability tests are standardized.

The test battery developed by Dorgeuille (1966) for his study of the amusias provides an example of a systematic examination that is quite comprehensive and yet not too long for practical application. It covers diverse aspects of musical function, as outlined in Table 1. In addition, Dorgeuille assessed the premorbid musical capacities of each patient by a check list that provided specific information about musical training in school, participation in band, chorus or orchestra, formal musical education and level of skill in instrumental performance, sight reading and writing music. Evaluation of whether or not the observed level of performance on a particular test was defective could then be made with

*Table 1*    Functions assessed in test battery of Dorgeuille (1966)

---

*I. Vocal expression*
A.  Patient is asked to sing familiar songs named by examiner.
B.  Patient is asked to sing melodies by imitation.
C.  Patient is asked to whistle a melody.
D.  Patient is asked to reproduce tones presented by voice, piano, etc.

*II. Rhythmic expression*
Patient is asked to reproduce rhythmic patterns tapped on a table.

*III. Writing*
A.  Patient is asked to copy a simple musical text.
B.  If task is appropriate for his musical background, patient is asked to transcribe a dictated melody.

*IV. Discrimination of sounds*
Patient is asked to indicate which of two tones is higher in pitch.

*V. Identification of familiar melodies*
Patient is asked to identify familiar melodies played on the flute.

*VI. Identification of types of music*
Patient is asked to indicate the types of music (e.g. dance, military, church) reflected in the playing of representative samples of each genre on the flute or the piano.

*VII. Identification of musical instruments*
Patient is asked to identify the instrument as characteristic pieces are played on the piano, violin, organ, etc.

*VIII. Reading*
If task is appropriate for his musical background, patient is asked to sight-read musical texts.

---

reference to the patient's premorbid capacity in this respect. Of course, limitation in musical background precluded giving tests assessing the reading or writing of music to many patients.

The test battery, and a systematic neuropsychological examination of language functions, praxis, perception and calculation, were given to 26 right-handed patients with brain disease. Thus it was possible to determine the associations among the different musical performances as well as to determine their relationship to locus of lesion, linguistic functions and perceptual capacities. The findings of this comprehensive study are considered in the next section.

A more global approach to the problem of assessing premorbid level was taken by Grison (1972) in her study of disturbance of musical function in patients with hemispheric disease. On the basis of anamnestic data, she placed each patient into one of six categories as shown in Table 2. Although less rigorous than the method employed by Dorgeuille, this categorization appears to be a useful and practical procedure.

*Table 2*   Levels of musical culture (adapted from Grison, 1972)

---

1. Showed no interest in music; did not care to listen to it or to sing.
2. Occasionally sang familiar melodies such as nursery rhymes and regional songs; sometimes listened to music on the wireless.
3. Enjoyed singing and had a "repertory" which he maintained and augmented; was a critical listener of music on the wireless; bought gramophone records and listened to them frequently.
4. Played an instrument but was not trained in theory or sight-reading.
5. Played an instrument; fair sight-reading ability and general musical knowledge.
6. Was an excellent musician on both the practical and theoretical levels.

---

## CLINICAL AND PATHOLOGICAL CORRELATES

More often than not, disturbances in musical function occur in association with aphasic disorders. A survey of the cases reported in the literature suggests that about seven of every ten patients described as amusic suffered from one or another form of aphasia. Moreover, the type of musical disability manifested tends to conform qualitatively to the type of aphasic disorder shown by the patient. Patients with a Broca type of aphasia are likely to show oral-expressive defects without noteworthy concomitant impairment in musical perception or recognition. The occurrence of receptive musical defects is associated with either word-deafness or a Wernicke type of aphasia. Dorgeuille (1966) found five instances of musical agraphia in his series; four showed a concomitant verbal agraphia. He encountered six cases of musical alexia, three of whom showed a concomitant verbal alexia. A predominantly amnesic type of amusia is likely to be associated with corresponding amnesic difficulties in speech. For example, one of the patients in the series of Grison (1972) presented with an amnesic aphasia, characterized by word-finding difficulty and circumlocutions in association with fluent speech and mildly defective oral language comprehension. She showed no impairment in the discrimination of notes, melodies or rhythms and could hum melodies quite accurately. However, she had obvious difficulty in trying to retrieve the names of familiar tunes which she knew quite well.

Nevertheless, despite this close qualitative and quantitative association between disorders of music and language, there is incontrovertible evidence that the two spheres of activity are mediated by distinctive neurobehavioural systems. The long-standing observation that patients with severe expressive language disorder are able to sing is in itself sufficient proof of this. The same dissociation may be observed in patients with receptive language disorder. The word-deaf patient of Klein and Harper (1956) at first experienced oral speech "as an undifferentiated mass of sounds without structure or rhythm". Later, when his condition stabilized, he was able to perceive some familiar words and phrases correctly but was still unable to carry on a conversation. He even heard his own speech as indistinct and, except for vowels, was unable to repeat speech sounds correctly. Nevertheless, he was able to recognize most of the popular melodies played on a gramophone to him. Moreover, he was able to identify the voices of people familiar to him and even to identify different regional accents. Thus his capacity to apprehend the musical aspects of spoken language, as reflected in voice quality and accent, was retained within a setting of defective perception of individual word sounds.

Similarly, Assal (1973) has reported the case of a pianist with a fluent aphasia and marked impairment in verbal understanding, repetition, reading and writing. He could play the piano quite as well as before his vascular accident and detailed examination disclosed no changes in musical capacities that did not require verbal communication. He continued to play in a professional band specializing in light music.

Nor is the sparing of musical capacity in aphasic patients necessarily limited to relatively simple expressive and receptive functions. Luria et al. (1965) have described the case of a distinguished Russian composer who was rendered severely aphasic after a stroke sustained when he was 57 years old. Some six years earlier he had had a stroke with transient sensory, motor and speech disturbances from which he recovered completely. After the second stroke, he showed marked impairment in conversational speech, repetition and verbal comprehension, which persisted until his death at the age of 61 years. Nevertheless, throughout the three year period between his second stroke and his final illness, he completed a number of compositions begun before the stroke and wrote a substantial series of new compositions which were performed in public by leading artists and which "other musicians considered to be up to standard, and which did not differ significantly from the compositions of his earlier years". Post mortem examination disclosed a massive softening of the temporal and inferior parietal areas of the left hemisphere.

The fact that disturbances in musical function can occur in patients who are free of any aphasic disorder is equally cogent evidence for the independence of the two "language" systems. Patients with purely or predominantly oral-expressive impairment are about as likely to be non-aphasic as aphasic. However, it must be remarked that most of them do in fact show dysprosodic speech, which might be interpreted as another expression of a general defect in the oral production of sounds, rhythms and melodic intonations. Impaired perception of sounds, tonal sequences and rhythms is somewhat less frequently observed in non-aphasic patients as compared to those with receptive language disorder but numerous case reports indicate that it is far from being a rare occurrence.

Clinicopathologic correlations with respect to disturbances in musical function are much less abundant than for the aphasic disorders and only a limited amount of information about the site of lesions associated with the amusias has been amassed. Broadly speaking, predominantly expressive amusias with relative preservation of receptive capacities are associated with anteriorly situated lesions, for the most part compromising the frontal lobes, and defects in the perception and recognition of tones and melodies (with or without concomitant expressive impairment) are associated with the presence of disease of the temporal lobes. The analogy with the aphasic disorders, in which a predominantly expressive aphasia is likely to be associated with an anterior lesion and a predominantly receptive aphasia with a temporo-parietal lesion, is evident. There is, however, one quite fundamental difference. Appropriately situated lesions in either hemisphere can produce both expressive and receptive disorders of musical function in a right-handed patient while aphasia in such a patient is almost invariably an expression of left hemisphere disease.

Analysis of the clinical literature suggests that "pure" expressive amusia (vocal or instrumental) with preservation of receptive functions and without aphasia is most likely to be associated with anterior lesions of the right hemisphere. The case reports of Mann (1898), Jossmann (1926, 1927) and Botez and Wertheim (1959) illustrate this relationship. A predominantly expressive amusia in combination with a predominantly expressive aphasic disorder is associated with anterior lesions of the left hemisphere, as illustrated by the inability of many Broca aphasics to reproduce a heard tone or to sing a tune. Thus, setting aside the question of the presence or absence of an associated aphasic disorder, there appears to be no hemispheric bias in respect to the lesions that may produce a disorder of expressive musical function.

Disturbances in receptive musical capacities in combination with aphasic disorder have been found to be associated with lesions involving the middle and posterior parts of the first and second temporal gyri, the transverse temporal gyri and the anterior temporal region of the left hemisphere. The three surgically explored cases of Dorgeuille (1966) may be cited to illustrate this point. Case No. 19, a fluent aphasic, was examined three years after evacuation of an intracerebral hematoma located in the anterior part of the left temporal lobe. He made many errors in discriminating tones and could not identify the characteristic sounds of different instruments. He also showed defective reproduction of sounds and rhythmic patterns but he could identify and sing familiar melodies. Case No. 20, examined two weeks after evacuation of an intracerebral hematoma at the tip of the left temporal lobe, also showed a fluent aphasia with paraphasic speech, word-finding difficulties and mild impairment in oral speech comprehension. She exhibited impairment in the discrimination of tones as well as expressive musical defects. Case No. 22, an accomplished musician, was examined shortly before surgical exploration disclosed a glioblastoma occupying the middle and posterior parts of the first and second temporal gyri of the left hemisphere. She showed a fluent aphasia with significant impairment in oral speech comprehension. She could reproduce isolated tones accurately but showed evident defects in singing melodies with which she had been quite familiar. She would begin to sing the melody correctly but was not able to continue it to completion. She also showed impairment in the perception of tonal sequences.

Receptive amusia without concomitant aphasic disorder has been found to be associated with temporal lobe disease of either hemisphere or of both hemispheres (Schuster and Taterka, 1926; Pötzl and Uiberall, 1937; Pötzl, 1939, 1943; Spreen et al., 1965). These observations, taken together with the circumstance that so many patients with "temporal lobe" aphasia show intact musical capacity, has led to the supposition that music, unlike language, has bilateral hemispheric representation. This may be the case but the facts in themselves indicate only that the left hemisphere dominance characteristic of the mediation of language functions does not hold for musical functions. An equally plausible interpretation is that some individuals show dissociated dominance, i.e., they are left hemisphere dominant for language but right hemisphere dominant for music.

Henschen (1920) and, later, Kleist (1934, 1962) tried to establish extremely precise localizations of the cerebral areas mediating specific musical functions. Henschen, for example, localized a "center" for singing in the upper part of the third frontal gyrus, a "center" for oral musical comprehension in the left temporal pole and a "center" for reading music in the angular gyrus. On his part, Kleist related different aspects of musical perception to different parts of the temporal lobe, e.g. the discrimination of timbre to the transverse gyri and the apprehension of melodic patterns to the architectonically delimited *subregio magna dorsalis* (Hopf, 1954) on the lateral surface of the temporal lobe. These attempts to establish precise anatomic correlates for specific performances often have been derided as being the product of sheer fantasy. In fact, they emerged from painstaking analysis by serious, well-informed investigators of the data available to them; but it is clear that our current fund of anatomical and clinical information is far too meagre to provide substantial support for these essentially speculative inferences. Yet they are not without heuristic value in pointing up the necessity for detailed anatomical study and careful clinical investigation.

The idea that each hemisphere makes a distinctive contribution to receptive and expressive musical performance has been proposed. For example, Barbizet (1972; Barbizet et al., 1969) has advanced the concept that the right hemisphere participates primarily on the perceptual and executive levels of musical activity while the left hemisphere mediates the recognition and memory of musical structures, the symbolic processes in reading and writing music and the higher level integrative functions involved in musical composition.

Only a few definitive statements can be made about the interrelations among the diverse musical deficits. It is clear that there can be a dissociation between expressive and receptive functions. A patient can show significant impairment in singing and instrumental playing without noteworthy perceptual deficit. Conversely, a patient with perceptual defects can be shown by appropriate methods of examination to have intact executive capacities. The abilities to reproduce isolated sounds and to sing a melody may be differentially impaired; however, they are usually lost together.

On the other hand, failure to produce a familiar tune when given its name, which is essentially a form of amnesia, frequently occurs within the setting of intact expressive capacity. Impairment in the reading and writing of music shows a close association. There is frequent dissociation between the ability to discriminate isolated sounds and the capacity to recognize melodies or to identify their type (i.e., church music, folk song, etc.). Observations such as these provide some theoretical justification for attempts, such as that of Kleist, to search for distinctive anatomical bases for different aspects of musical reception.

## CONCLUDING REMARKS

As this survey indicates, a substantial body of information has been amassed about the disturbances in musical function that may occur as a consequence of brain disease. The characteristic forms which these disturbances take have been well described and some broad correlations between them and the sites of the causative cerebral lesions have been established. Yet our knowledge of the neurological aspects of the problem is still quite fragmentary and major questions remain unanswered.

The nature of the relationship of the amusias to aphasic deficit is one such question. That the two groups of disorders tend to be closely associated is evident. But why one aphasic patient with a focal lesion will show concomitant disturbances in musical function while another patient with a similar type of disorder and lesion will show no musical disabilities is a complete mystery. Obviously, a major determining factor, the nature of which is unknown to us, is operating to produce such individual differences. It is possible that the contribution which each hemisphere makes to the mediation of musical function varies quantitatively from one individual to another. If this should prove to be the case, it could provide an explanation for the individual differences that are observed clinically. But, of course, whether this is in fact the case is not known. Thus a basic question about the hemispheric distribution of the neural mechanisms underlying musical function is posed and remains to be answered. Reliable knowledge about interhemispheric relations in this respect no doubt would go far towards helping us understand a cognate problem, namely, why some patients are rendered amusic as a consequence of disease of the right hemisphere while the majority of patients in this category are not affected.

A number of questions that are perhaps less basic in nature but still of considerable clinical importance also remain unanswered. The relative frequency and severity of disturbances of musical function in patients with brain disease have never been studied. Whether there are sex differences in this regard is unknown. Nor has any attention been given to the question of the frequency and qualitative nature of musical disabilities in left-handed patients. Investigation of this last issue in the field of the aphasic disorders has generated findings that have given much insight into the relations between handedness and hemispheric cerebral dominance for the language functions (cf. Benton, 1965; Subirana, 1969; Hécaen, 1972). Comparable study of the question in the field of the amusias might be as fruitful.

These investigative possibilities presuppose the application of objective and reliable methods for assessing diverse musical performances in relation to premorbid capacities in large groups of patients. Happily Ustved's (1937) strictures about the gross inadequacy of the techniques typically employed in the examination of patients no longer holds. Although much still needs to be done in the way of standardization of procedures and the gathering of normal values in defined populations, nuclear test batteries that can serve as models for further development are now available, thanks largely to the work of Wertheim and Botez (1959) and Dorgeuille (1966). The prospects that methodologically sound clinical assessment, coupled with employment of some of the experimental approaches described in other chapters of this volume, will significantly advance our understanding of the amusias appear to be quite bright.

# REFERENCES

ASSAL, G. (1973) Aphasie de Wernicke chez un pianiste. *Rev. Neurol.*, **29**, 251.

BALLET, G. (1896) *Le langage intérieur et les diverses formes de l'aphasie.* Paris, Alcan.

BARBIZET, J. (1972) Role de l'hémisphère droit dans les perceptions auditives. In: *Le monde de l'hémiplégie gauche* (J. Barbizet, M. Ben Hamida and P. Duizabo, eds.). Paris, Masson.

BARBIZET, J., DUIZABO, P., ENOS, G., and FUCHS, D. (1969) Reconnaissance de messages sonores: bruits familiers et airs musicaux familiers lors des lésions cérébrales unilatérales. *Rev. Neurol.*, **121**, 624.

BENTON, A. L. (1965) The problem of cerebral dominance. *Canad. Psychol.*, **6**, 332.

BOTEZ, M. I., and WERTHEIM, N. (1959) Expressive aphasia and amusia. *Brain*, **82**, 186.

BOUILLAUD, J. B. (1865) Sur la faculté du langage articulé. *Arch. gén. Méd.*, **I**, 575.

BRAZIER, M. (1892) Du troubles des facultés musicales dans l'aphasie. *Rev. Phil.*, **34**, 337.

DALIN, O. (1745) Berättelse om en dumbe, som kan siunga. K. Swenska Wetensk. *Acad. Handlingar*, **6**, 114.

DÉJÉRINE, J. (1892) Des différentes variétés de cécité verbale. *Mém. Soc. Biol.*, **27**, 1.

DÖLLKEN, A. (1935) Ueber Amusie und Spielzeitstörungen. *Z. Neurol. Psychiat.*, **154**, 32.

DORGEUILLE, C. (1966) *Introduction à l'étude des amusies*. Thèse, Paris.

DUPRE, E., and NATHAN, M. (1911) *Le langage musical: étude médicopsychologique*. Paris, Alcan.

EDGREN, J. G. (1895) Amusie (musikalische Aphasie). *Dtsch. Z. Nervenhlk.*, **6**, 1.

FEUCHTWANGER, E. (1930) *Amusie: Studien zur Pathologischen Psychologie der akustischen Wahrnehmung und Vorstellung und ihre Strukturgebiete besonders in Musik und Sprache*. Berlin, Springer.

FINKELNBURG, F. C. (1870) Asymbolie. *Berlin klin. Wschr.*, **7**, 449.

FISCHER, A. (1867) Ueber zentrale Sprachstörungen mit besonderer Berücksichtigung der Aphasie. Dissertation, Berlin.

GOWERS, W. R. (1875) On a case of simultaneous embolism of central retinal and middle cerebral arteries. *Lancet*, **2**, 794.

GRISON, B. (1972) *Une étude sur les altérations musicales au cours des lésions hémisphériques*. Thèse, Paris.

HÉCAEN, H. (1972) *Introduction à la Neuropsychologie*. Paris, Larousse.

HENSCHEN, S. E. (1920) *Klinische und anatomische Beiträge zur Pathologie des Gehirns, Teil 5: Ueber Aphasie, Amusie und Akalkulie*. Stockholm, Nordiska Bokhandeln.

HOPF, A. (1954) Die Myeloarchitektonik des Isocortex temporalis beim Menschen. *J. Hirnforsch.*, **1**, 208.

JELLINEK, A. (1933) Zur Phänomenologie der Amusie. *Jahrb. f. Psychiat. u. Neurol.*, **50**, 115.

JOSSMANN, P. (1926) Motorische Amusie (Demonstration). *Zbl. Neurol. Psychiat.*, **44**, 260.

— (1927) Die Beziehungen der motorischen Amusie zu den apraktischen Störungen. *Mschr. Psychiat. Neurol.*, **63**, 239.

KLEIN, R., and HARPER, J. (1956) The problem of agnosia in the light of a case of pure word deafness. *J. ment. Sci.*, **102**, 112.

KLEIST, K. (1928) Gehirnpathologische und lokalisatorische Ergebnisse über Hörstörungen, Geräuschtaubheiten und Amusien. *Mschr. Psychiat. Neurol.*, **68**, 853.

— (1934) *Gehirnpathologie*. Leipzig, Barth.

— (1962) *Sensory Aphasia and Amusia: the Myeloarchitectonic Basis*. Oxford, Pergamon Press.

KNOBLAUCH, A. (1888) Ueber Störungen der musikalischer Leistungsfähigkeit infolge von Gehirnläsionen. *Dtsch. Arch. klin. Med.*, **43**, 331.

LURIA, A. R., TSVETKOVA, L. S., and FUTER, D. S. (1965) Aphasia in a composer. *J. neurol. Sci.*, **2**, 288.

MANN, L. (1898) Casuistische Beiträge zur Hirnchirurgie und Hirnlokalisation. *Mschr. Psychiat. Neurol.*, **4**, 369.

OPPENHEIM, H. (1888) Ueber das Verhalten der musikalischen Ausdruckbwegungen und des musikalischen Verständnisses bei Aphasischen. *Charité Ann.*, **13**, 345.

PÖTZL, O. (1939) Zur Pathologie der Amusie. *Z. Neurol. Psychiat.*, **165**, 187.

PÖTZL, O. (1943) Bemerkungen zum Problem der kortikalen Vorgänge bei der akustischen Wahrnehmung. *Mschr. Ohrenhlk.*, **77**, 422.

PÖTZL, O. and UIBERALL, H. (1937) Zur Pathologie der Amusie. *Wiener klin. Wschr.*, **50**, 770.

PROBST, M. (1899) Ueber die Lokalisation des Tonvermögens. *Arch. Psychiat.*, **32**, 387.

PROUST, A. (1866) *Arch. gen. Méd.* Cited by Ballet (1886) and Henschen (1920).

— (1872) De l'aphasie. *Arch. gen. Méd.*, **I**, 147.

SCHUSTER, P. and TATERKA, H. (1926) Beitrag zur Anatomie und Klinik der reinen Worttaubheit. *Z. Neurol. Psychiat.*, **105**, 494.

SPREEN, O., BENTON, A. L., and FINCHAM, R. W. (1965) Auditory agnosia without aphasia. *Arch. Neurol.* **13**, 84.

SUBIRANA, A. (1969) Handedness and cerebral dominance. In: *Handbook of Clinical Neurology*, Vol. 4 (P. J. Vinken, G. W. Bruyn, M. Critchley and J. A. M. Frederiks, eds.). Amsterdam, North-Holland Publishing Co.

USTVEDT, H. J. (1937) Ueber die Untersuchung der musikalischen Funktionen bei Patienten mit Aphasie. *Acta med. Scand.*, Suppl. 86.

VIGNOLO, L. A. (1969) Auditory agnosia: a review and report of recent evidence. In: *Contributions to Clinical Neuropsychology* (A. L. Benton, ed.). Chicago, Aldine Publishing Co.

WERTHEIM, N. (1963) Disturbances of musical functions. In: *Problems of Dynamic Neurology* (L. Halpern, ed.). Jerusalem, Hadassah University Hospital.

— (1969) The amusias. In: *Handbook of Clinical Neurology*, Vol. 4 (P. J. Vinken, G. W. Bruyn, M. Critchley and A. M. Fredricks, eds.). Amsterdam, North-Holland Publishing Co.

WERTHEIM, N., and BOTEZ, M. I. (1959) Plan d'investigation des fonctions musicales. *Encéphale*, **48**, 246.

—— (1961) Receptive amusia: a clinical analysis. *Brain*, **84**, 19.

# 23

W. H. TRETHOWAN

# Music and Mental Disorder

> . . . Madness in great ones
> must not unwatch'd go
> (*Hamlet*, Act iii, Scene 1, line 196)

This chapter discusses the effects of mental disorder upon musical creativity, defined here in its widest sense, so as to include instances not only of frank mental illness but also abnormalities of personality or character severe enough to cause some disability or to give rise to eccentricities of conduct which may transgress generally accepted bounds of normality. We are not concerned with performers but composers, regardless of the fact that these include many who were also accomplished executants, often in the virtuoso class. While eccentricity is not unknown in performers – the pianist, Vladmir Pachmann for example – these, while allowing for occasional emotional display when under stress, seem on the whole to be fairly stable, despite the popular stereotype of the temperamentally volatile opera singer. Indeed it is unlikely that any performer of the first rank, confronted as he inevitably must be by severe competition and ruled by an intensity of purpose sufficient to carry him through the daily ordeal of hours of arduous practice, can afford to be temperamentally self-indulgent and yet remain at the top of his profession, However, this may not be so true of composer-executants: as exemplified by Busoni, Chopin, Liszt, Paganini or Rachmaninov.

There are several questions to be answered: the first being that of prevalence. How common is mental disturbance among musicians as compared with those having no discernible creative powers? Secondly, where abnormality is evident, how characteristic is this? Thirdly, what is the effect of mental disorder upon musical output, and upon its quality? As these are not distinct questions, but interrelated, it may not prove possible to give them separate answers.

Before attempting the task, some consideration needs to be given to the justification for undertaking it in the first place. As Philip Heseltine (alias Peter Warlock) said of Delius – "It is the music that matters not the man"

(Heseltine, 1922). In view of his own profound psychological problems he might well have said the same of himself. Likewise, Erwin Ratz is reported to have said to de la Grange:

"I want to tell you Mahler's music is so much more important than his biography. In fact I don't think his biography is important at all!" (Sutcliffe, 1974).

The justification for turning personal matters into public property is that knowledge of them may lead to a better appreciation not only of the man but of his music also. Furthermore, not all composers would agree with Heseltine. Thus, in 1907, Grieg, who too had his problems – although in his case these were probably largely due to severe respiratory disease – wrote to Percy Grainger:

I have always found that they are mistaken who would divide the artist from the man; on the contrary, the two are indissolubly wedded one to the other. In the man can be found the parallels of all the artist's traits (Beecham, 1959).

Among other things, it is tempting to believe that Grieg may have had in mind how much Grainger's customary ebullience was reflected in his music.

Finally, we may perhaps care to agree with Thomas Carlyle who, giving his views on the propriety of biography, stated:

No man lives without jostling and being jostled; in all ways he has to elbow himself through the world, giving and receiving offence. . . . To paint man's life is to represent these things. Let them be represented, fitly, with dignity and measure; but above all let them be represented (Carlyle, 1838).

\*          \*          \*          \*

Before exploring the vexed question of prevalence, some prior consideration should perhaps be given to whether there is any absolute association between mental instability and musical creativity. While in the main we are inclined to think not, or at the most to believe that if there is any such relationship, this is likely to be only of an indirect kind, such consideration cannot be avoided if for no other reason than that the investigator does not have to look too deeply into the lives of very many composers, including some of the most eminent, before becoming aware of their eccentricities, some of which, at least, can be construed as evidence of frank mental disorder. Despite this, it soon becomes apparent that the vulgar notion of the mad genius is an overstatement which, if it is not to obscure more important issues, must be put aside. Thus, while Henry Raynor (1972) has made the point that the 19th century invented the legend of the great unappreciated genius, misunderstood, neglected and held in contempt by his contemporaries, so, in the 20th, must we beware of further compounding this stereotype by adding mental derangement to its qualities.

The concept of the mad genius has not, furthermore, been confined to composers, but has been liberally applied to painters, poets and playwrights, to scientists and inventors, to all those, in fact, who have that particular quality of mind which lesser men are apt wrongly to regard as visionary; but after all is said, there appears to be no firm evidence that mental instability is conducive to creativity. Indeed, in the case of frank mental illness the reverse almost certainly obtains. An empty vessel – demented, as it were – produces only a hollow sound; a cracked bell – intolerably distorted harmonics. The essential qualities must have been present in the first place; there being no evidence whatsoever that those in whom these qualities are lacking are, by virtue of mental disorder, capable of undergoing some kind of metamorphosis into genius, or anything remotely resembling it. When a musician does become mentally ill but is nevertheless able to continue with his creative work, at least for a time, it is likely that he does so in spite of his derangement and not because of it.

As with mental illness, so with alcohol or drugs: this, despite William James's view that alcohol has the power "to stimulate the mystical faculties of human nature" (James, 1902). What needs to be better understood, and especially by those who believe that it is possible to achieve some entirely new-found inspiration via alcohol or drugs, is that the effect of these upon the central nervous system is essentially subtractive or disintegrative, particularly in regard to the function of the higher brain centres.

This is relevant, for there are a number of composers who have become addicted to alcohol, although only one example of drug dependence can be found. This was Bernard van Dieren (1884–1936), whose addiction was probably of iatrogenic origin, in that he was prescribed morphine in order to combat the pain of chronic gall-bladder disease (Lowbury, 1975). There may well have been more to his addiction than this. Van Dieren was an unusual and possibly highly eccentric person. Of mixed Dutch and Irish extraction he was, according to Sacheverell Sitwell (1947), a man of prodigious memory, an expert bookbinder, carpenter and electrician who "had the appearance of and was dressed like an alchemist of the 16th Century". He is also said to have been a crack pistol-shot.

In the case of those composers who suffered from alcoholism all the usual kinds of causes appear to have been operative. Tchaikovsky confessed not only to an over-fondness for brandy, but to "secret tippling" (Gould, 1906), possibly in an attempt to numb his neurosis. Alcoholism is, in any event, known to be common among homosexuals. This conceivably,

although it has not been expressly stated, may also have been the reason for
Mussorgsky's downfall, for not only did he die of drink when aged 42, but
there are suggestions that he too had some emotional difficulties in his
relationships with women (Von Riesemann, 1935). Scriabin, whose
sexuality was also probably abnormal, is said to have drunk heavily as a
young man and continued to do so until later in his life when he appears to

Figure 1    Bernard van Dieren. Self-portrait.

have gained some degree of inner relief from tensions by becoming engrossed in seemingly spiritual matters, following which he became more temperate. Beethoven, who had a penchant for fortified wines (Cooper, 1970), died of cirrhosis of the liver, as did Satie (Myers, 1948) – although it is not certain in the case of either that the cause was entirely due to drink. Beethoven, indeed, apart from his very obvious emotional problems suffered from a chronic intestinal disorder.* Perhaps, therefore, he was inclined to drink more at times than he should have done to dull his discomfort, not to mention the misery of his deafness.

However, neither Beethoven nor Tchaikovsky probably had alcoholic propensities to anything like the same extent as did W. F. Bach, Moeran, Mussorgsky and Lambert; or were possibly as intemperate at times as Reger or Glazunov, whom Darius Milhaud, on a tour of Russia in 1926, found "cut off from the world by a veil of vodka fumes" (Milhaud, 1952). Another with an undoubted tendency towards alcoholism was Peter Warlock, whose rumbustious beer-swilling habits can be regarded as intrinsic, at least to one side of his character, as is perhaps reflected in his drinking songs.

Although there is no evidence in the case of any of these composers that their alcoholic habits had any directly beneficial effect upon their music, the possibility of some rather more indirect effect could be argued. Busoni, for example, stated that he was in the habit of taking a glass of wine to help him to relax before he began to compose; just as at his later recitals he would often take a glass or two of champagne before starting to play. It may have been this, together with his sometimes convivial way of life, which gave rise to the rumour that he was an habitual drunkard. The idea has, however, been strongly refuted both by Dent (1933) and van Dieren (1935) who apparently knew him well. Apart from this instance, many gifted artists, including musicians, are known to have hedonistic tendencies (Singer, 1932), the suggestion here being that a more than ordinarily developed capacity for sensual pleasures, including those of the table and the bed, may have lent colour, if not impetus, to creativity. Delius is a good case in point (Fenby, 1971): for while in the end he suffered from tabes dorsalis and on this account paid dearly for his earlier indulgences in the pleasures of Paris, his behaviour at the time was probably entirely in character. Indeed, much of his music seems to reveal this sensual characteristic. But although Delius was at one time known to have been a

---

* According to Professor Walter Smith, Beethoven may well have suffered from Crohn's disease (regional ileitis) which could, apart from his deafness, have accounted for all his other symptoms as well as his cirrhosis (Smith, 1975).

*bon vivant* (Jefferson, 1972), there is no suggestion whatsoever that he was at any time an alcoholic.

* * * *

One of the difficulties in trying to establish the prevalence of mental disorder among musicians, or among any other group of creative artists, is bound up with the matter of trying to define what is normal or not. But apart from this, who is to be included in the group under scrutiny? For example, if a number of musically knowledgeable persons were asked to name 30 European composers whom they would consider as coming within the category of genius (whatever this term really means) or those among the most gifted, there would probably be a reasonable consensus, but if asked to name a larger number, increasing divergencies would soon become apparent.

At the other end of the spectrum, and in contradistinction to those whose names, musically speaking, are household words, are the serried and earnest ranks of "church-cum-hymn-and-anthem" composers, together with a largish number who have written operas or music for the stage who, while they may have enjoyed some success in their own day, have since vanished into relative obscurity, so that were it not for Grove's dictionary we should probably know nothing of their existence. Although few might care to go so far as van Dieren (1935), who, in his book *Down Among the Dead Men*, seems to suggest that to be a forgotten composer is almost a matter of chance, there is some need for caution in making invidious assumptions about seemingly obscure composers. It is, for example, salutary to recall that J. S. Bach was much more highly regarded in his own day as an organist than as a composer, so that after his death little attention was paid to his works until, almost a century later, interest in them was revived, initially by Forkel and Rochlitz (Schweitzer, 1911) and subsequently by Mendelssohn and Samuel Wesley (Scholes, 1955).

It is difficult to know where to draw the line, for while it may be easy to distinguish a musical genius from a mere hack, there is nevertheless a rather ill-defined frontier having boundaries broad enough to conceal some who might, on closer scrutiny, turn out to be composers of real merit, but whose works due to a variety of circumstances are currently neglected. It is this, perhaps more than anything else, which presents what seems to be an insurmountable difficulty in establishing the prevalence of mental disturbance among composers. Even if we were to agree to go to the absurd lengths of including all of those who, at one time or another, had so much as a single one of their compositions published, this would clearly throw no useful light on the matter. Furthermore, it is likely that the information necessary to make an adequate assessment of their mental stability would, in most cases, be insufficient.

Difficulties of determining prevalence are also bound up with the problem of establishing adequate controls. This task when carried out contemporaneously is challenging enough; historically it is obviously impossible, but neglecting such difficulties, efforts have been made to try and settle the problem. Thus, the German psychiatrist, Ernst Kretschmer, although referring not only to composers, was in no doubt that the proportion of neurotics, psychopaths and the frankly insane was very much higher in geniuses than in lesser men. He observed furthermore:

In contrast to stable, limited talent which is inherited, true *genius* occurs almost invariably as a non-repeatable, non-inheritable phenomenon. In addition *degeneracy* is a demonstrably important factor. The posterity of persons of genius almost always shows a tendency to die out rapidly; frequently the man of genius himself has no direct descendants (Kretschmer, 1934).

While the notion of degeneracy has an old-fashioned ring, there appears to be much truth in what Kretschmer said. It is, for example, remarkable how many composers of eminence have remained single — though, like Paganini, not necessarily celibate or childless. Balakirev, Beethoven, Brahms, Bruckner, Chopin, Handel, Liszt, Mussorgsky, Ravel, Satie, Schubert and Wolf are some of those whose names spring readily to mind. Others, such as Tchaikovsky and Gesualdo, married disastrously; while some such as Berlioz, Mahler, Rossini, Scriabin, Warlock and possibly Charles Ives and Cesar Franck seem to have had considerable marital problems. Even Mozart and Schumann, who had relatively sizeable families, seem to have passed little or nothing of their musically creative genius on to their children, although one of Schumann's sons, Felix, had some talent as a poet, some of his poems being set by Brahms as solo songs. Musically there are relatively few father-and-son combinations to be found. Leopold and Wolfgang Mozart may be regarded as one exception. Nevertheless, and even though Wolfgang clearly inherited his father's musical talents, Leopold did not have the genius of his son. The same applies to the brothers Haydn. Joseph is usually hailed as a musical genius but not his undoubtedly talented brother, Michael. Again there have been families with several gifted members, but usually only one musical giant among them. Examples include the Couperins; Johann Strauss, his father and brothers; the Puccini family; and, of course, the Bachs.

At first sight the Bach family appear to contradict Kretschmer's hypothesis. Closer inspection may, however, suggest that their example could be the exception which turns out to prove the rule. Covering seven generations, many members of which were cantors, organists and town musicians who gained considerable reputations in their own day, the growing musical genius of the Bach family undoubtedly reached its peak in the person of Johann Sebastian Bach (1685–1750), following which it began fairly rapidly to decline. Although four of Bach's sons, Wilhelm Friedmann, Carl Philipp Emmanuel, Johann Christoph Friedrich and Johann Christian Bach all achieved considerable musical eminence in their own right, they seem to have passed little or nothing of their own genius to future generations. It is a reflection perhaps of hard times and the difficulties of child-rearing that of J. S. Bach's 20 children – seven by his first wife, 13 by his second – nine died within five years of birth and most of them within a much shorter period of time. Of the other 11 the majority seem to have remained unmarried. Only four bore children, of whom only one, Wilhelm Friedrich Ernst, son of Johann Christoph Bach, appears to have become a musician, being cembalist to Queen Louise of Prussia and music teacher to her children. He was the sole direct descendant of the great Cantor present at the unveiling of the Leipzig monument in 1843 (Schweitzer, 1911), and although he had two daughters he himself was the last of the male line.

Apart from the fact that none of J. S. Bach's male issue survived beyond a second generation, what perhaps might also be construed as further evidence of the impending dissolution of the Bach family soon began to show itself. Wilhelm Friedmann Bach, who has been hailed by some as the one who most inherited his father's genius (Terry, 1928), seems to have developed not only alcoholic but psychopathic tendencies also, including such a degree of indolence as to lead him, when organist at Halle, to try and execute a commission for some music for a university festival by passing off some of his illustrious father's work as his own. Soon after this he gave up his post, left his wife and daughter and became both a vagabond and increasingly addicted to drink.

Bach had yet another son, Johann Gottfried Bernhard, who while not a composer was apparently an organist of some competence, and caused his father considerable distress on account of debts and other irresponsible behaviour until his death at the age of 24. Apart from any hereditary influences which may have been at work, as both Wilhelm Friedmann and Bernhard were sons of Bach's first wife, Maria Barbara, who died when they were aged only six and four years respectively, it seems reasonable to suggest that the premature loss of their mother may possibly have been a contributory factor. Finally, and despite the fact that such an occurrence could be construed as no more than coincidence amongst so large a family, Gottfried Heinrich, Bach's first son born to his second wife Anna

Magdalena, while surviving 39 years, appears to have been feeble-minded.

There is another possibly feasible way of tackling the problem of prevalence. This is by means of what might be called the *nomination method*, whereby a list of the names of artists appropriate to the subject matter is obtained from a number of experts. Those about whom there is sufficient agreement are chosen and then subjected to more detailed scrutiny. This essentially was the method used by Dr. Adele Juda (1953), who approached a number of academic bodies and men of known distinction in various specialist fields, asking them to name those German-speaking persons whom they regarded as the most gifted and creative born since the year 1650. Her final list included 294 names, of whom 28 were composers.*

Juda's data has since been re-analysed by Slater and Meyer, whose conclusion was that the main weight of evidence was, on the whole, on the other side – that is, against the generalisation that genius is characterised by mental abnormality (Slater, 1958).

Of those on Juda's list, one, Robert Schumann, was clearly manic-depressive and suffered on this account for most of his life. It appears that he had a strongly positive family history of this disorder. Two others – Gluck and Wolf – suffered in the end from dementia; as did Schumann apparently. As, therefore, only three all told suffered from major mental illnesses, the concept of an association between genius and gross mental instability proves difficult to sustain. However, there were four others, Bruckner, Franz, Liszt, and Loewe, who sought medical treatment at one time or another for some kind of nervous condition. Nine at least, including Bruckner and Liszt, were also regarded by both Juda and Slater as having fairly well-defined psychopathic tendencies. There was disagreement between them about Gluck and Schubert, whom Juda saw as psychopathic while Slater did not, and in the case of Beethoven, where the reverse obtains. As some of the others whom Juda listed were also of fairly marked cyclothymic disposition, it can be concluded that the prevalence of what could be regarded as evidence not of overt madness but of at least some degree of mental instability among these 28 Austro-German composers is really quite high, those affected being not too far short of half their number.

Turning from prevalence to consideration of the kinds of mental disturbance from which composers appear liable to suffer, it must be stated that the conclusions put forward here are based on an examination of the

* Bach, W. F., Bach, J. S., Beethoven, Brahms, Bruckner, Cornelius, Franz, Gluck, Handel, Haydn, Hindemith, Liszt, Loewe, Lortzing, Mahler, Marschner, Mendelssohn, Mozart, Pfitzner, Reger, Schubert, Schumann, Stamitz, Strauss, J., Strauss, R., Wagner, Weber, Wolf.

lives of some 60 subjects, all currently deceased and selected largely because relevant information about them is fairly readily available. Bearing this bias in mind, it can be said that these subjects exhibited between them virtually the whole range of identifiable psychiatric illness or personality disorder, although not necessarily in the proportions in which such disturbances are found in the population-at-large.

Easily the commonest and most important of these are clinically recognisable affective disorders,* amounting in some cases to depression of such a degree that most psychiatrists would, today, recommend treatment. Whereas in some cases these states of depression were prolonged, leading to a very considerable reduction if not a cessation of musical output, in others more of a cyclothymic tendency is evident, leading to periodicity or to fairly rapidly recurrent mood swings and congruent fluctuations in creative activity. If four who are thought to have committed suicide are included,† and also several of the 13 who are thought to have been alcoholic, then not far short of half the subjects under consideration may probably be considered as being of melancholic temperament. In sharp contrast, it is only possible, with any degree of certainty, to identify one composer – Ivor Gurney – as having suffered from a schizophrenic illness.

Almost as many composers who showed signs of a mood disorder also exhibited neurotic or abnormal personality traits; although there is a considerable overlap between these two groups which are not, of course, mutually exclusive. One subject, Johann Strauss, suffered severely from phobic anxiety; a number of others had more or less marked obsessional trends. These include Bruckner, Lully, Mahler, Ravel and Satie; Scriabin and possibly Chopin and Dvořák also. Those who appear to have had some other form of personality disorder, with or without associated melancholic tendencies, include Beethoven, Berlioz, Busoni, Gluck, Liszt, Paganini, Pfitzner, Tchaikovsky, and Wagner, together with a number of others, some of whom have already been mentioned.

There are, in addition, a number who developed organically determined disorders, such as general paralysis. George Gershwin, who died aged 38 of a temporal lobe tumour, had his first seizure five months before his death, while actually performing his *Piano Concerto in F* (Rushmore, 1966). Acquired cerebral disease of this and other kinds must, however, be regarded as incidental and not wholly relevant to the main theme of this discussion. However, and as will be shown, there are certain aspects of the matter which are worthy of further consideration.

---

* Disorders characterised by fluctuations in mood and mental energy.
† Jeremiah Clarke, E. J. Moeran, Peter Warlock and possibly Tchaikovsky also.

The suggestion of a relationship between manic-depressive tendencies and creativity, or between melancholy and genius, is not new, but stems back to Aristotle, who observed that all those proficient in politics, philosophy, poetry or the arts, tend to be of melancholic temperament. Several 20th century writers have said the same of musicians (Singer, 1932; Schrade, 1964). Slater (1958) even went so far as to suggest that a cyclothymic disposition might, in some ways, be useful to a creative artist seeing advantage in the fact that the cyclothyme is, as a rule, extraverted and capable of strong emotion; a view shared by Onuf who regarded those of manic-depressive temperament as intensively responsive to emotional factors (Onuf, 1920). Thus such persons, if musically creative, are able to inject this heightened capacity for emotional experience into their music, but there is, perhaps, more to it than this. As already suggested, it is characteristic of affective disorders, of whatever type, that although it is the fluctuation of mood which may appear to be the primary feature this may turn out to be only a part or reflection of a much more profound disturbance, which being all-pervasive may affect every aspect of the physical and mental life of the sufferer, leading not so much to depression of mood but to a lowering of vital activity to the point where any kind of productive work, and in particular creative work, becomes quite impossible. Owing to semantic confusion, the sufferer and those around him, may describe this state of lowered vitality and reduced mental and physical energy as if it were primarily a disorder of mood when, as has been suggested, this may be no more than part of it. Thus Rimsky-Korsakoff gave a vivid personal description of how, in 1892, his own musical vitality was affected by a state of mental depression:

But lo and behold! One fine morning at the end of August or at the beginning of September, I was overtaken by an extreme lassitude accompanied by a sort of rush to my head and utter confusion of thinking. I was frightened in real earnest, and in the first few days even lost my appetite completely . . . Whenever I did remain alone, unpleasant obtrusive fixed ideas persistently crept into my head. I thought of religious ideas and of humble reconciliation with Balakireff. . . . But I had grown altogether cold to music and the thought of occupying myself with philosophic education pursued me unremittingly (Rimsky-Korsakoff, 1924).

Such fluctuations of energy which lead periodically to a state of comparative if not total inactivity seem to lend themselves to comparison with episodes which appear to resemble a kind of hibernation during which, however, the hibernator may be "gathering steam" for a further period of productivity which takes place as resurgence begins.

Confirmation of this is to be found in the letters which several composers have written about themselves and their work. Elgar ". . . ebullient one minute, downcast the next", when depressed – which appears to have been by no means infrequent – would write to his friends that he was giving up music; that he was sick of it and all connected with it. On one occasion he even went so far as to state ". . . music is a trade and I am no tradesman", possibly expressing, thereby, his continuing resentment at his relatively humble birth. Michael Kennedy has observed how Elgar's creative periods were usually preceded by a period of acute depression:

The (Enigma) Variations and Gerontius followed one such period; the bleak and despondent 1907 was followed by a burst of activity which produced two symphonies and a concerto (Kennedy, 1968).

Similar insights can be gleaned from the letters of Peter Warlock, of whom E. J. Moeran, who shared a cottage with him for three and a half years, stated:

Warlock's methods as a composer were dictated by the peculiarities of his temperament. For weeks he would be sunk in gloom unable to think of a note (Cockshott, 1955),

and as Warlock himself wrote in a letter to Colin Taylor in June, 1918:

I am grieved to hear that you have been labouring again in the toils of the fiend dejection – how well I know him too! He has treated me lately to a much longer spell in his society than I had any wish for. I think there are few influences more wearing than his; the inactivity, the consciousness of being void and sterile . . . I cannot write a note of music. I am utterly desiccated. . . .

However, within two months of writing these words, he suddenly composed ten songs in a fortnight (Gray, 1934). Warlock was not only manic-depressive, as his recurrent hypomanic and depressive episodes and his subsequent suicide clearly show, but a man deeply disturbed and divided in other ways, as was apparent to D. H. Lawrence who drew a cruel caricature of him as Halliday in *Women in Love* (1921).*

Other instances of the relationship between music and melancholy are not hard to find. There is, however, one example which deserves special mention, not only because it appears to be unique but because it is a musical statement of the matter (Figure 2).

This is the final movement of Beethoven's string quartet, Opus 18, No. 6, which he composed between 1798 and 1800, and which he entitled *La Malinconia*. The piece contains six alternating slow and fast sections. While

* A more charitable portrayal of Warlock is to be found in Aldous Huxley's *Antic Hay*, in the character of Coleman (Huxley, 1923).

Figure 2   Middle section of the final movement of Beethoven's String Quartet, Op. 18 No. 6, *La Malinconia* showing fast and slow passages.

the slow passages seem intended to convey a gloomy disposition, the fast ones are perhaps rather more phrenetic than elated, which, nevertheless, is not necessarily out of character. In view of its phasic quality the movement appears to be an attempt to describe, in musical terms, the fluctuations of mood and activity, to which the cyclothyme is subject. Beethoven's title leaves no doubt about this; it is indeed, the only composition which, it has been said, has made a psychiatric term immortal (Caldwell, 1972), and yet, as Joseph Kerman has observed, the piece:

plumbs melancholy in a curiously aloof speculative way . . . revealing an almost heartless preoccupation with its own harmonic meditations over those of the poor melancholic (Kerman, 1967).

Despite Beethoven's own acquaintance with despondency, it may be concluded, therefore, that *La Malinconia* is, perhaps, more of an intellectual description of melancholia than an emotional one. It certainly fails to arouse that degree of affective response in the listener that so many of his other works do, for example the third movement, *molto adagio*, of his later string quartet in A minor (Op. 132), the "Hymn of Gratitude".

The case of Robert Schumann (1810–1856) is undoubtedly the best documented example illustrating the relationship between periodic fluctuations in mood – in this instance of frankly manic-depressive proportions – and musical output. A histogram which relates the composer's annual output in terms of works either completed or, in a few cases, taken to the point of final abandonment, contrasted year by year with his prevailing mood state (see Slater, 1972), shows this clearly (Figure 3). From this it may be observed that Schumann's most productive years appear to have been 1832, 1840 and, above all, 1849, although the years 1850 to 1853 also saw the completion of a considerable number of works which, towards the end of this period, and due apparently to organic brain disease supervening, were of deteriorating quality, particularly perhaps his later choral works (Halsey, 1972). What is of greater interest is that these

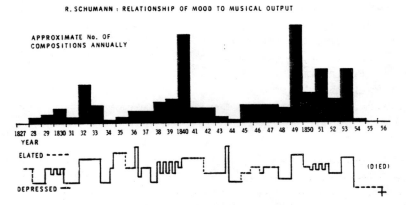

Figure 3   Histogram indicating Schumann's annual output of compositions (Slater, 1972).

productive years appear to have been preceded by periods of up to a year when the composer was predominantly depressed, as can be clearly seen during the period 1831 and 1834. In the six years preceding 1840 – one of Schumann's more prolific years – a gradual build-up of output is evident during which period there also appear to have been considerable fluctuations in his mood. Following this there was a fairly rapid diminution of his output and, with the exception of a short sharp upward swing at the end of 1843, a return the following year to deep depression. During the period 1845–47 Schumann's prevailing mood appears to have returned more or less to normal, so that he remained moderately productive until 1848, when despair overcame him once again, despite which he still appears to have continued to be moderately musically active, but as can also be seen this depressive phase led directly up to the year 1849, a year in which he was probably more productive than at any other time during the whole of his musical life, and one throughout which he remained in high spirits.

Cyclothymia is not, of course, the only type of disposition which may give rise to fluctuations in output. In some instances there occurs what may perhaps be called a creative pause due apparently to a depressive phase of much longer duration. Several examples of this are to be found.

One of the most striking is the case of Mily Balakirev (1837–1910), who retired in 1871, when aged 34, from music altogether and became a railway goods clerk. Apart from becoming quite obviously melancholic he also became intensely religious, which sudden conversion, it is said, occurred on the anniversary of his mother's death, which happened when he was ten years old. His state of depression lasted four years altogether, following which he recovered and set to work once more on his unfinished opera, *Tamara*. But even then he is said to have remained a man of rather narrow outlook and autocratic temperament, in whose case age tended to increase the less endearing aspects of his character (Garden, 1967).

There were clearly several different factors operative in bringing about Balakirev's mental illness. He was a man of compulsive character who had previously had a nervous ailment when aged 21. This, although described as "inflammation of the brain", was probably an unrecognised depressive bout. In any event, the illness seems to have left him irritable and prone to headaches. Apart from losing his mother when he was a child – a factor which has been thought to predispose to the development of a severe depression during later life (Munro, 1966) – Balakirev also had problems with his father, who was an unsuccessful civil servant and a gambler. Because of this he had to contribute to the financial upkeep of his sisters. To add to this in the years immediately preceding the onset of his depression he fell not only into financial difficulties but also suffered some professional reverses, including being ousted from the conductorship of the Russian Musical Society after having offended its patroness, the Grand Duchess Elania Pavlova.

The case of Giacchimo Rossini (1792–1868) is altogether more complex. By the age of 37 he had composed 36 operas. Then, in 1829, his career as an opera composer ended. Although often entreated to write further operas, he refused adamantly to do so. Eight years silence followed; then between 1837 and 1842 he completed his *Stabat Mater*, following which, and apart from a few relatively minor works, he again became musically silent until 25 years later, when he wrote his *Petite Messe Solonelle* which, despite its name, is by no means a minor work.

Rossini's cessation of creative activity when apparently at the height of his powers – the so-called "Great Renunciation" (Toye, 1934) – has given rise to much discussion. Schwartz (1965) states that the reason for it was that Rossini, who was over-attached to his mother – herself an opera singer although not of the first rank – became depressed following her death in 1827; his grief over this event being reactivated when his first wife, Isabella Colbran, from whom he had been separated for a number of years, also died. Isabella Colbran, a prima donna, between 1815 and 1823 sang leading roles in the first performances of no less than ten of Rossini's operas. Schwartz's interpretation of these events is that Rossini's ambivalence to his mother made it impossible for him to mourn her in a healthy way, and that his refusal to compose further operas could be construed as an expression of unconscious anger at her for having deserted him by dying – a psychoanalytically-based hypothesis of a not unfamiliar kind. There are several serious objections, however, to Schwartz's formulation. The first is that Rossini wrote two more operas after his mother died, *Le Comte Ory* and *William Tell* – one of his greatest successes. The second is that at the age of 27 – that is about two years before her death – Rossini had already announced his intention of stopping composing at 30, having by then, as Stendhal observed, amassed a considerable fortune, both on account of his own success as an opera composer and by marrying Isabella Colbran (Weinstock, 1968). Thirdly, although Rossini later fell ill this did not occur until 1832, some five years after his mother's death.

Rossini's prolonged illness was both of a physical and mental kind. He suffered from chronic gonorrhoea, and fearing a stricture catheterized himself daily; which practice may well have caused superadded infection and exacerbated his chronic urethritis. However, according to Riboli (1954), the torment which Rossini suffered on this account did not suffice to explain the strong physical and psychic prostration into which he fell, while Olympe Pélissier, who nursed him and later became his second wife, observed that he appeared changed "even more morally (i.e. mentally) than physically".

Riboli regarded him as manic-depressive which, in view of his previous outgoing personality, his pyknic somatotype, and the nature of many of his symptoms, seems likely. Among other things he is said to have suffered from psychic inhibition, loss of weight, debility, auditory illusions, delusions of poverty, fears of suicide, inability to eat and sleep, and moods of black despair. Like most manic-depressives his condition underwent considerable fluctuations. Thus in 1836 Mendelssohn found him "big and fat, in his most able and festive mood". It was soon after this that he completed his *Stabat Mater*. In 1839 his father died and he relapsed, but by 1844 he was better again and had begun to take interest in various musical activities. Again he relapsed, so that in 1852 Lombroso, who saw him then, stated he was "definitely mad" (Macalpine and Hunter, 1952); while in 1854 another visitor, Morgani, noted how "he gave vent to heavy laments and sighs, unexpectedly broke into sobbings and looking in the mirror accused himself of cowardice" (Weinstock, 1968). In 1855, when aged about 63, he began to recover once more and gradually to assume his old gregarious habits. This time he appears to have remained mentally well until shortly before his death.*

There are other more puzzling cases: for example, that of Paul Dukas (1865–1935) – best known perhaps for *The Sorcerer's Apprentice* – who appears to have given up composing in early middle age having, it is said, burned the unpublished products of over a quarter-of-a-century's labour (Scholes, 1955). As there seems to have been no evidence of mental disorder in his case, did he, like some others may have done, run out of "creative steam"? And what of Sibelius (1865–1957) who, having written his last major work, *Tapiola*, 30 years before his death, produced nothing but a handful of small-scale stuff thereafter? Although the evidence is not conclusive, it seems possible that alcoholism may have played a part (Layton, 1965). However, more needs to be known to account for Sibelius's later unproductive years. Layton states that he was undoubtedly irked by the lack of success of his works in Germany and "that his powers of self-criticism, always acute, definitely sharpened". There were also certain psychological shocks "among them the loss of a trusted friend and critic, Capelan". There is evidence, too, that the long-awaited *Eighth Symphony*, although never finally published, may have been in an

---

* Although the duration of Rossini's melancholia may seem surprisingly long, it should not be forgotten that such prolonged illnesses were not uncommon in the days prior to electroconvulsive therapy and antidepressant drugs.

advanced state of completion at the time of the composer's death (Layton, 1975).

Charles Ives (1874–1954) was yet another composer whose output came apparently to a sudden halt. Partly this may have been due to a heart attack in 1918, but possibly, according to Aaron Copland, because Ives had never had an audience, and had heard little or nothing of his music played, he may have become disenchanted with composing (Perlis, 1974). There is no suggestion to be made, however, that this cessation of Ives's musical output was due to mental abnormality. The more immediate neglect of his music seems to have stemmed from its complexity, its technical difficulty in performance, and possibly by reason of the expression of musical ideas too far ahead of his time for ready acceptance. However, following improvement in his physical condition and considerable revision of some of his work by the composer, the value of much of his music has come to be recognised, so that it has begun to assume a rightful place in the orchestral repertoire and much of it is now available in recorded form (Wooldridge, 1975).

Perhaps one of the most remarkable examples of all is that of the French poet, painter and composer, Henri Duparc (1848–1933), of whom Northcote (1949) has written:

Seldom has any creative artist laid so small an offering on the altar of fame as Henri Duparc. Some 14 songs, a symphonic poem, an orchestral nocturne, and a three-part motet comprise almost the whole of his existing compositions.

At the age of 72 Duparc explained in a letter to his publishers that all his songs were written before 1885, when he was aged 37, and that he had never been able to compose since then. Although it has been suggested, because he went blind at the end of his life (possibly due to tobacco amblyopia) and suffered from some kind of paralysis, that his inability to compose may have been due to a progressive neurological disorder, this does not appear to have been the case. While Alajouanine has suggested that he may have been manic-depressive (Koupernik, 1974), the real reason seems to be that Duparc, who probably always had neurotic tendencies, later became musically completely inhibited by increasing psychasthenia and obsessional self-criticism (Merle, 1933). Duparc apparently destroyed a good deal of his work, including the first act of an opera as well as some early piano pieces. He is said to have taken meticulous care over his works and to have subjected them to constant revision (Northcote, 1949). There is, however, nothing it seems to be found of Duparc's neuroticism in his songs, which are generally agreed to be of superb quality. One other, and probably again an obsessional symptom, was an idea from which Duparc suffered that a bird would come to his window at the same time each morning and trouble him with its warbling, and in some way interfere with his musical sensibility. Curiously enough all these kinds of difficulties seemed to have affected Duparc's musical life only; his gift for painting, which is said to have been considerable, seems to have remained unaffected.

In contrast perhaps, there can be seen in the case of the English poet and songwriter, Ivor Gurney (1890–1937), not only a cessation of musical output due to mental illness, but also a deterioration in the quality of his work. Gurney was invalided from the Army in 1918 after considerable suffering in Flanders, where he wrote much of his poetry and some of his songs. In 1922 he was admitted to a mental hospital with a diagnosis of delusional insanity, where he remained for the next 15 years until dying of tuberculosis. An examination of his medical records leaves no doubt that the nature of Gurney's illness was paranoid schizophrenia. This is confirmed by Professor E. W. Anderson (1974) who looked after Gurney for part of the time he was in hospital.

Although Gurney's mental illness is usually ascribed to his suffering in the trenches and was no doubt exacerbated by these privations, it seems clear that well before his admission to the mental hospital where he passed the remainder of his days he had had a whole series of nervous breakdowns, usually following the completion of any major piece of work. These recurrent episodes of nervous illness, which began as early as 1913, appear to have been largely of a depressive kind and accompanied by threats of suicide (Hurd, 1975). They must, however, be regarded as precursors of his later paranoid psychosis.

Gurney continued to write music for a time, even while in the asylum, but his later songs – those composed around 1925 – which are still in manuscript, and appear to be the last he wrote which were not subsequently destroyed, show not only a deterioration in their quality but are, in some instances, annotated with delusional statements which refer to such things as "electrical torture"* (Figure 4). Some of his poetry of about the same period is similarly annotated.

Other of Gurney's scrawls appear to reveal a confusion of ego identity, a common and important symptom of schizophrenia; this being further borne out by his statements that he was the author of Shakespeare's plays, that Beethoven and Haydn had never existed and that he had composed their music. On at least one of his manuscripts Gurney signed himself "L.

---

* It should be emphasised that this was well before the introduction of electroconvulsive therapy into psychiatry, and seems to have referred to Gurney's delusional belief of being influenced by the wireless.

Figure 4  Final page of Gurney's setting of W. B. Yeat's "All the words that I utter" showing some of his annotations. (By kind permission of Mrs. Joyce Finzi.)

van Beethoven of Louvain" – the pun being unwitting, not an attempt at humour, but a fairly typical example of schizophrenic thought disorder. Musically, Gurney's later songs show a considerable degree of structural deterioration with, according to Dr. Howard Ferguson:

unrelieved semiquaver movement so that the music tends to wander on without any real sense of direction . . . Each bar considered individually makes harmonic sense: it is only the ability to define and organise material, and to construct a coherent whole, that is altogether lacking (Ferguson, 1974).

This analysis fits in remarkably well with what might be the expected effect of a schizophrenic process upon the ability of an otherwise talented musician to compose.

In those composers who later developed organic brain syndromes, their ability to write music came not unexpectedly to a halt; in some cases more rapidly than in others. Possibly the two best examples are Robert Schumann, to whom considerable reference has already been made, and Hugo Wolf. Both, like Donizetti and possibly Smetana, are thought to have suffered from general paralysis (one variety of tertiary neurosyphilis), although in Schumann's case there still seems to be room for doubt, despite the fact that he clearly suffered (during the final years of his life) from some form of organic brain disease.

Although there may be fairly clear evidence of deterioration in Schumann's later music, not only, according to Dr. Eric Sams (1974), of the actual fabric of the musical material, but also in its relationship to verbal comprehension, this interestingly enough is much less obvious in the case of Hugo Wolf (1860–1903). Wolf suddenly became acutely psychotic when, in September 1897, after assembling a group of his friends to hear him play a piano arrangement of his unfinished opera, *Manuel Venegas*, he suddenly declared that Mahler had been dismissed from his position as Director of the Vienna State Opera and that he, Hugo Wolf, had been appointed in his place. This grandiose delusion not only startled his hearers but not surprisingly heralded his admission to Dr. Svetlin's asylum. For at least a year before this, however, it is on record that Wolf had Argyll-Robertson pupils – a sign strongly suggestive of neurosyphilis. Even before then, and during the rehearsals and performance of his one and only completed opera, *Der Corregidor*, in 1896, Wolf's behaviour seems at times to have been so outrageous that it must be concluded, despite his lifelong temperamental instability (he, too, had cyclothymic tendencies), that his judgement was even more grossly impaired than may have been usual. Nevertheless, little of Wolf's brain disease is revealed in his music.

In March 1897, six months before he went overtly mad, Wolf wrote his three *Michaelangelo* songs. Of the last of these – *Fühlt meine Seele* – Eric Sams has written:

This is not a perfect work, nor is it easy to grasp at first hearing. But the workmanship is so exquisite, the emotion so intense, that a man might be immortal for having written this one song. It was Wolf's last (Sams, 1961).

There is also, of course, *Manuel Venegas*, which Ernest Newman has described as a "pathetic fragment" showing however, "no signs of failing inspiration" (Newman, 1907). But while it is certainly not first-rate Wolf, it is nevertheless still difficult to understand how a man with so advanced, presumably, a degree of brain damage could have written it.

Sams has put forward the notion that in considering a composer's weakening of creative powers, it might be useful to divide this concept into component parts. He states:

If one such part were originality, I think I should concede that Wolf's last (*Michaelangelo*) songs do indeed show a deterioration in this respect which is not paralleled in (say) Brahms's last songs; or Schubert's, or (come to that) Richard Strauss's (Sams, 1974).

The fact that the ability to compose, in some cases at least, may, in the face of advancing organic brain disease, be relatively well-preserved, is an interesting finding deserving further consideration. Music, it is said, is the most abstract of all arts; and yet it is the power of abstract thought which appears to be the first casualty in the journey towards dementia. How can it be, therefore, that the pathological march of organic brain disease may be such, in some cases, as to leave whatever part of the brain is concerned with musical composition unscathed — at least until a relatively late stage?

It could be postulated that musicianship is primarily a temporal lobe function (possibly a non-dominant one) and that as the ravages of a disease such as general paralysis are prone, at least in the earlier stages, to attack the frontal lobes, the neuronal source of musical genius, if indeed there is one, may remain unimpaired until the later stages; but such a notion may over-value topography. A more likely explanation is that musical ability, especially when highly developed, tends to show itself at a very early age. There are many instances of this, Mozart probably being the most striking example. Thus, following the phylogenetic law — the last gained, the soonest lost — musicianship, in the face of a not too rapidly advancing dementing process, might be expected to remain relatively well-preserved until the end draws near. It should also be borne in mind that what a person with progressive brain degeneration can accomplish at any particular state of his disorder is a factor not of the diseased part of his brain, but of that which, up to that time, has remained intact (Jackson, 1884).

\*     \*     \*     \*

There remain to be considered in what ways the personality problems or emotional disturbances from which some composers have suffered may be reflected in the quality of their music. This is the most difficult of all questions to answer, for the pitfalls of subjectivity lie in wait for those indulging in even the most tentative speculations.

While there are many varieties of personality disorder, two principal groups stand out — the *hysterics*\* and the *obsessionals*. Of those in the first category perhaps the two prime examples are Hector Berlioz (1803–1869) and Richard Wagner (1813–1883). It has nevertheless to be said, in dealing with those kinds of personalities as are currently under consideration, that any attempt at a fairly conventional classification is likely to turn out to be highly inadequate, being relatively so crude as to do little more than rough justice to matters both delicate and of extreme complexity.

Berlioz's extraordinary behaviour when rejected by his fiancée, Camille Moke, in favour of Pleyel is nothing if not indicative of his tendency to dramatise. As soon as he heard about it he decided to go to Paris, shoot Camille, her lover, her mother, and himself. After purchasing the complete outfit of a lady's maid, which he intended to wear as a disguise, loading his pistols and putting into his pockets a bottle of strychnine and another of laudanum and after "wandering the streets of Florence with the sickly, restless air of a mad dog" (Cairns, 1970) he appears, after contemplating drowning himself *en route*, only to have got so far as Nice when he apparently recovered his senses. We are not told what happened to the pistols and the poison; however it is possible that Berlioz's failure to use them indicated a degree of faint-heartedness, well in tune with the hysterical character in which the most seemingly violent emotions may not penetrate much beyond skin deep. Reflecting on the matter Berlioz himself said:

"It would have made a fine scene. It really is a great pity it had to be dropped."

It should also be known that despite his apparent frenzy over the affair, he still found time to write a note regarding an alteration to his *Symphonie Fantastique*, the work which, more than any other perhaps, reveals his true nature.

Berlioz, despite his periodic exuberance, suffered from a variety of nervous complaints including, it is sometimes alleged, epilepsy. This he himself denied, and there seems no real reason to believe that the notion has any foundation in fact. However, a rumour to this effect may have grown out of knowledge that Berlioz was given to fits of frenzy, these emotional storms being provoked by frustration, arising either from difficulties in

---

\* The term hysteria has in recent years achieved a somewhat unfortunate connotation. It is used here to denote a flamboyant, demonstrative often histrionic, extravagant and extraverted personality type, capable not only of attracting attention but if, in addition, talented, of holding it.

getting his works performed or having to indulge in musical journalism for a living, which pursuit he appears to have detested (Rhys, 1937). Later Berlioz became depressed by the death of his wife from whom he had been for some time estranged, and even more so by that of his son (Hadow, 1926). As a result of this his last days, which have been described as empty and solitary (Scholes, 1955), were passed in a state of considerable despair.

It is almost impossible within so small a space to do justice to a character as colourful and-complex as Richard Wagner (1813–1883). Many might agree that his operas, if for no other reason than their size and scale alone, betray his expansive histrionic tendencies, but despite the esteem in which he is held there are many for whom his music has little appeal and who, perhaps like Rossini, regard it as "all sauce and no substance" (Weinstock, 1968). Wagner's most striking personality characteristic was his monstrous egotism, to which so much of his life bears evidence: his shameful treatment of his first wife, Minna; his affairs with Frau Wesendonck and others who took his passing fancy, and perhaps above all the outrageous manner in which he carried on with Cosima von Bülow, later to become his second wife but, whose husband, although a friend and colleague, Wagner more or less publicly cuckolded. Indeed it was even said of von Bülow that he not only owed his appointment as Kappellmeister to the Court of King Ludwig of Bavaria to Wagner's friendship with the King but to "his compliance as a husband" (Newman, 1914).

Add to all this Wagner's flamboyance, his pathological fondness for silk, satin and other creature comforts; his constant tendency to live beyond his means; his attitude to money – particularly that of others to whom his reputation soon became that of a reckless spendthrift – then his personality presents an image closely resembling that of Henderson's creative psychopath (Henderson, 1952):

There, you see it all – the egotism, the insanity of altruistic feeling, the unfeelingness, the eccentricity, the near-genius type, and yet coupled with violent tempestuous behaviour, which might break out at any time and in any way irrespective of what it might mean to the central figure and those in close association with it. There, too, you may perhaps discern – if you can think in such a way – the strange fascination and charm which such a person may exert.

These words were actually written of Lady Caroline Lamb, but, except for the fact that few would deny his real genius, Henderson's description might have served Wagner equally well. The testimony of his contemporaries bears this out. Thus Hanslick stated:

He talked incredibly much and rapidly . . . He talked continuously and always of himself, of his works, of his reforms, his plans. If he happened to mention the name of another composer, it was certain to be in terms of disdain . . . He was egoism personified, restlessly energetic for himself, unsympathetic towards and regardless of others (Hanslick, quoted by Newman, op. cit.).

There can be little doubt that this very streak of ruthlessness contributed greatly to Wagner's creativity and to the form which it took. His work could hardly have flourished had the flame of his self-esteem burned low.

This same streak of ruthless egotism is evident in the character of some other composers, although in no instance so obvious as in Wagner's case. Beethoven certainly had it – as evidenced by the extraordinary affair over the custody of his nephew, Karl, and also, perhaps, in some of his somewhat unscrupulous dealings with his publishers. Hugo Wolf, possibly, and Liszt and Richard Strauss seem to have had at least some of the same degree of egotistical endowment; but perhaps next to Wagner the most striking example may be that of Delius. How else could a man, blind, paralysed and tortured by lightning pains – a terrible symptom of the illness from which he suffered – continue to have composed music, even with the help of his indefatigable amanuensis, Eric Fenby, unless driven relentlessly onwards by a ruthless force of self-justification? If Delius, like Wagner, was in doubt of anything whatsoever, it was never of himself. This cannot be put down merely to his disease for there is ample evidence that before it took its terrible toll of him, Delius had all the necessary strength of self-purpose to carry him through to what must have been the bitterest end.

It has been said of Gustav Mahler (1860–1911) that the more expansive side of his nature is revealed by his attempt to create works of greater compass than, possibly, were within his powers. However, it is the obsessional aspects of his character which appear to be the more important, although these are reflected only secondarily in his music, largely in the detailed and minute instructions given in his scores; but this, as has also been postulated, is not necessarily evidence of an obsessive tendency, it could equally well be interpreted as the work of a master craftsman who knew just what he wanted and how to get it (Christy et al., 1970). However, although Mahler had a valvular lesion of the heart and died ultimately of bacterial endocarditis, his hypochondriacal concern about his cardiac condition – albeit iatrogenically induced according to Alma Mahler (1946) – clearly betrays obsessive trends, as probably does his excessive detestation of noise, excessive even for a musician and about which he complained in his letters to Alma, almost everywhere he went. He also had a number of other rather finicky habits.

Some other composers seem to betray obsessionalism in their music.

Anton Bruckner (1824–1896) appears to be a good example. Bruckner was not only obsessed with death and with corpses but was of a highly pedantic turn of mind, having a compulsion to collect diplomas, and a tendency to waste time – of which he stated that he never had enough – in endless revision of his scores (Schönzeler, 1970). Although strictly celibate he was fascinated by adolescent girls to whom he many times proposed and was invariably rejected. Bruckner also suffered a compulsion to count, which according to Redlich (quoted by Slater, 1958) shows itself in his music as a partiality for stiff regularities of periodisation sometimes approaching rhythmic monotony.

A repetitive phase has also been identified in several of the works of Antonin Dvořák (1841–1904) which it is thought the composer himself may not have recognised. This may be evidence of some degree of obsessionalism, accounting also perhaps for the fact that his earlier works tend to be long-winded and repetitious. Although there is not too much evidence of obsessionalism in Dvořák's non-musical life, it is recorded:

that he was fascinated by trains and kept track of schedules and the serial numbers of locomotives; even sending someone out to read them when he was too busy with music (Kantor and Pinsker, 1973).

Perhaps the most striking example is that of Erik Satie (1866–1925) who, although he lived alone in somewhat squalid surroundings in Paris and apparently at times in considerable poverty, dressed fastidiously and in so correct a manner as would befit a senior civil servant. Despite this, and when shortly before his death Satie was removed to hospital, his only toilet accessories were found to be a scrubbing brush and a piece of pumice stone. When his room was entered – no one was allowed in it during his life – his wardrobe was found to contain a dozen identical old-fashioned but brand new suits, an excessive number of shirts, collars, old hats and walking sticks and a cigar box containing several thousand pieces of paper, on which he had made curious drawings and extravagant inscriptions which spoke of "enchanted shores, pools and marshes in the time of Charlemagne". Satie's obsessional nature is further revealed both in his elaborate handwriting and the ornate manner in which he wrote out his music (see Figure 5) (Myers, 1948; Milhaud, 1952).

Constant Lambert (1934), who described Satie as the only modern composer whose music could at that time be described as abstract, likened *Gymnopèdies* – a short suite of three remarkably similar piano pieces – to musical sculptures, stating that:

Just as it does not matter in which way you walk around a statue, nor does it matter in which order you play the pieces.

Two of these pieces (the first and last) were later orchestrated by Debussy, who was taken to task on this account by Cocteau and others, on the grounds that Satie's original idea was misinterpreted and that the "transparent clarity and simplicity were clouded in an impressionistic haze" (Gowers, 1974). Certainly Debussy's treatment of the pieces considerably destroys their obsessional character.

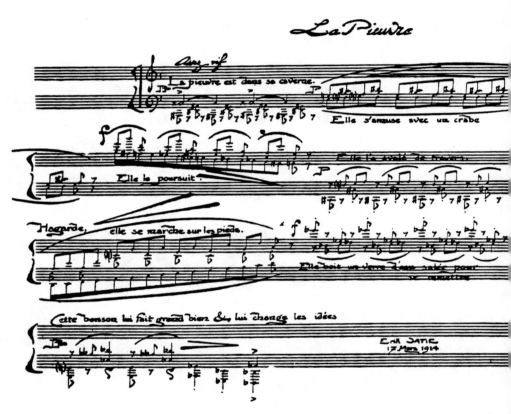

Figure 5    An example of Erik Satie's very precise musical notation and ornate handwriting. (By kind permission of Dennis Dobson, Ltd.)

Alexander Scriabin (1871–1951) could also be classed as an obsessional, although one cast in a very different mould from some of those already mentioned. He was very particular concerning his appearance and would spend hours preening himself before entering a room full of guests. His handwriting (like Satie's possibly) was said to have been perfect and symmetrically lettered; so much so that it is recorded that on these grounds alone he was once declared clinically insane – a somewhat slender basis, perhaps, for arriving at such a profound conclusion. However, many of his contemporaries also regarded him as mad on account of his sometimes strange behaviour (Bowers, 1974).

Further evidence of Scriabin's obsessionalism may be gleaned from his dislike of every-day financial transactions and his strange habit of putting on gloves before receiving or giving money to tradesmen.* As a child and during adolescence, Scriabin suffered from a variety of neurotic symptoms and on this account was periodically subjected to "cures". As he grew older this tendency to nervous disorder increased. In 1895, he consulted the eminent neurologist, Dr. Wilhelm Erb, and, it is said, gained complete relief from troublesome migrainous headaches after receiving psychotherapy. As he grew older, Scriabin seems to have become progressively immured in theosophy, oriental mysticism, satanism and a variety of eccentric semi-religious pursuits. He is said to have indulged in flying experiments, and on one occasion to have tried to imitate Christ by walking on the waters of Lake Geneva. Being unsuccessful "he settled for preaching to the fishermen from a boat" (Bowers, *op. cit.*).

Like other obsessionals, Scriabin's sexuality was as divided and disturbed as the man himself. Although twice married (*de facto*, on the second occasion), and the father of seven children, this was by no means the limit of his sexual activities. At one time he is said to have had a taste for very young girls and much older men, and caused a considerable scandal in Moscow in 1903 by seducing a 15-year old girl student at a school where he was music teacher. According to Bowers once again, Sabeneeff, a contemporary of Scriabin, referred to his "lust and utter depravity", which suggests that in addition to his heterosexual escapades he may also have ventured in other directions. While at the Conservatory his fellow students called him "Pussy" which, it is said, he did not appear to mind. It is also on record that he was greatly admired by his piano teacher, Zveryov, apparently one of Russia's most notoriously homosexual musicians.

Be this as it may, Scriabin's obsession with sex has probably never more clearly been revealed than in his *Poème de l'Extase*, which, without the composer's "foggy, turgid, prolix, diffuse, almost comically cosmic verse purporting to explain the music" (Lyons, 1971), is quite clearly as voluptuous an account of the sexual act as was ever expressed in any medium. Much of Scriabin's other symphonic works are said to express his interest in theosophy and like matters. Constant Lambert referred to the

---

* Any doctrinaire Freudian would unhesitatingly regard the equation money-paper-faeces–dirt as unequivocal evidence of the possession of anal-erotic, i.e. obsessional tendencies.

"opulent vulgarity" of his works, while Busoni, who was ruder still, described his piano sonatas, which have been considerably acclaimed, as "*une indigestion de Chopin*" (Dent, 1933). Not unnaturally the Soviets saw him as decadent, but it is difficult to decide whether it was Scriabin's music or his personality they disliked more.

When we come to consider those composers whose music may have been primarily influenced by fluctuations in mood, we are confronted by what is perhaps a real dilemma; the question being when a composer at one time writes music which is cheerful, gay and abandoned, and, at others, sad or solemn, whether this really is or is not a true reflection of his prevailing emotional state at the time. We should perhaps agree with Hindemith (1952) that a man who labours several months over a funeral piece does not, during all this time, necessarily remain in a funereal mood. What is much more likely is that his ability to compose music of this or any other kind indicates his ability to inject his experience of his own alterations of mood into his music, as and when he chooses. It might also be asked whether those composers of predominantly melancholic temperament are largely compelled to depressed musical utterances, whether those of predominantly cheerful disposition are given primarily to the writing of music which is carefree, euphonious and in a major key, and whether those who are cyclothymic, and familiar with both extremes, reveal their temperamental fluctuations in the variability of their compositions.

While it is possible to answer all these questions affirmatively, not being mutually exclusive, it is as well to be aware of the risks of over-simplification. None of the questions does justice to the complexity of the matter, for not only are there many shades of mood which lie between the extremes of deep depression and high-spirited elation, but a variety of other emotional states which, not being primarily determined by mood, lie qualitatively outside this dimension. Furthermore, although there may be considerable consensual agreement as to the portrayal, in musical terms, of moods such as gaiety and despair – by having resort to such simple devices as fast or slow tempi, major or minor keys and certain harmonic progressions which, having predetermined if not absolute associations, tend to invoke an appropriate response in the listener – such relatively concrete conventions are not only of limited effects, but they cannot possibly do justice to the subtleties of emotional expression which lie within the ambit of musical artistry, and which defy analysis other than in the most abstract terms. As Deryck Cooke has pointed out, music is "extra-musical" in the same sense that poetry is "extra-verbal". Thus, notes like words may have emotional connotations although in an entirely personal way (Cooke, 1959).

The matter has been taken further by Hindemith, who insisted that music cannot actually express a composer's feelings and that if he himself believes it does, then he deceives himself. What he really accomplishes is something learned by experience: that is he uses certain patterns of tone-setting which, he has learned by experience, correspond with appropriate emotional reactions on the listener's part. By his technique, therefore, he obtains the desired response. He went on to stress that although listener, performer, and composer alike can be profoundly moved by perceiving, performing or imagining music, the feelings evoked are not real feelings for, Hindemith insisted, if they were real feelings they would not begin and end precisely with the musical stimulus that aroused them. He stated:

Real feelings need a certain interval of time to develop, to reach a climax, to fade out again; but reactions to music may change as fast as musical phrases do, they may spring up in full intensity at any given moment and disappear entirely when the musical pattern that provokes them ends or changes.

This is arguable in that it bears upon the nature of reality. There seems, indeed, no reason to suppose that a feeling which is musically evoked and which on this account may be short-lived, and not necessarily intense, is for this reason not a *real* feeling. Also, and apart from this, there are, surely, many musical pieces which having been heard, but not immediately succeeded by something fresh, may linger and leave behind them an affective state in the mind of the listener which may persist for a considerable period of time.

Bearing these things in mind consideration may be given to the songs of Peter Warlock (1894–1930), which appear to provide a striking illustration of the qualitative effects of cyclothymia upon musical content; this quite apart from that of the wider influence of mood upon unevenness of output, which in Warlock's case has previously been considered. Currently, Warlock is generally thought of as a minor composer – possibly *miniaturist* would be a better description – for most of his compositions consist of short songs. Nevertheless, there appears to be a growing body of opinion that many of them are of remarkable quality.

Warlock's songs fall stylistically into several fairly clear-cut groups. *Captain Stratton's Fancy, Good Ale*, and *Rutterkin* obviously reveal the more manic aspects of his character. In contrast: *Sleep, Rest Sweet Nymphs*, the exquisite *Balulalow, The Birds*, and a number of his other songs and carols reflect what could perhaps be most appropriately designated as a state of tender melancholy. Warlock's masterpiece is undoubtedly *The Curlew*, a setting of four poems by W. B. Yeats, which Kennedy (1974) has said "explain" (*reveal* might be a better word) the melancholy and despair which lay at the roots of his Jekyll-and-Hyde personality. It is certainly a piece of infinite sadness and tender beauty. However, there was clearly another more sinister and complex side to Warlock's character, one which has yet to be fully explored. This is suggested by the nature of certain of his other songs, which, in addition to being melancholic, have a decidedly macabre quality. These include *The Frostbound Wood*, *The Shrouding of the Duchess of Malfi* and, in particular, *The Fox* – which Constant Lambert is reputed to have said had "the smell of death about it" (Bishop, 1970). Lambert's prophecy was right: within a year Warlock committed suicide.

Allowing for an interval of just over 300 years, a comparison – possibly valid in certain respects – may be drawn between Warlock and the remarkable Carlo Gesualdo (1560–1613). It is probably no coincidence that Warlock, together with Cecil Gray, contributed to a biography of Gesualdo. Gesualdo, Prince of Venosa, had both strong melancholic and sadomasochistic tendencies. He murdered his first wife and her lover in a particularly sanguinary manner, having caught them, as he intended, *in flagrante delicto*. His second marriage was hardly more successful (Watkins, 1973). He himself enjoyed physical ill-treatment and employed young men to beat him during which it is said "he was wont to smile joyfully" (Gray and Heseltine, 1926).

Gesualdo, a contemporary of Monteverdi, was a composer of madrigals and motets, some of which must have been considered as quite remarkable at the time when they were written, both on account of their chromatic modulations and their not infrequent defiance of some of the more generally accepted rules of part-writing. Gesualdo's music certainly gained the disapproval of some academic musicians, in particular Dr. Charles Burney (1726–1814), probably England's first musicologist of note, who could find nothing in his music but "unprincipled modulation". For example, Burney regarded *Moro Lasso*, one of his most remarkable madrigals, as "extremely shocking and disgusting to the ear". In contrast, Constant Lambert (1934) categorised Gesualdo, along with Berlioz, Busoni and Schoenberg, as an orginal: – "One of the great isolated figures of music". Although one can do no more than this, it is fascinating to speculate just how much Gesualdo's melancholic temperament and deviant sexual tendencies are reflected in his music, some of which, even after the passage of three and a half centuries, is still remarkable to the ear.

One might look and find melancholic tendencies in the work of many others – or cherish the illusion of doing so: in Beethoven, Brahms, Rachmaninov, or Tchaikovsky; in the solemn and exquisite cadences which, as they die away, bring a sense of finality to the *"Crucifixus"* in Bach's *B Minor Mass*, a sense dispelled a moment later by the triumphant

"*Et Resurrexit*"; in Purcell's superb "*When I am Laid In Earth*"; in Gerald Finzi's tenderly moving *Dies Natalis*; and in the remotely plaintive lament of the softly speaking trumpet, which lulls momentarily the gathering storm that brings William Walton's *First Symphony* to its titanic close. Also, of course, in Elgar, particularly in the final movement of his *Cello Concerto* which so clearly reveals the disillusionment of his declining years.

There is one last point to be made. It has been said by his daughter, Imogen, that her father, Gustav Holst, who so often spent his time sunk in utter despair (Abraham, 1946), regarded *Egdon Heath* as the best of all his compositions (Imogen Holst, 1962). In spite of the sense of desolation which the piece at first seems to evoke, there emerges that degree of affective warmth, which, together with despair, is so characteristic of the creations of those who really know what melancholy means and which, when musically expressed, immediately arouses empathy. It is that self-same warmth which gives rise to the unique sense of emotional inundation which, whenever it is experienced, leaves the discriminatingly appreciative listener in little doubt that what he hears is music worthy of the name, and no mere sentimental artifice. Indeed, it is just that touch of melancholy expressed in some form or other which, if it does not mar the man, so often provides the piquancy which transforms his music from what might otherwise be no more than a passing pleasure into an unforgettable experience.

## REFERENCES

ABRAHAM, G. (1946) *British Music of our Time*, ed. A. L. Bacharach. London, Pelican Books.

ANDERSON, E. W. (1974) Personal communication.

BEECHAM, SIR THOMAS (1959) *Frederick Delius*. London, Hutchinson.

BISHOP, J. (1970) *Peter Warlock: 22 Songs and Candlelight*. Record sleeve, Norfolk, Galliard 4012.

BOWERS, FAUBION (1974) *The New Scriabin, Enigma and Answers*. London, David & Charles.

CAIRNS, D. ('1970) *The Memoirs of Hector Berlioz*. St. Albans, Panther Books.

CALDWELL, A. E. (1972) La Malinconia: Final movement of Beethoven's quartet op. 18, no. 6 — a musical account of manic depressive states. *J. Amer. Med. Women's Assoc.*, **27**, 241–248.

CARLYLE, T. (1838) *Sir Walter Scott. Critical and Miscellaneous Essays*. Vol. IV, 1899, London, Chapman and Hall Ltd.

CHRISTY, N. P., CHRISTY, B. M. and WOOD, B. G. (1970) Gustav Mahler and his illnesses. *Trans. Amer. Clin. and Climactological Assoc.*, **82**, 200–217.

COCKSHOTT, G. (1955) E. J. Moeran's recollections of Peter Warlock. *Musical Times*, **96**, 128–130.

COOKE, D. (1959) *The Language of Music*. London, Oxford University Press.

COOPER, M. (1970) *Beethoven, The last Decade*, London, Oxford University Press.

DENT, E. J. (1933) *Ferrucio Busoni*. London, Oxford University Press.

DIEREN, BERNARD VAN (1935) *Down Among the Dead Men*. London, Oxford University Press.

FENBY, E. (1971) *Delius*. London, Faber & Faber.

FERGUSON, H. (1974) Personal communication.

GARDEN, E. (1967) *Balakirev*. London, Faber & Faber.

GOULD, G. M. (1906) A biographic clinic on Tchaikovsky. *Boston Med. & Surg. J.*, **44**, 513–517, 552–557.

GOWERS, P. (1974) *Piano Music by Erik Satie*. Record sleeve, London, Saga 5387.

GRAY, C. (1934) *Peter Warlock*. London, Jonathan Cape.

GRAY, C. and HESELTINE, P. (1926) *Carlo Gesualdo, Prince of Venosa, Musician and Murderer*. London, J. Curwen & Sons.

HADOW, W. H. (1926) *Studies in Modern Music*. London, Seeley Service & Co.

HALSEY, L. (1972) The Choral Music. In: *Robert Schumann, the Man and his Music*. 350–389, ed. Alan Walker, London, Barrie & Jenkins.

HENDERSON, D. K. (1952) *The Psychopathic Personality*. Inaugural Postgraduate Lecture, Oxford University Press.

HESELTINE, P. (1922) *Frederick Delius*. London, John Lane the Bodley Head.

HINDEMITH, P. (1952) *A Composer's World. Horizons and Limitations*. Cambridge (Mass.), Harvard University Press.

HOLST, IMOGEN (1962) *Gustav Holst: Egdon Heath*. Record sleeve, London, The Decca Record Co., SXL 6006.

HURD, M. (1975) Personal communication.

HUXLEY, A. (1923) *Antic Hay*. London, Chatto & Windus.

JACKSON, J. H. (1884) Evolution and dissolution of the nervous system. Croonian Lectures. In: *Selected Writings of Hughlings Jackson*. Vol. 2 (1958), New York, Basic Books.

JAMES, W. (1902) *Varieties of Religious Experience: A Study in Human Nature*. London, Longmans.

JEFFERSON, A. (1972) *Delius*. London, J. M. Dent & Sons.

JUDA, A. (1953) *Höchstbegabung ihre Erbverhältnisse sowie ihre Beziehungen zu Physischen Anomalien*. Munich, Urban Schwarzenberg.

KANTOR, M. and PINSKER, H. (1973) Musical expression of psychopathology. *Perspectives in Biology and Medicine*, **16**, 263–269.

KENNEDY, M. (1968) *Portrait of Elgar*. London, Oxford University Press.

— (1974) *Peter Warlock: The Curlew*. Record sleeve, Hayes, Middlesex, EMI Records, HQS 1325.

KERMAN, J. (1967) *The Beethoven Quartets*. London, Oxford University Press.

KOUPERNIK, C. (1974) Personal communication.

KRETSCHMER, E. (1934) *A Textbook of Medical Psychology*. Trans. E. B. Strauss, London, Hogarth Press.

LAMBERT, CONSTANT (1934) *Music Ho!*. London, Faber & Faber.

LAWRENCE, D. H. (1921) *Women in Love*. London, Martin Secker.

LAYTON, R. (1965) *Sibelius*. London, J. M. Dent & Sons.

— (1975) Personal communication.

LOWBURY, E. (1975) Personal communication.

LYONS, J. (1971) *Alexander Scriabin*. Record sleeve, London, MacNeill Press, Deutsche Grammophon, 2530 137.

MACALPINE, I. and HUNTER, R. (1952) Rossini: Piano pieces for the primal scene. *Amer. Imago*, **9**, 213–219.

MAHLER, ALMA (1946) *Gustav Mahler. Memories and Letters*. Ed. Donald Mitchell, London, John Murray.

MERLE, F. L. (1933) *Psychologie et Pathologie d'un Artiste, Henri Duparc*. Thesis, University of Bordeaux.

MILHAUD, DARIUS (1952) *Notes Without Music*. London, Denis Dobson.

MUNRO, A. (1966) Parental deprivation in depressive patients. *Brit. J. Psychiat.*, **112**, 443–457.

MYERS, R. (1948) *Satie*. London, Denis Dobson.

NEWMAN, E. (1907) *Hugo Wolf*. London, Methuen.

— (1914) *Wagner as Man and Artist*. London, Jonathan Cape.

NORTHCOTE, S. (1949) *The Songs of Henri Duparc*. London, Denis Dobson.

ONUF, B. (1920) The problems of eugenics in connection with the manic-depressive temperament. *New York Med. J.*, **3**, 407–412.

PERLIS, D. (1975) *Charles Ives Remembered*. New Haven, Yale University Press.

RAYNOR, H. (1972) *A Social History of Music*. London, Barrie & Jenkins.

RHYS, E. (1937) *The Life of Berlioz*. London, J. F. Dent & Sons.

RIBOLI, B. (1954) Profilo Medico Psicologio de G. Rossini, *La Rossegna musicali*, quoted by Weinstock (1968) op. cit.

RIMSKY–KORSAKOFF, N. (1924) *My Musical Life*. London, Martin Secker.

RUSHMORE, R. (1966) *The Life of George Gershwin*. London, Collier-Macmillan.

SAMS, E. (1961) *The Songs of Hugo Wolf*. London, Methuen.

— (1974) Personal communication.

SCHOLES, P. A. (1955) *The Oxford Companion to Music*. 9th edn. London, Oxford University Press.

SCHÖNZELER, H. H. (1970) *Anton Bruckner*. London, Calder & Boyars.

SCHRADE, L. (1964) *Tragedy in the Art of Music*. Massachusetts, Harvard University Press.

SCHWARTZ, D. M. (1965) A psychoanalytic approach to the great renunciation. *J. Amer. Psychoanal. Assoc.*, **13**, 551–569.

SCHWEITZER, A. (1911) *J. S. Bach*. Trans. Ernest Newman, London, Black.

SHEAD, R. (1973) *Constant Lambert*. London, Simon Publications.

SINGER, K. (1932) *Diseases of the Musical Profession*. Trans. Wladimir Lakond, New York, Greenberg.

SITWELL, S. (1947) *The Hunters and the Hunted*. London, Macmillan.

SLATER, E. (1958) *The Problems of Pathography*, Presidential Address to the Psychiatric Section of the Royal Society of Medicine, 14 October (unpublished).

— (1972) Schumann's illness. In: *Robert Schumann, the Man and his Music*. 406–414, Ed. Alan Walker, London, Barrie & Jenkins.

SMITH, W. (1975) Personal communication.

SUTCLIFFE, T. (1974) Premeditated Mahler. *Manchester Guardian*, 22 April.

TERRY, C. S. (1928) *Bach: A Biography*. London, Oxford University Press.

TOYE, F. (1934) *Rossini, A Study in Tragi-Comedy*. London, William Heinemann.

VON REISEMANN, O. (1935) *Moussorgsky*. New York, Tudor Publishing Co.

WATKINS, G. (1973) *Gesualdo, The Man and his Music*. London, Oxford University Press.

WEINSTOCK, H. (1968) *Rossini: A Biography*. London, Oxford University Press.

WOOLDRIDGE, D. (1975) *Charles Ives: A Portrait*. London, Faber & Faber.

# 24

N. SCHIPKOWENSKY*

# Musical Therapy in the Field of Psychiatry and Neurology

Music is without doubt the most ancient of the arts. Unlike most other art forms it has its natural predecessors, for Nature is full of noises and sounds which, like birdsong, provide tuneful melodies. Songs attend man from the cradle to the grave, lulling him asleep in tender age and sounding his funeral obsequies. Songs accompany man during his hours of festival, love and affection, joy and grief, consoling him in slavery and lending wings to him in liberty. Yet man does not content himself with the resources of his voice alone, he constructs various wind, percussion and string instruments to express his inmost emotions with their sounds.

It is beyond my brief, as well as my competence, to consider the role of music in all aspects of social and personal life. I shall confine myself, therefore, to the prophylactic and therapeutic value of music in psychiatric and neurological practice.

Among primitive peoples healers resorted to song when giving medical advice. Apart from individual performances, ceremonies were conducted by a group of consulting doctors, with the participation of the patients' relatives and neighbours, and lasted for days (Radin, 1948; Densmore, 1948). In both these methods of treatment music was an essential component, either the healer himself or his attendants would sing, shake a rattle, or beat a drum. The songs were thought to have a supernatural origin, deriving from dreams or visions. At the same time instructions were received as to the course of the ritual, selection of patients and the curative practice in general by the healers who were in bizarre states of altered consciousness.

Music therapy attained its proper significance in the work of Orpheus (c. 1350 B.C.), a Thracian man of genius. This native of the Rhodopian mountains praised the cosmic harmony, which ought to illuminate man's mental life, to the accompaniment of a golden lyre. This healer-songster would tame wild beasts, that is, man's passions, by his enchanting music,

---

* Deceased 8th April 1976.

move rocks, that is, reach the bottom of even the most unfeeling hearts, cure patients and even revive the dead.

The ancient Thracian anticipated future scientific medical trends centuries before the development of Greek culture. The beginnings of Greek drama were laid in the Dionysiac festivals. The legendary Thracian king and healer Zalmoxis, mentioned by Socrates in Plato's "Charmides", held the idea of man's spiritual and bodily integrity as a whole, an irrevocable association of somatotherapy and psychotherapy. Orpheus, on the other hand, in his prophylactic and curative practice, employed music and poetry to restore harmony between Cosmos and man, living things and inorganic matter. His philosophy was the pith of Orphism which, through the medium of Pythagorean teaching, exerted considerable influence on the doctrines of Plato, Aristotle and other philosophers of ancient Greece. In all their teachings an important part was assigned to music in the fields of education, constructive interpersonal relations, art, religious ceremonies, and public life. Music was considered indispensable for the preservation of mental and bodily health of the individual and the cure of functional and even organic disease.

Bruno Meinecke (1948) stated that "psychiatric cases of various types were treated by song" (p. 75) both in ancient Greece and Rome. Aescalepiades, Celsus, and later Robert Burton, among others, recommended music for the treatment of mental disorder, first and foremost melancholia. Similar views penetrated Arabian medicine from the eighth century on. They developed in keeping with the political expansion and economic prosperity of the Islamic world, which attained its apogee between the ninth and twelfth centuries. Prominent exponents included Razes (850–923), Avicenna (980–1037), Avenzoar (1091?–1162), Averroes (1126–1198) and the Rabbi Maimonides (1135–1204), who, having enriched themselves with the knowledge of their Roman and Greek predecessors from Hippocrates to Galen, and having adopted their positive attitude towards music (Ammar, 1965; Ellenberger, 1974), transmitted both of them to the Occident. This is why music was also introduced into their mental hospitals. The latter were founded by the Arabs at least four centuries before similar institutions in Christian Europe.

Both cosmic and bodily harmony were regarded as made up from the co-operation of the four primordial elements of matter, earth, water, air, fire, as well as their corresponding fluids, blood, lymph, yellow and black bile, respectively.

The idea of an omnipresent harmony originally held by Orpheus, and then by Pythagoras and his disciples, penetrated much of the scientific work of antiquity and remained operative until recent times. As concerning the rhythm of matter, both in its organic and living varieties, this idea holds true. In the universe there is rhythm indeed, yet the latter can hardly be reconciled with harmony. Cosmic cataclysms, social calamities and individual sufferings are inconceivable as transformations of the universal harmony. The movement of matter has neither beginning nor end; it comprises many a consonance, indeed, but disharmonies too. Its rhythm remains wholly irrevocable whether periodic or aperiodic. Even if one were reluctant to accept the speculation of Hughes that music took its origin from dance, it is undeniable that both these arts are subject to rhythm. More precisely, this primary nature of rhythm accounts for its all-important role in the curative ceremonies of primitive tribes.

The belief in the curative power of music persisted in advanced civilisations of antiquity until the Renaissance. Miraculous effects were ascribed to it not only in cases of neurosis and psychosis but also in organic bodily disease. It was believed to cure sick people, resuscitate the dead, bring to an end psychotic epidemics such as tarantism as well as contagious ones. When appropriately applied it was claimed to have the property of preventing individual crimes and mob riots. Throughout the centuries there amassed an ample bibliography on iatromusic comprising single observations, studies and monographs. Strangely enough, therefore, even in recent times, when well-founded systems of musical therapy have been devised and applied in many countries throughout the world, not even a brief mention of them is to be found in textbooks or the voluminous handbooks of psychiatry published in various languages. The only exception I know is of the monograph by L. Wolberg (1967) who assigned one page to musical therapy, dealing briefly with its potentialities.

\*    \*    \*    \*

Methods of iatromusic may be divided into five basic varieties: background, contemplative, combined, performing, and creative musical therapy.

## Background musical therapy

Background musical therapy is heard at fixed hours in the humdrum hospital routine. It is transmitted by way of radio and television programmes or from record players and tapes. Although there is no strict selection in the programmes it goes without saying that excessively loud music should be avoided, so as to create a background of calm during working and eating, reading and talking. Entertainment should be arranged at least once a week, preferably on a Sunday afternoon so that the patients' relatives and friends participate.

## Contemplative musical therapy

Contemplative musical therapy presupposes the patient's initiation into the significance of art in general and of music in particular. Every session is preceded by concise information as to the composer's identity and the spirit of his work. The performance is followed by a free discussion about the emotions evoked. Contemplative musical therapy can be conducted either individually or collectively; in either case it is in keeping with the "Iso" principle (Altshuler, 1948) which had been anticipated by V. von Bekhterev as long ago as 1916. At the beginning the musical compositions are chosen to correspond with the prevailing mood of the patient. For depressive states they should have a tone quality of melancholy, in hypomanic patients the music should be replete with joy, yet always avoiding unrestrained frenzy. The various musical instruments are of uneven emotional value. Thus, in states of tension with anxiety wind instruments may intensify uneasiness, while this is mitigated by a trio of piano, violin and cello.

An individual approach enhances the patient's connection with musical therapy (Schmolz, 1971), facilitates the uncovering of morbid experiences ("communicative" musical therapy as Schwabe called it) and results in emotional enlivenment ("reactive" musical therapy in Schwabe's terminology).

The second approach consists in a technique based upon an enhanced level which aims at controlling sadness, soothing agitation, whether the patient be beside himself with joy or with rage.

In states of psychosis one starts by influencing the patients chiefly by rhythmic stimuli, then going on to melody and finally to harmony. Then music is used to stimulate imagination. Obviously these components are not autonomous in any piece of music, the music is arranged according to the predominance of the individual components, for example, rhythm in marches, melody in songs and harmony in tone poems, either for single instruments or full orchestra. The programme must be intelligible to almost every patient. Irrespective of the general technique, contemplative musical therapy must naturally be adapted to the patient's personality, the nosological classification of his disease, and its dynamic evolution from the beginning of the programme to its end.

## Combined musical therapy

Combined musical therapy is linked with overall influences by means of other therapeutic procedures. Unlike the background variety, it calls for a selection of musical compositions which should agree with the respective therapeutic approach by rhythmic, melodious succession of sounds, and at last by harmony, or by all three elements together.

Callisthenics are characterised by rhythm which is embodied not only in the timing of the movements but also in their smoothness, suppleness and continuity. Inspired by the emotion that music engenders, normal psychosomatic states are restored. Similar regularities obtain in the case of remedial dances. Here synchrony and co-ordination of pantomime and psychomotor activity are inseparable from the consonance of music and full co-partnership with the other participants. The patient, far from being a mere unit in the activity of couples or of larger groups as at a dance, feels himself a full member of a community which is equally striving towards liberation from psychopathological dominance. This is why remedial dances call for control by a choreographer who, in collaboration with the music therapist and the doctor, elaborates the programme in detail. This should be based upon folk round-dances if possible, or on compositions with folklore motives.

The third type of combined musical therapy consists in the induction, maintenance, and termination of hypnosis simultaneously with the performance of musical compositions. Franz Anton Mesmer (1734–1815) was the first to practise this approach. He would accompany his seances on "animal magnetism" with music which he sometimes played himself on a harmonica. The influence he exerted on his patients consisted of individual and collective suggestion which occasionally went on to hypnoid states. The important point is that Mesmer combined suggestion with music. Apparently this method is still employed by V. Ya. Tkachenko.

A group is formed of eight to ten selected neurotics with conspicuous sleep disorders. Reclining in easy chairs or on couches, they are instructed to shut their eyes and to allow themselves to be carried away by the melody of a Chopin nocturne, by Grieg's piano sonata, by Tchaikovsky's *Autumnal Song*, or by a similar composition. At the same time the suggestion is made to the patients that music is calming them and lulling them to sleep. The music continues throughout the whole of the forty-five minutes "sleep". The therapist then proceeds to individual contacts. For two or three minutes he promises that sleeplessness will subside and disappear along with the patient's neurotic ailments. Awakening is secured by suggestion made simultaneously with cheerful pieces which reinforce the patient's confidence in recovery. Such treatment is repeated eight to ten times daily. Musical hypnosis has been conducted in several balneo-sanatoria for patients with nervous disorders in Bulgaria (Bankya, Varshetz, Naretchen).

The "musical symbolic drama" (Leuner and Nerenz, 1964) consists in evoking suggestive images which reflect psychotraumatic situations of conflict, music merely playing the role of a catalyst in their evocation.

Autogenic training (Schulz, 1960) is the fourth variety of combined musical therapy, though only used exceptionally. Schwabe (1974) reported far better results from his "regulative musical therapy", which consists essentially in such a combination. He drew up a list of pieces suitable for all forms of musical therapy. A similar approach has been used by Teirich (1958).

Electro-sleep is the fifth technique which entails musical therapy. D. Traikov (Sofia), using an ingenious contrivance which is fitted to sound-emitters placed under each patient's pillow, switches on music and electrical current simultaneously to each patient, thus avoiding the noise of the loud speaker which disturbs some patients. In this way individuals are enabled to regulate the volume of sound.

The combination of music and painting (Reisch, 1971) constitutes a sixth variety.

The seventh, and final, variety of combined musical therapy consists in the association of poetry with music. Here again we recall Orpheus, whose songs were not only melodies accompanied by the lyre, but also verses in which his sublime philosophy was expressed in terms of harmony between Cosmos and Man. The patients themselves read aloud or recite verses — whether self-selected or recommended by their therapist — and this technique constitutes a variety of executive art therapy.

## Executive musical therapy

Executive musical therapy consists either in individual or collective singing and playing instruments. Its resources are manifold and are as yet insufficiently utilised. In every mental hospital a company of singers or choral society should be formed. Long-stay patients are particularly suited for participation. The chorus strengthens self-confidence and the patient's evaluation of his social worth. As a member of such a company the individual patient feels protected against the stress of solo performances by his partnership in a collective body pursuing the same end and impelled by identical motives. Moreover, the patients, knowing well that no polished performance is expected of them but merely a therapeutic effort, are not overwhelmed by feelings of inferiority. Should the chorus happen to attain a satisfactory aesthetic level, then the participants will feel rewarded by the admiration of the listeners; but even without such high attainment the patients' participation in a choir is likely to open their minds and broaden their cultural outlook.

The programme, which requires to be mastered in two or three meetings weekly each of an hour's duration, comprises chiefly folksongs and pieces with folklore motifs. Words and music must lend wings to the enjoyment of life, to the tender emotions inspired by the opposite sex, to love in the more general sense of *agape*, to the admiration of nature, and to warm feelings towards humanity.

It is a remarkable achievement when the direction of the chorus is conferred upon one of the patients, either temporarily or permanently. In this way the group dynamics are improved by a positive relationship between the conductor and the cast. The confidence shown in him enhances his assurance of success. Choral societies are to be found in many hospitals throughout the world. In Bulgaria they have been in operation at the mental establishments of Radnevo, Bjala, Lovetch and Lom for the last few years.

The formation of orchestras is a far more difficult problem. It has been mastered successfully in some hospitals, for example, in Canada.* Each mental establishment should at least possess a piano.

## Executive iatromusic

Executive iatromusic can be provided for children's mental and neurological departments with comparative ease. For such patients it is of major importance in the course of treatment and rehabilitation, and may be a decisive factor in patients with brain damage resulting from perinatal trauma. It produces a favourable response in victims of mental deficiency, behavioural disturbance, and neurosis, even in cases where concomitant neurological symptoms exist.

Gollnitz and Schultz-Wulf obtained encouraging improvement by graduating from the simplest type of rhythmic movements (clapping hands, stamping, exercises with balloons, balls, hoops, sticks) to the use of percussion instruments (beating a drum with hands or sticks, or playing the triangle, xylophone, or metallophone), and finally to the performance of

* Editorial footnote. In late nineteenth-century England the superintendent of Powick Asylum was a great believer in the value of music and formed an orchestra, presumably of staff and patients; the conductor of the orchestra was Elgar.

song and enacting fairy tales. Even earlier many workers (Bade, 1925; Semann and Corvinius, 1929; Scheiblauer, 1945; Teirich, 1958; C. Orff and G. Keetmann, 1959; Ch. Koffer-Ullrich, 1960; Preu, 1971) had stressed the positive effects of music in the development of healthy children as well as sick. Music improves the psychomotor functions in patients with cerebral lesions, stimulates their intellectual-mnestic activities, and balances personality disharmonies. Neurotic reactions, too, are beneficially influenced. Rhythmic musical therapy is applicable, moreover, in pyramidal, extrapyramidal and ataxic disorders provided that it conforms with the patients' ages and with their specific neurological syndromes.

## Creative musical therapy

Creative musical therapy is the fifth and highest variety of this type of treatment. As in the case of the other arts, it is rooted frequently in poignant experiences, from which catharsis is effected either by way of song or an instrumental composition.

To reduce the creation of works of high aesthetic value merely to psycho-cathartic processes would be an over-simplification of the intricate impulses involved. Still, it is fair comment to submit the view that the torments of parting with one's dearly beloved, grief over a deceased friend, oppression in slavery, and more generally the shattering of mental equilibrium as a result of splitting of the personality following interpersonal and social conflicts, have been often expressed by a process of musical transformation.

Combinations of executive and creative musical therapy were applied by Weise and Albert (1971) in the form of mimetic and gesticulatory expression of various powerful emotions (joy and grief, wrath and loathing, etc.), also by Koch and Bach (1971) in the form of group eurhythmics. Patients are encouraged to find for themselves the appropriate emotional types of musical pieces or else to determine the tempo of the movements by their own performances on percussion instruments. These same methods are also applicable to psychotic patients.

The methodical approaches of creative iatromusic have been cultivated and improved by Schwabe (1974). He divided them into melodic, rhythmic, and text improvisations which are performed by a chorus of patients. In the first variety a suitable melody and a given rhyme are put together; in the second it is suggested to them that they should create a new rhythm for a repeated melody; and finally the chorus writes the text to a given theme, say one of the seasons of the year. The last named embraces both poetic and musical creation.

The higher grades of musical therapy (melodic, rhythmic and text improvisations) presuppose, as a preliminary, a certain proficiency in choral work. This must be acquired before embarking upon the venture of collective creation of melodies, rhythmic cadences and texts. Only such musical therapists as themselves possess above average talents and a comprehensive experience of choral conducting are able to work their way up to such accomplishments. In my view they might also encourage some particularly gifted patients to play a musical psychodrama in which the melodies are created by the participants themselves at the moment of performance.

Musical therapy cannot be raised to the rank of a unique method, nor even to that of a most important one. It belongs to the category of cultural influences – theatre and opera, painting and sculpture, prose writing and poetry, performances intended to entertain and to give pleasure – which combine in liberating psychotherapy.

According to the first principles of liberating psychotherapy, the common task of the hospital staff and their patients consists in the realisation of the way in which the pathological situation is eliminated. The era of the old time asylums is over, yet nobody would go so far as to assert that in modern psychiatric and neurological institutions the environment and the trend of fundamental attitudes pervading the community are wholly beneficial to the patients. Clinical and social psychiatry have been substantially fostered in their development by the introduction of such aids as entertainment, occupational and cultural therapy into the humdrum life of mental hospitals, by transferring many of the psychiatrist's activities outside the walls of former "lunatic asylums" to out-patient departments, home care, industrial labour aiding therapy, and clubs formed by former patients who have been discharged cured. In spite of these undoubted successes reality falls short of ideal conditions almost everywhere. Here and there discrepancies may be deep enough to give rise, not without some reason, to criticism by "antipsychiatrists" (Szasz, Foucault, Cooper, Laing, Basaglia, etc.). Still, their attempts at reducing psychiatry to sociology and even to political science are as much unfounded theoretically as they are unavailing in practice. Yet their attacks remind us of something that has been realised by all true healers throughout the centuries, though they did not always put it into practice, namely, that we should beware of doing bodily harm, or of inflicting iatro-psychogeny upon our patients; moreover, we are under the obligation to prevent hospitalisation with all its consequences. Art in any form affords ample opportunities for combating hospitalisation and for preventing its harmful sequelae. In this respect music ranks highest because it is readily available and because it is economical of time and money. At fixed hours of the day iatromusic ought to be scheduled within the timetable of each mental hospital. The patients should be arranged in groups so that the music selected is most suitable for their individual personalities. Untoward effects of a hospital environment can be largely neutralised by iatromusic. As is well known, even in well organised and conducted modern establishments a wearisomely uniform trend of therapeutic and restorative procedures, as well as gaps in the daily schedule, still account for negative environmental influences on the patients.

Musical therapy contributes furthermore to the practical realisation of the second principle of liberating psychotherapy, namely, the elimination of the psychopathological dominance of emotional disorders, obsessional ideas, delusions, hallucinations, parabolic impulses, narcopathic addictions, and perversity of instincts. By the joint efforts of the psychiatrist and by the conscious co-operation of his patients it is possible to help them turn away from such pathological experiences, which are kept at a distance, contrary to generally adopted assertions which are held as definite tenets in blind dogmatism. The beneficial climate of the therapeutic community is a major prerequisite for this effect. Common efforts of staff and patients concentrate on the formation of propitious patterns of guiding experiences which are based on confidence in the future and on striving after some sublime purport of life by creative intentions and by overcoming the difficulties of personal readjustment.

Delusions are refuted by clearing up their incongruity with the reality of the surrounding world (as in schizophrenia, for instance), and with one's own behaviour (in cases of depression). Hallucinations lose their dominance when they are seen in a true light and recognised as ultraparadoxical externalisations of subjective states. Narcopathic addictions are within the range of one's own conduct. The patient's personality, in cases of psychopathy and neurosis, still remains able to determine itself by self-consciousness and self-knowledge. In psychoses its primordial liberty is restored by combined somato-therapy and psychotherapy. This ascendancy over the patients' psychic life aims at easing ways of access for sane dominants. Such ascendancies can be established more readily under the beneficial influence of occupational and cultural therapy. In this respect the potentialities of music are very considerable, though not unlimited.

It is a widely held opinion that mental patients are inaccessible to the verbal influence of the doctor. This is an exaggeration and consequently wrong. Yet one can hardly doubt that mental patients are accessible to influences by ways other than those utilising speech, as by handshaking, for instance. No doctor should omit this act when meeting his patient. A smile, a friendly look, a warm attitude on the part of the psychiatrist may prove helpful in establishing the contact. Music exerts an even deeper influence on the patients' personality and more particularly on their emotional life.

Iatromusic may also be incorporated within the third principle of liberating psychotherapy, namely, the shedding of introspection by concentrating the individual's activities upon the true values of life, such as his family, circle of friends, occupational duties, amusements and hobbies, and cultural interests.

Musical therapy, in all its varieties, and more particularly in choirs and orchestras, materially helps the practical realisation of the fourth principle of liberating treatment, namely, therapeutic silence. Patients, especially neurotics but also some psychotics, tend to talk incessantly about their own complaints and those of others. In this way they poison their family atmosphere, engender fears in their children and enrich their own illness with other people's symptoms, causing their disorders to flare up time and again owing to the signalling power of the spoken word (I. P. Pavlov).

The time occupied by any form of music secures, by its continuity, respite from talking about one's own ailments or those of others. It goes without saying that healing silence, like the other modalities of liberating psychotherapy, must be learned and mastered consciously with commonsense and feeling. It would not be contrary to the spirit of liberating psychotherapy, however, if it were aided by non-oral means too, such as occupational and cultural therapy respectively. Here also belongs iatromusic. The skilful combination of bodily influences (occupation, physical exercise, dancing, holidays, in addition to drug medication) with psychic ascendancy over the patients opens the way to the high road of recovery and rehabilitation. The doctor directs the patient's progress by combining direct and indirect psychotherapy, both oral and non-oral approaches, in a constructive influence on the patient's personality. The latter can go through the mental illness with enriched vital experience and with a broadened mental outlook only on that condition. These inmost foundations are the strongest shield against external stresses and the patient's own breakdown, for they are the best prevention of relapse into the morbid circle of his mental illness. Musical therapy is a valuable, though not indispensable, means of laying down such foundations.

# REFERENCES

ALTSHULER, I. M. (1948) A psychiatrist's experience with music as a therapeutic agent. In: *Music and Medicine*, ed. D. M. Schullian and M. Schoen. New York, Schuman, 266–281.

AMMAR, S. (1965) *En souvenir de la médecine arabe*. Tunis.

— (1969) La medecine de l'âme chez les arabes. *La Tunisie médicale*, 1, 1–8.

VON BEKHTEREV, V. (1916a) *The Importance of Music for the Aesthetical Education of Children from the First Days of Infancy*. Moscow.

— (1916b) Problems bound up with the therapeutical and hygienic significance of music. *Obozrenie Psychiatri Nevrol Exper Psychol.*, 1–4, 124.

CARAPETYAN, A. (1948) Music and medicine in the renaissance and in the 17th and 18th Centuries. In: *Music and Medicine*, ed. by D. M. Schullian and M. Schoen. New York, Schuman, 117–157.

ELLENBERGER, H. F. (1974) Psychiatry from ancient to modern times. *American Handbook of Psychiatry*, ed. by Silvano Arieti. 2nd edn, New York, Basic Books, 3–27.

DENSMORE, FR. (1948) The use of music in the treatment of the sick by American Indians. In: *Music and Medicine*, ed. by D. M. Schullian and M. Schoen. New York, Schuman, 25–46.

GOLLNITZ, G. and SCHULTZ-WULF, G. (1973) Rhythmisch-psychomotorische. *Musiktherapie*, Jena, G. Fischer.

KOCH, E. M. and BACH, O. (1971) Gruppenrhythmustherapie mit psychiatrischen Patienten. In: *Musiktherapie*, heruasg. v. Chr. Kohler. Jena, G. Fischer, 101–104.

LEUNER, H. C. and NERENZ, K. (1964) Das musikalische Symboldrama und seine psychotherapeutische Wirkung. *Heilkunst*, 77, 330–335.

MEINECKE, B. (1948) Music and medicine in classical antiquity. In: *Music and Medicine*, ed. by D. M. Schullian and M. Schoen. New York, Schuman, 47–95.

NERENZ, K. (1971) Das musikalische Symboldrama. In: *Musiktherapie*, herausgeg. von Christa Kohler. Jena, G. Fischer, 119–127.

ORFF, C. and KEETMAN, G. (1959) Grundlagen und Ziele des Orff–Schulwerkes. Mainz.

RADIN, P. (1948) Music and medicine among primitive peoples. In: *Music and Medicine*, ed. by D. M. Schullian and M. Schoen. New York, Schuman, 3–24.

REICH, P. (1971) Die Kombination von Musikrezeption. In: *Musiktherapie*, herausg. von Chr. Kohler. Jena, G. Fischer, 128–134.

SCHIPKOWENSKY, N. (1961) *Pathologische Reaktionen der Persönlichkeit—Neurosen und psychogene Psychosen*, Wien, Maudrich.

— (1965) *Iatrogenie oder befreiende Psychotherapie—Scheideweg jeden Arztes*. Leipzig, Hirzel.

— (1974) *Iatrogenie oder befreiende Psychotherapie, II. umgearbeitete und erweiterte Auflage in japanischer Sprache*. Tokyo, Bunkodo.

SCHIPKOWENSKY, N. *Liberating Psychotherapie versus Iatrogeny.* Detroit (Michig.), Wayne State University Press. (In the press.)

— (1974) Grundsätze der Thrakischen Medizin. *Academia Literarum Bulgarica, Thracia II.* Serdicae, 241–252.

— (1974) Die Antipsychiatrie in Vergangenheit und Gegenwart. *Fortschr. Neurol. Psychiatr.,* **42**, 291–311.

SCHMÖLZ, A. (1971) Zur Methode der Einzelmusiktherapie. In: *Musiktherapie* herausg. von Chr. Kohler. Jena, G. Fischer, 83–88.

SCHWABE, CHR. (1974) *Musiktherapie bei Neurosen und funktionellen Störungen.* Jena, G. Fischer.

SCHULTZ, I. H. (1960) *Das autogene Training.* Stuttgart, Thieme.

SIEGERIST, H, E. (1948) The story of tarantism. In: *Music and Medicine,* ed. by D. M. Schullian and M. Schoen. New York, Schuman, 96–116.

TEIRICH, H. R. (1958) *Musik in der Medizin.* Stuttgart, Fischer.

WEISE, K. and ALBERT, H. D. (1971) Psychomotorische Therapie auf der psychiatrischen Station. In: *Musiktherapie,* herausg. von Chr. Kohler. Jena, G. Fischer, 97–101.

# Index

7206E